weavers *of the* southern highlands

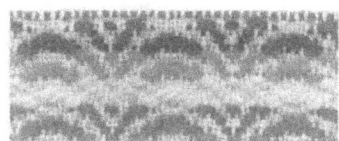

weavers
of the
southern highlands

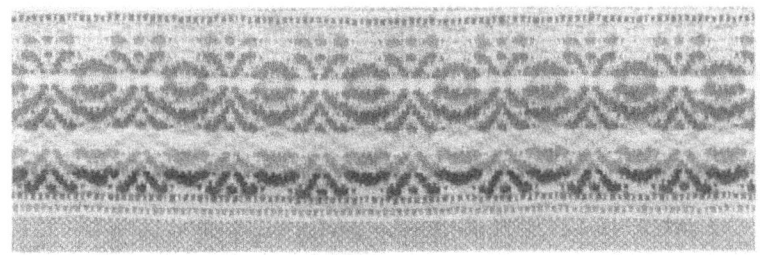

philis alvic

THE UNIVERSITY PRESS OF KENTUCKY

Copyright © 2003 by The University Press of Kentucky
Paperback edition 2009

The University Press of Kentucky
Scholarly publisher for the Commonwealth,
serving Bellarmine University, Berea College, Centre
College of Kentucky, Eastern Kentucky University,
The Filson Historical Society, Georgetown College,
Kentucky Historical Society, Kentucky State University,
Morehead State University, Murray State University,
Northern Kentucky University, Transylvania University,
University of Kentucky, University of Louisville,
and Western Kentucky University.
All rights reserved.

Editorial and Sales Offices: The University Press of Kentucky
663 South Limestone Street, Lexington, Kentucky 40508-4008
www.kentuckypress.com

Cataloging-in-Publication Data is available from
the Library of Congress.

ISBN 978-0-8131-9221-5 (pbk: alk. paper)

This book is printed on acid-free paper meeting
the requirements of the American National Standard
for Permanence in Paper for Printed Library Materials.

Manufactured in the United States of America.

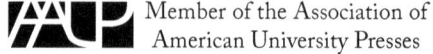

Member of the Association of
American University Presses

To my husband Gary Schroeder,
who has been a vital part of this book,
even before it began to take the form of a book.
He served many functions: facilitating the research,
assuming many unexciting tasks in the various research projects
and in the formation of the book, continually prodding me
to adopt new technology, and always encouraging me to keep going.

contents

List of Illustrations and Maps	viii
List of Appalachian Settlement Schools and Weaving Centers	xiii
Preface	xx
1. Foundations of the Appalachian Craft Revival	1
2. Common Threads	15
3. Berea College and Fireside Industries	35
4. Pi Beta Phi Settlement School and Arrowcraft	56
5. Appalachian School and Penland Weavers and Potters	75
6. The Weavers of Rabun	96
7. Other Mountain Weaving Centers	113
8. Weavers and Managers	135
9. Production	152
10. Financing and Fulfilling a Mission	169
Appendix: List of Oral History Interviews	190
Notes	193
Bibliography	212
Index	224

illustrations and maps

illustrations

Weaver at Loom	1
Walker Sisters	2
Family in Front of Cabin	4
Mary Sloop Looking at Weaving	5
Early Berea Weavers	7
Appalachian School Room	8
Early Gatlinburg	11
Pi Beta Phi Teachers	12
1½ Miles to School—Penland	13
View from the Weaving Shed	14
Daughters of the American Revolution	15
Olive Dane Campbell and John Jacob Niles	17
Southern Mountain Workers, 1926	18
Southern Mountain Workers, Speakers	20
First Southern Highland Handicraft Guild Fair	22
Southern Highlanders, Inc.	23
Cover—*Handicrafts of the Southern Highlands*	27
Penland's Weaving Institute	29
Rural Handicrafts Booklet	32
Allen Eaton and Tina McMorran	34
President Frost	36
Women Carding Wool	37
Hettie Wright Graham	39
Jennie Lester Hill	40
Ernberg and Weavers	41
Log House	43
Ballard with Weavers	44

Illustrations and Maps

Anna Ernberg	47
Mountain Weaver Boy	51
Labor Day Fireside Weaver	53
First Class Pi Beta Phi School	56
Chairs and Baskets	58
Redding Teaching Weaver	60
Aunt Lizzie Reagan	62
Izora Bringing in Weaving	63
Redding Gathering Weaving	65
Arrowcraft Shop in Snow	66
Meta Schattschneider	68
Shipping Room at Arrowcraft	69
Summer Crafts Workshop	70
Amy Burt with Children	76
Lucy Morgan Checking in Work	78
Weavers' Day	79
Winding Bobbins	80
Checking Pottery	82
Lucy Morgan at the Century of Progress	83
Ridgeway Porch	86
Flossie Perisho	90
Theresa's Wedding	92
Bonnie Willis Ford and Lucy Morgan	93
Jay Hambidge	97
Mary Hambidge	98
Eleanor Steele and Hall Clovis	99
Rock House	101
Early Weavers on Rock House Steps	102
Dye Shed	104
Weaving Shed	106
Farm with Sheep	107
Mary Hambidge and Vassos Kanellos	108
Mary Hambidge	111
Eliza Shirley	115
Light in the Mountains	116
Zada Benfield and Marian Brown	118
Crossnore's Log Building	119
Frances L. Goodrich	122
Shuttle Crafters	124

Illustrations and Maps

The Spinning Wheel	126
Eleanor Churchill	130
Churchill—Winding Warp	131
Churchill Weavers	133
Weaver with Yarn	135
Redding, McCarter and Izora Keeler	136
Sally Spark at her Loom	137
Weaver and Child	139
Penland Weavers Sewing	141
Weaver at Tallulah Falls	142
Emma Conley	145
Lucy Morgan at her Loom	146
Lily Mills Practical Weaving Suggestions	148
Tina McMorran	149
Weaver at Barn Loom	152
Woman at Ernberg Loom	154
Warping	155
Threading Heddles at Churchill	156
Coverlet Patterns	158
Conley and Lewis at Dyepot	160
Homespun Flyer	161
Tallulah Falls School and the Georgia Women's Club	163
Churchill Interior	165
Arrowcraft Interior	167
Berea Bags	170
Louise Pitman and ODC	172
Sales Area at Crossnore	173
Molly Moore	175
Early Arrowcraft Shop	176
Cora Morton Demonstrating	179
Arrowcraft Catalog	181
Tallulah Falls School and the Georgia Women's Club	184
Inside Clover Bottom	188
Craft House Porch	189

maps

Appalachian Settlement Schools	xi
Appalachian Weaving Centers	xii

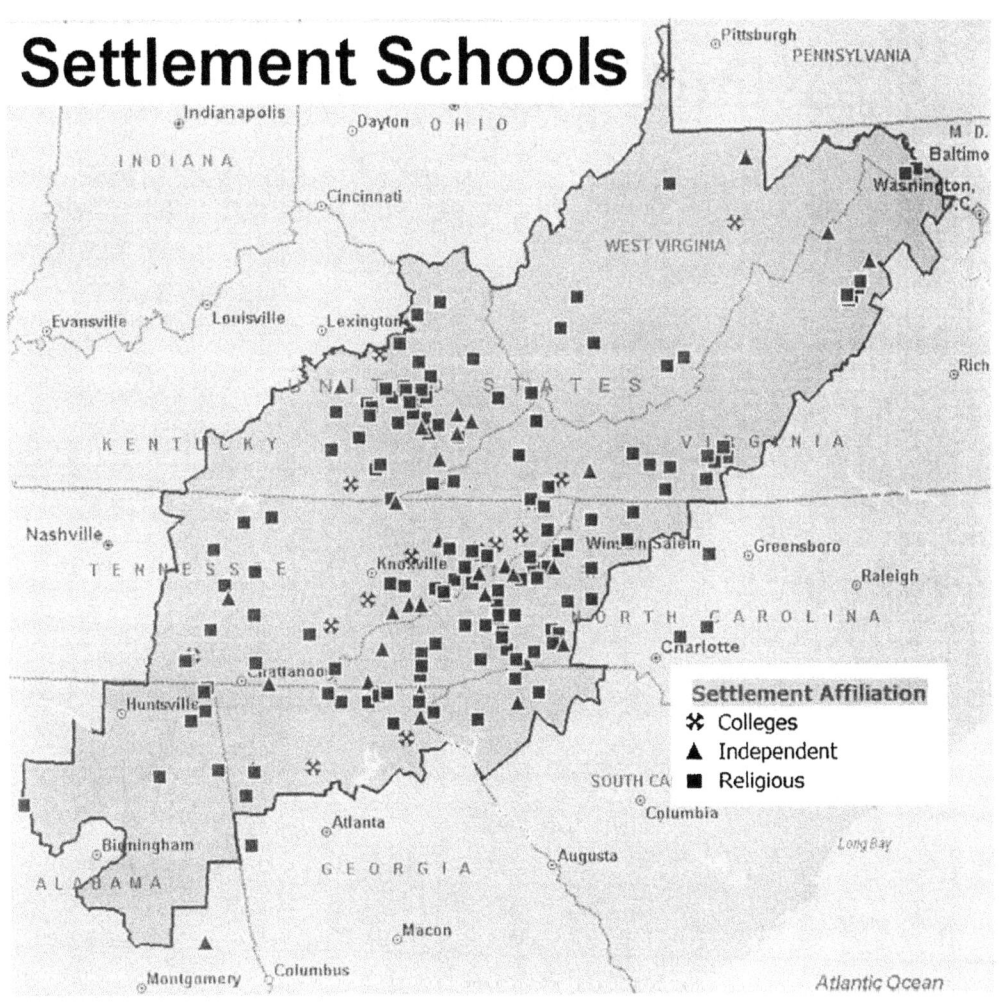

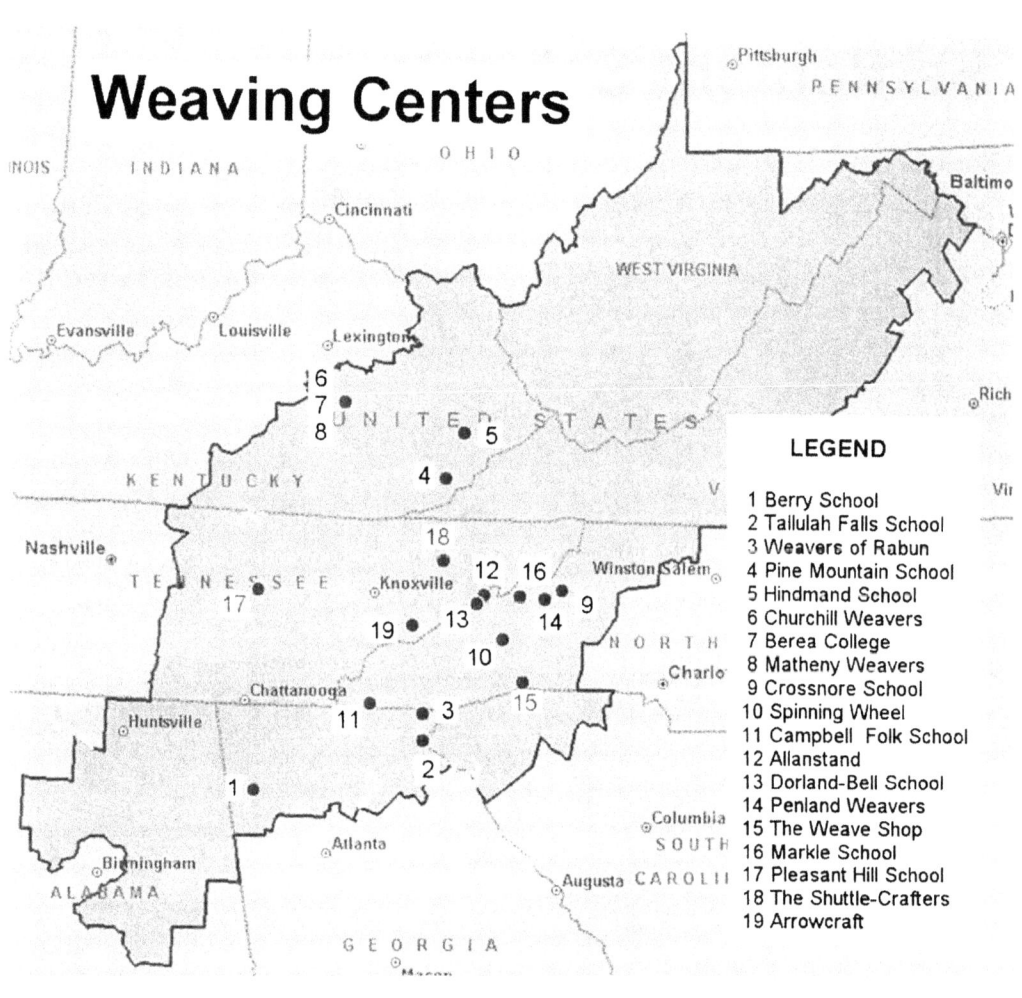

settlement school and weaving centers

Settlement Schools as identified by John C. Campbell [Olive Dame Campbell] in *Southern Highland Schools Maintained by Denominational or Private Agencies:* Russell Sage Foundation, 1920.

- ● Major Weaving Centers
- ▲ Schools that maintained major weaving programs
- ■ Outside traditional Appalachian Region
- ◆ County—city is unknown

Name	Town	Affiliation
Alabama		
John H. Snead Seminary	Boaz	Methodist Episcopal
Nottingham Primary School	Boaz	Methodist Episcopal
Rebecca McCleskey Home	Boaz	Methodist Episcopal
Tennessee River Institute	Bridgeport	S. Baptist Convention
Southern Industrial Institute	Camp Hill	Independent
Mallalieu Seminary ■	Dothan	Methodist Episcopal
Eldridge Academy	Eldridge	S. Baptist Convention
Flat Rock High School	Flat Rock	Methodist Episcopal
Gaylesville Academy	Gaylesville	S. Baptist Convention
Mountain Pine Industrial School	Long Island	Seventh Day Adventist
Beeson Academy	Pisgah	S. Baptist Convention
Georgia		
Blairsville Institute	Blairsville	S. Baptist Convention
McCarthy Settlement School	Cedartown	Methodist Episcopal
Bleckly Institute	Clayton	S. Baptist Convention
Piedmont College	Demorest	Congregational
Epworth Seminary	Epworth	Methodist Episcopal
Hiawassee Academy	Hiawassee	S. Baptist Convention
N. Georgia Baptist Institute	Morganton	S. Baptist Convention
Berry School ▲	Mount Berry	Independent

Settlement Schools and Weaving Centers

Mt. Zion Seminary	Mt. Zion	Methodist Episcopal
Jay Hambidge Foundation ●	Rabun Gap	Independent
Rabun Gap Industrial School	Rabun Gap	Independent
Rome Industrial School	Rome	Seventh Day Adventist
Nacoochee Institute	Sautee	Presbyterian (United)
Tallulah Falls Industrial School ▲	Tallulah Falls	GA Federation of Women's
Reinhart College	Waleska	Methodist Episcopal
Young-Harris College	Young-Harris	Methodist Episcopal

Kentucky

Annville Institute	Annville	Reformed Church
Athol Presbyterian School	Athol	Presbyterian (USA)
Barbourville Institute	Barbourville	S. Baptist Convention
Union College	Barbourville	Methodist Episcopal
Berea College ▲	Berea	Independent
Churchhill Weavers ●	Berea	Independent
Matheny Weaver ●	Berea	Independent
Stuart Robinson School	Blackey	Presbyterian (USA)
Witherspoon College	Buckhorn	Presbyterian (USA)
Brooks Memorial Institute	Canoe	Presbyterian (USA)
Canyon Falls Academy	Canyon Falls	Presbyterian (USA)
Carr Creek Community Center	Carr Creek	Independent
Dry Hill Community Center	Dryhill	Independent
Frenchburg School	Frenchburg	Presbyterian (United)
Carcassonne Community Center	Gander	Independent
Gray Hawk School	Gray Hawk	Reformed Church
Highland School	Guerrant	Presbyterian (USA)
Hazard Institute	Hazard	S. Baptist Convention
Hazel Green Academy	Hazel Green	Disciples of Christ
Beechwood Seminary	Heidelberg	Presbyterian (USA)
Hindman Settlement School ▲	Hindman	TN Federation of Women's
Houston Academy	Houston	Presbyterian (Assoc)
Turkey Creek Reformed Mission	Houston	Presbyterian (Assoc)
Lees Collegiate Institute	Jackson	Presbyterian (USA)
Krypton School	Krypton	Brethren
Sunnyside School	Levi	Presbyterian (USA)
Sue Bennett Memorial	London	Methodist Episcopal
Riverside Institute	Lost Creek	Brethren
McKee Academy	McKee	Reformed Church
St. Mary's Sewing School	Middlesboro	Protestant Episcopal
Morehead Normal School	Morehead	Disciples of Christ

Settlement Schools and Weaving Centers

Mount Victory Academy	Mount Victory	Presbyterian (USA)
Langdon Memorial School	Mt. Vernon	Presbyterian (USA)
Arkley Hall, Erie Home & School	Olive Hill	Methodist Episcopal
Oneida Baptist Institute	Oneida	S. Baptist Convention
John C. C. Mayo College	Paintsville	Methodist Episcopal
Matthew T. Scott Jr. Academy	Phelps	Presbyterian (USA)
Pikeville College	Pikeville	Presbyterian (USA)
Pine Mountain Settlement School ▲	Pine Mountain	Independent
Magoffin Institute	Salyersville	S. Baptist Convention
Harlan County Community Life	Smith	Presbyterian (USA)
Stanton College	Stanton	Presbyterian (United)
Cumberland College	Williamsburg	S. Baptist Convention
Mountain Cabin Quilters	Wooton	Independent
Wooton Fireside Industries	Wooton	Independent
St. John's Collegiate Institute	Knox ◆	Protestant Episcopal
Wentworth Agricultural School	Knox ◆	Protestant Episcopal

North Carolina

Allenstand Cottage Industries ●	Allenstand	Independent
Christ School	Arden	Protestant Episcopal
Asheville Home School	Asheville	Presbyterian (USA)
Asheville Normal School ▲	Asheville	Presbyterian (USA)
Biltmore Industries ●	Asheville	Independent
Pease Memorial	Asheville	Presbyterian (USA)
Spinning Wheel ●	Asheville	Independent
The Log Cabin Settlement	Asheville	Independent
Mitchell Institute	Bakersville	S. Baptist Convention
Mountain Orphanage	Balfour	Presbyterian (USA)
Lees McRae Institute	Banner Elk	Presbyterian (USA)
Golden Industrial Institute	Bostic	Independent
John C. Campbell Folk School ▲	Brasstown	Independent
Brevard Institute	Revard	Methodist Episcopal
Magnetic School	Buladean	Presbyterian (USA)
Yancey Collegiate Institute	Burnsville	S. Baptist Convention
Pisgah Industrial Institute	Candler	Seventh Day Adventist
Haywood Institute	Clyde	S. Baptist Convention
Laura Sunderland Memorial School	Concord	Presbyterian (USA)
Crossnore School ▲	Crossnore	Smith-Hughes Act
Farm School	Farm School	Presbyterian (USA)
Naples Rural School	Fletcher	Seventh Day Adventist
Maxwell Farm School	Franklin	Presbyterian (USA)
Morrison Industrial School	Franklin	Presbyterian (USA)
Glade Valley High School	Glade Valley	Presbyterian (USA)

Settlement Schools and Weaving Centers

St. Paul's Mission School	Glen Alpine	Protestant Episcopal
Mountain View Institute	Hays	S. Baptist Convention
Fruitland Institute	Hendersonville	S. Baptist Convention
Markle School of Industrial Arts ▲	Higgins	Independent
Dorland Bell School ▲	Hot Springs	Presbyterian (USA)
Jefferson School	Jefferson	Methodist Episcopal
Cowee Mountain School	Leatherman	Seventh Day Adventist
Patterson School	Legerwood	Protestant Episcopal
Davenport College	Lenoir	Methodist Episcopal
Mars Hill College	Mars Hill	S. Baptist Convention
Club House	Marshall	Independent
St. Thomas's School	Mill Spring	Protestant Episcopal
Mitchell Home And School	Misenheimer	Methodist Episcopal
Applachian Industrial School ▲	Penland	Protestant Episcopal
Penland Weavers And Potters ●	Penland	Independent
Lees Mcrae Institute	Plumtree	Presbyterian (USA)
Robbinsville High School	Robinsville	Independent
Rutherford College	Rutherford	Methodist Episcopal
St. Francis' School	Rutherfordton	Protestant Episcopal
Westminster School	Rutherfordton	Presbyterian (USA)
Saluda Seminary	Saluda	Congregational
The Weave Shop ●	Saluda	Independent
Sylva Collegiate Institute	Sylva	S. Baptist Convention
The Blue Ridge Weaver ●	Tryon	Independent
Tryon School	Tryon	Independent
Round Hill Academy	Union Mills	S. Baptist Convention
Valle Crucis Industrial School	Valle Crucis	Protestant Episcopal
Washington Collegiate Institute ■	Washington	Methodist Episcopal
Weaver College	Weaverville	Methodist Episcopal
Wesley House	Winston-Salem	Methodist

South Carolina

Six Mile Academy	Central	S. Baptist Convention
Frances Willard School	Landrun	Independent
Long Creek Academy	Mountain Rest	S. Baptist Convention
North Greeneville Academy	Tigerville	S. Baptist Convention
Spartan Academy	Wellford	S. Baptist Convention

Tennessee

Pine Burr Studio	Apison	Independent
Athens School, U of Chattanooga	Athens	Methodist Episcopal
Ritter Home & Industrial School	Athens	Methodist Episcopal

Settlement Schools and Weaving Centers

Baxter Seminary	Baxter	Methodist Episcopal
Beersheba High School	Beersheba	Methodist Episcopal
King College	Bristol	Presbyterian (USA)
Wesley Settlement House	Bristol	Methodist
Smoky Mountain Academy	Butler	S. Baptist Convention
Watauga Academy	Butler	S. Baptist Convention
Horse Creek School	Chuckey	Presbyterian (United)
Weslyan Academy	Chuckey	Methodist Episcopal
Cosby Academy	Cosby	S. Baptist Convention
Ebenezer Mission	Del Rio	Presbyterian (USA)
Doyle Academy	Doyle	S. Baptist Convention
Lynn Bachman Memorial School	Farner	Presbyterian (USA)
Pi Beta Phi Settlement School ▲	Gatlinburg	Independent
Camp Creek School	Greeneville	Presbyterian (United)
Cedar Creek School	Greeneville	Presbyterian (United)
Paint Creek School	Greeneville	Presbyterian (United)
Shelton School	Greeneville	Presbyterian (United)
Tusculum College	Greeneville	Presbyterian (USA)
Zion School	Greeneville	Presbyterian (United)
Grace Nettleton Memorial Home	Harrogate	Independent
Lincoln Memorial University	Harrogate	Independent
John Black School	Hartford	Presbyterian (USA)
Stoctons Valley Institute	Helena	S. Baptist Convention
Carson And Newman College	Jefferson City	S. Baptist Convention
Livingston Academy	Livingston	Disciples of Christ
Hiawassee College	Madisonville	Methodist Episcopal
Maryville College	Maryville	Presbyterian (USA)
McLemoreville Collegiate Institute*	McLemoreville	Methodist Episcopal
Milligan College	Milligan College	Disciples of Christ
Providence House	Monteagle	Protestant Episcopal
Smoky Mountain Seminary	Moraine	Presbyterian (USA)
John A. Patton Community Center	Pikeville	Methodist Episcopal
Pleasant Hill Academy ▲	Pleasant Hill	Congregational
The Shuttle-Crafters ●	Russelville	Independent
Murphy College	Sevierville	Methodist Episcopal
Pittman Community Center	Sevierville	Methodist Episcopal
St. Mary's-On-The-Mountain	Sewanee	Protestant Episcopal
Chilhowee Institute	Seymour	S. Baptist Convention
Burritt College	Spencer	Independent
St. Andrew's School	St. Andrew's	Protestant Episcopal
Washington College ◆	Washington	Presbyterian (USA)

Walkers Valley Settlement	Blount ◆	TN Federation of Women's Clubs
Inamuch Mission	Hamilton ◆	Protestant Episcopal
Greenbrier Valley Settlement	Sevier ◆	TN Federation of Women's Clubs
Fall's Gap Settlement	Unicoi ◆	TN Federation of Women's Clubs

Virginia

Martha Washington College	Abingdon	Methodist Episcopal
Stonewall Jackson College	Abingdon	Presbyterian (USA)
Shenandoah Community Workers	Bird Haven	Independent
Blackwells Hollow School	Boonesville	Protestant Episcopal
Virginia Intermont College	Bristol	S. Baptist Convention
St. Peter's-In-The-Mountains	Callaway	Protestant Episcopal
St. Phoebe's Hall	Callaway	Protestant Episcopal
St. Mark's Mission	Dante	Episcopal
Blue Ridge Industrial School	Dyke	Protestant Episcopal
Emory And Henry College	Emory	Methodist Episcopal
Harris Mountain School	Endicott	Presbyterian (USA)
St. John's-In-The-Mountains	Endicott	Protestant Episcopal
Christian Training School	Fancy Gap	Christians
Ferrum Training School	Ferrum	Methodist Episcopal
St. Andrew's-On-The-Mountain	Fletcher	Protestant Episcopal
Girls' Industrial School	Fosters Falls	Presbyterian (USA)
Grundy Presbyterian School	Grundy	Presbyterian (USA)
Oak Hill Academy	Kindrick	S. Baptist Convention
Cecil Mission School	Lydia	Protestant Episcopal
St. James Mission School	Lydia	Protestant Episcopal
Rosemont	Marion	Independent
Frazier Mountain School	Mission Home	Protestant Episcopal
Mission Home	Mission Home	Protestant Episcopal
Bethesda School	Ocala	Presbyterian (USA)
Mountain Neighbors ●	Oldrag	Independent
Lee Institute	Pennington Gap	S. Baptist Convention
Harris-Cannaday Memorial School	Pizarro	Presbyterian (USA)
Simmons Gap	Sullivan	Protestant Episcopal
Blue Ridge Academy	The Hollow	Presbyterian (USA)
Lower Pocosan Mission School	Towles	Protestant Episcopal
Upper Pocosan Mission School	Towles	Protestant Episcopal

Settlement Schools and Weaving Centers

West Virginia

Alderson Baptist Academy	Alderson	N. Baptist Convention
Alleghany Collegiate Institute	Alderson	Methodist Episcopal
Morris Harvey College	Barboursville	Methodist Episcopal
Bethany College	Bethany	Churches of Christ
St. Andrew's-On-The-Mountain	Charles Town	Protestant Episcopal
Patty C. Stockdale Memorial School	Colcord	Presbyterian (USA)
Davis And Elkins College	Elkins	Presbyterian (USA)
St. Andrews's	Harper's Ferry	Protestant Episcopal
Lewisburg Seminary	Lewisburg	Presbyterian (USA)
West Virginia Synodical School	Madison	Presbyterian (USA)
Salem College	Salem	Seventh Day Baptist
Mountaineer Craftmen's Coop ●	Preston ◆	Independent

preface

Elsa Regensteiner and Lurene Stone introduced me to the intricacies of weaving while I was a student at the Art Institute of Chicago in the early 1960s. Even though Mrs. Regensteiner based her course on the Bauhaus experimental approach, she augmented our free inquiry with lectures on textile theory. We were assigned no text, so I eagerly sought out books about weaving at the Chicago Public Library. This was just before the major explosion in craft writing, so I didn't find much. As I searched the stacks for anything relating to weaving, I came across Allen Eaton's book *Handicrafts of the Southern Highlands*. I devoured the chapters relating to weaving, as well as the wonderful images by Doris Ulmann.

Since that time, I have carried around in my head the Appalachian pictures of the young girl seated at the loom and the old woman with a lace collar at a large old loom. I never visited the southern Appalachian Mountains until later in my life; by that time I had a husband, three sons—and lots of weaving paraphernalia. During my husband's first college teaching job in South Carolina, I inquired about joining the Southern Highland Handicraft Guild, and was informed that I lived one county outside the applicable region. I countered that a very famous mountain, King's Mountain, lay partially within York County, but the Guild, refusing to waver from John C. Campbell's definition of Appalachia, declared me ineligible. I did manage to visit some of the sites mentioned in Eaton's book—Penland School, Gatlinburg, Berea College, and the John C. Campbell Folk School.

In 1976 we moved to Murray, Kentucky, where my husband took a position in a teacher education project and I completed the Certificate of Excellence of the Handweavers Guild of America. I found it difficult to develop an artistic career in a small town in far western Kentucky, so I began writing about weaving as a way to publicize my work. Magazines obligingly let me illustrate my articles with my own woven pieces.

In 1988 the Kentucky Arts Council awarded me a special small artists' development grant. My husband drove me to the Hambidge Center in the northeastern corner of Georgia for three glorious weeks of weaving, walking in the woods, and enlightened dinner conversation. One evening the director, Ray Periotti, mentioned that the founder of the center had been a weaver. I quipped that the building filled with looms—known as the Weave Shed—had given me a clue. He asked if I was interested in seeing examples of Mary Hambidge's clothing and weaving from her business. Well, I was hooked—they were beautiful. When my husband came to collect me, I knew I had to return someday.

On a trip to Lexington that fall, I walked into the offices of the Kentucky Humanities Council and inquired if they would give me money to study a woman who had lived in Georgia. I guess my answer to the question—"Why would Kentuckians be interested in a

Preface

woman in Georgia?"—was sufficient. Virginia Smith took me into her office and explained how to write a grant proposal, offering to help me through the process. Following her directions, I applied and was awarded $500 dollars more than I had requested; I was also told to hire a folklorist. I was going to protest that Mary Hambidge had considered herself modern and not part of the folk tradition, but I was advised to keep quiet and work with the folklorist.

After a phone interview, Roby Cogswell, a folklorist with the Tennessee Arts Council, became part of my team. I was off on a fascinating adventure that lasted over a dozen years, involving a couple hundred very generous people, several places in the mountains that have adopted me, and, of course, the pursuit of documents and objects about weaving. I started this work believing that you needed a Ph.D. to gain access to archives, but Liza Kirwan of the Archives of American Art assured me that this wasn't the case. I also found that my activities in the craft world opened doors for me. I appreciate all of the folklorists and the Appalachian and women's studies scholars who took me seriously when I approached them about my research. They gave me confidence whenever I doubted my qualifications for academic inquiry. And I will be forever grateful to Nancy Grayson, then of the University Press of Kentucky, for suggesting that I combine my separate research projects into a book.

It is hard to credit all of Emily Wolfson's contributions to this project—she has always been there when I needed her, even when I didn't know I required assistance. She has been an audience for sharing exciting finds and for listening to me complain. As a native Kentuckian, one of the founders of the Kentucky Guild of Artists and Craftsmen, an activist in other arts organizations, and an excellent artist and weaver, Emily helped me to fit together the pieces of the puzzle that my research uncovered.

My brother, Donald Alvic of the Environment, Energy and Resources Center at the University of Tennessee, kindly let himself be drawn into my research. Having a geographer in the family has proven useful.

Roby Cogswell acted as an advance man, introducing me to the folklore community, where I met Jan Davison, David Brose, Gail Matthews, Doug DeNatale, Georgia Weir, and others who were willing to discuss theories and share contacts and resources.

With my first Humanities Council grant, I realized that I was onto a very good way to fund my research. The grants have covered supplies and travel expenses, allowing me to pursue research that I could never have undertaken on my own. My method has remained the same over the years. I study a weaving center by traveling to the site and locating as many resources as possible in the form of documents, people associated with the activities of the place, and artifacts. I document as much as I can, which usually involves a lot of copying and photographing. I analyze the materials, after which I write a booklet and compile a slide/tape presentation. Most of the projects have been completed in the wonderful, nurturing atmosphere of the Hambidge Center. In day-long public library residencies, I demonstrated weaving, showed the slide/tape presentations, displayed weaving from the centers and books about Appalachia, and talked with people about the significance of weaving in the mountains. In all, I received major grants from the Kentucky Humanities Council, the Tennessee Humanities Council, the North Carolina Humanities Council, and the Folklife Program of the North Carolina Arts Council. I also received mini-grants for programs from Humanities Councils in Kentucky, Tennessee, North Carolina, Illinois, and Georgia. The staffs of the various funding agencies became very involved in the projects, often making excellent suggestions. Harlin Gradin of the NCHC and Beverly Patterson of the NCAC extended themselves beyond their job descriptions, patiently dealing with my concerns and contributing to my research. I presented a total of forty-two programs in public libraries in small communities throughout the middle South. These libraries, run by dedicated librarians, serve as beacons of culture for their communities. I thoroughly enjoyed talking with hundreds of active and inquisitive people during these residencies.

During the summer of 1989, I embarked on my first study at the Hambidge Center. My expectations, timeline for completion, and budget were all totally unrealistic. With the help of Joan McLaughlin, who was writing a book on Mary Hambidge; Ray Periotti, who provided a environment for research and assisted in many small ways; Karen Schaller, who shared her own notes on the clothing of Mary Hambidge; and many others in and around the Betty's Creek area of northern Georgia, I fit together the pieces of the motivation and work of Mary Hambidge. Over the years, Mary Creety Nikas Beery has shared many stories about Mary Hambidge, as well as materials in her possession. Artist and frequent Hambidge resident Laurence Holden and his wife, Lynn, became good friends as we talked about Mary and her work, and about our feelings regarding art and life. Judy Barber, whom I first met in her capacity as Hambidge board member—she later became director of the center—listened to my stories and always made me feel welcome in the place we both love.

Robert Marshall Shepherd wrote me a letter after he saw a show of my woven wall textiles based on Mary Hambidge and her life. After spending his career in New York City, he had retired to Kentucky to research his family roots. He told me many engaging stories about Mary Hambidge and showed me correspondence from her spanning more than twenty years.

In 1991 I chose to study weaving in Gatlinburg because I knew it would be better documented there than at most other sites. The Pi Beta Phi Fraternity consented to let me explore the archives of their school in Gatlinburg and to delve into the records of their weaving program. The staff of Arrowmont School and Arrowcraft provided space, allowed me free access to their materials and to the fabric collection, and answered all my questions. With her quiet efficiency, Arrowmont Director Sandra Blain made my study much easier. Communications staff assistant and librarian Cynthia Huff placed resources at my disposal and allowed me to report on my progress and express my frustrations. Former director Marian Heard greeted my research with encouragement and talked about her many years at Arrowmont. She gave me a glimpse into the lives of the women who organized the crafts production and education in Appalachia. She stands as an example of someone able to maintain high standards while remaining inclusive. Artist and writer Bernice Stevens, who first came to the Summer Craft Workshops in Gatlinburg in 1946, told many wonderful stories about craft development in the Tennessee mountains, and about the progress of the Southern Highland Handicraft Guild. These women continued to respond to my phone calls and invitations to visit long after this project was over.

In 1992 the research expanded considerably with concentration on the Penland School. The staff of the school allowed me to move in, outfitting me with an office key, a desk, phone and message privileges, and access to a copy machine. As unofficial staff historian, Kat Conley outlined the history of weaving at the school, putting at my disposal many of the materials she had collected over the years. Suzanne and William Ford of Chinquapin Inn at Penland, where I stayed during this study, also took an active part in the project. Sue introduced me to many people connected with the school and with the weaving, and listened to my progress reports. Bill told of his childhood in the unusual creative environment of the Penland School, of his

Preface

parents, Bonnie and Toni, and of Penland's founder, Lucy Morgan. The staff at the Diocese of Western North Carolina at Black Mountain gave me access to the archives of the Appalachian School and other Episcopal Church records. Louise Morgan generously shared scrapbooks she kept of the Penland School and the weaving program and related many wonderful stories of her aunt Lucy Morgan. Weaver and textile historian Sadye Tune Wilson of Nashville not only gave me much encouragement, but she also gave me a hardcover copy of Allen Eaton's *Handicraft of the Southern Highlands,* which I have filled with Post-it Notes and flags over the years.

In an earlier project, I had spent a short time in the archives at Berea College researching background information on the Appalachian Craft Revival; in 1993 I finally got around to a full study of the weaving at Berea. Loyal Jones, then director of the Appalachian Center at Berea College, pointed me towards many of the significant pieces of the Berea puzzle and discussed the implications of crafts development. Garry Barker, then assistant director of student crafts at Berea College, always had his door open when I called to talk. As he had worked for the Southern Highland Handicraft Guild, served on the Guild's board, and written about craft promotion, he had special insights, which we discussed at great length. The Special Collections staff at the Hutchins Library at Berea College—especially Shannon Wilson—found and copied an amazing amount of material for me and listened to my theories as they evolved. While I was working on the Berea project, Julie Sowell, at the time curator at the Appalachian Museum at Berea College, was doing research for an exhibition on Berea's student craft program. We joined forces, often making two copies of documents in the archives so that we could cover more territory jointly. We talked at great length in an effort to understand the personalities and events that had shaped Berea's history. Sally Wilkerson, former Fiber Arts Professor at Berea College, contributed many interesting stories of her life as a student and instructor at Berea. Arturo Alonzo Sandoval, Fiber Arts Professor at the University of Kentucky, welcomed me as his houseguest, thus contributing substantially to my research resources. Lila and Richard Bellando discussed the Churchills and permitted the use of written materials, business records, photographs, and fabric samples of the Churchill Weavers. The Appalachian Community Development Association of Cincinnati, Ohio, also provided a grant to collect oral histories.

Anita Bugg and the staff of WKMS-FM, the public radio station at Murray State University, mixed the sound for my slide/tape presentations and turned many of my oral history interviews into radio programs.

Back in 1994—when I still thought writing a book would be easy—the Appalachian Center at Berea College gave me a grant for continuing research in preparation for a book on Appalachian Craft Revival weaving. Helen Lewis, then serving as interim director of the Appalachian Center, willingly discussed evolving ideas for the book and encouraged me to tell stories.

In 1995 the Kentucky Foundation for Women funded a grant, "Weaving a Better Life," to conduct further oral-history interviews with women connected with the Appalachian Craft Revival. This grant was matched by the Craft Revival Project of the McKissick Museum at the University of South Carolina. Doug DeNatale and I talked several times about the extensive goals of the McKissick project at the time he applied to the National Endowment for the Humanities. After receiving the NEH grant, Jane Przybysz took over as director of the project and challenged me on many points, helping me to clarify my positions.

Even though the editor at the University Press of Kentucky assured me that I had already

Preface

done sufficient research to write this book, I undertook a study of the Weaving Room at the Crossnore School in 1998. Ellie Hjemmet, at the time manager of the weaving program, insisted that I take up the research that she had begun. Joe Mitchell, director of Crossnore School, Inc., provided work and living space for this study, as well as other resources of the school. Dr. Emma Fink, daughter of the school's founder Mary Martin Sloop; and Virginia Hartley, granddaughter of Weaving Room manager Mrs. Newburn Johnson, provided a great deal of information and encouragement. Francis and Helen Luce, Francis and Peggy Hamlin, and others from the Avery County Historical Society and Museum assisted in the project and in the exhibition of weaving held at the Museum. The staffs of many of the departments of the Wilson Library at the University of North Carolina at Chapel Hill and at the State Archives in Raleigh helped me locate valuable information.

I have been pleased and a little surprised at the open-hearted welcome I have received at the places that I have studied. Not only the major sites, but also the 'others' have supplied me with documents, objects, and people that relate to their individual histories. Knowledge of these places has been preserved by caring people, who like me thought that this stuff was important. I have tried to respect that many of these places are still running schools, businesses, or social service agencies and am grateful that they allowed me to impose on their busy schedules.

I have continued to consult all of the people I mentioned in individual projects as my ideas about people, events, and places took shape over the years. Sometimes friends have been drawn into this project to listen to me talk—both Carol Baugh and Joanie Pigford shared contacts and always had eager words for my work. Finally, I want to thank Betsy Adler, whom I first met during her tenure as folklorist for the Kentucky Humanities Council. She became a close friend after I moved to Lexington. She has commented on the manuscript for this book, addressing questions of scholarship, suggesting additions, and tidying up my grammar.

I have included a list of all of the oral history interviews that I have conducted. I cannot express sufficient gratitude to the people who made time in their busy lives to talk to me. So many people welcomed me into their homes when I called. As we often sat on the front porch, a former weaver would apologize for not being able to remember enough to be useful to me. I would always assure them that I wouldn't ask hard questions about names and dates. When we got to talking, they would invariably relate enlightening stories about the weaving, the managers, and earlier times in the mountains. Talking with these women became my education, allowing me to place in perspective information I had gathered from other sources. I have attempted to tell their stories in a manner of which they would approve.

Since the mid-1990s I have made five international trips as a volunteer consultant in weaving techniques, product design, and crafts marketing. While this work has taken me away from my writing, it has also contributed to my understanding some of the topics covered in this book. As I talked to craftspeople in Peru, Morocco, India, Nepal, and Armenia, I realized the similarities between the problems they face today and those encountered in Appalachia one hundred years ago.

Throughout the process of collecting information, developing products for grants, and writing this book, I have continued to weave. The experience of researching has influenced the wall textiles that I weave. As this phase of my research is now complete, I know that I will continue to collect information on weaving in the Appalachian region. My own weaving and the weaving of Appalachia will continue to be entwined.

foundations of the appalachian craft revival

Early Weaving in the Mountains

Even over a hundred years ago, weaving was associated with the southern Appalachian Mountains. Perhaps this perception occurred because weaving survived as a household art longer as part of subsistence mountain living or because the local color writers who set their adventure tales in the southern mountains referred to "damsels in homespun" or "youth in rugged trousers of handwoven jeans." Around 1900, many social service workers in the region encouraged weaving to promote economic development among women, which also strengthened the association between the Southern Highlands and weaving.

"Hand spinning and weaving were at the foundation of the revival of handicrafts in the Southern Highlands, and weaving continues to be the principal home industry there to this day," wrote Allen Eaton in his definitive history of the Appalachian Craft Revival, *Handicrafts of the Southern Highlands*.[1] Weaving centers coordinating the production and marketing of goods led the revival of crafts produced in the home as a means of supplementing the income of families. The Fireside Industries of Berea College, Kentucky; Arrowcraft at the Pi Beta Phi Settlement School in Gatlinburg, Tennessee; and the Penland Weavers and Potters at the Appalachian School in Penland, North Carolina, were the largest and most active of the weaving centers. While they shared the same goals and many practices, they differed from each other substantially.

The Weavers of Rabun in the northeastern corner of Georgia started from other assumptions and their growth was predicated on different principles than the mainstream centers of

Berea College published this photograph of a weaver in several issues of the *Berea Quarterly*, which was circulated to the supporters of the college in the late nineteenth and early twentieth centuries.

Craft Revival weaving. Founded by Mary Hambidge and supported by a patron, this operation marketed its goods through different channels than the other centers. A closer look at these mountain weaving establishments, as well as several dozen others documented by Eaton, emphasizes the importance of weaving in the Appalachian Craft Revival and within crafts development in the United States.

The Craft Revival leaders encouraged weaving among the grandchildren and great grandchildren of women who had woven out of family necessity. The frontier families that settled Appalachia brought with them knowledge and equipment for home textile production, but most women readily gave up the many arduous tasks of cloth production when commercial fabrics became available. With the revival, the objective for weaving changed from personal use to income generation. The types of products also changed with the emergence of this new purpose of selling handwoven products to other people. With this economic incentive, looms again appeared in homes throughout Appalachia.

"In the 'yesteryears' this country was a community of weavers, but after the war, 'store cloth' was cheap so that one woman after another put the old loom aside, but many of our neighbors today know how to spin and weave though it has been 'a tol'able long spell' since any of them have done such a thing," observed Carolyn McKnight Hughes, who was the industrial arts teacher at the Pi Beta Phi Settlement School in Gatlinburg in 1915.[2] She was referring to the period after the Civil War. She explained in her article in *The Arrow* aimed at the school's sponsors that many women still knew how to weave and a few even possessed the skills for making "kivers," but the weavers were all old and lived in remote parts of the mountains.

After the Civil War looms fell idle and were stored in barns, but some weaving continued in all of the southern mountain states. In Tennessee, Emma Bell Miles witnessed weaving preparation near her home outside of Chattanooga. One of the stories in *Spirit in the Mountains,* published in 1905, contains a description of a woman warping a loom. The account is so accurate that Miles must have witnessed the task herself.[3] At Little Greenbrier, also in

The Walker sisters carried on the family traditions of spinning and weaving. All but one of the Walker sisters stayed on their family's land in Little Greenbrier after the government moved the rest of the residents during the creation of Great Smoky Mountains National Park.

Tennessee, five of the seven Walker sisters born in the 1870s and 1880s continued weaving in their family home even after the Great Smoky Mountains National Park took over their land in the 1930s.[4]

A unique historical document from North Carolina describing people and their occupations also mentions weaving. Between 1841 and 1916, Jake Carpenter listed the death dates, often accompanied by brief notations on the lives of the deceased, for the Three Mile Creek area of Avery County, North Carolina. Uncle Jake used his own method of spelling in his roster of names and in his commentary. Next to the men's names Carpenter most often recorded "farmer" and "soldier," noted a couple of blacksmiths, and commented on a few who made good whiskey. He identified several weavers, all of whom lived long lives. In 1875 Lily Wisman passed away at the age of eighty-two; Uncle Jake observed that she spun and wove all of the clothing that her family wore. He identified seventy-two-year-old Peg Chatem as a spinner and weaver when she died in 1886. In 1895 Miney Inglish, who lived until the age of ninety-three, was listed as a weaver only. Franky Berlison, a weaver and spinner, died at the age of eighty-six in 1896. During the last twenty years of his record keeping, no other names of weavers appeared.[5] Except in a few rare cases, the complex skills of yarn preparation, dyeing, and weaving were not passed down to the next generation of women.

In her 1913 book *The Carolina Mountains*, Margaret Morley wrote about the daily life of women, which contained a section on weaving and dyeing. She observed that looms could no longer be found in the larger and more prosperous communities, but in "the remoter regions, far from railways and summer visitors, they are still in common use. With what pleasure one recalls certain high valleys where under the shadow of blue domes and green slopes one finds in every second house a great loom taking up half of the room!"[6] Frances Goodrich found weavers in the hills around Brittain's Cove near Asheville; they helped her recreate traditional weaving products to sell to northern customers. Established weavers Elmeda Walker and Aunt Cumi Woody sold coverlets through Goodrich's Allanstand Fireside Crafts.[7] In the early 1920s, Lucy Morgan walked from Penland to visit old Susan Phillips on her farm near Bakersville in Mitchell County, North Carolina. Aunt Susan had woven most of the fabric used by her family, but her daughters continued only with spinning, not weaving.[8]

In the journal Katherine Pettit kept at the turn of the twentieth century, when she and several friends set up summer camps in the mountains of eastern Kentucky, there are references to weaving found in homes: "She had an attractive comparatively clean room with homespun coverlid and blankets on the bed. She showed us her loom and promised us to teach her grand daughter to spin and weave."[9] Albert Anglin remembered that as a child early in the century, he handed threads to his mother as she dressed her loom in their Rockcastle County Kentucky home.[10]

Two renowned mountain weaving families turned their household skills into weaving items for sale during the Craft Revival: the Mast family of Valle Crucis, North Carolina, and the Dougherty family of Russellville, Tennessee. Eaton described Allie Josephine Mast, whom he designated by her married name, Mrs. Finley Mast: "She lived with her sister, Mrs. Robert Mast, in the old cabin on the Mast homestead which was built in 1812. Together they worked on two looms even older than the cabin."[11] While demonstrating weaving at the first fair of the Southern Highland Handicraft Guild, Sarah Dougherty described her weaving center, the Shuttle Crafters, as a place to practice "the arts of our grandmothers." She meant that very literally, displaying "examples of weaving of five consecutive generations" of her family.[12] Another mountain family, the Pigmans of eastern Kentucky, also worked in a continuous tradition, cherishing articles woven by generations of their female line. Una Pigman taught weaving for many years at the Hindman Settlement School, while her sister Winnie Pigman Day wove for several weaving centers, including Hindman, Carr Creek, and Quicksand.[13] Since these sisters worked for others, they did not generate the publicity of the other two families, who proudly claimed their ancestors in promotional materials.

Weaving never completely died out in the southern Appalachian Mountains after the Civil War, but neither did every home have a loom. Textile production skills ceased to be passed down in families after inexpensive commercial textiles became readily available. In a few hollows and up a few creeks, old women continued to weave household necessities, but they were the exceptions. After the general abandonment of the looms, the spinning of wool persisted, with yarn knitted into men's socks. While weaving required many complex skills, the simpler task of spinning could be done after other household chores were completed.

Seeking and Defining a Mission

Appalachian settlement schools revived weaving as part of a program of comprehensive reforms that not only addressed problems in education, but also confronted concerns about health care, recreation, and household economy. The mountain settlement school movement had no central guiding agency, and it even lacked a common motivation. The term "movement" is only applicable in hindsight to this collection of individual institutions engaging in similar activities. Beginning before the turn of the century and continuing through the 1920s, schools sprang up all over the mountains, with backing from Protestant denominations, social service agencies, and even lone individuals with privately raised funds. In 1920 John C. Campbell listed over 150 of these schools.[14]

While most of these mountain ventures began as schools, their work was based on the principles of the settlement house movement. Copying the English model for working among London's poor, settlement houses in the United States multiplied rapidly in northern cities, working among immigrant populations. The first settlement workers in London summarized

The settlement workers went to remote areas of the Appalachian Mountains to help educate children and to work on social problems.

Foundations of the Appalachian Craft Revival

their mission: "to bridge the gulf that industrialism had created between rich and poor, to reduce the mutual suspicion and ignorance of one class for the other, and to do something more than give charity, university men would live in a poor neighborhood of a great city. They would make their settlement in the slums an outpost of education and culture."[15] In the United States, the settlement ideal still required that reform workers live among the poor as beacons of a better lifestyle, influencing by example. The settlement workers learned firsthand about local conditions and responded to needs they perceived in each community. They believed in the power of progressive education, organized collective action, recreation, modern hygiene, and preventive medicine—all cloaked in activist, liberal Christianity.

The southern mountain workers also eagerly tackled difficulties in education, recreation, and health, but they faced economic problems not found in cities. In the remote areas of the mountains, where the sponsored schools served as community development centers, most families practiced subsistence farming, with cash income derived from men working part-time in logging, mining, and other short-term manual labor jobs. The women worked only on the farm and in the house. The mountain workers proposed crafts as a way to supplement the family's income while not substantially altering the rural lifestyle. Among the crafts, weaving became the handwork most commonly promoted among women.

In their formative years, all the weaving centers put out pamphlets to inform patrons about their activities. In addition to presenting items for purchase, these early brochures put forth each center's mission and history. These publications stated two major goals: 1.) to save or revive the lost art of weaving, and 2.) to help women by providing them with paid work. A third objective often crept into these statements of purpose, having to do with the virtues accrued by throwing the shuttle, although the exact nature of this value varied depending on the center. These small-format publications, each consisting of only a few pages, aimed their message at a population far from the mountain production centers. Included with the mission statement were usually several photographs of finished goods, a weaver at a loom, and a building (either a weaver's home or the center).

Mary Sloop surveyed the weaving made at The Weaving Room of Crossnore School, Inc., which started a school-based weaving program in 1920.

These publications focused first on saving weaving. A Berea College Fireside Industries' pamphlet from the first decade of the twentieth century set forth goals under the heading of, "What we 'aim for to do.'" The list began, "to preserve so far as possible the simple life of the mountains, and to build upon what is best in their present customs and traditions." The text continued by extolling the virtues of handweaving, and ended with a presentation of products for sale. The declaration of principles that began Crossnore's brochure stated first, "To keep alive an almost forgotten art." A 1925 Appalachian School brochure professed the desire to save this lost heritage under the title of "Revival of Colonial Weaving."[16]

Emphasizing the revival aspect of their work, the centers attempted to connect themselves with Appalachian weaving and weavers of the past. All of the centers referred to information about weavers, described weaving for household use, or claimed to be carrying on the tradition of weaving overshot coverlets. Frances Goodrich linked her efforts to those of a specific, older weaver: "It is our misfortune that we went to Allanstand too late to see Aunt Polly, but we know her thrifty and artistic nature from the work she left behind." Often the weaving matriarch took a more generic form, as in Crossnore's pamphlet: "We dye with the old-fashioned 'indigo blue pot' like our grandmothers did." Winogene Redding presented chatty and appealing vignettes describing the weavers, their relation to their work, and their families in her final reports for Arrowcraft and in articles she wrote for Pi Beta Phi's *The Arrow*. In November 1929, Redding recalled, "One woman told me recently of seeing years ago, her grandmother's and grandfather's church clothes that her grandmother had woven. The dress was made of very fine dark brown homespun wool and fashioned with a series of ruffles, short and full, down the entire length of the skirt. The man's suit was much more gay as the trousers were woven of colored striped homespun and the woven cotton shirt was made with a ruffle around the vest-like front. They were beautifully sewed with tiny, wee stitches, the happy result of months of work." She concluded this section of mountain weaving tales with the sentence, "Thus was weaving when our country was young and the family clothing and bedding depended upon the ingenuity and art of the womenfolks."[17]

Mary Hambidge emphasized her modern use of weaving while still claiming the mountain heritage. In a pamphlet describing the work of the Jay Hambidge Art Foundation, she extolled the traditions as being akin to many of her own goals: "Here they had continued to practice their skills in carding, spinning and weaving, which they had always used in their daily life. They still clung to the early American pattern of living, close to Nature, with Agriculture as their chief means of livelihood."[18]

Although the informative brochures listed the preservation of the art of weaving first, the second goal of providing financial help to families was actually the primary motivation behind the revival of weaving. An Allanstand Industries pamphlet expressed the sensitivity required in promoting this economic development: "The two or three women who made a home together in the little cottage near the school-house found many avenues of approach to their neighbors, but a problem faced them such as meets every one who sets himself to social service, namely, how to bring material help to those neighbors without hampering them, or injuring their self-respect." They settled on reviving the "old time crafts which were fast disappearing," which would bring "habits of self-help to many" through the generation of additional income.[19]

Berea explained the school's involvement in marketing crafts in the following manner: "The industries are carried on in the mountain homes, under our guidance, and bring some income to those homes which is commonly used for the education of the children." After the direction of Berea's Fireside Industries passed to Anna Ernberg, she reinforced the economic value of the weaving: "If we can put a little ready money into that mountain home, entrusting

In the late nineteenth century, Berea College started buying weaving from community women and the mothers of students, soon directing manufacture under the name of Fireside Industries.

to the mother, whose ambitions and faith in the children are, perhaps, the greater, we shall be quite sure to add to the comfort and beauty of the home and to the encouragement of all aspirations for the young people of the household."[20]

The writer of one Crossnore pamphlet presented the financial goal more directly: "To provide a way by which the many mountain mothers may earn money which they need more than you can imagine, and long for, with a longing you have never known." This message was aimed at middle-class women, who purchased items through churches and social service agencies. While the school helped children, the weaving offered possibilities for their mothers: "Married as mere girls, with almost no education, they have watched the wonderful development of their younger sisters or their daughters, till their own privations and limitations have loomed large." A few of Crossnore's small catalogs end with a blatant sales pitch: "LIFE is a different thing to these 'hidden heroes,' as I call these mountain mothers, and you help to produce the result when you enable us to sell their finished product. SO, WHO WILL BUY?"[21] None of the readers doubted the financial significance that their purchases brought to Appalachian women.

A 1924 Penland pamphlet pointed out the disintegration of the family that occurred when local people were forced to seek factory work outside the mountains. The weaving "makes it possible for the people to stay in the mountain home with its high ideals, and to do there a work which brings economic independence while at the same time satisfying a natural artistic taste and an inborn creative impulse." In *The Story of the Penland Weavers*, Bonnie Willis Ford stated the goals of the weaving: "At the beginning of the community project, a two-fold purpose was established which was, namely—to perpetuate the native arts and crafts, and through them to provide for the people of the community a more adequate means of livelihood. Throughout all of the ensuing years, although the weaving has grown to large proportions, there has never been any other objective."[22]

The economic benefit of weaving appeared in *The Arrow* as part of the reports to the Pi Beta Phi membership about the progress of their settlement school. Winogene Redding described a woman who quit working in the fields for "inside" work: "For some women like this one weaving is emancipation from tending the crop; for others the money it brings means new shoes, a new dress for one of the children, a poke of meal for the family or a new and coveted piece of furniture. One energetic woman has built an attractive modern home with the proceeds from her weaving."[23] There is a strong emphasis on the jobs provided to women and the economic benefits to the family in all of Redding's writings.

The third objective that was tucked into the early justifications for weaving programs had a moralistic tone, although the writers did not agree on what the exact benefits were. In 1909 Frances Goodrich exclaimed, "our aim and hope have been to bring interest and thrift and self-help to many." Later in her life, Goodrich reflected on her mountain work: "In the younger women who were learning to weave and keeping at it, I could see the growth of character. A slack-twisted person cannot make a success as a weaver of coverlets. Patience and perseverance are the first necessity, and the exercise of these strengthen the fibers of the soul." She claimed benefits for the next generation: "One who has had to do with hundreds of mountain girls in their teens has told me that never did she find one to be of weak and flabby character whose mother was a weaver; there was always something in the child to build on."[24]

Anna Ernberg believed that weaving exemplified the best qualities in mountain life: "How can we better make them 'hold up their heads' and believe in their own possibilities than by paying honor and giving just recognition to this skill and thrift which belong to them as an inheritance?" In her 1913 article in the *Berea Quarterly*, Ernberg presented desirable qualities felt by the weaver: "In seeking to glorify rural life it is an immense advantage to have some definite occupation of a dignified and worthy character which may enliven the loneliness of a life which must be largely shut in."[25] The act of weaving, itself good, resulted in the practitioner acquiring good traits.

By the 1920s, over 150 schools like the Appalachian School in Penland, North Carolina, were located in remote areas along the ridges of the Appalachian chain of mountains. They were usually sponsored by Protestant denominations.

Foundations of the Appalachian Craft Revival

Although Bonnie Ford only listed two objectives for the Penland revival of weaving, the 1924 pamphlet about the Appalachian School stated a third: "Weaving gives an outlet for minds that are keen, and an opportunity for the expression of native artistic and creative ability." The pamphlet continued, "Women gain a new importance in the eyes of their husbands and a new self-respect." Earning money improved the women's stature within the household while providing redeeming personal benefits. Crossnore, too, professed additional, although vague, gains for the weavers aside from the much-needed income: "To these hungry minds the weaving lessons opens new fields." The women became somehow better as they threw their shuttles, having occupation for their minds while adding to the family income. Mary Hambidge invested the act of weaving with basic values: "To preserve and develop this precious remnant of American heritage into something higher and more far reaching in scope, while at the same time keeping its inner value of simplicity, honesty, and practicalness, became the primary objective of the Foundation."[26]

Saving the dying art of weaving became a pretext for promoting the economic development of women. Even though they stated the mission in two parts, the second goal of providing an income achieved the first objective of saving weaving in the mountains. Because the southern mountain workers sought to improve the general quality of women's lives, they turned to an activity that they felt had virtue in itself. They professed that weaving awakened creativity and built character—while earning money. After they became better known for their products, the weaving centers abandoned this moralistic tone about the virtues of weaving.

The writers of these tracts were well aware of the audience that received this publicity and the nature of the organizations that distributed them. In most cases, the women who wrote these pamphlets possessed similar education and background to the women who read them. Through these pamphlets, the organizers defined their mission for themselves as well as outlining motives for potential buyers. Their words conveyed the sincerity with which they approached their cause. While the writers occasionally overdramatized their message, always evident is the earnestness of their personal dedication to social betterment through providing women with a way to earn money. While this may read as a sales pitch, it expressed deeply held beliefs.

The booklets circulated through the women's networks made up of arts organizations, church groups, and community social service associations. Even though many Protestant denominations, states Federation of Women's Clubs, the Daughters of the American Revolution, the Pi Beta Phi Fraternity, and other women's organizations supported weaving centers, they also relied on their individual members to buy the products. Women inevitably drew into sales ventures other women's groups they felt would sympathize with the cause. Although directed at women of means, these pamphlets were an appeal for the sale of items, rather than a call for charity. The pamphlets functioned as marketing vehicles, juxtaposing the mission statements with descriptions of items, prices, and shipping instructions.

Foundations of Thought

"The revival was not marked by a sudden turning of large numbers of workers to handwork, but rather by gradual renewing of interest and activity in the old-time arts in different parts of the mountains quite independently of one another," observed Eaton at the outset of his study of the Appalachian crafts.[27] The workers who revived crafts didn't arrive as a unified group or part of any organized movement, but rather filterd into the mountains around the turn of the twentieth century, gradually introducing crafts as a form of economic development.

The leaders, grounded in several different social and religious movements of the period, forged their own pragmatic philosophies independent of one another. They borrowed heavily from the Social Settlement Movement that had worked among immigrants in major cities; the Arts and Crafts Movement, which established handicraft societies on the English model; the Country Life Movement, which encouraged diverse and fulfilling lives in rural areas; and the Social Gospel Movement, which promoted Christian work and sharing among the worthy poor. These Progressive-Era women—and a few men—did not stand idly by but rather leapt in when they saw wrongs of the world that needed righting. The educated women, who made up most of the leadership of the Appalachian Craft Revival, subscribed to the legend "Not for Herself, but for Humanity," as found in the literature from the Women's Building at the World's Columbian Exposition held in Chicago in 1893.[28] Young women of the time, raised to think of family and the less fortunate before their own needs, often sank their energies into social causes. The southern mountains attracted many young women who planned to spend a year or two in meaningful work before returning home and assuming the more traditional roles of wife and mother. While some of these women did return home, others spent the rest of their lives in the mountains.

The women who worked in the southern Appalachian Mountains received support from a broad-based women's network of arts organizations, church groups, and community social service associations. Although Protestant denominations founded the majority of the schools and community centers, other organizations made significant contributions as well.[29] The Georgia and Kentucky Women's Clubs, the Daughters of the American Revolution, and the Pi Beta Phi Fraternity each sponsored at least one school in the mountains. But whether or not the schools received direct support from a specific agency, the broader women's network of organizations provided a forum for fundraising and for the sale of items produced at centers. While most of the women could not be counted on for large sums, they gave consistently to benevolent appeals.[30]

Like the development of the Appalachian settlement schools, the weaving centers sprang from no single ideology. They loosely followed the working models established at Allanstand near Asheville and at the Fireside Industries of Berea College. The centers coordinated activities and marketed items, with the women weaving in their own homes. Within these general parameters, each center forged its own unique structure influenced by local support, the physical setting, the parent institution, and the personalities of the principal players. Comparing their stories both enhances the similarities and explains the differences between places.

Four weaving centers—the Fireside Industries at Berea, Arrowcraft at the Pi Beta Phi Settlement School in Gatlinburg, the Penland Weavers in Penland, and the Weavers of Rabun in Rabun Gap—will be examined closely because they span a broad range of defining variables. They are located in the mountain regions of four states: Kentucky, Tennessee, North Carolina, and Georgia, respectively. Each started in a different decade: Berea, in the 1890s; Gatlinburg, 1912; Penland, 1923; and Rabun Gap, mid-1930s. The founding of each center also had roots in different organizational structures: Berea was associated with an independent school, Gatlinburg was the philanthropic activity of a national women's organization, Penland was affiliated with a church mission effort, and Rabun Gap was the product of one woman's imagination.

The small Seiver County community of Gatlinburg, Tennessee, as seen by the Pi Beta Phi teachers in the early part of the twentieth century.

The Southern Mountains: Setting the Scene

The geography of the southern Appalachian Mountains both gave cohesion to the work and presented a great obstacle to development. Olive Dame Campbell summarized her husband's definition of the Southern Highlands as follows: "those three belts of the Appalachian Province, designated by the Geological Survey as the Blue Ridge Belt, the Greater Appalachian Valley and the Allegheny-Cumberland Plateau. The steep front of the Blue Ridge to the east, the broken irregular face of the Allegheny-Cumberland Plateau to the west and the upper reaches of the Coastal Plain to the south, distinguish the Highland proper from the country adjacent and in many respects not dissimilar. In all this region, reckoned on a county basis, covers some 112,000 square miles."[31] The schools and the craft centers that were managed by people coming from outside the mountains tended to be located in remote areas rather than in established population centers. On a map of the region, the dots representing institutions for education and crafts development are sprinkled along the eastern and western Appalachian ridges—avoiding the central valley.[32]

Even back in the nineteenth century, Berea College was the easiest mountain institution to reach. An 1877 brochure from the school describes the area: "Berea is a small village, delightfully located among the foot-hills of the Cumberland Mountains, and just upon the famous 'blue-grass' region of Central Kentucky. It is accessible by stage lines from Lexington and Richmond, by railroad from Louisville."[33] At this time, the railroad stopped eight miles from Berea, but a Berea station was established after the school grew and developed.

In sharp contrast to the relative ease of reaching Berea, Elizabeth Clarke Helmick remembered her arduous journey to reach the Pi Beta Phi School in 1912:

> Army life on the frontier, among Indians, in isolated Army posts, and actual war experiences should have prepared me and made me more enduring for that awful first trip from Knoxville to Gatlinburg. However, even after these twenty-four years which have elapsed, that ride through swollen rivers, over miles of uncharted stony trails, up precipitous mountain sides and down into cavernous ravines, over roads overhanging the mountain sides or temporarily widened by anchored logs when we looked over the tree tops into the rushing waters of the Little Pigeon River two hundred feet below, comes afresh to my mind as one of the unforgettable experiences of my life.

Although an arduous journey, she thought it worth the effort: "When we rounded the curve

Elizabeth Allen Clarke Helmick of the Phi Beta Phi Settlement School Committee, on the far right, poses for a picture with several teachers from the 1916–17 school year.

in the road that brought to view the magnificent grandeur of the Gatlinburg scenery, like a woman being delivered of her first child, the previous tortuous four hours were entirely forgotten for the moment, and my soul was spurred to ecstatic adoration and sympathy for the place."[34]

When Winogene Redding arrived at the Pi Beta Phi School in 1925, traveling was still a problem. She described visiting the weavers, who "lived distances from the school that were separated by rocky or muddy roads." In 1928 she finally secured an automobile for some of her travels, but in the early years she used other modes of transportation. "The first year I walked and walked, sometimes as much as twenty-five miles a week to reach the women who wanted to learn to weave. . . . The next year I decided to save myself so much walking so I rode a horse to the most distant homes." As Redding described Gatlinburg in 1925, the "town could not boast of a lawn mower, baby carriage, church every Sunday, coal or electric stove, and only the Teachers' Cottage had both a bathroom and a furnace." After the establishment of the Great Smoky Mountains National Park, Winogene wrote that in 1945 Gatlinburg included "a telephone exchange, public library, post office, four churches, a four-lane highway with sidewalks."[35]

When Muriel Early Sheppard described her trip to the Appalachian School, up the hill from the tiny village of Penland, it was a much less difficult journey than the one Helmick experienced, but she still presented an austere landscape: "The school is reached by a circuitous road up a steep grade hanging along a narrow shoulder with a magnificent prospect of the Cane River Mountains and the narrow Ledger valley." In her 1932 newspaper article she graphically set the school in the Toe River Valley section of North Carolina. "The buildings are scattered informally over the hilltop known as Conley Ridge which juts into the river valley at Penland at the foot of Bailey's Peak in a wooded promontory and runs back in a circular sweep past the foot of the Otter Knobs, enclosing a shallow inner valley along whose sunny slopes extend 30 acres of orchards belonging to the school farm. The entire farm holding embraces 224 acres with 3 acres under cultivation in corn and wheat, and three acres of gardens."[36]

Lucy Morgan recalled her first arrival at the Penland Station. Miss Amy Burt greeted the new teachers with "'The wagon's for your baggage. We'll walk.' She waved her hand in the general direction of Conley Ridge. 'It's just up there a little way. The road's too rough for riding. Going up there in a wagon would shake your teeth out.'" Although the route was

Foundations of the Appalachian Craft Revival

After the train made the flag stop at the small Penland settlement, those desiring to go to the Appalachian School faced either a very bumpy wagon ride up the hill or a shorter but steep climb.

shorter, the walking path up the mountain proved very steep, even for Lucy, "born and reared in the mountains and all my life had been accustomed to walking." When students later came to the Weaving Institute, many of them took the train, transferring at Johnson City for the train to Penland. Even with improvements to the road, many of the students chose the path for the walk up the hill to the school.

After Lucy received from Bishop Horner a Model T Ford roadster with a pickup truck rear, she toured nearby resorts to sell weaving. In the early 1930s, the roads in the North Carolina mountains left much to be desired. "Between us and Spruce Pine there was still a tremendous mud hole; the state kept a team of mules and a driver there, and when a car came along they didn't even wait for it to get stuck. The driver automatically hitched the mules to the bumper and pulled the car through."[37] Even though Spruce Pine, just a few miles away, viewed itself as a progressive community with modern conveniences, Penland remained isolated, reached only with great effort.

In her 1935 book *Cabins in the Laurel*, Muriel Earley Sheppard presented both a physical and cultural picture of the Toe River Valley. The wife of a mining engineer, Sheppard arrived in the area in the late 1920s. In her book she recorded her observations and repeated regional stories and folktales. Appalachian writer John Ehle, after noting that the local people did not care for their portrayal in the book, wrote in the foreword to the reprinted edition: "This book is Muriel Sheppard's picture of Appalachians—let each writer have his own—perhaps the best non-fiction portrait we have." The photographs accounted for part of the negative local reaction to the book. Photographer Bayard Wootten traveled from her studio in Chapel Hill to record the people in their home settings using natural light. Some area inhabitants resented her images of old men in overalls and women in long work dresses. One woman who knew the pictured subjects observed, "She wanted to photograph them like that, those people had nice clothes."[38]

The paved roads that today wind their way into mountain communities only hint at the

Spinners on the Weaving Shed porch at the Hambidge Foundation in Rabun Gap, Georgia, look south towards Betty's Creek.

perils of travel in former times. Mary Martin Sloop recounted the daylong ox cart ride in 1911 from Plumtree to her new home in Crossnore, North Carolina: "And though we had few possessions, it was still a difficult task to move a family over six or seven miles of mountain trails—they were hardly roads in those days—and few vehicles could stand the jolting." At this time the small community of Crossnore proclaimed a population of twenty-three: "Down in the village one could count three houses, a combination schoolhouse and church, and one store."[39]

Mary Hambidge settled in the far northeastern corner of Georgia. "The valley where the Weavers of Rabun work is full of the murmur of water and the soft mist-colored shadows of the Blue Ridge Mountains that nudge the irregular horizon. The water is clear, rock-happy Betty's Creek, which flows close by this unique mountaincraft colony in Rabun County, Ga., not far from the little town of Dillard. The blue hills have names like Ridgepole, Joe Gap and Pickens' Nose, Gulf Mountain and Stillhouse Mountain."[40] The beauty of the area attracted Mary Hambidge and she valiantly—and vainly—fought to keep her property from being bisected by the straightened surfaced road reaching from Dillard to the North Carolina line.

Such rugged physical settings played a part in the development of all of the centers. Even though many of them were situated within ten miles of the county seat or some other sizable town, the lack of adequate roads prevented easy access. Most of the weavers lived on small farms near the school or center. In the early part of the twentieth century, transportation consisted of walking, riding a horse or mule (sometimes pulling a sled for hauling), and—where roads permitted—using a wagon. Weather conditions often made roads impassable.

2

common threads

The histories of weaving at Berea, Gatlinburg, Penland, and Rabun Gap record their individual development, but these places shared several events, people, and other connections. The weaving centers started independently of each other, with different organizational structures, but they professed common founding principles. Their leaders came from similar backgrounds and held similar beliefs. Periodically the craft production centers joined together for mutual benefit, sometimes in self-generated ventures and sometimes in opportunities provided by others. The federal government also influenced and participated in Appalachian crafts development in several ways.

Organizations Promoting Crafts for Economic Development

In 1905 Martha S. Gielow founded the Southern Industrial Education Association to promote and raise money for crafts development in the Appalachian Mountains.[1] Gielow centered her operations in Washington, D.C., with later auxiliaries in Philadelphia and New York, among other cities. The association ran an annual craft exhibition, called an "exchange," under the patronage of the First Lady in residence at the White House. First developed to help impoverished gentlewomen after the Civil War, the exchange system marketed handmade

The Daughters of the American Revolution sponsored their own schools and gave generously to others on their approved school list, such as the Crossnore School in North Carolina.

work through a women's network. When more women sought income during the late nineteenth century, independent exchanges emerged in all major United States cities.[2]

The Southern Industrial Education Association sold handmade items, and each year reported the sales figures in its quarterly newsletter. From 1916 through 1918, the amount remitted to producers nearly tripled, from $2,886 to $8,363.15.[3] After First Lady Ellen Wilson saw weaving examples in the 1913 exchange, she commissioned textiles from weavers Josie Mast and Elmelda Walker of North Carolina to redecorate President Wilson's bedroom in the White House, which was known as the Blue Mountain Room and housed the Lincoln bed.[4]

Martha Gielow and others raised money by selling craftworks and by soliciting individual contributions. The Southern Industrial Education Association supported "Field Welfare Workers," who taught and promoted craft production. The Association contributed handwork funds to programs at established schools, rather than starting schools of its own. The 1919 Southern Industrial Education Association newsletter stated that the association "has no schools exclusively its own, but co-operates with settlement schools in isolated districts by furnishing equipment for industrial training and salaries of industrial teachers and of extension workers who visit the remote cabin homes and give the parents help and suggestions which are eagerly received." By paying tuition fees to schools, the association "provides scholarships for deserving children who are eager for a chance but whose parents are without funds necessary to pay their expenses."[5] In 1918 the association aided seventeen schools, including the Hindman Settlement School and the Pine Mountain Settlement School in Kentucky, Lincoln Memorial University in Tennessee, the Lees McRae Institute and the Crossnore School in North Carolina, and the Berry Schools in Georgia.

Industrial training encompassed a broad range of living skills. The Southern Industrial Educational Association organized "for the purpose of giving the boys and girls in the remote mountain sections training suited to their local environment that shall enable them to go back to their mountain homes carrying with them knowledge of carpentry, agriculture, care of stock, sewing, cooking, housekeeping, simple nursing and care of infants, and domestic hygiene and sanitation."[6] Among the subjects for girls, weaving alone offered a potential source of income—the other skills were part of the female's domestic role. In 1925, the association itself disbanded "owing to changed circumstances," but the New York Auxiliary and several other individual members continued promoting industrial education in the southern mountains.[7]

John C. Campbell originated and directed the Southern Division of the Russell Sage Foundation. He traveled throughout southern Appalachia, collecting and disseminating information on a wide range of human activities. He gathered and shared information about the southern mountain workers, who in many cases did not know of the endeavors of others because they sprang from different sources. A friend wrote of Campbell's headquarters: "His office in Asheville became a clearing house for the mountain work. His knowledge and advice were sought by workers on the field. The representatives of various agencies supporting work in the mountains consulted him about plans and problems. Prospective donors sought his opinion as to the worthiness of particular objects to which they had been asked to contribute. Prospective teachers and community workers would turn his office into an employment agency."[8]

Margaret Olivia Sage formed the Russell Sage Foundation when she inherited $65 million following the death of her husband in July 1906. The charter of the foundation stated that the income from the endowment be applied "to the improvement of social and living

Olive Dame Campbell pictured with John Jacob Niles, who traveled in Appalachia with photographer Doris Ulmann, examine handcrafted wooden animals made by the Brasstown Carvers.

conditions in the United States of America." The governing document laid out the means for accomplishing this task: "research, publication, education, the establishment of charitable or benevolent activities, agencies and institutions, and the aid of any such activities, agencies or institutions already established."[9] The foundation's mission was to identify and study social problems, and then to publicize social conditions and injustices.

After John C. Campbell graduated from Andover Seminary in 1895, he chose service as an educator at schools in the southern Appalachian Mountains over a career as a Presbyterian minister. He taught at Joppa, Alabama, and Pleasant Hill, Tennessee, and also served as president of Piedmont College in Demorest, Georgia. After his wife died of an extended illness, he sought rest on a trip to Scotland, his ancestral home. He met Olive Dame, touring with her sister and mother, on the ship and they saw each other several times in Scotland, finally returning to the United States on the same vessel. They married in 1907; on their honeymoon in Europe they discussed social service activities they might pursue in the southern mountains. John began a survey of southern Appalachia for the Russell Sage Foundation in 1908 with a grant of $3,000 for expenses, receiving no compensation for his services.[10] In October 1912, the Russell Sage Foundation officially created the Southern Highlands Division headquartered in Asheville, naming Campbell secretary in charge of all activities.

From the autumn of 1908 to the spring of 1909, Campbell and his wife traveled extensively in the mountains, learning about the area and meeting workers in the field. Although Campbell reported his activities to the foundation, he resisted publishing the findings of his studies because he feared alienating the agencies as he compared and generalized about the complex problems they faced. However, he began writing *The Southern Highlander and His Homeland,* which his wife Olive finished after his death in 1919 and the Russell Sage Foundation published in 1921. In the preface Olive noted John's reservations about writing about a people who lived in a geographical area but were not "socially homogeneous. Many statements applicable to the remote rural folk who were the particular object of his study were not true of their urban and valley kinsfolk, yet to differentiate groups in discussing phases of life common to all was not easy."[11]

John C. Campbell realized that many of the people he met while studying mountain life did not know about the work of others involved in similar efforts, even when they were working in the same general vicinity. He organized the first gathering of mountain workers, which was held in Atlanta on April 24, 1913, with "thirty or thirty-five in attendance."[12] The program listed "Industrial Teaching" as one of the six discussion topics. After this initial success, the Conference of Southern Mountains Workers usually met in late March at the Farragut Hotel in Knoxville. From the very first, the meetings mixed lectures by experts about some aspect of mountain work with group discussions on specified topics. The conference participants clarified their missions, studied perceived regional difficulties with help from consultants and statistical studies, shared achievements, and gathered inspiration from each other. After the death of John C. Campbell in 1919 at the age of fifty-one, Olive Dame Campbell assumed management of the conference. By 1930 the Conference of Southern Mountain Workers attracted 125 participants from church missions, independent schools, health centers, handicraft cooperatives, and national social service and government agencies.[13]

The Conference of Southern Mountain Workers introduced a quarterly publication called *Mountain Life and Work* in April 1925. In his introduction to the first issue, William J. Hutchins, president of Berea College, noted the complexity of understanding the mountains in times of

Participants at the Conference of Southern Mountain Workers, held in Knoxville, Tennessee, on April 6–9, 1926, stand on the steps of the Lawson-McGee Library, where the meetings took place.

economic and cultural change. The conclusion of the introduction read, "Our editors have been promised the co-operation of the foremost students of the mountain problem. They believe that this magazine may become a present day interpreter of the mountains to themselves and to the country; and an organ of inquiry, investigation, instruction to the hundreds of mountain workers who are willing to make needful sacrifices, but do not care to die as the devotees of 'misguided loyalties.'"[14] The magazine contained summaries of lectures and discussion groups from the annual conference, histories of settlement schools and other mountain organizations, analyses of perceived mountain problems, thought-provoking articles by experts, and profiles of accomplished mountain people and others who led lives of exceptional service to the region.

Olive Dame Campbell functioned as helpmate to her husband, but she also pursued her own interests. As she traveled in the mountains with her husband, Olive collected ballads. Later she recruited the eminent English musicologist Cecil Sharp, who expanded on her fieldwork and then coauthored *English Folk Songs from the Southern Appalachians*.[15] After John's death, Olive began adapting the Scandinavian folk-school model to rural Appalachia, an idea that she and her husband had often discussed. Following a year in Scandinavia spent studying their adult education program, she wrote a book about Danish folk schools and founded the John C. Campbell Folk School at Brasstown, in far western North Carolina.[16]

Olive, who graduated Phi Beta Kappa from Tufts College in 1903, taught high school English before her marriage. While she propelled others into action, most progressive ideas concerning crafts development can be traced back to her.[17] Olive maintained a lively correspondence with John M. Glenn, director of the Russell Sage Foundation, in which she informed him about projects in the mountains and secured funding.

Allen Eaton also championed Appalachian crafts at the Russell Sage Foundation, serving as facilitator to several development projects. In 1920 Eaton joined the Department of Surveys and Exhibits at the Russell Sage Foundation, having a joint appointment with the American Federation of Arts until 1929. Then Eaton developed the foundation's Department of Arts and Social Work, which he managed until his retirement in 1946. The purpose of his department was "to study the influence of arts in everyday living, and to bring a larger measure of beauty, either created or enjoyed, into the lives of all people."[18] Interpreting his mission broadly, Eaton promoted crafts development, cooperated with many agencies, and demonstrated the importance of art produced in varying situations and by diverse groups of people. Born and educated in Oregon, Eaton taught at his alma mater, the University of Oregon, and served in the Oregon legislature until negative reaction to his pacifist leanings during World War I drove him to seek employment in the East.[19]

Olive Campbell involved Eaton in the Conference of the Southern Mountain Workers. He organized meetings of the mountain craft centers that led to the formation of the Southern Highland Handcraft Guild. After many years of research, the Russell Sage Foundation published Eaton's *Handicrafts of the Southern Highlands* in 1937—and it remains one of the most informative texts on Appalachia crafts and their revival to this day.[20] He organized exhibitions featuring mountain crafts and produced two short films in cooperation with the Department of Agriculture.

Although most influences on crafts development in the southern Appalachian Mountains came through organizations, both chance and intense interest drew Chicago educator and weaver Edward F. Worst to the area. He inspired Berea's Edith Matheny to weave, he spoke at the Conference of Southern Mountain Workers, he encouraged Berea College's Mountain Weaver Boys, he studied traditional weaving found in the mountains, and he taught at Penland's Weaving Institute for many years. His 1918 book *Foot-Powered Loom Weaving,* one of the earliest books aimed at the home handweaver, provided technical information and weaving patterns.[21] A member of Chicago's group of progressive educational reformers, Worst taught manual arts in public schools, developed a program of manual arts at the Chicago Normal School, and then supervised the manual arts training for the Chicago Public Schools from 1912 to 1935. Between 1910 and 1920, he operated Lockport Home Industries in his hometown of Lockport, Illinois. The main activities of the Lockport Industries were production weaving and pottery.[22]

Alliances of Production Centers

Through the work of Olive Dame Campbell and the Conference of Southern Mountain Workers, different mountain agencies began identifying common problems in their craft programs. During her study of Scandinavian folk schools, Campbell had visited a cooperative crafts shop in Finland and envisioned a similar organization for the southern mountains. At her invitation, both Allen Eaton and Edward Worst participated in meetings of the Conference of Southern Mountain Workers, in which they stressed the importance of handicrafts in rural life and planted the seeds of cooperation between existing craft groups. Eaton followed his 1926 conference address, "Mountain Handicrafts—What They May Mean to Our Home Life and to the Life of Our Country," with a similar talk to the same group in 1930. Worst spoke on "Handwork for the School and Home" at the 1927 conference and led a roundtable discussion group in 1928.[23] By focusing the discussion of crafts production for home use and economic development, these experts made it easier for schools and handicraft centers to share their experiences.

At the Conference of Southern Mountain Workers in 1926, Olive Campbell suggested forming a crafts association.[24] After discussing handicraft production during several conferences, representatives from seven centers convened at Penland just after Christmas in 1928 to

Some of the speakers at the 1926 Conference of Southern Mountain Workers: Olive Dame Camplbell is next to Helen Dingman from Berea College, standing at the far right of the first row; Allen Eaton is the last person to the right in the third row.

plan the formation of a crafts association. Allen Eaton reported that while it snowed, the group

> considered: the economic significance of handicrafts in homes and schools; influence of the crafts upon the character of the workers; necessity of keeping standards of craftsmanship high; disposing of work not up to standard; protection of designs originated by others; use of native materials; use of attractive and permanent colors in weaving; methods of marketing employed in other countries such as Canada, Norway, Sweden, and Denmark; creation of new objects and new designs to meet market requirements; methods of financing these industries and of paying workers; cost of production and its relation to selling price; partial use of machinery in hand-made articles; commissions allowed to dealers and consignment plans; extent of output in the industries represented at the meeting; and possibilities of extending markets.[25]

This agenda could have supplied enough conversation for years. Enough common interest existed among the groups for the creation of an organization, but the formal commitment to join together occurred a year later, at a meeting at the Spinning Wheel in Asheville. Even though they kept low profiles and exhorted others to take on leadership roles, Olive Dame Campbell and Allen Eaton generated most of the ideas behind the cooperation of craft agencies.

The new organization chose the name Southern Mountain Handicraft Guild, exchanging "Mountain" for "Highlands" in 1933. At the 1930 spring meeting of the Conference of Southern Mountain Workers, a brief two-page constitution was passed unanimously. Article II set out five objectives for the organization:

> (1) To bring about cooperation among all agencies and individuals interested in conserving and developing the handicrafts of the Southern Mountains and to encourage a wider appreciation of these crafts.
>
> (2) To raise and maintain standards of design and craftsmanship and to encourage individual expression.
>
> (3) To study cost of production, competition, marketing, and the other problems concerning the handicrafts.
>
> (4) To gather and give to members information on methods and sources of materials; to hold short courses and to provide other instruction and help at such times and places as desired by members.
>
> (5) To perform any other work incidental to the accomplishment of the purposes of the Guild.[26]

The Guild brought the production centers together as a common trade organization, which jointly promoted their image, maintained standards, and tackled production and marketing problems. Within this structure each center maintained its own business autonomy, including control over prices, wages, production methods, and existing distribution channels. Because the Guild's organizers came from social service backgrounds, they understood the value of education. The Guild proposed education plans for the buying public and for its own members. Even though the first Guild objective mentioned "conserving" handicrafts, it never advocated reproduction of traditional items. The mission of "conserving and developing handicrafts" referred to the process of hand production, not the product.

At the Guild's inception, its constitution established three categories of membership:

producing centers, individual craftsmen, and friends, each with separate dues levels. The initial membership in the spring of 1930 consisted of nine producing centers—including Berea College's two slots for Fireside Industries and Woodwork—one individual, and two friends. By October 1933 the Guild had grown rapidly to twenty-five production centers, twelve individuals, and nine friends. During the first twenty years, production centers dominated the Guild's membership and its management structure. In later years, as college-educated craftspeople gravitated to the mountains because of the market opportunities and the inexpensive lifestyle, individuals assumed Guild leadership.[27]

During its early years the Southern Highland Handicraft Guild met twice a year—in the spring, in conjunction with the Conference of Southern Mountain Workers, and in the fall, at a member site. Agenda items included discussing common problems of production and marketing, sharing approaches to difficulties found within their institutions, and planning exhibitions and sales opportunities.

Frances Goodrich transferred ownership of her Allanstand Cottage Industries shop and business to the Guild, propelling the newly formed crafts organization into crafts retail sales. Olive Dame Campbell reflected on the gift: "It was the latter part of February in 1931 when she called in Clementine Douglas, Marguerite Bidstrup and myself and unfolded her plan for giving the entire Allanstand business to the Guild. I remember well how we sat over the fire and talked through the whole momentous matter, which was consummated not long after."[28] Since the Guild's assumption of Allanstand's management, it has operated sales areas in Asheville, North Carolina, and other locations with varying success. Since 1980 Southern Highland Handicraft Guild operations have been based in the Folk Art Center on the Blue Ridge Parkway on the eastern edge of Asheville; the facilities include a large shop, an auditorium, workshop rooms, a gallery, a library, and administrative offices.[29] The Guild has maintained its original operational structure, although through the years the membership has changed from dominance by production centers to individual craftspeople.

The Southern Highland Handicraft Guild held its first fair in 1948 on the grounds of the Pi Beta Phi School in Gatlinburg, Tennessee.

To present products and educate the buying public, beginning in 1948 the Guild sponsored an annual fair. Pi Beta Phi hosted the first fair, with tents outside for demonstrations with displays and sales held inside the school. Since very few consumers realized the amount of work that hand construction involved, members demonstrated their crafts as an educational component of the fair's activities. The demonstrations helped justify the cost of items to visitors who would be able to observe the time and complex techniques required in hand construction. A weaver sat at a loom, deftly throwing the shuttle while manipulating foot pedals to raise the harnesses in a memorized pattern sequence. Potters skillfully formed vases, drawing the shape from a lump of wet clay as the potter's wheel rotated before them. The fair continued in Gatlinburg in the same format in 1949, moving to the new Civic Auditorium in Asheville for the 1950 event. The fair expanded to two per year, at first alternating between spring in Asheville and fall in a new auditorium in Gatlinburg until eventually both fairs were moved to Asheville.[30] The basic structure of having makers selling directly to the consumers, demonstrating their crafts, and providing a range of items for sale within each of their booths proved a very successful method of selling crafts, and the general fair format has been copied by many other regional and state crafts groups.

In 1934 the Southern Highland Handicraft Guild formed a committee to advise the Tennessee Valley Authority about establishing their craft marketing enterprise.[31] Within five years of the formation of Southern Highland Handcraft Guild, the federal government began promoting Appalachian crafts through an organization called Southern Highlanders (using a name bewilderingly similar to that of the Southern Highland Handicraft Guild) as part of economic development under the TVA's social mission.[32] On May 7, 1935, the Southern Highlanders incorporated in the state of Tennessee, with the TVA as the biggest stockholder, and craft production centers and individuals buying shares for five dollars apiece. Like the TVA, the Southern Highlanders' service area encompassed the large geographic area touched by the Tennessee River and its tributaries, including all of Tennessee and extending into the mountains of Virginia, Kentucky, and North Carolina. The largest stockholders came from the ranks of the long-established craft production centers in the mountains: Allanstand Cottage Industries, Arrowcraft, Berea College, the John C. Campbell Folk School, Churchill Weavers, the Markle School of Handicrafts, and the Spinning Wheel.[33]

During its first two years of operation, the Southern Highlanders received subsidies from the TVA as a demonstration project. Southern Highlanders proposed "to facilitate the marketing of handicraft products by opening up new markets, to provide more economical handling, to furnish advice and information on styles, designs, et cetera, which, when used, will produce products more acceptable to consumers, and to assist the producers in securing a greater cash income."[34] As part of this mission it established its first shop and managed its operation from Norris, Tennessee, which had turned into a popular tourist site as a result of construction on the first TVA dam. After opening four other shops, the Southern Highlanders quickly pared

The Tennessee Valley Authority's demonstration project in craft economic development, the Southern Highlanders, Inc., published a catalog and maintained stores in Rockefeller Center in New York City and at the dam site at Norris, Tennessee.

down their retail outlets to Norris and Rockefeller Center in New York City. The other three locations—the Patten Hotel in Chattanooga, the Chickamauga Dam site in Tennessee, and the Palmer House in Chicago—lasted only a short time due to disappointing sales.

To reach a larger buying public than might walk in either of its stores, the Southern Highlanders produced a twenty-four-page picture catalog offering chairs, small tables, baskets, toys, pewter bowls and plates, brooms, small wooden items, jewelry, and a large variety of textiles. The woven articles included baby products, guest towels, table linens, men's neckties, and scarves and shawls. The catalog did not identify which centers produced which items, although the final page listed fifty-two member organizations.[35]

Within five years of its inception, the Southern Highlanders started negotiating a merger agreement with the Southern Highland Handicraft Guild. Many issues complicated the talks, including the larger geographical area served by the Southern Highlanders, the incompatibility of standards, and the TVA-owned stock. The merger finally occurred in 1951.[36]

Joint Promotion of Mountain Crafts

In the early part of the twentieth century, the Southern Industrial Education Association showed crafts brought together from many different parts of the Appalachian Mountains. In Washington, D.C., the association organized an annual exhibition, with auxiliaries sponsoring bazaars in other cities.[37] Because the Southern Industrial Education Association raised money through a network of socially conscious middle-class women's groups, the crafts items it sold became identified with the southern mountains. While individual craftspeople might have exercised personal creativity in producing any particular object, the techniques used were not practiced exclusively in Appalachia. When First Lady Ellen Wilson selected and commissioned crafts for the Mountain Room of the White House, Appalachian arts received recognition at the highest level.

Not until 1930 did craft cooperatives show their crafts work to other mountain producers. Allen Eaton coordinated the first craft exhibition at the Second Presbyterian Church of Knoxville in conjunction with the annual meeting of the Conference of Southern Mountain Workers. His working committee consisted of representatives of the Pi Beta Phi School, Crossnore School, and the John C. Campbell Folk School. Notices requesting items had been sent to 24 centers, but "eight previously unknown groups had sent in their work, making 32 centers represented." Eaton observed that "this first comprehensive exhibition was a surprise to members of the Guild as well as to visitors, for with a few exceptions the centers themselves had little idea what others were producing."[38] This exhibition, which displayed hundreds of craft products in a gallery format (with works hanging on walls, rather than on tables as at a bazaar), confirmed the purpose of the newly formed handicraft Guild—helping members envision future joint promotions. The centers carefully compared the range of products, especially noting quality and price.

Encouraged by the success of the 1930 exhibition and a few subsequent shows, the Guild contemplated an exhibition on a major scale—for a new organization, it thought big. Allen Eaton, in his capacity as Russell Sage Foundation representative, agreed to assemble articles for display from members of the Southern Highland Handicraft Guild. The American Country Life Association included the exhibition in its annual conference program, and through Eaton's influence, the American Federation of Arts took on the responsibility of touring the show. By working together, these four organizations made *Mountain Handicrafts* an exhibition with wide scope and distribution; it was a project that the Guild could never have attempted on its own.

The first showing of *Mountain Handicrafts* occurred in August 1933 at the American Country Life Association's convention in Blacksburg, Virginia. The exhibition then circulated during 1933 and 1934 to the Corcoran Gallery in Washington, D.C., the Brooklyn Museum in New York City, the Decatur Art Institute in Illinois, the Joslyn Memorial Museum in Omaha, the New Municipal Auditorium in St. Louis (in connection with the National Folk Festival), the Everhart Museum in Scranton, the Milwaukee Art Institute, the Norfolk Museum in Virginia, and the new Art Museum at Berea College in Kentucky. When the show visited Brooklyn, the museum suggested that patrons buy pieces, emphasizing the social benefit of the revival of crafts by schools in Appalachia: "Almost all the items in the exhibition are for sale, affording visitors an opportunity to help a group of worthwhile people, and at the same time procure handmade objects of great charm and practical value."[39]

Moving the display of mountain crafts from tables to walls and pedestals failed to liberate it from its roots in social service work. While the exhibit presented the objects with greater reverence, the identification labels neglected to include the names of individual makers. In the fine arts it is understood that artists are recognized for a personal style and unique expression. In *Mountain Handicrafts,* as in other promotional vehicles of Appalachian crafts, the creator remained a generic mountain artisan, rather than an individual artist with a personal history. Doris Ulmann's photographs accompanying the exhibition reinforced the concept of the universal Appalachian craftsperson. Although some portraits identified the photographic subject, nothing connected any of the craft items with a specific person.

The exhibition traveled in eighteen boxes, weighed a total of 2,827 pounds, and required at least two hundred feet of wall space as well as several display platforms. Thanks to the Russell Sage Foundation's sponsorship and volunteer efforts from the participating craft agencies, the exhibition rental fee totaled only $37.50, with an additional 20 percent discount extended to chapters of the American Federation of Arts. The shipping costs, assumed by the exhibiting agency, far exceeded the rental amount.[40]

The *Mountain Handicrafts* catalog contained a great deal of information about the 582 pieces shown, including the type of each item, and the size, material, and place of origin. Weaving dominated, making up approximately half the show—298 of the 582 pieces were identified as woven. While the catalog listed 582 items, any single item might include identical pieces in multiple colors or represent a set of related items, such as a doll's table and chairs. Aside from weaving, the exhibition also included sixty-eight wood carvings, fifty-seven baskets, twenty-nine pieces of furniture, nineteen brooms, seventeen dolls, and eight quilts, as well as hard-to-categorize items such as toasting forks, decorative sugars, hooked rugs, wooden bag tops, pewter bowls, and shuttles. The Cherokee Reservation in North Carolina submitted eight beadwork baskets and ten other Indian crafts pieces.[41]

Twenty-eight centers and three individuals of the Southern Highland Handicraft Guild—almost the entire membership—contributed items to *Mountain Handicrafts.* In all, twenty production centers exhibited weaving. Of those twenty, half sent exclusively woven articles, while four others contributed mostly weaving. Clearly, weaving dominated the exhibit in both the number of items and the number of participants. Of the eleven crafts producers that sent no weaving, five specialized in a single category such as woodcarving. Several of the centers not sending any woven goods either produced weaving but chose not to show any at the time, or established their weaving department at a later date.

Mountain Handicrafts showed the artistry and skill of the Southern Highland Handicraft Guild members in major city museums and introduced a wide national audience to the Appalachian Craft Revival—in settings that conferred credibility. In the catalog, Eaton proclaimed that the "primary purpose of the exhibition is educational," but explained how readers could order items to be delivered after the show's tour. Quoting William Morris of the English Arts and Crafts Movement, Eaton admonished people to "have nothing in your home which you do not know to be useful or believe to be beautiful."[42] In inviting exhibition visitors to buy, Eaton's appeal offered several rationales: these items were both useful and beautiful, and the expenditures were supporting a worthy cause at the same time. As this exhibition traveled in 1933 and 1934—some of the darkest days of the Depression—the show's participants were pleased about the recognition, and appreciated the sales.

In 1937 Allen Eaton organized another exhibit, this time for the Department of Agriculture. In it, he featured products from the southern mountains among other works from rural areas around the country. The Rural Arts Exhibition opened in November 1937 in a "gallery especially constructed for the purpose in the patio of the Department of Agriculture Administration Building" in Washington, D.C.[43] In addition to serving as curator, Eaton also designed the exhibition, featuring eighty large photographs of country scenes and craftsmakers in the entrance and displaying crafts on two tiered shelves like large steps built around the room, with a fountain in the center. Eaton described his gallery presentation concept: "All these were arranged, not as arbitrary divisions, or geographically, but rather as one large harmonious picture with articles placed wherever their form, color, or texture contributed most to the display."[44]

The exhibition, which "featured mainly the things that country people make with their hands," included 427 numbered entries.[45] Again, the actual number of pieces was much higher because multiple items were grouped in a single listing. For example, number 29 was 29 small scarves and number 285 was 73 baskets. Even though Eaton proclaimed that "every State, Territory, and possession of the United States was represented by handicrafts, photographs, or both," the craftspeople of the southern mountains contributed a higher percentage than other areas, with over 100 listed items.[46] A major part of the submissions came through the Extension Services of different states. In this show, with everything from pottery to pewter tankards and corn shuck mats to a Sioux bridle, weaving comprised the largest category, with over 100 pieces. In gathering the items, Eaton intended to show the ingenuity of rural people during the Depression, pointing out the many benefits of crafts. "But understanding and sentiment for the handicrafts has come to many during these years when so many of our people were forced to fall back upon their resources, their hands, their minds, and spirits for the solution of vital problems; and many thousands of our people have found in handicrafts economic, social, educational, and esthetic returns which, as we have opportunity, we shall understand better."[47]

Over 20,000 people visited during the three weeks of the exhibit, including many top government officials—even President Roosevelt. As had been done in other exhibitions, Eaton stressed the economic significance: "We have referred literally hundreds of people to the makers of the objects that were on display, and of the actual objects which were sent to us for exhibition with selling prices marked on them, we sold over $1,800.00 worth."[48]

Allen Eaton's book *Handicrafts of the Southern Highlands,* published in 1937 by the Russell Sage Foundation with photographs by Doris Ulmann, continues to be the most informative text on the Appalachian Craft Revival.

The most enduring joint promotional project of the Appalachian Craft Revival was a book about mountain crafts, although it was originally intended only as a history and survey of current practices. In 1937 the Russell Sage Foundation published *Handicrafts of the Southern Highlands,* by Allen Eaton. The book began as a suggestion for a study of the "mountain industries problem." In 1928 Olive Dame Campbell wrote to John Glenn, head of the Russell Sage Foundation, suggesting that a survey be conducted to explore the relationship between "crafts and the program for social improvement, which all of the schools really have at heart, however blindly they go about it. And if there is a connection, what is it and how is it related to the matter of perfection of output and economic return."[49] She recommended that Allen Eaton conduct the study because he got along with people better than Edward Worst did. Embracing progressive theory, the Russell Sage Foundation believed that studying and publishing information about social problems resulted in positive change.

Handicrafts of the Southern Highlands provided a history of handwork in Appalachia, described craft skills, and chronicled the development of the Craft Revival centers. Also, although often overlooked, the book included a list of problems facing handicraft production and suggestions for dealing with them. While never intended as a sales vehicle, the appealing format of Eaton's book promoted southern mountain crafts to a wide audience. More than one hundred illustrations, half of them by internationally distinguished photographer Doris Ulmann, provided enduring images of the craftspeople and their work.

Eaton led many other diverse projects focusing on southern mountain crafts. For the Department of Agriculture, Eaton oversaw the making of a twenty-minute black-and-white film about crafts in the mountains called *Old Crafts: New Horizons*. Started in the late thirties, the planning of the film stretched over many years, taking an unusual turn with the advent of World War II, when the script evolved to include the war effort, positing that among the reasons for fighting was preserving the values of the southern Appalachian Mountains. In addition to presenting panoramic views of the mountains, *Old Crafts: New Horizons* showed Berea College, the Pi Beta Phi School, Penland, the Spinning Wheel, the John C. Campbell Folk School, and several independent craftspeople. Eaton stressed both the beauty of the product and skill of the maker. Another film, *Patterns of Rural Art,* shorter but in color, accompanied the Rural Arts Exhibition in Washington. Some of the same footage appeared in the second film.[50]

Major national recognition for southern mountain crafts came in 1942 when the popular women's magazine *House & Garden* devoted its entire June issue to Appalachia. The magazine's editorial board concentrated on Appalachia at the suggestion of mountain native Samuel Clemens Beard Jr., a history professor at the University of Illinois, after he responded to the June 1941 issue on the Pennsylvania Dutch country.[51] Unfortunately, this national exposure for Appalachian crafts came at a time when the country was focused on the more pressing problem of gearing up for World War II in both Europe and the Pacific.

The magazine showcased handmade items in features and articles, included a map with crafts sites, and showed advertisements for mountain-produced and mountain-inspired home accessories. All five magazine editors and a photographer toured the mountains, creating many of the articles themselves. Within their standard picture-magazine format, they produced pieces with homey, captioned photographs of children and family settings. The editors worked closely with Appalachian craft groups, listing the member organizations of both the Southern Highland Handicraft Guild and the Southern Highlanders, Inc. Several features demonstrated the Guild's influence, including an article by Allen Eaton; a two-page spread on coverlets and quilts with a picture of an Arrowcraft weaver making yarn into a skein on a reel; a profile on generations of weavers in the Doughtery family of Russellville, Tennessee; and a picture piece on contemporary crafts. "Homes of the Handicrafts" showed photographs of the Hillcrafters' Guild on Christmas Ridge in Berea, the J.C. Campbell Folk School, the Berry Schools' first building, Berea's Log House, the Spinning Wheel in Asheville, the Arrow Craft Shop, the weaving studio at the Penland School, and the interior of the Southern Highlanders' Shop in Rockefeller Center, thus directing the consumer to many of the mountain sales shops, ending with the sophisticated urban showroom.

Many of the twenty-one articles on Appalachia appeared to confirm contemporary stereotypes of the region. But on closer investigation, some of the pieces with condescending headlines offered reasonable content, such as the "Furriner's Guide," which contained a travel guide to festivals and historical sites. The full-page picture of a bride in sunbonnet and full-length cotton work dress being swung in a washtub by two stalwart youths "to bring her luck" seemed particularly contrived. The history professor who suggested this issue authored a piece about quaint mountain speech patterns. While pictures of school children in bib overalls hearkened back to a simpler lifestyle, the features and advertisements depicted products designed for the sophisticated consumer. The magazine predicted a Southern Highlands trend in home furnishings, picturing an idealized country home that included many items inspired by Appalachia.

Common Threads

Government Involvement in Crafts

While state and federal governments never played a major role in the promotion of hand production, several state-administered federal programs had a significant impact on handicraft programs. Many weaving programs associated with schools accepted money from the federal government designated for vocational education. The United States Congress passed the Smith-Hughes Vocational Education Bill on February 23, 1917, thereby entering into a partnership with states to provide training in agriculture, home economics, and trades and industries. The Pi Beta Phi School in Gatlinburg, the Penland School and the Crossnore School in North Carolina, and many other schools instituted programs and paid part of teachers' salaries with Smith-Hughes funds. Berea College never sought federal funding, resisting the regulations that inevitably accompanied the allocation of public monies.

In North Carolina, George W. Coggin assumed a post in the vocational education division of Trades and Industries on September 25, 1919. He administered the Smith-Hughes program and guided the development of training programs until his retirement in 1953. During his tenure, most vocational instruction concentrated on traditional industrial skills, such as auto mechanics or the building trades, but Coggin also encouraged small programs in hand production. In the late 1930s Coggin addressed a national meeting of vocational educators about his state's textile classes. He reported that "textiles" comprised half of North Carolina's trade extension programs, referring to the industrial textile industry that had experienced amazing growth in the South in the early part of the twentieth century. The courses included cloth analysis, mill arithmetic, and loom mechanics. Instruction in carding, spinning, and weaving meant learning skills for machines that automated these processes. Halfway through his address he switched from talking about industrial production training to "one other phase

Students and teachers from an early 1930s Weaving Institute held on the porch of Ridgeway Hall at the Appalachian School at Penland. Standing at the upper left of the picture is Edward Worst, with Lucy Morgan next to him.

of our program which may or may not be considered textiles. . . . this is Hand Loom Weaving." After a brief description of the mountain regions of North Carolina and its inhabitants, he outlined the program. "Those who can secure looms for their homes weave at odd times and get the teacher to help them as they may need it. You may question the efficiency of such a plan but it gets almost unbelievable results. You must remember that these people are keen and resourceful." Several times during his written text, Coggin stopped reading and told stories of this mountain brand of resourcefulness.[52] At the end of his talk, Coggin described the success of the 1937 Weaving Institute at Penland, where North Carolina residents received free instruction, funded in part by Smith-Hughes.

The North Carolina vocational education department began by supporting Crossnore and Penland, but by the mid-1930s other centers also received Smith-Hughes money for teaching weaving. Classes at Hayesville, Canton, Franklin, Boone, and Greensboro appeared in North Carolina vocational reports for many years, while a few other programs only showed up for short periods. All of these weaving centers except Greensboro were located in mountain communities. Among the hundreds of North Carolina vocational education programs, George Coggin encouraged a few handweaving programs as a pet project of his, rather than as serious training for employment. When Congress allocated money for vocational education programs in skilled trades, handweaving received recognition only because a few enterprising educators figured they could squeeze crafts under the regulations.

In 1941 Louise Moore analyzed the Smith-Hughes craft education programs for the federal government. Her research took her to Crossnore, Penland, and Gatlinburg in the Appalachian Mountains and to New Hampshire and Vermont. She visited sales venues in Boston, New York, and Asheville to study the merchandising of handcrafted products. She reported favorably about the teaching of weaving: "A relatively small expenditure has resulted in widening wage earning opportunities for many persons with some handcraft skill, or interest in acquiring skill, who, without instruction, would have been incapable of producing or marketing salable articles." But Moore also cautioned that "experience seems to prove that the markets for hand made articles are limited, that these markets can be ruined by too large a production of articles of no great artistic merit, originality, or local interest." Since economic development supplied the impetus for crafts training, she concluded that there was "little justification for expenditure of Federal funds to foster handcrafts in localities with ample industrial opportunities for employment."[53] Although cautious about quality, Moore recommended crafts for rural areas with limited options, mentioning the remote sections of Appalachia.

In 1933 and 1934, the Women's Bureau of the Department of Labor examined Appalachia crafts production. The Women's Bureau undertook the study of mountain handicrafts as part of the preparation for the Tennessee Valley Authority's venture into crafts marketing. Under the direction of Bertha Nienburg, three researchers fanned out over the mountains and into the Tennessee valley to gather statistics and interview workers. In 1935, the Department of Labor published "Potential Earning Power of Southern Mountaineer Handicraft," a report based on the information gathered from the research.[54]

Even though the document focused on the economic value of hand production, the Women's Bureau took the opportunity to further a current agency goal—the elimination of home-based workers. Within the same time period as the mountain research, the Bureau documented and published abuses of women working piece-rate in their homes, noting states' legislative efforts to abolish the practice of home labor.[55] On the first page of this report "prepared to acquaint the consuming public" with abuses among home-based workers, the Women's Bureau enumerated its reasons for its position. Home workers assumed all costs of the workspace and usually bore all of the equipment costs. The industry only paid for work up to a certain standard, with materials being charged against the worker for inferior production. The employer usually required delivery of the finished goods and felt no responsibility for providing continuous work. While the Women's Bureau promoted laws for curtailing home-based labor, the ultimate goal was to concentrate workers into factories, where working conditions could be regulated.

The crusade against home-based work colored many of the findings in the final report on the Appalachian Mountains; statistics gathered in field surveys were used to reinforce its conclusions.[56] The researchers sent into the mountains used two instruments to record their findings, a one-page form for individuals and a two-page form for production centers. They gathered data about 10,576 workers, 95 percent of whom were women.

The Women's Bureau found abuses of labor in the candlewicking, quilting, and chair caning industries, which thrived on pools of cheap labor. Candlewicking employed over two-thirds of the survey population, with the second highest number engaged in quilting. While this Department of Labor study exposed the exploitation of workers in these three craft categories, the final report failed to give a true picture of Appalachian handicrafts because these major offenders operated primarily outside the mountains. The quilting was concentrated in central Kentucky and chair caning in western Kentucky. Although located in the foothills of northwestern Georgia, the candlewicking business employed jobbers who recruited homeworkers in the mountains.

Nienburg's analysis also distorted the actual picture of mountain production because she divided the production centers into four categories: semi-philanthropic, schools, cooperatives or home extension, and commercial. Unfortunately, crafts in the mountains could not be separated as neatly, because many centers spanned two or more categories. Nienburg declared that "Ninety-one percent of all craftfolk were engaged by commercial centers. Only 3 percent received some employment through the semiphilanthropic centers." This presented an incomplete view of the actual situation.[57] The misclassification of many of the mountain programs, coupled with the unusually large number of craft workers engaged in candlewicking, quilting, and chair caning, skewed the percentages.

However, the Nienburg report presented some provocative statistics. In the gross sales for 1933, candlewicking came in first, followed by quilting, with weaving pulling in third place. The amazing statistic is not that candlewicking produced $1.2 million in sales, but that weaving was able to generate almost $200,000. Candlewicking and quilting represented large commercial ventures, whereas weaving encompassed many small centers operating throughout the mountains. A comparison of sales figures for 1929 with those from 1933 reveals that candlewicking doubled its gross sales during that period, while the figures from weaving were cut in half. During this period the average earning for workers in candlewicking dropped by 50 percent, while wages for weavers stayed substantially the same. It appears that the commercial businesses took advantage of the Depression to pay workers less, while the weaving establishments maintained their previous wage scales.

The TVA followed the model of the Southern Highland Handicraft Guild when it established Southern Highlanders, rather than adopting the recommendations presented in the Nienburg report, which they commissioned. Even though Bertha Nienburg delivered a talk at the 1934 Guild meeting requesting assistance in implementing her suggestions for centralizing craft production, no action followed.[58] While the report failed to record conditions in mountain crafts production accurately, it gathered some significant information about the lives of the makers. For example, weavers grew or raised most of the food consumed by their families. Even though the survey instruments imposed a rigid data-gathering format, the researchers occasionally jotted comments on the backs of forms—providing valuable insight into local conditions.

The Department of Labor had a far more significant impact on mountain crafts when it enforced the minimum wage Fair Labor Standards Act of 1938. The mountain craft centers first tried to obtain exemption status, but eventually they complied. World War II delayed the implementation of a minimum wage for home-based work in crafts. In 1946 and 1947, Arrowcraft compiled detailed records on the exact time required to wind warps, dress looms, weave, and finish articles, and then computed the amount the weaver received for the piece, finally arriving at her hourly wage.[59] Although it was always difficult to calculate the exact time spent on home production, the centers attempted to comply with the law by increasing piece-rates in compliance with government regulations.

In another federal government program, the Extension Service promoted crafts activities—or "rural arts," as the agency referred to them—as a part of its wider mission. In 1914 the Smith-Lever Act mandated the creation of the Extension Service as part of the Department of Agriculture. While some of the nutrition, home, and lifestyle improvement programs proved easier to promote, "Home agents across the nation found handicrafts a drawing card useful among otherwise indifferent women."[60]

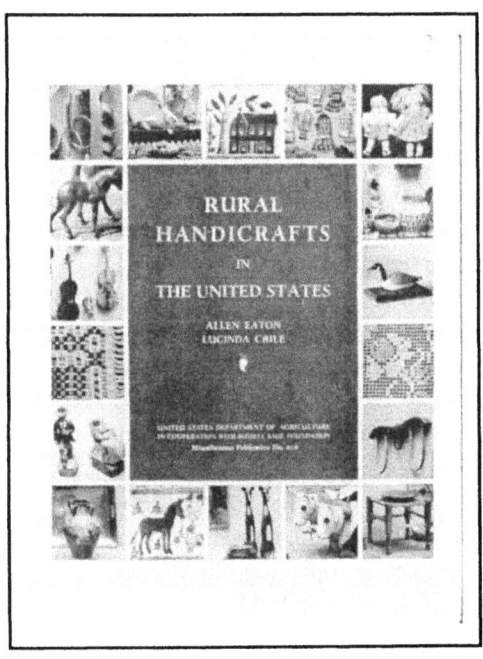

In the 1946 Department of Agriculture publication *Rural Handicrafts,* Allen Eaton reported on the exhibition put on by the Department of Agriculture, and Lucinda Crile summarized the findings of a survey about rural arts in the United States.

Through state and county Extension Services, in the late 1930s the government conducted a study of the extent and kinds of arts practiced by rural Americans. Seventy-five percent of all rural women and girls engaged in some type of arts activities. The overwhelming majority practiced traditional female needle arts: knitting, crocheting, quilting, embroidery, and other forms of sewing.[61] Few women ever realized any income from their craft—rather, they made things for home use or as a leisure pursuit. Confining themselves mostly to home improvement topics, home demonstration agents rarely promoted crafts that required complex skills or special equipment.

Education in the Crafts

In the twentieth century, Appalachia achieved distinction not only for the production of handicrafts but as a good place to learn craft skills. The Penland School of Crafts and the John C. Campbell Folk School in North

Carolina, and the Arrowmont School of Arts and Crafts in Tennessee drew students from all over the United States as well as from other countries to study in one or two-week classes. Many other schools and recreation centers throughout Appalachia also provided both extended programs and workshops in crafts education.

Historically, mountain settlement schools taught crafts as part of their industrial arts programs; starting in the early 1920s, many received financing through the Smith-Hughes vocational education act. The weaving centers either taught weavers the skills they needed during home visits or else the weavers utilized skills they had already learned in school. The leap from teaching local people skills for production to providing instruction to visitors from outside the mountain region came in 1929 when Lucy Morgan welcomed weavers from other parts of the country to a workshop conducted by noted Chicago educator Edward Worst.

Earlier in the twentieth century, Olive Dame Campbell and others in the crafts community assumed that Berea College would take the leadership in crafts education because of the school's extensive crafts student labor program. Missionaries, settlement workers, and even Lucy Morgan received training at Berea during its concentrated winter terms. But Anna Ernberg's apprentice style of teaching required more time than most of these adult learners could afford to spend. And even though they followed the Berea Fireside Industries model in establishing their own weaving centers, they desired more concentrated direct instruction in weaving skills.

In the late 1920s Lucy Morgan realized that providing instruction for visitors would publicize her own weaving center's efforts while creating an additional source of income. The Penland Weaving Institute made it possible for a student to have a concentrated experience with a master weaver in a short space of time. Aside from presenting beginners with basic weaving instruction, the knowledgeable craftspeople could acquire higher levels of skill or learn unusual techniques. Within a few years, the Weaving Institute evolved into the Penland School of Crafts, with concentrated workshops scheduled in many different craft areas, taught by a distinguished faculty recruited from around the country. A few weeks in a lovely setting with the joys of immersing oneself in the process of acquiring specialized techniques, all available at a modest cost, appealed to an increasingly larger population. Propelled by circumstances and always recognizing a good idea, Lucy Morgan developed the short-term craft workshop format that is now a widely followed model.

As the Southern Highland Handicraft Guild grew, the need for training members in design and additional techniques became evident. Olive Dame Campbell summarized the survey of crafts production and availability of educational programs as: "On January 6, 1944, the General Education Board [of the Rockefeller Foundation] granted the Southern Highland Handicraft Guild a fund of $6,000 for an exploratory year, looking toward a Craft Education project in the Southern Highlands, as a basis for a training and research program in handicrafts."[62] The University of Tennessee released Marian Heard, Associate Professor of Related Arts, for six months to travel throughout Appalachia so that she could assess the need for educational programs. Heard traveled 13,533 miles, visiting 166 individual craftspeople, 38 schools, and 29 craft business organizations gathering information. She recommended that craft education opportunities be expanded through colleges, short workshops, and at the local level through home demonstration Extension agents and vocational education programs.[63] Although the Southern Highland Handicraft Guild received a grant from the General Education Board to expand their educational programs, problems with its tax status prevented it

Allen Eaton discusses a tapestry made by Tina McMorran, Arrowcraft weaving supervisor. Eaton taught a course on crafts and design at the early Summer Craft Workshops held by the University of Tennessee at the Pi Beta Phi School in Gatlinburg, Tennessee.

from receiving the money for several years. However, the Guild instituted workshops on its own, the first ones being conducted at Penland in September 1945.[64]

In the summer of 1945, the University of Tennessee began offering Summer Craft Workshops at the Pi Beta Phi School facilities in Gatlinburg. In the early 1960s, Marian Heard influenced the Pi Phis to rededicate their mission to crafts education, which created the Arrowmont School of Arts and Crafts.[65] Over the years, the J.C. Campbell Folk School also found that craft classes appealed to people coming from outside the mountains to study in concentrated workshops.

While special scholarships have always been available for people in the area, the craft schools relied for operating expenses on the tuition paid by people from outside the region. Summer classes especially attracted public school teachers. The mountain environment appealed to people escaping cities in pursuit of a purposeful diversion or increased proficiency in craft techniques. For several of the major craft production centers, the selling of skills provided a more enduring pursuit than the selling of handcrafted products. Students taking classes at these schools today know little of their histories, never suspecting that many of them started as weaving centers.

3

berea college and fireside industries

Most Kentuckians and Appalachians—along with a good portion of the United States population—associate the name "Berea" with the word "college." Berea College not only dominated the town that bears its name but played a leading role in supplying the educational, spiritual, and social needs within the self-designated area it served, the southern Appalachian Mountains. The college led the revival of weaving in the mountains and served as a model for many other weaving cooperatives.

Within the Berea community, four major weaving establishments grew during the early part of the twentieth century: two directed by the college and the other two independent enterprises. The college-sponsored weaving included the Fireside Industries, which eventually employed hundreds of area women working in their own homes and girls participating as part of the student labor program. As the college grew, the need for more labor opportunities produced the Mountain Weaver Boys. Difficulties of working within the college structure led to the development of the Matheny Weavers and the Churchill Weavers. As one sorts through the stories of the personalities and the controversies, it is easy to lose sight of the real operations of these businesses. Whatever problems there might have been, thousands of yards of fabric and hundreds of different items in dozens of patterns came from the looms in and around Berea. The college production will be examined here—the other concerns will be dealt with later.

Berea's weaving played many roles in the mountains. In *Handicrafts of the Southern Highlands,* the 1937 survey of crafts in the mountains, Allen Eaton proclaimed that the Appalachian Craft Revival began in 1893, shortly after William Goodell Frost assumed the presidency of Berea College.[1] The Craft Revival started with weaving. Under the direction of Frost, Berea strove to lead the educational, economic, and social efforts conducted throughout the southern Appalachian Mountains. Weaving fit into the category of economic development for women, plus it had some allied social benefits. The college provided area women with an outlet for the production of their looms and inspired other mountain communities to adopt weaving programs. Whether Berea offered direct assistance or not, the Fireside Industries served as a model for the development of weaving cooperatives throughout the mountains.

In 1855 minister and abolitionist John G. Fee built a one-room school on Berea Ridge in Madison County, Kentucky, with financial help from Cassius M. Clay and northern friends. During most of the first fifty years, Berea maintained a policy of being open to all races and both sexes. In 1904 the Kentucky legislature passed the Day Law, which prohibited institutions where "persons of the white and Negro races are both received as pupils for instruction." After a lengthy court battle to maintain integrated education, Berea College reluctantly gave

William Goodell Frost assumed the presidency of Berea College in 1892 and soon began advertising that the college would buy weaving from women as a way to defer educational expenses for their children.

in to the new state policy. With financial help from Andrew Carnegie, the college established a separate independent African-American school called the Lincoln Institute in Shelby, Kentucky.[2] The mission of Berea College refocused to concentrate exclusively on meeting the needs of the "mountain whites" of Appalachia.

Throughout most of its history, Berea College maintained an elementary school, a high school, and a vocational school, as well as normal or teacher preparation and adult education programs—in addition to the undergraduate college. Since Berea sought pupils from areas lacking extensive financial resources, the school always provided its students with opportunities to pay for their education. In 1892 the incoming college president William Goodell Frost persuaded the college trustees to pass a resolution allowing free tuition. All students worked a set amount of time to cover tuition fees, and either paid cash or worked additional hours for their room and board. Some student labor choices included operations needed to keep the school running, such as laundry work, clerical assistance, or washing dishes. Other labor options developed skills such as forestry, woodworking, printing, hotel and restaurant management, or needlecraft. Although only a small number of students worked in the craft industries, the college publicity about the labor program featured crafts. A student seated at a loom or constructing a broom made an effective picture in the college's appeals for money.

Shortly after Frost began as president of Berea College, he discovered the promotional value of presenting college donors with woven coverlets purchased from mountain homes. During the last part of the nineteenth century, the English Arts & Crafts Movement extended the influence of John Ruskin and William Morris across the ocean to the major cities of America, cultivating a fashionable market for handcrafted items. Always on the lookout for new avenues of raising money, President Frost saw the possibilities in encouraging handweaving. Selling handcrafts also fit in well with his general promotion of the mountains. In an article acquainting the country with mountain problems, Frost observed that "Spinning, in fact, has helped to form the character of our race, and it is pleasant to find that here in Appalachian America it is still contributing to the health and grace and skill of womankind."[3] Because the mountain people practiced arts and crafts forgotten by industrialized society, Frost presented the items they made by hand as possessing unique value.

In recounting the early history of crafts at Berea College, an often repeated story has President Frost requesting a local woman to weave half a dozen coverlets for him. A bit put out, the weaver then describes to him in detail the work involved in shearing sheep, picking and carding wool, spinning the yarn, collecting dyestuffs, dyeing the wool, dressing the loom, and then finally weaving. The weaver concludes, "It would take we'uns nigh one year or more afore we could have that many 'kivers' woven. It's no child's play to weave a 'kiver,' President."[4] Production of woven goods required many diverse skills and took a long time, with many of the tasks tied to specific seasons of the year. This tale of the weaving process nicely illustrates Frost's assertion of the competence and work ethic among the women of the mountains.

A student recruiting letter dated November 27, 1897, urged young women to come to Berea with the promise that they could "earn nearly their whole expenses" by working three hours a day. The letter suggested that mothers would be able to secure money for the deposit and initial expenses by selling weaving to the college. "Each girl must send in $1 now to engage a room, and bring as much as eleven dollars with her. To help her make up this money the College will buy good homespun linen at about 40 cents a yard, lindsey and jeans at 50 cents, dress flannel 60, coverlids $4, pair wool blankets $5."[5]

Most mountain families had put away their looms when commercially woven fabrics became cheaply available after the Civil War. Even though the memory of weaving existed and disassembled looms could still be found in barns, the craft was no longer passing from mother to daughter as one of the necessary household arts. With the promise of money, out the looms came and once again women took up weaving. But the weaving produced as a result of the college's new demand lacked the skill acquired from continuous practice. Academic researcher Max West described this problem in a 1904 *Bulletin of the Bureau of Labor* article: "It was found that the recently woven coverlets were inferior to some of the older specimens which had been preserved, in that the patterns failed to 'hit in the seam,' and also because the less permanent aniline dyes were being used in place of the original indigo and madder. The college therefore undertook a revival in the quality as well as the quantity of the work."[6]

In response to this poor quality, Berea conceived the Homespun Fair as the main vehicle for promoting higher standards. First held in 1896 in conjunction with the Berea College Commencement, the event encouraged younger people to take up handcrafts and rewarded good craftsmanship. Thousands of people attended Berea's graduation exercises, so an exhibition offering money prizes and selling crafts attracted considerable attention. In addition to several categories of weaving, the fair presented awards for natural dye formulas, baskets, knitting, woodworking, and leatherwork. Unfortunately, after several years problems arose. In her 1909 annual report, Mrs. K.U. Putnam, chair of the Homespun Fair, observed that the same participants tended to win the prizes every year.[7]

Several women in the mountains around Berea produced woven goods for sale by the college. President Frost prevailed on a local woman, Susan B. Hayes, to take up weaving again. Even though she had not woven for some time, Frost and her husband expressed confidence in her abili-

Berea College women carding wool in preparation for spinning it into yarn for use in weaving.

ties. Several daughters in need of school expenses also acted as an incentive for Mrs. Hayes. In a college-owned house, Hayes established weaving operations, offering weavers wool fleece, natural dyestuffs, cotton yarn, and other weaving and spinning supplies.[8] She also assisted college faculty member Josephine Robinson in purchasing handwoven goods for resale to college supporters. Head of the Ladies Department and professor of mathematics, Miss Robinson also knew how to weave. In 1898 she added to her other responsibilities, chairing the Homespun Industries committee. In her second year as director, Miss Robinson exhibited "homespun fabrics" to women's groups in Brooklyn, Rochester, Providence, Chicago, St. Paul, Minneapolis, and at the Pan-American Exposition in Buffalo.[9] Her leaflet "Repair that Loom" combined some practical suggestions with encouraging the resumption of weaving in the home.

In 1899 the *Berea Quarterly* reprinted an article from *The Outlook* of September 1898, in which President Frost referred to "fireside industries of past ages." Eaton credited Frost with bestowing the term "fireside industries" on the weaving and other textile crafts. Both the English and American Arts and Crafts Movement promoted domestic industries that could be carried on around the family hearth. The term "fireside industries" connoted a romantic charm Berea found useful in marketing. An update on the "fireside products" in the 1900 *Quarterly* identified a chief difficulty in reviving weaving, noting "a feeling among the people that these noble industries were old-fashioned and something rather to be ashamed of!"[10] By selling weaving to college supporters, Berea gave mountain women pride in this accomplishment as well as economic assistance. A once necessary household skill converted self-sufficiency production to the manufacture of luxury items, for which consumers paid a good price.

In her 1902 annual report to the college president, Robinson took credit for training "the best available weavers until they can do work equal to the best done anywhere." She concluded that "the foundation is now laid for the introduction of artistic weaving of any sort desired, a foundation without which no such work could ever be done." Robinson paved the way for the expansion of the industry. By February 1902 the *Berea Quarterly* offered for sale coverlets in a variety of sixteen patterns, either made to order or already completed; jeans and handspun linen fabric; and wool blankets. "We have now some 2 dozen good 'kivers' on hand, which will be sent (purchaser to pay express) for $7.50 each; half a dozen of special size and fineness, for $12.50 each; and 1 dozen smaller than standard size, unmatched in seam ('don't hit') or otherwise a little less desirable for $6 each."[11] The price was determined by the quality and size of the item.

During 1902 weaver and interior designer Candace Wheeler visited Berea College and helped develop plans to expand the weaving program and suggested products. As a leader of the Arts and Crafts Movement in the United States, Mrs. Wheeler established workshops for the hand-production of textiles and encouraged many other people to start craft ventures. In a pamphlet promoting the organization of home weaving industries, Wheeler offered this assessment: "Certainly no conditions could be more favorable than those existing in the Cumberland Mountains, where wool and cotton grown upon the rough farms are habitually spun, and woven, and dyed in the home-cabin."[12] Although she exaggerated the amount of weaving in the mountains around Berea, it served as an example of the distinctly American handcrafted work she championed. In a 1930 newspaper article in the *Berea Citizen*, Eleanor Frost, wife of the college president, credited Candace Wheeler with being the "real founder of homespun in Berea" because she had seen the potential for weaving and envisioned what the industry could become.[13]

In 1901 President Frost hired Hettie Wright Graham to be full-time coordinator of Berea College's community weaving program, but poor health forced her retirement within a few years.

In the early part of the twentieth century, Berea employed a full-time weaving director, Hettie Wright Graham of Flushing, New York. Mrs. Graham lived in and managed the industry for less than two years from Clover Bottom Cabin. The college moved the 26 x 28-foot former Baptist church-house, described as a "heartening example of log architecture," from nearby Jackson County to the campus to serve as weaving headquarters.[14] Outfitted with handwoven textiles, the building showed an example of comfortable living. Another cabin, originally used to board some of the college's first teachers, provided additional space for the weaving program.

In her short tenure, Graham developed a workforce of twenty spinners and weavers, most of them working in their own homes; the college paid for finished pieces. She tried to secure adequate and reliable supplies of wool and flax for spinning. She introduced the weaving of rag rugs, which sold for "about $1.00 per square yard." The rag rugs used ticking scraps obtained from a Cincinnati manufacturer for weft.[15]

Hettie Wright Graham embarked on an ambitious plan of promoting the weaving through lectures and exhibitions in major cities. In January 1902 she wrote to President Frost, "I find everywhere the greatest interest. It is only necessary to tell what we are doing and a cordial invitation to show our work comes."[16] Sales occurred through two presentation avenues: notices in the *Berea Quarterly* and exhibitions.

During the Commencement of 1903, a fellow Quaker visited Mrs. Graham in her weaving cabin; he reported on his stay in a Quaker publication. The unidentified visitor presented his observations of the weaving and the campus. He observed that "President William G. Frost wore a suit of brown 'linsey-woolsey,' which looked as if it would wear till it went out of fashion, if men's suits ever do go out of fashion." The writer included his observations on mountain work: "Many people with the missionary spirit are now trying to do settlement work in the mountains though the conditions differ so greatly from city work that it hardly seems the same. These mountain people are American citizens, self-respecting and even proud. They are often shy and reserved and do not like to be exploited. One needs to have the right feeling to be of real service to them." He obviously thought that Berea approached their work sensitively because he wished those "who have money to spare would take an interest in this school."[17]

Mrs. Graham failed to return to Berea in the fall of 1903, illness remaining the official explanation for her absence. Difficulties in managing the business aspects of the Fireside Industries contributed to her not resuming her post. In a letter to President Frost she complained that she believed worry about taking inventory shortened her life by five years. She reasoned, "It must seem foolish to a mind like yours that I cannot master the details of so simple a business as mine, but you know the proverbial tendencies of artistic natures do not run that way."[18]

With Hettie Wright Graham not returning to the college, the management of the Fireside Industries fell to the head of the Domestic Science Department and laundry supervisor, Jennie Lester Hill. The first woman to receive a Bachelor of Arts from Berea College, Hill had proven an able administrator in her college responsibilities, although she was not a weaver. Under her guidance Berea students started weaving with cotton and linen and making netted lace. In her 1907 annual report to President Frost, she observed about the community program that "the weavers themselves are taking a greater pride and interest in the work and are hunting up old 'drafts' and practicing new combinations of patterns." A weaving draft provided loom threading information on four parallel lines for a specific pattern similar to music notation. Many of the pattern drafts collected by the weavers had been kept in families for over one hundred years.[19]

Jennie Lester Hill, who was the first woman to receive a Bachelor of Arts degree from Berea College, headed the Domestic Science Department. She assumed responsibility for the weaving program after the departure of Hettie Wright Graham.

A brochure called *Not Exactly a Commercial Scheme* listed the college's main priority as "the great labor of school and extension work" while noting that the mountain families needed the money, often using it for school expenses. Under Mrs. Hill's direction, the Fireside Industries offered wares as part of the college's "gigantic but cheering task of helping our contemporary ancestors." In explaining the venture into retail sales, the college stated: "We first showed these products merely to prove the capacity of our mountain clients." However, this reluctant sales brochure continued, "We shall handle as many of these products as our limited strength permits, hoping thus to enlist a wider interest and larger support for Berea College."[20] Evidently a conflict existed between operating a handicraft business and the wider mission of the school. The school wanted the sales but only if it could remain untainted by commercial motives. Higher principles rather than mere monetary gain guided the tone of the college's marketing. In addition to textiles—coverlets, yardage, and rag rugs—Hill's small sales pamphlet offered an iron oil lamp and an oak table.

In a brief piece in the *Berea Quarterly* for 1910, Hill demonstrated a talent for advertising copy, writing engaging stories that the consumer would find compelling. She presented a coverlet as a "second-class one, just the thing for summer camp or bungalow." The description of a bright red, white, and blue coverlet ended with the suggestion: "Just the thing for a boy's room. Teach him patriotism while he sleeps!" Another story tugged at the reader's social concerns, describing why the college purchased less than top quality merchandise: "That old one bought because a girl must have money or leave school. This other one taken to encourage a new weaver."[21]

For several years Jennie Lester Hill recommended that the Fireside Industries needed the attentions of a full-time supervisor without any other heavy duties. Even though she believed in the work of the industry, the number of workers diminished under her reign. By 1911—the year after Mrs. Hill's retirement—the department was run by the sewing instructor and only four weavers remained.

On April 18, 1911, President Frost offered Anna Ernberg of New York City $550 for ten month's work plus a two-month vacation as the full-time head of Fireside Industries. His lengthy letter described Berea as a missionary school, and gave exact dollar amounts for the school's finances and salaries for female staff. In the responsibilities he outlined for her, he expected her to travel in the mountains three months of the year "to gain the confidence of the mountain women," and to make sales trips to the North. "Now for the weaving itself," he continued. "We do not wish to introduce forms of weaving which are new and foreign to the people here but to encourage and develop the forms which have been handed down by tradition from the old English and Scotch sources. I have inferred that your own work was learned in Sweden. Of course it is much alike and may involve some better elements but it seemed to us better to preserve that which is traditional and familiar to the older women in the mountains."[22]

Grace Tabor, "a charming writer on art, gardening, etc.," wrote to Eliza Calvert Hall about discovering Anna Ernberg, "a native of Sweden—(the daughter of an officer of the Swedish Army)—and an expert in all kinds of weaving." In *The Book of Handwoven Coverlets*,

In 1911 Berea College engaged Anna Ernberg to manage the Fireside Industries. She expanded the weaving program to include many students, who covered their tuition with their labor.

published in 1912, Hall quoted Tabor: "I brought Mrs. Ernberg to the notice of President Frost of Berea, and she was engaged to succeed Mrs. Jennie Lester Hill, under whose superintending the Department of Fireside Industries had become justly famous."[23]

William Wade, a weaver and a prominent figure in deaf education, also played a significant role in advocating for Ernberg. In February of 1911 Wade forwarded a letter to President Frost that had been written to him by Ernberg. She declared her desire to leave the overcrowded metropolitan area of New York City for a pastoral setting, indicating a favorable knowledge of Berea College. In the letter, Anna evaluated several traditional coverlets, praising the pattern weaving for its beauty and simplicity of design. Also, she sent Wade "a pillow that I made for you as thanks for the photos and may be more as a tribute to the lover of old handweaving, as I have been struggling good many years to have it known and have never met anybody that did care for it as you seem to do." In this personal communication—obviously intended only for Wade—Ernberg's remark about coverlet weaving suggested to Frost that she would respect the mountain traditions. Wade also backed Ernberg by contributing to her relocation expenses, asking Frost to keep this kindness anonymous.[24]

Anna Ernberg gladly accepted President Frost's offer to be the superintendent of the Fireside Industries. Educated in her native Sweden, she came to the United States in her midtwenties with her husband Hjalmar. During her years in New York, she taught weaving at Pratt Institute and Teachers' College at Columbia University. In the fall of 1911 at age thirty-seven, she assumed her duties at Berea College and moved into the weaver's cabin in Berea with her two sons.[25]

Less than a year and a half after arriving in Berea, Ernberg's article for the *Berea Quarterly*, "Ruskin's Ideal for Humble Homes," rambled on about the illustrious history of handweaving, with particular emphasis on Sweden's place in it. Finally, toward the end of the piece, she managed to tie weaving heritage to her work at Berea: "I shall not need to show anything new, nothing foreign, but would like to see the weaver of today make a fabric as good as her mother and grandmother made." Even though Ernberg spent most of the article extolling international weaving, she claimed the local weaving tradition for her current endeavor. She concluded with a statement of mission: "And I am sure the mountain homes have been waiting for some such opportunity as this. . . . An artistic product going forward in the family loom will be an educating and uplifting influence for the household. And how much will it mean for the mother of a family to have a resource of her very own for securing the money she so much desires for home comforts or the education of her children!"[26]

During Ernberg's early years at Berea and well into the 1920s, Jennie Hill's catalog continued to be reproduced with only slight variations. The coverlet pictures remained the same in the Ernberg edition, with curtains and rugs with overshot patterns added as new items. Anna contributed her own philosophy in a few new paragraphs: "We are not running a shop with stock on consignment. All the products sold by us are made under our direction, material supplied when so needed. This helps us in standardizing and assures us a good quality when the worker herself does not know enough to choose the best. The worker is paid immediately for her work, as we feel that 'immediate help is double help,' and most of our mountain workers cannot afford the outlay for material, neither to wait for returns of her labor until her products are disposed of."[27] The distinction Ernberg made between consignment and purchasing for resale was significant for both of the reasons she stated. First, with the college acting as the direct purchaser of the products, it controlled design and quality. When dealing with mail-order sales, the product delivered should be consistent with the product advertised. Second, the worker received payment when she delivered the items to Berea. In the consignment system, the worker would have been paid only after the goods sold. Most of the time, several months would have elapsed before the maker received any money. This control made business sense while providing the best condition for the worker.

Immediately after World War I, Ernberg wrote *An Appeal to the Women of America*, in which she urged awareness of the needs of mountain counties, "where not a single man who was called claimed exemption." She recommended charity a little closer to home: "We are confident that the patriotic women of America will respond to this call from the lonely and isolated cabins in our mountains, as they have to those more insistent appeals from stricken Europe." The second half of the pamphlet contained testimonial letters supporting the work of the Fireside Industries. Mountain women expressed their gratitude for receiving weaving assignments through the college. Eminent people, such as social worker Jane Addams and investigative writer Ida M. Tarbell, attested to the value of handcrafted work, particularly that produced under Anna Ernberg's guidance.[28] This publication concentrated on fundraising without listing products.

Not content with the two leaky cabins assigned to the weaving program, by 1913 Ernberg used her sales trips in the East and North to raise additional money for a building fund. In her appeals for funds, she referred to the planned two-story structure as the "Log Palace," but after its completion in 1917, the official name became the Log House. The structure provided ample room for the increasing supply of looms, product finishing spaces, a sales area, and, on the second floor, an apartment for Ernberg. Complaining that her planned storage shed had not been built, Anna set about to secure additional money for another log building. On May 21, 1921, an elaborate ceremony commemorated laying of the cornerstone for a second struc-

Not content with the small leaky cabins assigned to the weaving program, Anna Ernberg raised money to build the Log House, finished in 1917; it provided space for the weaving and the craft sales, and also had an apartment for Ernberg on the second floor.

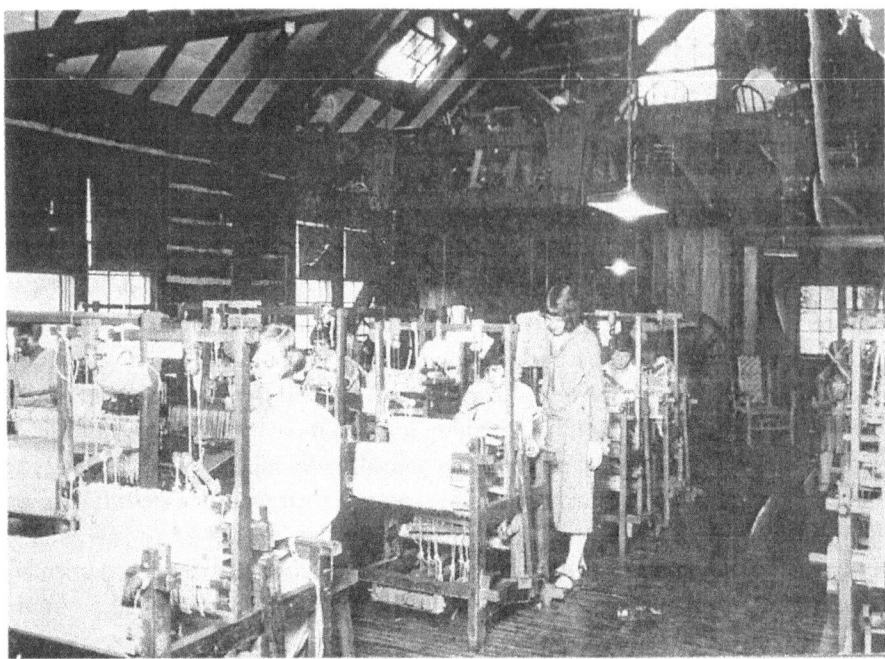

Ernberg constructed another cabin behind the Log House for the looms. Because the Kentucky Lieutenant Governor Thurston Ballard donated the money for this structure, it was named Sunshine Ballard after his wife.

ture behind the first. Most of the money came from the lieutenant governor of Kentucky, Thruston Ballard, with the new building bearing the name of his wife, Sunshine Ballard.[29]

During the year that construction began on the Ballard building, Fireside activities involved 112 homes that supplied items for sale, 23 students who worked half days, and 114 girls who worked in two-hour labor shifts. The women who worked in their own homes spun, wove, sewed, knotted and tufted bedspreads, netted fringe, pieced quilts, and made baskets. The students who wove half days covered all of their college living expenses, while extending their studies over more years. Half-day students typically worked at the looms; those working fewer hours did some weaving but mostly hemmed or did other finishing work. In her 1921 final report, Ernberg reminded the president that her department had been conceived as extension work for community women, rather than students with labor assignments. "We all know that student labor cannot be self-supporting and I do not think we ought to wish it to be as we surely want to feel that our work with them has some educational value that cannot be counted in dollars and cents."[30]

Student labor demanded more supervision—and a different type of supervision—than dealing with community women. The student workers who worked two-hour shifts presented special problems for the Fireside Industries. Without adequate periods of concentration, the students were not able to develop diversified weaving skills. As a result, they commonly received assignments in finishing work, which could be more easily stopped and started. The two-hour-a-day workers came from the Academy or Foundation schools; they weren't older and more mature college students. Ernberg lamented that the short-time workers affected her financial balance because they did not produce at the consistently high level of the other workers and required more attention.

Students rarely returned to work at Fireside once they had been trained. Every quarter some students transferred to other labor assignments, and many returned home after dropping out of school. In the annual report of 1926, weaving assistant Eleanor Stockin observed on the labor situation, "It is easy to see the difficulties of keeping up a steady production of work, up to our standard, with such a shifting group of workers. Out of one hundred and sixty-eight girls, only thirty-two remained with us the entire year."[31]

Anna Ernberg traveled to major cities in the East and North to sell the products of Fireside Industries. Berea College supporters and donors provided their homes for exhibitions and sales, or arranged for her to appear before sympathetic groups. Women's Clubs, the Daughters of the American Revolution, church groups, and various art organizations were among the groups that requested Ernberg as speaker, often after individual members had heard her message elsewhere. The college, Appalachia, and the worthy weaver were all part of the sales package. This approach to marketing represented the purchase of items as a missionary activity. While Ernberg never doubted the quality for the price she offered, she also stressed the good that buying the item would do.

Local newspaper articles highlighting these events played very heavily on contemporary Appalachian stereotypes. One Boston news item began, "Mrs. Anna Ernberg, called 'the director of the fireside industries' at Berea College, Kentucky, has for four years lived in a state of complete isolation from the world in order to help the ignorant mountaineers and moonshiners in their struggle for knowledge and means to gain a livelihood." Another newspaper featured the headline, "Tales of Southern Mountain Life Are Strange As Fiction" with the sub-headline, "Woman Who Works in Hills to Educate Americans Recounts Battle for Existence." Although such newspapers may have exaggerated the squalor, the consistency of the accounts suggests that Anna herself dramatized her work in this fashion. Even when newspaper articles avoided succumbing to unpleasant stereotypes, the unique nature of Berea College played a prominent role in marketing the products. In a report on a 1930 trip, *The Duluth Herald* began with a straightforward introduction, "Workers at Berea College Tell About School Affairs," and continued with the school description: "A college where students may not use tobacco. Where co-eds may not wear silk garments. Where students may not use automobiles at college. But where no one is barred because of poverty."[32] During this particular event, a recent Berea graduate accompanied Anna Ernberg and sang mountain ballads.

One speech that Ernberg gave during her sales trips concluded with this note of mission: "I appeal again. Don't rob our mountain women of their inheritance of this kind. Let us try to understand and encourage and help her to appreciate and instead of robbing her, try to bring a little beauty and aesthetic uplift in her lonely life of doing without."[33] Whatever Ernberg said, it produced results. She sold great quantities of the handwork, raised money to build her Log Palace, and secured donations to the college. She often made repeat performances in her circuit of favorable cities.

Before coming to Berea, Anna Ernberg had designed a small wood counterbalance loom that could be assembled without hardware. Weaving on these looms was much easier than on the large cumbersome looms common in the mountains. Even though the counterbalance loom's action was of the same type as on traditional looms, the better-engineered Ernberg design required less force to operate it. Also, the looms were available in narrower sizes, perfect for weaving the smaller and more popular items. That the small looms required less space was also a considerable advantage. In an agreement with President Frost, the college woodworking department manufactured these looms and paid Anna a five-dollar royalty for each one sold.[34] Ernberg did not seek a patent on her design because she expected and encouraged local craftsmen to use the loom as a model for making equipment used by the many weaving cooperatives springing up throughout the mountains. Ernberg was also willing to defer her royalty payments when Berea's Fireside Industries and other southern philanthropic institutions bought looms for the purpose of increasing weaving in the region.

By her tenth year at Berea, Anna Ernberg's salary had more than tripled, a reflection of the confidence that President Frost placed in her.[35] However, complaints about Ernberg mounted as well. While Anna could be quite charming—as her abilities as a speaker and fundraiser attested—she could also be exacting, brusque to the point of rudeness, and querulous. She annoyed college administrators because of her impatience with visitors—including donors to the school—and because of her opposition to the school's edicts. President Frost made excuses for her because he believed in her work. In 1920, shortly after leadership of the college passed from Frost to William J. Hutchins, the two men exchanged letters in which they discussed "the weaving situation," among other things. Conflicts between student labor and the faculty and jockeying for position among the different academic departments precipitated the exchange of letters. Hutchins described Ernberg's tenure at Berea as follows: "I understand that she built up a department, which now extends its influence into a good many homes in the mountains, which more than supports itself, which furnishes a most attractive form of advertising for the college. I understand that Mrs. E. is herself somewhat domineering, somewhat hard upon the girls and women who work for her, that she is not always gracious to guests, and that she is naturally sensitive and high strung with regard to her status etc." Despite this criticism—after having heard Ernberg's version of events—Hutchins commented that "on the whole [he had] won a great admiration for the woman." Frost's clarification began by noting that Ernberg had "found a market, making friends and securing introductions among the 'donor class'" and "set a standard of excellence that is near to perfection."[36] Ernberg fought hard for her beliefs and refused to submit graciously to authority.

During his tenure, Hutchins studied, evaluated, and reexamined the Ernberg "situation" many times over many years. Ernberg displayed perceptive self-awareness in one remark to President Hutchins: "May I ask you also to believe that even if you will not find me very diplomatic or tactful that you shall always find that I am honest, frank, and truthful, and that I have no fear at all in promising to be always loyal and faithful to you in the small part I have in Berea's work." In 1922 the royalty payments of the Ernberg Loom erupted as a major controversy. When Hutchins requested that Ernberg relinquish her royalties from the loom sales, Ernberg wrote back: "If I had written a book before I came to Berea and had a royalty on the same would you ask me to give up that royalty now since we have a living salary?"[37] Hutchins defended the withdrawal of the royalty payments on the grounds that Berea now compensated the faculty adequately and provided a retirement system. In any case, the governing Prudential Committee's policy that targeted Ernberg's extra compensation had actually been developed to curtail the activities of physics and automobile mechanics teacher David Carroll Churchill. Even though Churchill thought he had a prior agreement with Hutchins allowing him to supplement his salary, the committee refused to let him start a loom manufacturing business.[38]

When New York journalist Ida Tarbell named Anna Ernberg one of the fifty outstanding women in America in 1930, she erroneously identified Ernberg as the founder of the Fireside

Berea College and Fireside Industries

Industries at Berea College. While never claiming to have started the weaving program, Ernberg did allow that "Mrs. Frost and others have very kindly said, that my department begins with me."[39] Under Ernberg, the Fireside Industries developed into a major student labor employer, considerably expanded home-based textile crafts, and influenced most of the Craft Revival weaving centers in the mountains. She and President Frost agreed on the importance of weaving as a "fireside industry," which contributed to family finances and to the quality of life within the home.

Ida Tarbell compiled her list of fifty women from among living Americans, including in her criteria the "Ability 1) to initiate or create; 2) to lead or inspire; and 3) to carry on." Such notable women as Helen Keller, Frances Perkins, Margaret Sanger, Jane Addams, Mary McLeod Bethune, Edith Wharton, Willa Cather, and Amelia Earhart made the list. (Tarbell herself would not have been out of place on her own list for her pioneering muckraking work as assistant editor of *McClure's Magazine* and, later, as owner and associate editor of *American Magazine*. Her major accomplishment was exposing the inner workings of John D. Rockefeller's oil monopoly.) Only one other woman was recognized for southern mountain work—Martha Berry, founder of the Berry Schools in Georgia.[40] Ernberg and Tarbell both belonged to the Pen and Brush, a literary and art club in New York, and their friendship continued after Ernberg moved to Kentucky, with Tarbell visiting her in Berea on several occasions.

In time, President Hutchins became a defender of Anna Ernberg. In a letter to the Prudential Committee, he answered the allegations of Anna's misappropriation of funds: "My general judgment of this has been that she had identified herself so completely with the Fireside Industries that in turn she has identified the Fireside Industries with herself." For this reason he excused Ernberg's casual system of accounting for petty cash. This letter, dated February 15, 1932, examined alternatives to her continued employment, concluding:

> If we were considering the Fireside Industries merely as a commercial enterprise, I think we should still have to think long and carefully as to whether we could do better than to retain Mrs. Ernberg in her job. She keeps the building immaculate. Her work is regarded as the standard of all the work of the [Southern Highland] Handicraft Guild. When I brought a friend from Boston into her Fireside Industries with the thought that she with her wide knowledge of weaving might give us some valuable information, the woman simply said to me that the half has not been told, that we were doing things far and away ahead of the work done in Boston.[41]

Controversy surrounded Ernberg, and the administration dealt with it by hiring others to take on some of her responsibilities, especially those that required contact with the public, where Anna's personal style was most likely to cause a problem. For this reason, retail sales on campus separated from the Fireside Industries, although the shop continued in the Log House. The finishing of goods fell

Anna Ernberg managed the Fireside Industries of Berea College with a stern but able hand for 25 years.

under a separate supervisor, as did the teaching of weaving. Because of growth in production and numbers of people to be supervised, the business needed extra help.

During the sixteen years that Ernberg served under the reign of William Hutchins, the operations of the Fireside Industry expanded considerably, regressing only once during the Depression. In the mid-1920s, numbers peaked at about 170 mountain homes supplying products and over 250 girls employed throughout the year in the log buildings on campus.[42] She designed items, ordered materials, taught student workers, managed weaving and finishing operations, kept time and pay records, supervised home weavers, directed marketing, traveled for school promotion, and taught the required Sunday School class. Ernberg's complaints of overwork were amply justified.

During Ernberg's first ten years at Berea, the Fireside Industries' sales increased tenfold, from $1,408.07 to $15,787.89.[43] In the academic year of 1928 sales reached the highest figure at over $34,000. However, the major drop in income occurred a few years into the Depression in 1932, when the nation's belated realization that the economic reversal after the 1929 stock market crash would last far longer than initially expected. During this same year, however, Anna's "field expenses" dropped to about one-quarter of the figure from the preceding year. Without her personally pitching the benefits to the students and community women, the weaving sales declined considerably.

Every year all Berea College departments, services, and student labor units filled out an accounting form for the Treasurer. Under the "Expenditure" column, the Fireside Industries annual accounting included all materials, labor, freight, sales trips, staff salaries, and overhead expenses such as water, heat, and light. Income came primarily from sales and donations. Materials, labor, overhead, and other actual cash outlays were added together as expenses and then subtracted from income, to determine the "Net Gain."[44] Examining the figures in the gain and loss columns does not accurately reflect the financial situation because huge inventories carried by Fireside Industries counted as assets on the plus side of the equation. While this may be a standard accounting practice, the addition of inventory to income distorts the bottom line. In reality, most of the recorded profit existed as merchandise that remained unsold on the shelves of Fireside Industries.

During the twenty-five years that Ernberg was at Berea, Fireside maintained a close balance between expenses and income, posting steadily increasing numbers until the Depression, when it decreased. Fireside Industries employed a large number of student workers—this fulfilled a major objective of the college, superseding the business goal of making a profit. No other manager since Ernberg's time generated as great a variety of items, dealt with as many students, produced as many pieces, or ran the industry as efficiently.

Smaller items comprised most of the production because they were easier to sell, required less skill to make, and fit into shorter labor periods. The numbers demonstrate this vividly. During the eight months between August 1935 and March 1936, the accounts indicate that 5,451 pieces were sold. Finger towels led the list at 1,729, followed closely by "scarfs" and shawls at 1,460, while purses ran a distant third at 685. While the small pieces sold easily, dozens of them needed to sell to bring in the revenue of just one large item. Eighteen coverlets brought in a total of $489. Overproduction, always a problem, continued especially in purses—almost 1,000 more were made than were sold.[45] The need to keep students busy outweighed the market justification of letting demand regulate production or supply levels. Over the entire history of Fireside, the conflict between running a business and providing work for the college's labor program was always present.

A small note to this production tally indicates that "mountain products or outside" items, of which 6,454 were sold, generated a total of $8,283.65. Unfortunately the record fails to breakdown either quantities or types of products. Fireside cut the number of items purchased from community women during the Depression, when the decline in discretionary purchasing power affected middle-class women. Ernberg wrote to Hutchins in 1931 that her first obligation must be to supply the students with work. She explained why she bought fewer of the larger items from community women and expressed regret at having to turn these women away: "Nobody can know how my heart has ached and how I have suffered with them, knowing that their needs on account of the drought last Summer, have been larger and greater than ever. . . . It is hard to have to refuse people when all they ask for is some work to do, and knowing that perhaps they may be suffering hunger and cold."[46] When hard times forced a choice, the college favored student workers, denying community women income from an industry originally started for their benefit.

In the early 1920s Fireside Industries first offered weaving instruction, separate from the labor program. Anna Ernberg felt that the instruction was already incorporated into the student labor program and should have been sufficient for those who really wanted to learn weaving. She thought that girls would learn the process and then develop their own weaving businesses, using her Fireside model. But demand for weaving instruction forced her to offer classes, even though she considered the interest a "fad." Ernberg could not conceive of weaving as a leisure-time activity. In her heritage, students learned crafts skills as apprentices—not in classes. Miss Anna LaGrange Walker assumed the role of weaving instructor at the Fireside Industries. For three years the Academy taught weaving classes, but Ernberg fought for all weaving to be under Fireside. In 1934 Walker summarized the growth of the weaving classes over a ten-year period; it had started with thirty students and reached sixty-eight that year. Most of the students came from the Academy or high school; the next highest group was "auditors." College students only took weaving in the summer, which was when most of the auditors attended.[47]

Many of the weaving teachers in the Appalachian Mountains went through the Berea program. Ernberg believed in the growth of weaving cottage industries, but felt that those interested should serve an apprenticeship under her, rather than simply being taught how to develop a business. Whether or not the teachers came from Anna Ernberg's program, Berea set the standard for other weaving cooperatives.

In 1920 a Berea Normal student, Zada Benfield returned home to Crossnore, North Carolina, and helped establish a Fireside weaving program at the new high school. Her co-founder, Clara Lowrance, was also trained at Berea, and she continued the program until her retirement. Sarah E. Boyce accompanied her husband—both were Berea graduates—to the Pleasant Hill Academy in Cumberland County, Tennessee. In the mid-1930s she started a weaving business run out of her home. The founder of the "Little Loom House" in Louisville, Kentucky, and publisher of "Kentucky Weaver," Lou Tate graduated from Berea College in 1927. She learned to weave in a summer class under Anna Walker. The college supported her research on traditional coverlet patterns.[48]

Lucy Morgan started her own Fireside Industries at the Appalachian School in Penland,

North Carolina, after learning to weave from Anna Ernberg in the winter of 1923. The college secretary, Marshall Vaughn, wrote to President Hutchins about Lucy's less-than-favorable experiences: "Mrs. Ernberg gives her just as little as she can get by with when she should give her all she has in her belfry or as much as the lady can take during the time of her stay."[49] He reported that Lucy Morgan had withdrawn her recommendation for Penland students to come to Berea to learn weaving.

Through her student and assistant, Marguerite Porter Davison, Anna Ernberg had a profound influence on the course of American handweaving. Miss Porter was studying at Berea's Normal School in 1912 when she met Waldo Davison; in 1916 they married. She dedicated *A Handweaver's Source Book,* which contained over two hundred drafts for overshot coverlet patterns, to Anna Ernberg. Davison's *Handweaver's Pattern Book,* a meticulous investigation of the variations in weave structures, continues to be one of the most consulted resources used by handweavers.[50]

Anna Ernberg retired at the end of the summer of 1936. Like many other Berea faculty members, she complained that the hard work had ruined her health, and she did have a heart condition. After an extended illness, she died on April 1, 1940, at the age of sixty-six.[51] With exaggeration befitting her stature, Ernberg's tombstone in the Berea cemetery extended the dates of her supervision of the Fireside Industries from 1911 to 1940. Following this erroneous date is a fitting eulogy:

> Not Until The Loom is silent
> and the shuttles cease to fly
> shall God unroll the pattern
> and tell the reason why
> The dark threads are as needed
> in the Master's skillful hands
> as the Threads of Gold and Silver
> in the pattern He has planned.[52]

Mountain Weaver Boys

Aside from the weaving of the Fireside Industries, Berea College developed another student-labor program that produced woven yardage. In late 1922, the college contacted noted educator and weaver Edward Worst of the Chicago Public Schools about locating a person to direct men's weaving. In reply, he suggested a possible applicant and commented, "I am indeed pleased to know that the textile work is at last being extended to the young men at your school. It has been my experience in public school work that where the boys are given an opportunity to weave, they do it better than the girls."[53]

A few years later, in 1926, Howard Ford took up the job of creating the program. After attending normal school in Michigan, Ford taught at the Appalachian School in Penland, North Carolina, later continuing his education at Berea College. When he took up residence again in Berea, he energetically attacked the many problems associated with developing a fly-shuttle loom industry and formulating a business strategy. Within two years he had male students producing wool yardage. Worst responded to a gift of overcoat fabric from a "mountain boy weaver" in 1929: "The material, in every respect, is equal to anything I have ever seen

A Berea College student weaves at a fly-shuttle loom. In 1926 Howard Ford began tackling the many problems involved with starting a new weaving industry at the College—The Mountain Weaver Boys.

that came from a foot power loom. I am sure that if you have any doubts as to Mr. Ford's ability, the product he is now turning out will convince you that he is a capable young man. The only experience he had ever had with a loom before going to you was the short time he spent with us in Chicago. You certainly are to be congratulated in having one who could make so great a success in so short a time."[54]

During the more than two years it took Ford to get things up and running, he solved many technical difficulties before developing a reliable fly-shuttle counterbalance loom. John Kay had invented the fly-shuttle attachment to the loom in 1733. A spring mechanism propelled the shuttle, which greatly increased weaving speed. This invention was one of the principal factors leading to the industrial revolution in the British textile industry.[55]

The new student-labor weaving program bore the official name of Mountain Weaver Boys. Ford designed a logo depicting a cabin on a mountaintop. A small publicity brochure described the fabric: "A genuine homespun is made from a single ply yarn, every fiber of which is virgin wool. We build in our own woodshop the looms on which homespun is woven. Our yarns have a very hard twist to make them wear and they are carded and spun in a picturesque water-powered mill up in the Great Smokies."[56] Although billed as "homespun," commercially produced yarn was used to weave the fabric. The term referred to the textured look of the cloth, rather than handspun materials. Small folders contained fabric swatches in an array of colors, from which clients ordered yardage for a suit or overcoat.

During the school year ending in June 1930, George R. Bent took over as head of the Mountain Weaver Boys. He first tackled disposing of an inventory of substandard fabric and yarns, and then launched into the production of high-quality suiting. Bent, who later assumed the role of marketing Berea College crafts, demonstrated an understanding of business practices. He reduced excessive overhead by increasing production, thus spreading the cost of producing goods over more items. In his first annual report, he recommended that the still-limited production be carefully placed. "I have discouraged men from buying where I could not see that they would show it to influential friends. I have tried definitely to sell to men who meet other men of money and influence. These men are wearing on their backs a walking ad for Berea."[57]

Bent knew that a market needed to be created, even for the weavers' high-quality product. He secured an exhibition area in Boone Tavern, a hotel and restaurant that Berea College ran as part of the student labor program. Promotional devices called attention to the best qualities of the fabric and capitalized on the school name. A small tag secured to each length of yardage certified the fabric to be virgin wool and handwoven at the Berea College Student Industries. Also, with each piece of material came a satin label identifying the fabric as "homespun," with the names of the school and craft and a picture of a boy at a loom. When sewn inside the finished garment, the label reminded the wearer of the origin of the fabric throughout its long life.

By calling a new line of blankets a "Sarvice" Blanket, Bent realized the marketing potential of associating products with Appalachia. In his 1932 annual report, he pointed out that the name derived from the Sarvice Tree (a local mountain pronunciation of the serviceberry tree with blooms of white flowers in the very early spring), thus tying the product with the region and associating it with utility. He named blanket patterns after local creeks: Pretty Run, Pigeon Wing, Yallerjacket, and Whoopferlarrie. An assistant in the department designed a popular woman's sport coat. Despite Bent's marketing improvements, when Ernberg-trained Bess Ledford took over as director in 1933, the Mountain Weaver Boys still operated at a financial loss.[58]

Bent understood business, but it took Ledford, who knew about weaving, to turn the industry into a profitable enterprise. She consolidated the yardage line, keeping the best-sellers, reevaluating the colors, and offering a more lightweight wool for women. Under her guidance, the production line expanded to include men's lounging robes, scarves, couch throws in Scottish plaids, and men's neckties coordinated with the "homespun" suiting.[59] Apart from the Berea walk-in trade, items were sold through catalog mailings and consignment exhibitions. The college discovered that men who liked the fabric often did not know of a tailor who could make custom garments. So the college identified a network of tailors in major cities to accomodate orders for suits and coats. For those clients who came to the campus, garments could be sewn at the school.

Sometimes a need for handwoven fabric arose at the college. David Gilliam wove 198 yards of cloth in over 198 hours for the cover of the 1937 Chimes, the college yearbook.[60] In addition to this prodigious output, Gilliam received commendation as a model student. Bess Ledford praised him as early as 1934 when he was an Academy sophomore. "He tries hard to cooperate in every way possible to perfect his weaving. He takes suggestions and criticism beautifully and profits by them. He is a delightful worker and a very good student."[61]

In June of 1941, Ledford recommended that the sales area in Berea be expanded and remodeled into a more attractive space. Her year-end summary of sales figures indicated that three-quarters of the business originated in the Berea shop, while only one-quarter came in by mail. Unfortunately, the coming of World War II curtailed wool supplies, which limited production. During 1941, the last year of Ledford's management, twenty-four students found employment at the Mountain Weaver Boys, with boys doing the weaving and girls finishing the products.[62]

During the late thirties and forties, the income from the men's weaving compared very favorably to that of the Fireside Industries. Some years the gross sales figures were higher than that of the female weaving industry. After the Mountain Weaver Boys began showing profits, their margins became much higher than Fireside's.[63] Clearly the fly-shuttle and the limited product line enabled a much smaller number of workers to succeed, when judged by profitability. The Mountain Weaver Boys continued as a college labor choice for many years, but eventually merged into one weaving operation under the Fireside Industries.

Labor Day

At the end of the 1921 school year, Berea initiated an annual celebration recognizing their student industries and labor program that included a parade, awards, contests, and prizes. Berea's Labor Day occurs near the end of the school year in May, rather than on the national holiday commemorating labor on the first Monday in September. Berea College views Labor Day as "a day set aside in recognition of the labor activities which are, not incidental to the school program, but a vital part of it."[64]

During the many competitions traditionally held on Labor Day, two or three independent judges evaluated the students' performance in designated tasks. The day's events included competitions drawn from specialized skills developed within individual industries. Among dozens of contests were "Napkin Folding by Boone Tavern, Boxing Beaten Biscuits by the Candy Kitchen, Wrapping Family Bundles by the Laundry, Sheep Shearing by the Livestock Farm, Stuffing Baby Zebra by Needlecraft, Egg Grading by Poultry, Lacing Waste Basket by Woodcraft, and Canvas Folding by the Fire Department." Fireside Industries competed in several contests, with Bobbin Winding, Weaving Finger Towels, and Hemming Baby Bibs among the usual events. William H. Danforth of St. Louis, a long-time member of the college's Prudential Committee, established cash prizes for students who had come up with creative ideas or products in their labor assignment.[65] In a report on the Labor Day activities, an observer commented that the final awards ceremony "reminded one again of the dignity and democracy of labor."[66]

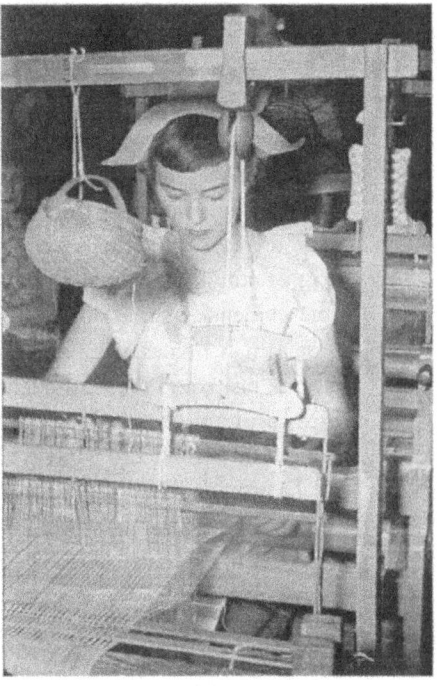

Berea College's Labor Day celebrated all of the different jobs students preformed on campus with a parade and contests in labor skills areas. The Fireside Industries weavers dressed in costumes for the event.

In the early years of Berea, student labor functioned as a self-help program enabling young people without financial resources to cover school expenses. During the Frost years, many of the labor assignments could be regarded as training opportunities in professions that students might follow after leaving school. In the Hutchins administration, the focus shifted to the educational value of labor.[67] Whatever the particular focus of the labor program, the dignity and democracy of labor has always been promoted and celebrated.

Berea's Influence

In examining the history of weaving at Berea, William Goodell Frost deserves credit for seeing the potential in weaving, first as a tool for promoting the college and then as a means of achieving economic development. The weaving and spinning fit in with his scheme for developing education at Berea. By focusing the mission of the school on Appalachia, Frost committed himself to raising vast sums of money. The students lacked the resources to pay for their own advancement, but were willing to work for their education. However, their labor alone could not cover the costs involved in maintaining and expanding an institution. More donors and larger contributions from patrons were needed to support a growing student body. Frost made the case for the college very appealing, but always fought against the negative stereotypes of mountain people. Frost presented handwoven coverlets to college supporters as tangible evidence of the worthy traits that mountain people possessed. The coverlets from Appalachian homes attested to the mastery of complex skills, the ability to work at long difficult tasks, and the aesthetic sensibilities of these isolated people. Because of the colonial revival in home decorating and handcrafted promotions by the Art and Craft Movement inspired by Ruskin and Morris, a donor was able to see the value in a gift of a coverlet.

Frost understood the economic possibilities of weaving, both for the weavers and for the college. By purchasing woven goods, the college presented women with a way of making money that made use of known skills and could be pursued in their homes. Although unknown, the several local women who first worked with Frost in developing the weaving deserve credit for demonstrating the economic viability of the products of the loom.

When Anna Ernberg was called to the task of building a weaving program at Berea, she found herself in philosophic agreement with President Frost, and proceeded to set the standard for the Craft Revival within Appalachia. The Fireside Industries she developed became the model for dozens of programs throughout Appalachia. In the types of items produced, design, quality of craftsmanship, and price, Berea College led the way. Its influence might have been even greater, if only Ernberg's personality had not been so prickly.

Berea College encouraged others to begin weaving within Berea, either by design or in response to actions taken by the school. As Berea became known as a community where weaving flourished, individuals and small home businesses established weaving operations in the area. Within the college itself, the Mountain Weaver Boys grew as an industry separate from Fireside, with the purpose of creating labor opportunities for male students. Former college associates started the other two major weaving ventures in Berea, Matheny Weavers and Churchill Weavers. Edith Matheny probably would have remained a hobbyist weaver making items for friends and family if it had not been for the deficiencies she perceived in the college weaving program. After she struck out on her own, the effort brought out her talent in dealing with people, her artistic curiosity, and her managerial abilities. When D.C. Churchill decided that he did not function well within the college structure, he pursued an interest that had been sparked during his years as a missionary in India. His weaving business succeeded because the talents of Churchill and his wife Eleanor complemented each other. To deal with the ever-increasing scope and complexity of their operation, they constantly invented mechanisms, refined procedures, and introduced new items.

Berea led the Craft Revival of the southern Appalachian Mountains by serving as an example of successfully managed crafts industries. Although the school hoped to inspire the students to start cottage industries when they returned home, not many small businesses modeled on the college craft production appeared. A far greater influence resulted from participation in the Conference of Southern Mountains Workers, established by John C. Campbell. Helen Dingman, a Berea College sociology professor, served the Conference in many capacities over the years, including executive director and editor of the publication *Mountain Life and Work*. President Hutchins was one of the leaders of the Conference of Southern Mountain Workers. The handicraft round-table discussions at the conference's annual meeting in Knoxville led to the formation of the Southern Highland Handicraft Guild. Understanding the significance of a cooperative effort for craft promotion, President Hutchins headed the college's delegation himself.

4

pi beta phi settlement school and arrowcraft

"In the 'yesteryears' this country was a community of weavers, but after the war, 'store cloth' was cheap so that one woman after another put the old loom aside," wrote Caroline McKnight Hughes.[1] The passing of weaving skills from one generation to the next had not continued within families following the Civil War. The revival of handweaving occurred because there was again a reason to weave: people from outside the mountains would pay "cash money" for the products from weavers' looms.

The story of weaving in Gatlinburg in the early part of the 1900s is made up of two major strands, which are joined by a third thread toward the middle of the century. First, weaving started as part of the Pi Beta Phi Settlement School program, both for students and for community women. Second, weaving led the crafts promoted as cottage industries by the Arrowcraft Shop, a division of the Pi Beta Phi School. Later on, weaving was a significant part of the Summer Craft Workshops, which grew into the Arrowmont School of Arts and Crafts. Because of the sponsorship of Pi Beta Phi, educated women guided the activities at Gatlinburg through the school's entire development and it provided adequate staffing and financing, unlike most organizations in the mountains.

The Pi Beta Phi School

In 1912 a school convened near the confluence of Baskins Creek and the Little Pigeon River in the small village of Gatlinburg, Tennessee. The women of the national collegiate Pi Beta

The Pi Beta Phi Settlement School opened in Gatlinburg, Tennessee, in 1912. The first class included several children of Andy Huff, who owned the local sawmill.

Phi Fraternity had decided at their 1910 convention in Swarthmore, Pennsylvania, to embark on an educational philanthropic project among "mountain whites."[2] The Pi Phis knew of the work of the Southern Industrial Education Association and of the pioneering work of the Hindman Settlement School in the mountains of eastern Kentucky. They were aware of the unmet demand for basic education in the southern mountains. The Washington Alumnae Club had submitted a proposition to start a school, to be dedicated on the fiftieth anniversary of the beginning of the fraternity in honor of their founders. In April of 1867 twelve young women attending Monmouth College in Illinois had founded the first fraternity for women, I.C. Sorosis, based on the model of men's fraternities. Soon the Greek letters, Pi Beta Phi, once a secret motto, became the name used by members to describe themselves, shortening it to "Pi Phis" in most of their literature. They chose the arrow as their symbol.[3]

In the summer of 1910 a committee of three Pi Phi women—Emma Turner, May Lansfield Keller, and Anna Pettit—traveled to the Appalachian Mountains and investigated sites for a school. The Grand President, Keller, went on to Gatlinburg alone, after the three had already visited several eastern Tennessee communities. She reported back to the membership that the isolated town in Seiver County presented the ideal situation. "Illiteracy is perhaps not so bad as represented, but the advantages for higher work are nil, and household economies, scientific farming, etc. are unknown quantities."[4] Anna Pettit, another member of the investigation team, stopped at Allanstand Cottage Industries near Asheville, North Carolina, on her return home. Under the direction of Presbyterian missionary Frances Goodrich, Allanstand produced and sold a variety of crafts manufactured in homes. Pettit reported, "We visited the exhibition room of Allanstand Cottage Industries where examples of the work of the mountaineers are sent for sale. I was amazed at the skill shown in the weaving and basket work."[5] The seed for wider work was sown early in the Pi Phi commitment to the mountains.

As might be expected of educated women, the Pi Phis did not embark on their school adventure uninformed. A recommended reading list on Appalachia consisting of seventeen books and nineteen periodical articles was distributed to members of Pi Beta Phi.[6] These materials presented Appalachia as a curious place, isolated and cut off from the strides of progress experienced by the rest of the United States. Regional color writers such C.E. Craddock (pseudonym for Mary Murfree), John Fox Jr., and Martha Gielow portrayed the emerging romantic stereotypes of the mountain people in fiction. Authors involved in "solutions" discussed the "mountain problem" in thoughtful and informed articles. William Goodell Frost, president of Berea College, and Samuel T. Wilson, who wrote for missionaries entering the Appalachian field, fall into this group of concerned writers. Not all of the works agreed with the Pi Phi endeavor. Writing in *The World's Work,* Thomas Dawley Jr. promoted relocating mountain people to jobs in lowlands cotton mills, concluding that "The people must go to the industries—to places where they can earn a living.... To try to keep them there by schools and churches is useless."[7] Travelogues with curious anecdotes about local inhabitants comprised the remainder of the suggested reading.

In the pamphlet sent along with the recommended reading list, the head of the fraternity, Emma Harper Turner, observed, "It will prove intensely interesting and of value when the time comes for us to consider definite things in regard to our definite school." But Elizabeth Helmick, the treasurer, hit on a more pressing need for all members to "buy" into the idea of work in the mountains. "It is earnestly hoped that this question of money support will not be a millstone in this magnificent undertaking, and that the members of Pi Beta Phi will promptly send to the treasurer as generous a remittance as they possibly can."[8]

In a report to the Pi Beta Phi membership, the settlement school committee laid out the objectives of the school project. "What we wish to do is to join in the effort to show them how to use their own resources, to develop industries suitable to their environment, and to lead more happy, healthful lives. We want to help, insofar as we can, to educate mountain boys and girls back to their homes instead of away from them."[9] Most mountain workers professed similar missions. This widely held desire proposed to make life more rewarding within the area, rather than encouraging outward migration of the inhabitants

The Pi Phis knew of the work of Jane Addams and the urban settlement houses modeled on the English settlement movement begun by Oxford University students. As with the urban settlement concept, Pi Phis would live among those they helped, and learn as well as teach. A 1917 report observed that "indeed, these mountain people taught us many valuable lessons in living. I believe that each earnest Pi Phi worker in this Fraternity enterprise received from her experience in Gatlinburg a gift in the life that led to better understanding and a greater appreciation of her inherent opportunities."[10] Most of the women that came to Gatlinburg from the North and Midwest to teach at the school stayed only a year or two, but some spent the rest of their lives in the mountains, either as teachers or as wives of local men. One teacher, Henrietta Huff, wrote of her experience many years later, "During the three years I taught at our Settlement School, not only did I fall in love with the beautiful mountains and the fine people living here, but also in particular with a certain young man by the name of James N. Huff, who was in the first class of 1912 and whose father, Andy J. Huff, was responsible for keeping the Pi Phi School here in that first year."[11]

In addition to the weaving, the Pi Phis sold many baskets and chairs produced by families in the Gatlinburg community.

Early on, the Pi Phis realized that helping the children also meant alleviating health and economic concerns of their families. Within the first year of the school's operation, a part-time nurse joined the staff. This service soon expanded into a full clinic run by a nurse, dealing both in preventive health and in treatment of diseases and accidents.

While health problems suggested adopting certain obvious strategies, economic difficulties did not present such direct solutions. In 1915, head teacher Mary O. Pollard observed that "Many of the women make exquisite patchwork quilts, and some still make the hand woven coverlets and blankets. If a sale could be found for these articles, many might undertake the work."[12] Within the year, teacher Caroline McKnight Hughes came to engage in "business and industrial work." Typical of the school's faculty, she belonged to Pi Beta Phi from northern schools—the

University of Minnesota, Cooper-Union in New York City, and teacher training from Prang Normal School.[13]

The first loom appeared at the school during 1915, and a notice in *The Arrow* anticipated another donation of three more looms by the Pi Phis of Springfield, Missouri.[14] Aside from the school weaving program, Hughes saw potential in community-based weaving, assessing the situation as follows: "Many of our neighbors today know how to spin and weave though it has been 'a tol'able long spell' since any of them have done such a thing." She encouraged interest in textile crafts by organizing a spinning bee with prizes. "I want the industrial work of our school to be given a thorough trial for I believe it will be the salvation of these people."[15]

When the school first conceived of the idea of selling crafts, they had planned to act as an agent for consigned goods, where the maker received payment only after the item sold. However, the workers did not understand the concept of consigning goods for later sale. A 1916 school report from Elizabeth Helmick, who served as both chairman and treasurer of the school, explained an unanticipated expense—payment to weavers and other "industrial" workers for their products. "They cannot understand our scheme of being their agent in selling their wares, but insist upon 'spot cash,' 'hand-go, hand-come' money, or they will not work." She continued, "They do not seem to care enough about having those comforts of which they know not, which their work would eventually bring them, to work and wait for its sale."[16] Cash in hand served as a motivating force, while the promise of future rewards did not. Because the craftspeople received direct payment for their goods, the school became the employer.

After the first year of the school's operation, the Pi Phis asked for and received a commitment of support from the community. Gatlinburg granted the Pi Beta Phi school thirty-five acres, and many school buildings appeared in rapid succession. By the early 1920s the school had grown from fourteen pupils and one teacher to over 130 students and five teachers. The Pi Phi teachers, who came from several Midwestern states, lived in the Teachers' Cottage on the school grounds. Some of the students boarded in school dormitories. In addition to the educational pursuits, the school organized sports teams, a debating society, plays presented for the community, special health clinics, a small farm, a canning club, a library, and, during World War I, a Red Cross chapter.[17]

In 1931 Mattie Huff, a graduate of the Pi Beta Phi Settlement School, pledged Pi Beta Phi in Ames, Iowa; her sister, Blanche, joined a year later. Andy Huff owned the Mountain View Hotel in Gatlinburg, and his children made up a good percentage of the first school class. One of the students from the first class, Sue Huff Cox, later returned to Gatlinburg to teach at the school she had attended as a child.[18]

Caroline Hughes supervised industrial work, including weaving, for only a couple of years. Several other teachers taught this subject for short periods of time, with Mr. and Mrs. Norman Pickett assuming "industrial" duties the longest. By 1924 a former student, Allie McCarter, headed the weaving at the school.[19] The weaving classes were taken by upper elementary grades and some high school girls. Sometimes the Arrowcraft weaving supervisor taught weaving in the school, but more frequently another teacher, often a graduate of the school, assumed responsibility for the weaving classes. The federal Smith-Hughes Vocational Education Bill, administered by the state, funded the industrial subjects of agriculture, boys' shop, weaving, and domestic science.

The Pi Phis educated the children of the Gatlinburg area, with increasing financial responsibility assumed by the state and county agencies, until the school system completely transferred to local control in 1966.[20] At that time, the new elementary school was named the Pi Beta Phi School in appreciation of the fraternity's work.

Arrowcraft

Community crafts became a separate entity within the school structure because of the program's success. In her 1924 report, the chairman of the Settlement School committee wrote, "Our development of the weaving must go on. We must inspire new designs, new combinations of colors and originality in the weaving of rugs, coverlets and baskets." She continued, "Let me add here that for the first time in our history has the fire-side industries been a financial success." The income figures she referred to were weaving sales at $2,304.27, with the baskets bringing in a slightly higher amount at $2,695.42.[21] As with Berea College, the term "fireside industries" refers to craftspeople producing items in their own homes for cooperative sale.

Weaving in the Gatlinburg area entered a new phase in 1925 with the arrival of Winogene Redding. Boston Pi Phis had visited the craft school in Boston, where Redding was studying weaving, and recruited her for the settlement school in Gatlinburg.[22] Born in Nova Scotia, she grew up near Boston, in Wollaston, Massachusetts. She had already read of the women that had gone to the mountains to work, and thought that she would try it for a short time, maybe even staying a year.

Gene later described her journey to Gatlinburg and her first interview with Evelyn Bishop, the school director: "She said I was to teach weaving. My next question was 'how and to whom,' and she left me to my own devices when she said I was to find my job and make it." Winogene certainly did "make it." She rounded up about a dozen weavers right away, and had them weaving either her designs or new color combinations of patterns they already knew. In less than a year, Redding had recruited a weaving force of thirty women, rejuvenated the school's weaving program, and even inspired most of the teachers to take up weaving after they finished their classroom duties.[23]

Winogene Redding worked for the Pi Phis for more than twenty years over several different stints. She established procedures that continued with only slight revisions through the years and under other supervisors.[24] The weavers received assignments, wove and finished

Weaver Ainer Maples sits at her loom, watched by Mary L. Ownnby and weaving supervisor Winogene Redding.

items in their homes, and received payment by the piece. After Winogene designed an item, she helped the weavers learn the necessary skills by traveling to their homes. The school supplied materials, with the costs later charged against the finished products. Furnishing yarns secured a lower price because the center could buy them in bulk and guaranteed standardization of materials. On average, twice a month each weaver would present completed items to the supervisor to be checked for craftsmanship. In home-based operations, quality control is maintained by constant vigilance on the part of the manager. Workers paid by the piece have an incentive to produce as many items as they can quickly, and quality suffers if not strongly enforced. By assigning projects to match the tastes and skills of each weaver, the supervisor was able to minimize problems.

Gene liked to talk, and she talked loudly. When she first came to the mountains she was unsure of how to approach mountain women. The school nurse, Phyllis Higginbottom, suggested flowers as a topic of conversation. During Redding's visits to recruit weavers and get them going on projects, she took the advice: "The subject of flowers was my conversational backlog for months to come."[25] Although her style and background differed greatly from the people she supervised, she related to the weavers effectively. She worked hard and tackled projects with enthusiasm. The final reports that she wrote to the Pi Phis each year included much more than just a summary of the finances. She told engaging stories of the progress of the department and the place of weaving in the lives of the women of the mountains.

During Gene's early years, the weaving headquarters resided in the basement of one of the school buildings; storage and shipping happened in whatever space was available. During 1926 two Pi Phis decided to open a shop for tourists in Stuart Cottage on the school grounds. The Arrow Craft Shop name, derived from the Pi Beta Phi arrow symbol, soon became condensed into one word, Arrowcraft. In May, the shop's first month of operation, sales reached almost $1,000, about three times the amount recorded for the same month in the previous year. By 1929, the Pi Phis found it necessary to operate the shop all year long, moving it into the original school cottage located near the intersection of Baskins Creek and the main road through town.[26] As Gatlinburg grew, this site proved an excellent location, and successive shop expansions replaced the original building.

From its inception, the Arrow Craft Shop did not supply items for local consumption but rather for sale to visitors to the area. Tourists to the mountains traveled through Gatlinburg and easily found their way to this unique shop selling attractively displayed handcrafted items. One tourist recounted a visit: "Through the doorway we saw into another room, and there we found the loveliest things imaginable. Laid out on and hung over the most attractive bed, which looked to have about 200 years to its credit, were scarfs, towels, pillows, and bags, all handwoven, and the finest linen and wool with the loveliest patterns and colors."[27] The tourists wanted a memento of the visit to the mountains or a small gift for friends at home. Textile pieces were attractive to travelers because they packed easily and did not break.

Aside from the direct financial support of Pi Beta Phi, fraternity members contributed to "their school" by buying an array of products offered in *The Arrow*. They also purchased from displays at annual Pi Beta Phi conventions. Items designed particularly for the Pi Phis, either with the arrow logo or in their colors of light blue and maroon, included bookmarks, guest towels, and tote bags. Most of them were luxury or decorative items, but they were still small and inexpensive enough to fit within the impulse buying budget. Alumnae clubs throughout the country organized sales events, most of them occurring on an annual basis. During the

Aunt Lizzie Reagan came to the Pi Beta Phi School as housekeeper for the teachers—soon she had an old barn loom set up for her to weave.

early years, Pi Phis purchased items primarily through their alumnae clubs, with the Arrowcraft shop representing only a small percentage of the total income. In the mid 1930s the business expanded in the Gatlinburg shop because of the increasing number of tourists investigating the area of the proposed new national park. A catalog offered mail-order items to general customers. Before this, the Pi Phis could buy items through *The Arrow*, but mail-order purchase was not available to the general public. During the last decade of Arrowcraft, near the end of the twentieth century, about a third of sales came from the shop, another third from Pi Phi purchases, and the remaining third from the catalog.[28]

The Arrowcraft catalogs carried pictures of the items, prices, and some product information. The catalog presented weaving, baskets, chairs, and stools to mail-order customers. Unlike most of the other weaving centers, no mission statement, institutional purpose, or even an Appalachian connection created an additional inducement to purchase. A flier from 1936 listed the item, the fiber, the color, the size, and the price. The pictures grouped pieces together. The cover carried the name of the shop followed by the "Pi Beta Phi Settlement School, Gatlinburg, Tennessee," but contained no explanation about the connection or anything about the work. However, the cover picture did feature Aunt Lizzie Reagan seated at her large traditional mountain loom, which conveyed the visual message of handcrafted products. Aunt Lizzie worked at the school as housekeeper for the teachers, and she is mentioned in several articles in *The Arrow*.

Arrowcraft did not feel the need to generate a specific marketing strategy based on promoting the region and the mission. Well-designed items, made from good materials and skillfully crafted, gave value for the price and did not require additional promotion. However, it was implied that each purchase helped not only the school but the mountain people as well. In *The Arrow*, Gene Redding kept the fraternity informed of the goals of the weaving program: "We want those who buy our weaving to realize that they are not buying just an article,

Pi Beta Phi Settlement School and Arrowcraft

but that they are supplying some woman with contentment and perhaps food; they are helping us to work out an economic problem of widespread influence for progress; they are helping to keep the Arrow Craft Shop and the Weaving Department in the community. . ."[29]

Big changes occurred in Gatlinburg when all the pieces finally came together to create the Great Smoky Mountains National Park. By the late twenties a highway connecting Gatlinburg and Knoxville was built. The first Pi Phis had reached Gatlinburg by a difficult path, part of the way struggling up a creek bed. The government bought land and moved people from the park area. A branch of the Pi Beta Phi School at Sugarlands (now the site of a National Park Visitor's Center) was closed because of the relocation. In the early years of the Depression, local men worked on a rotating basis, developing roads and trails within the park. In 1940, after many years of construction, President Franklin D. Roosevelt dedicated the national park, the second in the eastern part of the country.[30]

In preparation for the many visitors expected at the largest national park east of the Mississippi, Andy Huff constructed an addition to the Mountain View Hotel, which also included a branch of the Arrowcraft Shop. Like the Baskins Creek store, this shop displayed a loom, and manager Georgia Duffield gave frequent weaving demonstrations.[31] Since most visitors had only scant knowledge of cloth production, the loom served as an educational tool. In addition to satisfying the curiosity of the consumer, Duffield's descriptions of the complex process of setting up the loom and the thread-by-thread progress of weaving the fabric, helped justify the high cost of the hand produced work to potential buyers.

With the development of the park came tourists, and many other businesses sprang up in Gatlinburg because of the increased traffic. Allen Eaton observed, "Among these outlets for weaving in Gatlinburg at this time are Mary F. Ogle, Wiley's Shop, Smoky Mountain Handicrafts, M & O Tea Room, Bearskin Craft Shop, Mrs. Amos Trentham, and the LeConte Craft Shop."[32] Gene Redding complained that she trained weavers who either set up for themselves or went to work for others. Even though Redding believed that the ultimate goal of the weaving program was to provide income for women, she resented training the competition for Arrowcraft.

Who were the weavers of Arrowcraft? Looking at the earnings lists, the names of Clabo, Carver, Husky, Maples, McCarter, Ogle, Ownby, Reagan, and Watson appear many times. They are the names of Gatlinburg. Less common names appear, too, but since most of the names belonged to married women, it is impossible to find out the

Izora Keeler walks three miles to bring her finished weaving into Arrowcraft, crossing Baskins Creek a total of 17 times on the way.

exact family lines. In the first twenty years of Arrowcraft, mothers with children in the home formed most of the workforce. As Arrowcraft grew older, so did the average age of its weavers. Two, and sometimes three, generations of the same family wove for Arrowcraft. Gene Redding reportedly said that she couldn't say anything about anybody, because everyone was kin.[33] At one point seventeen members of the McCarter family worked for Arrowcraft.

Between 1935 to 1945, 242 different women wove for Arrowcraft, with at least 90 employed at any one time. The Census Bureau listed the population of Gatlinburg as 75 in 1930, with growth to 1,300 by 1940. The relocation of families out of the national park area was responsible for the rapid increase. During the next ten-year period, the 1950 census data showed an increase of only one, to make 1,301.[34] Given that many of the weavers lived outside the boundaries of the town, a remarkable number of women profited from weaving within this small area.

The statistics on weavers for the ten-year period indicate the part-time nature of the work: in addition to working part-time hours during the week, most weavers only worked part of the year. In this record of individual earnings, half of the weavers made below $150, with only a relatively small number making more than $300 a year. Roughly half of the weavers worked six months or less, with only very few receiving a check in all twelve months.[35] In a draft for an article for *The Arrow*, Redding wrote about the deciding factors affecting the acceptance of work assignments: "Gardening time is almost here, then comes canning time when weaving rightly takes second or third or fourth place."[36] The weavers set their own priorities and determined their own work schedule.

Arrowcraft supplied work, but the weavers controlled when they worked. In her 1944 Final Report, Redding explained production short-falls for some items: "If we pushed them, they were inclined to give up entirely so it seemed to be the best policy to pet them along and get what we could when we could. That sounds a poor way to do a business but it is my experience that it works best with these mountain women." The weavers liked staying at home with their children and they enjoyed the flexibility of their own work schedule. Even when the area offered other employment opportunities, the women that continued weaving said that they did not like the idea of having a boss. They did not want someone standing directly over them telling them what to do.[37]

In its report "Potential Earning Power of Southern Mountaineer Handicraft," the Women's Bureau of the Department of Labor took a firm stand against home-based workers. As part of the study done for the report, interviewers talked to nineteen craft households that worked for Arrowcraft. In response to the question of whether anyone in the household would be able to work at a center, most replied, "None." Only two indicated that they would travel to a center to work, and four others indicated that a sister or daughter might be willing to do that. Two said definitely that they didn't want to work outside the home. When asked about work preferences, most signified that they would do anything.[38] They wanted work, but something that could be done while still maintaining their lifestyle.

With the passage of the Fair Labor Standards Act in 1938 establishing the minimum wage, the federal government began examining wage practices in mountain handicraft work. Redding's 1940–41 Final Report conveyed her alarm: "The greatest and most serious development as far as our weaving is concerned to take place during the year is the effect that the application of the Fair Labor Standards Act will have. The Southern Highland Handicraft Guild had been carrying on negotiations with the U.S. Department of Labor since last March."[39]

Because the weaver was paid by the piece rather than by the hour, the government assumed that the crafts workers earned less than the amount set out in the law. Within the Southern Highlands Handicraft Guild, a debate raged about seeking an exemption from the law or evading compliance in some way. Allan Eaton wrote a seven-page letter to the Department of Labor requesting an exemption for workers in home-based handicrafts.[40]

The government did not get around to seriously investigating the wage laws until after World War II. To demonstrate that weavers earned the prescribed amount, Arrowcraft embarked on a major study to calculate the time involved. In 1946 and 1947, this study of forty-one weaving projects recorded warp preparation, actual weaving time and finishing. The warp preparation figure was divided by the number of pieces and added to the weaving and finishing time to arrive at the total amount of time spent on one piece. The number of pieces completed in an hour was multiplied by the amount paid per item to get the hourly wage. The weaving supervisor reporting the results of the study observed, "I think we have every reason to feel that we are doing well by our weavers, that the government can't help but agree when it makes sufficient comparisons throughout the country, and that we ought not be disturbed too much by the government in our efforts to do what we can."[41]

The law set the minimum wage at 30 cents an hour in 1939, which rose to 40 cents in 1945. Most weavers in the sample group earned between 45 and 50 cents an hour. Twelve weavers made less than 40 cents, while thirteen made more than 50 cents an hour. Of course

During World War II Winogene Redding drove around the Gatlinburg area, picking up completed work from the weavers. Mary L. Ownby stands to the left and Cora Morton to the right, as Gene checks in pieces on the car.

the speed of the individual weaver determined the wage. Cora Morton made 42 cents an hour weaving the Whig Rose mats, while her daughter Jane, a faster weaver, wove the same pattern for 46 cents.[42] All of the figures represent a best-case scenario, without taking weaver error into account.

In 1945 Gene Redding wrote that she had "designed 246 different woven articles in hundreds of colors" within the past ten years. Not all of these items remained in production during the entire period. Less popular articles were dropped from production, while new ones were added. Weavers produced aprons, bags, bibs, baby blankets, bed jackets, bathmats, coverlets, neckties, pillows, placemats (most with matching napkins), potholders, scarves, shawls, and finger and guest towels. Each of these categories had a variety of design and color options. In the nine years from 1936 to 1944, five different designs of baby bibs graced the line, with a total production of 13,580. Seventeen choices tempted the placemat customer. Production for the ever-popular mat in the Whig Rose pattern came to 16,332, which did not include the longer table runner. In contrast to the staggering production numbers for these small items, only 207 coverlets were woven.[43] However, considering that coverlets constituted the high end of the scale in time, materials, and final cost, this number nevertheless represented a substantial output.

Winogene Redding designed items for three distinct populations: tourists, Pi Phis, and catalog consumers. Although some overlap occurred in the variety of items that appealed to these different groups, designing for each required special considerations. Redding understood the needs and tastes of the middle-class woman who purchased products from Arrowcraft. Tourists bought placemats, guest towels, and other small items. The sales events sponsored by Pi Beta Phi featured more luxury pieces. Only the most popular pieces—those that had proven mass appeal—were included in the catalog. For mail-order sales, the production needed to be consistent and could not differ from the catalog picture.

The production line contained very few items that actually would have been present in a mountain home in the early part of the century. Only the coverlets came directly from the

Just three years after opening, the Arrowcraft Shop expanded, moving into the original school building next to Baskins Creek in 1929.

mountain tradition of weaving. While marketing did not suggest the replication of mountain originals, the appeal in the shop and at alumnae sales stressed that the women who wove the pieces lived in the mountains.

A 1946 pricing sheet lists the retail sales price of the fringed Whig Rose Mat at $1.25, with materials costing $0.18 and the weaver receiving $0.38. At this time, a bib sold for $0.75, with the weaver getting $0.35 and only $0.05 worth of yarn. A $40 coverlet used $10.25 in materials, with the weaver receiving $12.[44] The general formula for figuring the retail price was to double the sum of materials and labor. Most pricing in the crafts world follows a similar computation—but for the wholesale price, not the retail price. The budget for the designer, her staff and expenses should have been calculated in as part of the production cost for the wholesale price. Then this wholesale figure should have been doubled, covering the shop overhead and profit to determine the retail price.

Arrowcraft absorbed both the costs of managing the weaving and running the shop into a single overhead amount. For the expenses of running the weaving business and the shop to come out of the same markup, it meant that both units functioned with extreme efficiency. Amazingly, Arrowcraft even showed a profit during most of its life. Gross sales numbers for Arrowcraft attest to a steadily growing business. The gross sales for 1930 were over $28,500, rising to $43,000 by 1940, with 1950 sales at $126,000. With the Arrowcraft system of calculating prices, the weaver received a much higher proportion of the sales price than she would have with a more standard accounting method. For the 1946–47 fiscal year, Arrowcraft paid almost $40,000 to weavers, out of a gross sales figure of just over $100,000.[45] Arrowcraft could only figure prices using this method because they controlled both production and sales. Wholesale opportunities created problems because no margin existed to pay the wholesale commission.

While Pi Beta Phi provided income to the weavers, they considered their mission to be greater than merely a financial one. By the fall of 1932, monthly weavers' meetings became officially organized under the name of the Gatlinburg Weavers Guild. As a major incentive to attend the meetings, the weavers received checks for their month's work there. While having a central program, each Guild meeting also served as a social occasion, with shaped-note singing and refreshments. Gene described the meetings during the 1937–38 school year: "We celebrated Aunt Lizzie's 80th birthday at one, Christmas at another, the April meeting was 'baby day' when all babies born to weavers during the year were brought in for display. Mr. Coe gave a talk on hens at one meeting and so it goes—anything of interest that comes our way is used for programs."[46] Speakers presented programs on gardening, household management, the growth of the area, and—of course—weaving-related topics.

By the late 1930s, the Weavers Guild was writing and producing plays for the summer tourists. The play "Store Britches" had a run in 1941, for seventeen performances. Of the play, Redding wrote, "Lula Mae Ogle who weaves our coverlets wrote the story of a family whose daughter started to go courting with two men at once and how the old granny rescued her from the predicament." Lula Mae carried on the coverlet-weaving tradition of her mother, one that went back many generations. The weavers used the profits from many years of summer plays for an emergency fund to finance several trips for the group. In 1941 among the withdrawals was an entry reading, "Five weavers have borrowed from the fund to get glasses, one to pipe water into her house and one to pay for an X-ray of her husband's stomach."[47]

In the early 1930s, the Weavers Guild and the school P.T.A. were the only two organized groups in Gatlinburg. "Civic improvements will be a big issue locally in the next few years, and here are two groups of women beginning to realize that they can do things," Redding observed.[48] The workers at the Pi Beta Phi School felt that they prepared both the children and the women of the community for challenges that would come with the changes brought about by the coming of the national park. In addition to providing economic assistance to women, the Weavers Guild experiences prepared them for collective action. This fit in with the urban settlement house idea of organizing for social change that motivated many Pi Phis. Residents could assess local situations and join together to meet common needs. The Garden Club, founded in 1937, is one of the community organizations started by the Weavers Guild.

Over the years, seven women served as weaving supervisors with Arrowcraft, with a few others filling in between permanent managers. Winogene Redding stands as the most important person in establishing an identity and charting the course for the weaving industry. She spent twenty-two years in the position, in four different stints. Meta Schattschneider took over in the mid-1940s, leaving a few years later for a college teaching position in New Mexico. During her three years, Arrowcraft expanded to over 120 weavers during 1947 in the prime winter weaving months.[49] Women had more time to weave during the winter because garden and household chores demanded less of their time.

Meta Schattschneider assumed management of the weaving during one of Redding's absences from Arrowcraft. She conducted an extensive study of the time it took weavers to complete projects.

Tina McMorran took over supervision of Arrowcraft weaving in 1948 and continued in that position until she retired in 1957. She stepped into the position of weaving manager through a set of chance circumstances. In the summer of 1947 she took a weaving class under her friend and fellow Oregonian Mary Elizabeth Starr Sullivan at the Summer Craft Workshop, jointly sponsored by the University of Tennessee and the Pi Beta Phi School. During her time in Tennessee, McMorran impressed the Pi Phis with her abilities. So when Meta Schattschneider vacated the position, they persuaded McMorran to return as weaving manager in the early spring of 1948.[50]

Decisive downsizing of the weaving department began under Tina McMorran, although the reasons for this action are not clear. Her annual report for 1949–50 states: "Following instructions from Committee, after the last annual meeting, our department has operated on a greatly reduced budget, which I hope is showing the desired results."[51] Her cost control measures included cutting the number of weavers, decreasing inventory, and designing items that required yarns already on hand. Sales could not keep pace with production capacity, and the response was not an attempt to increase sales but rather a cut in production. This approach of balancing production with sales may have reflected a loss of interest by the Pi Phis, or it may have been the reaction of a very cautious governing board with little business experience.

Reflecting her quiet personality, McMorran tended toward muted colors in her designs. She continued with the same line of products at Arrowcraft and introduced the very popular tote bag as well as several garments. She also put into production pictorial wall hangings utilizing several different techniques. Under McMorran's direction, Arrowcraft wove special commission fabrics for church dossal and altar cloths. During her time at Arrowcraft, she attended a workshop with noted weaver and designer Dorothy Liebes. Although this failed to enliven McMorran's palette, Liebes's influence was seen in the introduction of reflective lurex metallic yarn.[52]

Winogene returned for her final four years of tenure in 1958. By increasing the number of weavers again, she tried to attain the sales figures she had posted ten years earlier. But the tide had turned; after only modest success, she left Arrowcraft for the final time—with sales figures heading down. The next two supervisors each only stayed a year; both suffered problems resulting from low sales and decreased budgets. In the final report of 1965, weaving manager Bess L. Mottern observed, "Arrowcraft has not kept up with the times. Your survival depends on immediate change, as the craft business is a highly competitive business."[53] She complained of a lack of freedom in designing and questioned the wisdom of continuing the production of small, inexpensive items rather than expanding into a higher-end market.

In the mid-1960s, Nella Cook Hill assumed the head of the weaving department. A graduate of the Pi Beta Phi School in Gatlinburg, she had worked for Arrowcraft in the shipping department and had assisted several weaving designers. Nella learned weaving from her mother, who had woven for Arrowcraft. She related that the money her mother earned from weaving helped considerably in supplementing her father's income from his job with the county roads department.[54] In fact all eight of the Cook girls learned to weave, but the one boy did not. Six Cook sisters worked for Arrowcraft at various points in its history, assuming jobs in shipping, buying, sales, bookkeeping, weaving, and management.

Two of the Cook sisters, Nella and Faye, coordinate orders to be shipped to Pi Beta Phi alumnae clubs to sell to members.

As the Gatlinburg downtown grew and evolved, eventually offering primarily mediocre souvenirs for tourists, Arrowcraft maintained its integrity by selling fine handcrafted work. A wide variety of crafts from throughout the Southeast graced the display area next to the weaving. Under Hill's direction, the weaving continued as the only craft production actually supervised by Arrowcraft. Baby bibs, potholders, pillows, bags, aprons, afghans, stoles, scarves, guest towels, napkins, and placemats persisted as the weaving staples.

At the end of the business day on May 14, 1994, Arrowcraft closed its doors and ceased operations. Visitors to Gatlinburg probably didn't even notice, as the shop changed hands and continued operation as one of the Southern Highland Handicraft Guild stores.[55] The demise of the shop and the weaving would have probably taken place several years earlier if not for the dedication of the Cook sisters. At the time of the closing of the business, Veryl Cook Monhollen served as manager, Faye Cook headed shipping and craft selection, and Bernice Cook Roberts functioned as bookkeeper. Nella Cook Hill retired in March, just before the end of Arrowcraft.

Arrowcraft saved over 550 production items, representing close to 70 years of operation. Examples dating from the 1930s represent all of the designers and the full range of work woven. For many of the pieces, the exact weaver has been identified. The work is now part of the permanent collection of the Arrowmont School.

Summer Craft Workshop and Arrowmont

In 1945 Pi Beta Phi, in cooperation with the University of Tennessee, offered the first "Summer Workshop in Handicrafts and Community Recreation" in Gatlinburg. The workshops took place at the school's facilities, using craft equipment transported from the Knoxville campus of the University of Tennessee. An article in *The Arrow* announcing the workshops anticipated this expansion of the school mission: "For years those closely associated with, or vitally interested in the future of, the Pi Beta Phi Settlement School, have had a vision—a picture of a nationally known Handicraft Center to which Pi Phis and other lovers of beauty would flock to study under leaders in the handicrafts, to enjoy the loveliness of the Smoky

Starting in 1945, the University of Tennessee conducted the Summer Craft Workshops at the Pi Beta Phi School facilities in Gatlinburg. Both teachers and students came from around the country to engage in weaving and a variety of other craft subjects.

Pi Beta Phi Settlement School and Arrowcraft

Mountains, and to learn first hand of Pi Beta Phi's contribution to Gatlinburg and to the handicrafts of the Southern Highlands."[56]

Weaving occupied a major place in the course offerings during the early years of the Summer Craft Workshop. The course schedule contained several weaving classes divided between two instructors, as well as Textile Decoration, Recreational Crafts, and Metals—Craft Design, Pottery, Enameling, and Art Related to the Home were soon added. The summer school invited faculty from all over the country to teach in Gatlinburg. In the early years Berta Frey, well known for her articles and books on pattern design, taught weaving. Arrowcraft designers Winogene Redding and Nella Hill also taught classes at Arrowmont.

During the summers from 1947 through 1950, Allen Eaton, author of *Handicrafts of the Southern Highlands* conducted a course described as "Craft Design—Analysis of the craft field; historic background; social and economic implications; present day factors influencing design, techniques and productivity."[57] The three-week workshop schedule allowed for students taking other classes to attend at least some of his lectures. A 1948 review of the workshop observed: "Mr. Eaton has pioneered in stressing the social values of the arts and no one could come in contact with him without becoming imbued with a fine and growing appreciation of all manner of things made by the human hand and a love of people who made the things."[58]

Even though other commitments prevented Marian Heard from directing the first workshop, she guided both the inception and logistics of the program. By 1946 she was serving as codirector of the Summer Craft Workshop and later took on full responsibility. Marian Heard had majored in ceramic design at Alfred University and received a master's degree from Columbia University. She moved south to the University of Tennessee in 1936 in order to establish the craft unit in the College of Home Economics. In 1944 she conducted a survey of crafts activity for the Southern Highland Handicraft Guild to ascertain the need for continuing education among craftspeople.[59]

During the late 1940s and the 1950s, enrollment in the Summer Craft Workshop hovered at around seventy-five students, spread over two sessions. About two-thirds of these students took classes for credit, with the largest portion receiving graduate credit. The majority of students were women, either teachers or extension workers. During this period, students came from over twenty-five states, and one or two other countries were represented.[60] From the very first, the workshop tried to include local weavers, announcing that "Scholarships for work in the summer session will be given to local weavers and handicraft workers whose abilities are such that they can profit from this advance instruction in color and design."[61] During the 1960s enrollment increased to near one hundred.

When Sevier County assumed complete responsibility for elementary and high school education in the early 1960s,[1] the Pi Phis considered a new mission for their Gatlinburg facilities. The successful Summer Craft Workshop under the direction of Marian Heard indicated an unmet need for quality instruction in crafts. Heard and Dr. Lura Odland, Dean of Home Economics at the University of Tennessee, proposed an expansion of the craft program. The Pi Phis enthusiastically approved the idea: "The Centennial Project has now picked up the torch and will carry on to make the former Settlement School the greatest Art and Craft Center, and a wonderful Memorial to the Founders of PI BETA PHI DURING ITS SECOND CENTURY."[62]

By winter 1968 the name had changed from "Summer Craft Workshop" to "Arrow in the Smokies" to "The Arrowmont School of Arts and Crafts." Pi Beta Phi headed a successful campaign to build a major studio building. In designing the structure, architect Hubert Bebb considered the specific needs and uses of the space. The functional and tasteful building included customized art studios, an auditorium, a central art gallery, a library resource center honoring Marian Heard, a book and supply store, and the administrative offices.[63] The new building was built adjacent to the existing craft facilities of the former high school. Arrowmont used several of the Pi Phi buildings to house the students, including a barn that had been transformed into a residence, complete with dormitories and semiprivate rooms.

In 1970 the class format changed to offer one and two-week sessions throughout the summer. This innovation came with the new craft facilities, and the total summer enrollment dramatically increased from around 300 at the beginning of the decade to 650. The craft school continued to attract students from throughout the country.

The school followed the model established at the Penland School, where recognized teachers from around the country presented specialty classes. When the format changed to one and two-week sessions, every student selected just one topic for intensive study. Although the school accommodated beginners, most of the classes focused on students already possessing basic crafts skills. With its well equipped studios, Arrowmont continues to offer in-depth classes in ceramics, enameling, woodturning, surface design, jewelry, and various other crafts subjects. Although the looms are still there, weaving no longer attracts many students. The Arrowmont program continued to grow under the leadership of Sandra Blain, who was promoted from assistant director to director in 1979; she retired in 2001. Arrowmont and Arrowcraft operated under separate boards and were managed by separate directors under the sponsorship of Pi Beta Phi Fraternity.

Alice Zimmerman and Bernice Stevens didn't make it to the first Summer Craft Workshop, but the two art teachers from Evansville, Indiana, signed up for the third workshop in 1947 and immediately became regulars. They had been seeking a place in the mountains to spend summers and engage in artistic activity. After developing an ambitious craft program in the Evansville public schools, the two women took early retirement and moved to the mountains where each resided until her death. On a mountain just outside Gatlinburg, they built twin houses, from where they could see both Mt. LaConte and Clingman's Dome. A shared studio between their houses provided a space for crafts. Along with ten other artists, they founded the Twelve Designer Craftsmen, which continued as a marketing cooperative and shop for ten years.[64] Although Zim and Steve are hardly typical in any way, they are examples of the many artists who have been attracted to Gatlinburg because of Arrowmont.

Fostering Leadership

Just as the Pi Phis believed in fostering leadership within the local Gatlinburg community, they also promoted leadership within the general region. The women from the Pi Beta Phi Settlement School always attended the Conference of Southern Mountain Workers and early voiced the need for an Appalachian crafts agency. Although representatives of the Pi Phi School missed the 1928 Penland meeting to discuss the formation of a guild, they signed on as a charter member of the Southern Mountain Handicraft Guild, which officially began at the Spinning Wheel in Asheville just after Christmas in 1929.[65] This federation of craft cooperatives banded together to address common problems, seek broader markets, and exhibit crafts.

In the early years of the Guild, members gathered in both the spring and fall meetings. During the spring of 1931 a Guild meeting took place at the Mountain View Hotel in Gatlinburg, just after the Southern Mountain Workers conference in Knoxville. At this gathering, Frances Goodrich astonished the new organization by offering to turn over ownership of the Allanstand Cottage Industries in Asheville to the Guild. With this new affiliation, renamed the Allanstand Guild shop, wholesale marketing became a new venture for Arrowcraft. In 1932 the spring gathering again took place in Gatlinburg. The Guild admitted "the Cherokee Indians" to membership and established a library, starting with twenty books.[66]

Arrowcraft continued to exert significant influence on the course of the Guild. Winogene Redding and several prominent women from other craft centers formed an inner circle that determined the mission, standards, and procedures of the Southern Highland Handicraft Guild. After leaving Arrowcraft in 1945, Redding went to work for the Guild as director of education. She had held the Guild positions of president and vice president, and later went on to lead the Standards Committee. Marian Heard also sat on the Guild board. In the mid-1940s she led a survey of crafts activities in the southern Appalachian Mountains, funded by the General Education Board of the Rockefeller Foundation.

Under the sponsorship of the Tennessee Valley Authority, the Southern Highlanders, Inc., began offering shares for membership in 1935. The purchase of $75 in stock made Arrowcraft among the top four stockholders of this new corporation specializing in crafts marketing. Weaving from Gatlinburg ranked among the top sellers in the Southern Highlander shops.[67] Arrowcraft could sell wholesale to Southern Highlanders because it took only a small commission, as opposed to the standard markup of retail outlets. Southern Highlanders employed Winogene Redding at their Norris facilities during one of her short absences from Arrowcraft.

On July 26, 1948, the Southern Highland Handicraft Guild opened the first "Craftsman's Fair" on the grounds of the Pi Beta Phi School for four days. This first Guild fair differed greatly from fairs today, which have individual artists booths, cooperative displays, and entertainment. Craftspeople from all over Appalachia demonstrated their arts in tents on the school grounds; they included weaving, spinning, dyeing, quilting, and rug hooking, as well as the making of chairs, brooms, baskets, corn shuck seats, carved figures, and pottery. Exhibitors contributed items to a combined display inside the school, rather than displaying items in booths. "After a tour of the many skillfully arranged exhibits, the visitor walked into the salesrooms; the two back class-rooms of the high school building were teeming with activity."[68] Gatlinburg became a regular site for the fair, which later moved to an indoor space after the town built an auditorium.

Influence

The early Pi Phis came to the mountains of eastern Tennessee as teachers. Even though their principle mission was to the children, they recognized the needs of families. Weaving for Arrowcraft provided women with a way to earn money while still maintaining control of their own schedules in their own homes. The Summer Craft Workshop grew into Arrowmont, which today exists as one of this country's premier craft institutions. Arrowcraft and Arrowmont led and served as models in crafts marketing, organization development, and crafts education.

Throughout the history of the shop and the school, the Pi Phis provided concerned guidance in solving problems that they noticed. In later years, Arrowcraft suffered from excessive central management, rather than allowing the development of an appropriate business strategy in response to market forces. Fiscal conservatism, rather than knowledge of commonly held business practices, governed the Pi Phis decisions.

The fraternity comprised of many chapters and alumnae clubs, generously supported the school in Gatlinburg. Individual Pi Phis contributed to their fraternity's philanthropy by buying from Arrowcraft, attending craft classes, and contributing money. Because of this continuous support by Pi Beta Phi, the school and the weaving program never suffered the stifling financial burdens of most other mountain ventures.

In a short article for *The Arrow*, coverlet weaver Lula May Ogle expressed her appreciation for the work of Phi Beta Phi: "They have done more for us by just living the better life among us than they could have if they had gone about teaching us in any other way. Mountain folks as a rule don't take dictation readily." This echoes the sentiments of other Gatlinburg residents who appreciated the leadership by example and the opportunities afforded by education. Ogle listed specific benefits bestowed by the Pi Phis, ending with the purchase of the weaving, "thus giving the woman of a family a wage to add to the living expenses."[69]

5

appalachian school and penland weavers and potters

The story of weaving at Penland starts with the Appalachian School at the whistlestop town of Penland in the mountains of North Carolina. Penland is located in Mitchell County, which sits at the northwest edge of the state, adjacent to Tennessee. Penland's early tale of weaving is Lucy Morgan's story too, although she doesn't enter the picture immediately. Lucy's older brother, Rufus Morgan, developed the Appalachian School under the direction of Junius Horner, Bishop of the Episcopal Diocese of Western North Carolina. Bishop Horner approached the young Morgan while he was still attending seminary in New York City. He proposed either teaching at one of the two already established Episcopal mountain schools or starting another school at Penland. The Seven Springs Farm and Industrial School founded by Baptist Wesley B. Connolly preceded the Episcopal venture at the same location. After graduating from seminary, Rufus Morgan brought his new bride, the former Madeline Prentiss of Falls River, Massachusetts, to live in a cabin up the hill from Penland. The first Appalachian Industrial School classes were held in rooms added onto a farmhouse, the principal building of the former Baptist school.[1]

The grandparents of Rufus and Lucy moved their family from Virginia to near Franklin in North Carolina after the Civil War diminished their fortune. This part of North Carolina—along the border with Georgia—is mountainous with deep valleys. One of the sons married into the Siler family, which had settled Macon County; this union produced nine children, of which six, including Lucy and Rufus, grew to adulthood. Lucy Calista Morgan was born on September 20, 1889, in Cartoogechayne, west of Franklin.[2] The family put a premium on education, and all of the children availed themselves of the meager educational opportunities offered in the mountains and, with the help of friends, gained higher education. Lucy's older brother paved the way for her higher education.

The Appalachian Industrial School trained students in farming and the household arts in addition to the regular academic subjects. In 1914 a school announcement proposed weaving as an option for girls: "Besides this, they will be taught, as soon as we are able to furnish equipment, to spin and weave, and to sing and play, and such other arts as will cultivate their minds and brighten their lives." In this first year of the school, three girls and two boys made up the complement of boarding students, while twenty-five pupils came from the area as day students.[3] When Rufus and his family left Penland after a few years for church work in South Carolina, he maintained an interest in the school's welfare.

By the end of World War I, the Appalachian School settled into a mission for younger children who lacked care because of a death in the family or other traumas. Students within walking distance continued to attend the school. Because of the inclement mountain weather

Amy Burt, who taught at the Central Michigan Normal School in Mount Pleasant, also directed the Appalachian School at Penland.

that often inhibited travel, the school extended the term through the summer, with the major vacation in the winter. Amy Burt assumed direction of the boarding school during the summer of 1918.[4] Rufus and Amy had become acquainted while at Columbia University in New York. Miss Burt taught history at Central Michigan Normal School in Mount Pleasant. When first assuming leadership of the Appalachian School, Burt spent summers and later moved to the area for year long residence.

In 1920 Amy Burt greeted Lucy Morgan when she arrived by train in Penland to assume the role of elementary teacher. Lucy described the small community of Penland, which sat astride the Estatoe River, (known locally as the Toe River), as "the station and five houses," with "a post office and a general store." They had the luggage carried by wagon and climbed the steep path to the school. On the suggestion of Rufus, Amy Burt had arranged for Lucy's teacher training at Central Michigan and even provided her with housing.[5] Shortly after she assumed the job at Penland, a school pamphlet described Lucy in the following terms: "artistic, original, and has keen intellectual ability, with deep human sympathy and love of children."[6]

Amy Burt promoted child-centered, process oriented education, which had recently been popularized by progressives, among them University of Chicago educator John Dewey. The Appalachian School brochures from the mid-1920s detailed the philosophy: "The workers in this school seek to gain such intimate knowledge of each child that individual needs may be understood. The teachers try to help each child obtain the greatest possible development, both in home and in school life." The brochures continued, "Nothing is really learned until it is acted upon. Therefore school should make opportunities for the pupils to have some real experiences of the things he studies in books."[7] In 1923, forty students attended the school, nineteen of them boarding. Opportunities and facilities expanded: "The school has an excellent library of seventeen hundred volumes." There was an infirmary with a nurse in attendance, and the beginning of a community-based weaving program.

The Appalachian School grew during the 1920s to over one hundred students, with considerably more students boarding than arriving every day from the immediate neighborhood. The salaried staff grew from five to ten by the end of the decade.[8] By the 1930s the physical plant of the school included many new buildings. The largest structure had been built with money from the United Thank Offering by the Episcopal Diocese—it was first known as the UTO Building and was later renamed Horner Hall following the death of the Bishop. Ridgeway, a two story wooden building, housed the major school classrooms, while Morgan Hall and Laurel Cottage served as residences. The farm consisted of several buildings.

In the late twenties Katharine Califf, a recent agriculture graduate from the University of Kentucky, came to manage the farm that not only provided some income for the school but fed the children. The children did farm chores and were often photographed with dogs, horses, or cows. Katharine and Lucy bought a cabin from the school for $500. Probably because Katharine always wore pants around the farm, the school children dubbed Lucy and Katherine "Ma" and "Pa." Miss Califf served the school in many capacities including treasurer and temporary superintendent before she left to manage her own farm.[9]

Gladys Chisholm, who conducted classes for the early grades for many years, assumed the duties of principal in the mid-1930s. She also taught folk dancing and wrote and produced plays for the children to perform. The entire community attended her quite elaborate costumed productions. Her photographic album dated 1932 contains many pictures of her productions, including one labeled *Weavers Play*. No indication is given whether the title meant that the play was about weavers or acted by them.[10]

Rev. Peter Lambert Jr. came to the Appalachian School in 1934 as rector and eventually took over directorship of the school, remaining until it closed in 1964. The Penland School bought the buildings and the land of the Appalachian School in 1965.

Fireside Industries of The Appalachian School

In the winter of 1923 Lucy Morgan made a decision that would change her life forever. A bright young girl from the Appalachian School wanted to attend high school in Berea, Kentucky, but her father refused to let her travel from home alone. Lucy agreed to accompany Bonnie Willis to the Berea Academy, then a department of Berea College, and help her get safely established. Lucy, who declared that she had always planned on learning to weave, said that this excursion afforded her the opportunity to join a new weaving class given by Anna Ernberg, director of Fireside Industries at Berea College.[11] Since the Appalachian School term extended from April through mid-December, Lucy occupied her nine weeks of winter vacation with weaving. In addition to observing the Fireside Industries under Ernberg, Lucy met Edith Matheny, who ran a home-based weaving business.

By the time Lucy returned to the Appalachian School, her original idea of teaching weaving to the older schoolgirls had evolved into a community weaving project. She set about establishing her own Fireside Industries, modeled after the ones she observed at Berea. Her new weaving program offered "an economic and spiritual value. Work on these farms is exceedingly hard."[12] Most of the families around Penland farmed, and they provided almost all of their own food. Many of the men mined feldspar, mica, or other minerals; others worked in the seasonal lumber trade. Women raised and provided for children, preserved food, made clothing, and performed many of the farm chores. In an area that offered few opportunities for women to earn money, they readily took up weaving.

In *Cabins in the Laurel,* Muriel Earley Sheppard summarized Lucy's reasons for encouraging weaving: "She wanted to help them, and she knew that whatever they did to earn money must be done at home, for most of them were mothers of families. The work must also be easily portable, because at that time there was no good road on the mountain, and raw material must come and the finished product go out on a human back if a horse or mule were not available."[13] Both Sheppard in her words and Morgan in her actions assumed that weaving would serve as part-time employment and not disrupt a family's lifestyle. Because of the lack of adequate transportation for the workers, an industry run from a central location would have been impossible.

All of the mountain weaving centers that solicited contributions or relied on the sympathy of consumers advertised their origins. Repeating these stories made explicit either a connection with weaving traditions or the worth of the endeavor. While there may have been variations from one retelling to the next, the basic message was never altered.

Lucy Morgan often recounted the tale of the first weaver to take a loom home. After Mrs. Henry Willis (Aunt Adeline, as she was known in the community) set up the loom on the porch of her cabin, Lucy helped her warp and start the project. Aunt Adeline's mother had woven "the necessary articles of clothing and household furnishings for a large family," as had most women in this isolated mountain community. When Aunt Adeline's husband delivered her first batch of finished rugs to the school, he was paid the enormous sum of slightly over twenty-three dollars. Word traveled fast and the entire community along Conley Ridge Road had been apprised of the exact amount before he even reached home. Lucy may have been exaggerating when she related that, "The next morning before I could get up, there were women at our door asking for looms."[14] They ordered twelve more looms from Berea, because so many women had requested work. Lucy then traveled to the weavers' homes to instruct them in the basics of weaving.

By January of 1924, less than a year after Lucy herself had learned to weave, her Fireside Industries offered over twenty different types of items for sale through a brochure. Many of the articles utilized plain weave, but some required more advanced skills. Plain weave, the easiest type of weaving, has a simple over/under interlacement of threads. Aunt Adeline wove her rugs in "Log Cabin," a plain weave design created by alternating light and dark threads in a pattern that suggested stacked logs. Several common overshot patterns required threading the warp on the loom to a specific pattern and then following intricate sequences for foot treadles that raised harnesses for the insertion of weft, or filling threads. By 1925 the list of

Lucy Morgan, seated, checked completed work the weavers brought in and distributed assignments for their next project.

items produced included bags, baby blankets, bureau scarves, capes, card table sets, coverlids, dress material, luncheon sets, rugs, scarves, and table runners.[15]

Lucy purchased Ernberg counterbalance looms manufactured by the Berea Student Industries, a labor program at Berea College. In comparison with the heavy, rough-hewn looms common in the mountains, the Ernberg looms operated with much greater ease. Even though both looms had the same type of counterbalance mechanism, the lighter, harder wood and the precise ratio of components made the new smaller Berea looms much more efficient to operate. Lucy loaned the looms she had brought back from Berea to weavers. Many of the weavers purchased their looms by paying a little money at a time until the total debt was paid off, or else their husbands copied the Berea model.[16] Later a local man, Bascum Hoyle, took up the manufacture of the looms.

Securing weavers and producing an array of articles proved to be the easy part of the weaving operation. According to Bonnie Willis Ford in her booklet on the history of Penland weaving, "The great task ahead lay in finding a market for the articles in order that it might be possible to furnish work for more women who were now looking forward to it so eagerly as a means of establishing themselves on a basis which more nearly approached economic independence."[17] She summed up the persistent problem of selling the production. Also, cash flow was a problem, because supplies had to be bought and weavers paid upon delivery of the items.

Morgan and Burt activated their network of women friends to sell weaving; later they expanded to Episcopal Church members, who bought pieces to support the Appalachian School. Although he was averse to the weaving at first, Bishop Horner supported the effort after Lucy demonstrated that the Ernberg looms were much easier to operate than the old mountain looms. He furnished a Model T Ford with a truck bed, and Lucy made her way over rough roads to nearby tourist resorts and fairs with stacks of woven goods.[18]

Thanks to support from a friend, the Fireside Industries set up a booth at the North Caro-

On Weavers' Day, workers line up in front of the Weaving Cabin, built with logs donated by weavers' families.

lina State Fair in Raleigh in the fall of 1924. This trip led to more economic support than sales alone when a visitor suggested that George W. Coggin, State Director of the Vocational Training Division, would probably be interested in the work. Coggin visited Penland early the next year and indicated the availability of funds under the Smith-Hughes Act for Vocational Education to support weaving instruction. The state agreed to furnish half of Lucy's salary provided she established a regular teaching schedule. In these development years, the school paid Lucy only the school's portion of her salary, absorbing the states contribution. She willingly worked for half of her proposed salary, never seeing anything amiss with the arrangement.[19]

Lucy carried on her weaving operations from Morgan Hall, the Appalachian School building that her brother had built as his home. She taught the weavers in their own homes, but state money dictated that more formal instruction be offered at a central location. The institution of Weaving Day, held once a week, was created to meet the requirement that the weavers gather regularly. The meeting soon outgrew the facilities, and the weavers planned to erect a new building. Bonnie Ford related that "it was decided that they should build cooperatively a community cabin which would serve as the weaving center. The weavers and their husbands agreed to contribute the logs from the timber on their own small farms, and to donate labor in building of the cabin in which they would all be share-holders."[20] On May 5, 1926 a log-raising took place for the 30 x 18-foot Weaving Cabin. Although the location on the far end of the school property seemed far from most of the other buildings, the site was directly opposite the cabin that Lucy and Katharine had purchased.

Ten especially fine photographs illustrate a 1928 brochure of the Fireside Industries of the Appalachian School. Bayard Wootten, a Chapel Hill photographer and a cousin of Lucy Morgan's, traveled to Penland to document the activities in the new weaving cabin. The pictures depict an attractively decorated and sunny cabin with many windows. In the (obviously staged) photographs, the women spun wool yarn, wove, or otherwise engaged in handwork. A backlit photograph of a young girl seated at a loom was the inspiration for the silhouette logo of the weaving industry.[21]

In the early days, the cabin housed five looms and the weavers gathered twice a week for Weaving Day. An article in *The Spirit of Missions,* an Episcopal publication, reported thirty looms in the community during 1927, a figure that grew to sixty-four by 1930.[22] Wednesday became Weaving Day, during which the weavers learned new patterns, turned in completed work, received new assignments, finished items that required handsewing or knotting, and socialized. Some of the weavers who did not own "warping bars" wound the forty to sixty yards of warp for their looms while at the center.

As the sponsor for the Appalachian School, the Episcopal Church helped promote weaving in several ways. The Penland weavers provided "liberal commissions" to women's auxiliaries running sales

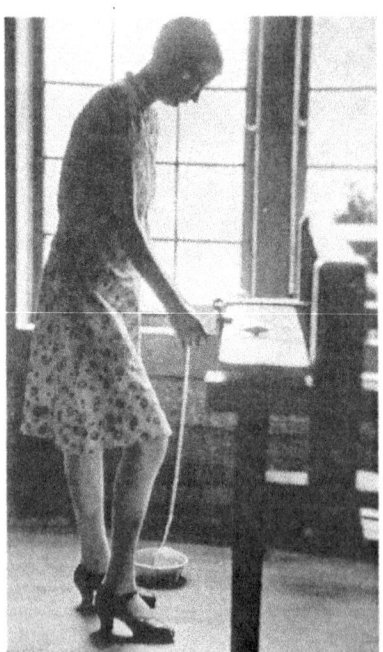

A young woman in Penland's Weaving Cabin stands winding bobbins for weaving.

events. Through church publications, members were asked to "help the weaving industry and, therefore, the school by giving Miss Morgan the names of gift shops in your vicinity."[23] Lucy Morgan regularly took woven goods to be sold at the national General Convention of the Episcopal Church. In 1926, the weaving center's first year of attendance, the New Orleans convention participants purchased $1,400 worth of weaving.[24]

During the early years of weaving at Penland, expenses considerably outweighed income. Lucy Morgan financed most of the losses from her personal savings. In 1923, the first, partial year of operation, the receipts from weaving totaled $223.45, with expenses of $1,109.25. By the second year revenues almost equaled expenses, the weaving bringing in about $4,500 with the outlay being just under $5,000. Even though the operation functioned in the red, funds continuously flowed to the weavers. By 1927 the weaving budget had grown to over $10,000, bringing almost $2,000 of profit to the Appalachian School.[25] While more sales naturally meant more profits, this brightening financial picture actually reflected the state's vocational contribution to management expenses.

Penland Weavers and Potters

The tale of the evolution of the Fireside Industries into the Penland Weavers and Potters is a complex one. The change involves the disassociation of the Appalachian School from the weaving business, as well as several substantial alterations and additions to Lucy Morgan's original vision of a business created to provide economic help to women of the area.

With the early success of the weaving, Lucy Morgan desired to improve her own skills at the loom so that she could better direct the operation. Since she expressed her dissatisfaction with Ernberg's lack of generosity, a return trip to Berea was not warranted.[26] She explored other possibilities for instruction. Like many other weavers of her day, Lucy owned Edward F. Worst's *Foot Power Loom Weaving*, one of the very few texts then available on hand production. Worst, director of manual training for the Chicago public schools, organized the Lockport Home Industries, which began as a weaving center and later expanded to include other crafts. Allen Eaton, whom she had met at the Conference of Southern Mountain Workers, contacted Worst and arranged for Lucy to travel to Chicago for nine weeks of study on a multi-harness loom in Worst's studio. Impressed with Lucy and her work in the mountains, Worst refused remuneration for his services, requesting only that she share her new knowledge with others.

Lucy invited Worst to see her weaving operation. In the summer of 1928 he took up the invitation to Penland, where he demonstrated multi-harness linen weaving to local weavers. Impressed with the weaving center at Penland, Worst encouraged expansion into pottery. That same summer, Worst sent C.W. Fowler, a potter from his own studio, to begin the work. In the fall of 1928, Frederick H. Koch, founder and director of the Carolina Playmakers at the University of North Carolina, visited Penland, and bestowed the name Penland Weavers and Potters to the business that now included both crafts.[27]

Even though the pottery never achieved the same commercial success as the weaving, the name stuck. Some pieces sold locally, but inconsistent quality control and shipping problems plagued the endeavor.[28] Pewter production proved a far more significant addition to the commercial venture, even though it was never incorporated into the name. Lucy acquired a basic knowledge of working pewter while visiting a friend in New York. She returned to Penland with molds and taught high school boys to hammer pewter. While the weaving employed

In 1928 Penland added a pottery, gaining with it a new name, Penland Weavers and Potters.

females, metal work was seen as a male occupation. Later, when the metal work included copper, women decorated the plates and trays. Ralph Morgan, Lucy's nephew, earned part of his university and medical school expenses by working pewter for Penland.[29]

Through roundtable discussions at the Conference of the Southern Mountain Workers annual meetings, leaders of different Craft Revival activities realized that a joint effort in marketing and education would benefit all of them. Under the guidance of Allen Eaton and with the blessing of the Russell Sage Foundation, representatives of eleven centers gathered at the Weaving Cabin at Penland amid the snows of late December in 1928. Another meeting a year later in Asheville produced the formal organization of the Southern Mountain Handicraft Guild, whose name was quickly changed to the Southern Highland Handicraft Guild.

Bonnie Willis, the young girl that Lucy had escorted to school in Berea, returned to Penland in 1931 to help Lucy run the weaving center. By this time, Bonnie had graduated from both the Academy and the College at Berea and taught English in high school. On June 3, 1930, Bonnie married Howard Ford, who had taught at the Appalachian School. Howard gained the nickname that stuck for life when someone at Penland thought he looked Italian and jokingly called him "Toni." Ford continued a close association with Penland even though he worked as a vocational educator in many parts of the country and consulted in countries all over the world. Bonnie, Toni, and Lucy built a house together, with a small room and sleeping porch for Lucy, across from the weaving cabin.[30]

Bonnie, always organized and efficient, kept the books for the weaving and the craft school and saw that everything in both ventures ran smoothly. While Lucy deserves credit for founding the activities on Penland hill, Bonnie's attention to detail insured that they continued. Over the years Bonnie wrote publicity materials, several brochures, and magazine articles about the weaving and the school. In her booklet *The Story of the Penland Weavers*, she presented an accurate and intimate account of the history of the weaving center. She championed the weaving because she knew firsthand the value that the extra income brought to the community. Weaving money made it possible for her and her younger sister, Flossie, to attend school at Berea. Each session of the Penland School, a play written by Bonnie related the history of the Craft Revival in the community. The story has two older women discussing how much the weaving contributes to the area and a girl discovers that she does not have to take a mill job in Marion but can find work without leaving the mountains she loves.[31]

The Depression eventually descended upon the southern mountains, although a little later than it hit the rest of the country, and not with the same force. The families around Penland farmed, providing most of their own food, and they had considerable experience making do with what little they had. However, the Depression affected the markets for the wares of the Penland Weavers and Potters. Tourists no longer generously bought the work that Morgan displayed from the small log cabin built on her truck bed. Lucy hit upon the idea of exhibiting at the Century of Progress planned for Chicago in 1933. She tried to convince the Southern Highlands Handicraft Guild to jointly present crafts at this world's fair, but Penland was the only center that raised any money for the trip. The communities of Spruce Pine, Bakersville, and Penland pledged a total of $500 for expenses, and performances by the Penland Playmakers contributed to the fundraising efforts.[32]

After considerable negotiations with the Century of Progress bureaucracy, Lucy finally got Penland included in the Chicago fair. Depending on who's telling the story, either Lucy's determination and charm won over the fair's officials, or Worst and/or several important Chicago Episcopalians influenced the controlling powers. Most likely it was their combined efforts that secured the spot in the fair near Lake Michigan. When the Penland exhibit passed through Kentucky on its way to Chicago, the *Lexington Leader* wrote that the "small motorized log cabin attracted considerable attention.... The cabin, called the 'Travelog,' will form

Lucy Morgan traveled to the 1933 Century of Progress exhibition in Chicago in a Ford truck with a small log cabin built in the back. This cabin, along with another constructed on the site, formed the Penland display.

one section of the exhibition building. The other section is being constructed at Penland and taken to Chicago in parts to assemble on the grounds."[33] Ralph Morgan and Toni Ford met with some resistance from organized labor in Chicago when they began hammering together the Penland exhibit.[34]

In a Charlotte newspaper piece, the author lamented North Carolina's lack of participation in the World's Fair. "And yet if it were not for one lone teacher at the Episcopal school for mountain boys and girls at Penland, North Carolina, the state that has so much industry and so much wealth that it is the second largest federal tax paying state in the union, would not be represented at this Century of Progress exposition."[35] This article, written during the second year of the fair, explained that sales at the fair contributed to the economic rescue of mountain weaving and told of the help given by Chicago Episcopal Church women in maintaining the display.

Morgan understood how to attract publicity to her work and gave even the sophisticated Chicago papers something to write about. Newspapers pictured spinners, weavers, wool carders, basket makers, and mountain musicians. One caption under a picture of a man in bib-top overalls playing a violin read, "Hoedowns and log-cabin dances from the North Carolina mountains will be heard by the world's fair visitors through the skill of 'Doc' Hoppes shown with the faithful fiddle he plays in his native 'Hoot Owl Holler.' He is a descendant of a brother of President Buchanan."[36] Edward Worst helped to find people to carry on the demonstrations when weavers and spinners from the mountains could not travel to the city.

In the first year of the fair, sales cleared up the backlog of weaving inventory and made enough money to reimburse Paul Bernat for credit advanced. The Bernat family owned a large yarn business and published the craft magazine *The Handicrafter,* which concentrated heavily on weaving. In her history of Penland, Bonnie Willis Ford tried very hard to give an unromanticized and honest assessment of the 1933 fair experience: "While no large amount of money was made, the experience brought benefits in advertising, in new contacts, and best of all in furnishing a full summer's work to the weavers that were worth more than money." Providing work is the important theme that echoes throughout her history of the weavers. Sales the second year of the fair did not live up to expectations, but Bonnie put a positive spin on it: "People admired who could not buy; the circle of friends grew larger."[37]

The weaving survived as a result of the trip to Chicago, but it did not prosper. Lucy appealed unsuccessfully to the Episcopal Diocese to pay outstanding bills. She then wrote requesting a separation of finances:

> In our good years, you claimed the profits of the weaving to help with the expenses of the children's department. Now that the lean years have come, can you in turn help with our weaving bills? I know the answer is: 'Insufficient funds.' I accept that, of necessity, and I shall not regret what was done in the past, if you will promise me that, providing that I can manage to get bills paid, and keep things going without an appropriation from you, you will allow the weaving, in the future, to put away the profits of good years (if ever there be any) to take care of the lean ones.[38]

Penland assumed responsibility for its own debts and controlled its own financial destiny from the time of this letter in 1934, but ties between the Diocese and the Penland Weavers were not officially severed until five years later.

The success of the summer Weaving Institutes prompted the legal dissolution of ties between the church and the Penland Weavers and Potters. While the weaving struggled to survive, the summer classes proved the biggest accomplishment of the Penland enterprise on Conley Ridge. And the students and visitors to the emerging school provided a new market for the weaving, pewter, and assorted other products made by craftspeople in the vicinity of Penland. Although the weavers never again attained their pre-Depression numbers, they continued in crafts production for many decades.

The Penland Weavers and Potters even survived for several years after Lucy retired and left the area in 1962. But by then the focus of Penland had changed from production weaving to the craft school. It was Bonnie Ford who kept the weaving alive. She balanced the books of the school until the fall of 1976, when she suffered a stroke and died just months before her scheduled retirement. She had planned to expand her pamphlet on Penland into a book, dispassionately telling the story of the now famous school that had begun with Lucy Morgan's desire to revive the dying art of weaving and provide paying work for women.[39]

Penland School of Handicrafts

As with many really important things in this world, the Penland School of Handicrafts started without design—a series of auspicious events contributed to its inception. Lucy Morgan, always ready to seize opportunities, saw possibilities and encouraged many to help in its development. A summer vacation by a weaver and educator turned into a workshop, then expanded into the Weaving Institute, and finally grew and evolved into a prestigious craft school.

The Penland School story begins in 1928 with Edward Worst's visit and demonstration of multi-harness linen weaving to the Penland weavers. The next summer Worst returned and spent more time with the weavers. Lucy asked Worst if he would again come to the mountains the next summer and offer a full week's instruction. "He readily consented with the provision that there should be no remuneration; and in August of 1930, he conducted the first weaving institute at Penland."[40] Even though Weaving Institute announcement brochures number from 1930, in her book Lucy Morgan established the inception of the school a year earlier: "It was in August 1929 then, that I consider the Penland School of Handicrafts was born. That was the year we had our first outside students."[41]

The expansion of an informal demonstration for local production weavers into an international and highly acclaimed craft school happened in many small steps, the first being the inclusion of other participants in the Worst workshop. "Being neighborly, Miss Morgan invited craft workers from nearby mountain schools to attend Mr. Worst's courses with the result that they as well as the local weavers had a wonderful week's experience."[42] A much wider audience learned of the Worst workshop through a small article in the July/August 1930 issue of *The Handicrafter*: "Another institute is being held this summer, and Mr. Worst, who is one of America's greatest weaving authorities, will conduct the sessions. The sponsors of the Institute have been kind enough to extend an invitation to outsiders, and those interested in attending can write Miss Lucy Morgan, Director of the Appalachian School, Penland, North Carolina, for further information."[43]

Mrs. Cumi Woody, a renowned mountain weaver, traveled from her home about forty miles from Penland when Worst visited, and she returned for several more summers. Lucy Morgan observed the dialogue been Aunt Cumi and Worst: "It always seemed mighty American and so right to me, this man from the great metropolis in serious though lively confab

At the early Weaving Institutes at Penland, looms lined the porch of Ridgeway at the Appalachian School.

with this dear old lady of the isolated mountain region in the Southern Highlands, each giving and receiving information about a subject in which they were both tremendously interested."[44] Worst showed particular interest in Aunt Cumi's knowledge of natural dyestuffs. In her 1912 coverlet book, Eliza Calvert Hall pictured one of Cumi Woody's coverlets and identified her as an Allanstand Cottage Industries weaver.

In the early years of the Penland Weaving Institute, the workshop promoted a mountain experience along with weaving instruction. In *Mountain Life and Work* Bonnie Ford described the extra activities—demonstrations of pottery and pewter making, visits to weavers in their homes, and stories beside the fireplace: "The city people were delighted with the mountain setting and the appetizing meals of fried chicken and country ham prepared for them by experts." In true mountain style, Lucy engaged her extended family in entertaining the guests. And to her, this family consisted of all within the neighborhood who encouraged and benefited from her work with the weavers. "What an evidence of the spirit of democracy when city folk met mountain folk on a common basis of work and fellowship, each a dream come true—studying with a great teacher!"[45] In 1932 the Weaving Institute began to offer other craft courses—Toni Ford taught pottery, Worst's son instructed in basketry, and two occupational therapists offered courses in leather and woodcarving.

In *The Handicrafter*, Paul Bernat wrote about an Appalachian excursion to several weaving cooperatives, one of which was Penland: "A few weeks spent in the Southern mountains, jaunting from craft center to mountain school, demonstrated to me the rapid strides that were being made in the development of indigenous crafts as well as in the introduction of new ones." As part of his trip he attended the 1930 Weaving Institute, commenting that although he did not come for the instruction, he thought that others should. He enjoyed the trappings of the experience: "There was an evening spent at a mountain cabin, buried in one of the hollows, listening to an old inhabitant picking the banjo, and this will be ever memorable."[46]

The Penland School grew very quickly, from eighteen students taking one-week classes in 1932 to eighty-three students taking four-week classes in 1935. The longer sessions included two weeks of instruction with Worst and two preliminary weeks for beginning weaving students. Several factors contributed to this rapid expansion. Worst definitely drew students. He visited Penland each summer until his death early in 1949. The mountain experience attracted many students, with several attending again and again. With increasing demand, Lucy expanded both the course offerings and the facilities. She realized that the workshops met a need for crafts education and sought more diverse options for the increasing number of students. Good publicity was the most important element that propelled the Weaving Institute into prominence. Bonnie Willis Ford wrote articles on the progress of the school that appeared regularly in both *Mountain Life and Work* and *The Handicrafter*. Publicity continued throughout Morgan's tenure, with features in newspapers all over the country and in several national magazines.

The Weaving Institute occupied whatever space they could find around the Appalachian School. Looms lined the porch of the old Ridgeway Hall, while Morgan Hall served as a teacher's residence. Plans to deal with the crowded facilities took shape during the summer of 1934. Over one hundred people donated $2.50 or more towards the purchase of a log for the new building.[47] Among those in the 1934 summer session who initiated the construction of this building were Helen Allen, educator and textile collector from the University of Wisconsin, and Berta Frey, author of technical handweaving material. Workers at other mountain schools, including Olive Campbell and Marguerite Butler from the J. C. Campbell Folk School and Mary Sloop from Crossnore School, also made contributions. Other friends of the weaving, such as Paul Bernat, Clementine Douglas of the Spinning Wheel, Frederick Koch of the Carolina Players, and David Churchill of Churchill Weavers, also donated. Several local residents pledged as well. From the very start, this new building, designed to hold both classrooms and sleeping facilities, was called the Edward F. Worst Craft House.

The first subscriptions collected for the Craft House included only those local people directly connected with the school. Penland area residents gathered subscriptions for the new building because they considered their own interests advanced by the expansion of the weaving program into education for a wider community. Their intentions—under the banner of "OUR APPRECIATION"—declared that the money be used for the purchase of windows for the "craft house, which's now being erected by local labor and which will be used for the purpose of advancing the weaving industry and thereby furnish employment to those in Penland and Mitchell County who are interested in the art of weaving. By our contribution we wish to make known our sincere appreciation to the Penland Weavers for the good work they have done and are now doing for our community which is putting Penland on the map because of the widespread interest the mountain hand craft work is creating through out the nation."[48] And the local Penland weavers benefited from Worst's visits by attending the Weaving Institute. Records of the 1935 class show that twenty-three of the eighty-three students came from the local community.[49]

The Worst Craft House established the model for expansion that Penland used for subsequent additions to the facilities. Lucy dreamed big, considerably bigger than the actual need at the inception of the project. She recruited an amazing variety of people to buy into her vision and help make her ideas a reality. Sometimes useful people presented themselves, such as M.D.R. Beeson, an architect from Johnson City, Tennessee, who volunteered to draw up plans for the Craft House. The first structure of the independent craft school was built into a hill, with a stone foundation basement creating a ground floor in the front, two log stories, and dormitory in the attic. Morgan both motivated and inspired. She also took risks by obligating money above the amount raised and borrowing against her own life insurance.

The log-raising for the Worst Craft House took place in May 1935 on Lucy's property adjacent to the Appalachian School farm. Bayard Wootten photographed the log-raising festivities, capturing the important figures of Edward Worst and Bishop Robert Gribbin, as well as several local women in their Sunday best spoofing at rolling logs. The 1935 summer Weaving Institute took place in this structure long before its final completion.[50] The new building created space for looms, private rooms and communal housing, offices, a stage for dramatic performances, a gift store, and a lounge. In one of the many Penland traditions, students gathered in the lounge for tea and listened to Lucy Morgan tell stories about the school and the origins of the weaving. Many friends of Penland donated parts of the building, with the class of 1935 purchasing windows and doors. From the first usage of the new building, looms flooded out onto the spacious porch, which ran the length of the Craft House, reminiscent of the weavers lined up on Ridgeway's long front porch.

When the need arose at Penland, people had a way of presenting themselves to meet the challenge. Rupert Peters materialized to supervise the weaving program just at the moment when the school expanded its capacity. Peters worked as Director of Visual Education for the Kansas City public schools and learned to weave at Penland in the summer of 1935. He went to the mountains in order to find a hobby for his wife, Myrta, who had lost her hearing. In an article about Peters in a publication concerned with hearing disabilities, the author noted the unusual case in which "an absorbing life interest came to a person with perfect hearing as the result of a hearing loss to some one else."[51]

Peters approached his own weaving in a precise and analytical manner, imparting information in structured and organized lessons. As supervisor of the weaving room, he always wore a tie and ran a disciplined studio with the help of several assistants. Other teachers came in for special instruction for short periods of time. When he retired, Peters and his wife moved to Penland and built a home on the stretch of road between the Appalachian School and the Craft House.

Students continued to come from throughout the country to take classes at Penland. A 1938 brochure announced the summer activities for the Ninth Annual Weaving Institute. Two three-week sessions offered first weaving for beginners, followed by the advanced class. Rupert Peters taught weaving fundamentals in the early session before Edward Worst arrived to teach special techniques. The looms numbered fifty at that time. A special notice in the class brochure warned students that looms could not be used for long individual projects. If one desired to weave "a coverlet, yardage for suiting, or draperies for her home," the weaver could be accommodated either before or after the regular sessions.[52]

The brochure briefly mentioned courses in spinning, vegetable dyeing, and pottery. Clyde P. Miller of Milton, New York, the only instructor named other than Worst and Peters, taught metal work and jewelry making. As in previous summers, additional projects were offered for all participants, mixing mountain folk culture, craft skills, and entertainment: "The way to weave chair bottoms of hickory splits will be taught as it has been done in the mountains for generations. This and other crafts perfected in their native environment will be passed on to the Institute students by the mountain people themselves." Several of the small craft projects took place around the fireplace in the evenings. And "in addition to the work planned there are always students who share with the group some special craft, and this spirit of give and take is one of the joys of the Institute." Penland evolved into a blend of technical instruction by distinguished teachers, local heritage crafts, hobby projects, and the general exchange of good ideas between participants.

This 1938 brochure advised students to bring "simple clothing such as wash dresses, warm sweaters and low heeled oxfords." Note that in addition to indicating the casual dress code, this quote implies that women comprised the student body, as no comparable list of men's clothing followed. Class lists bear out this supposition, although husbands frequently accompanied their wives. Many of the names in the lists were accompanied by an occupation and a place of residence. Teaching was the most common profession, and many held other positions in higher education. Occupational therapists and social service workers filled out the ranks. The class photos indicate that even those listed without a vocation were not young students. By this time in the school's history, the student body numbered over one hundred, coming from over twenty states.

Students spending the summer at Penland experienced more than just classes and the allied craft projects. Students went on either organized day trips or informal touring parties to Grandfather Mountain, Linville Falls, Roan Mountain, Blowing Rock, Wiseman's View, Mount Mitchell, Roby Buchanan's stone cutting shop on Cane Creek, or the Minpro Feldspar mill. And, of course, each session included a "visit with Doc Hoppas, local musician and story-teller at his home in Hoot Owl Holler, who on his moon-lit porch will sing the traditional ballads of the hills to the accompaniment of his banjo, and tell humorous tales out of his own experience."

This inclusive package of activities could all be had for the registration fee of $5 plus a tuition of $5 per week. The room and board charge was $2.50 or $3 per day, depending on whether a dormitory or a double occupancy room was desired. A student for six weeks at Penland paid $35 in tuition and $126 for a semi-private room with shared bath and board, for a total of $161. Of course, these figures did not include the costs of materials or extra recreational travel.

The state of North Carolina contributed federal money from the Smith-Hughes Act for vocation education, which helped pay Lucy Morgan's salary as director of the weaving operation, and later expanded its support to include Penland's summer teaching faculty. Edward Worst continued to donate his services free to the school. One of the provisions for state assistance stipulated that North Carolina residents receive free tuition.

Even though the title of Weaving Institute continued for several years, the name Penland School of Handicrafts came into use in 1935. The Penland Weavers and Potters, which for several years functioned separately from the Appalachian School, legally switched to operate under the Penland School umbrella at the time of its incorporation in 1938.[53] Even though Bonnie Ford kept meticulous books of the school's finances, implying the independent operation of the institution, in reality Lucy owned all of the land, the Worst Craft House, and much of the other school property. Lucy's will from this period left all of her real estate, money, and personal property to the Penland School.[54]

Many workers and their families from the Penland Weavers and Potters, as well as others

Flossie Perisho, sister of Bonnie Ford, taught at Penland School under the management of both Lucy Morgan and Bill Brown. She met her second husband when he studied weaving at Penland.

living along Conley Ridge, found jobs with the growing school. Cooks, office workers, construction and maintenance people, and other service personnel came from the immediate area. Teachers and class assistants were also drawn from the local population. Emma Conley collected natural materials and dyed yarn in huge steaming cauldrons. In addition to sharing her skills in dyeing, she taught spinning. Due to her knowledge and generous personality, she became a favorite demonstrator at many of the functions Penland attended, such as the Southern Highland Handicraft Guild Fairs. Bonnie Willis's sister, Flossie, who also attended the Berea Academy, returned to Penland after the early death of her young husband. Lucy tried to interest Flossie in the business side of the school, but Flossie found that she preferred crafts. Under both the Morgan and Brown regimes at Penland, Flossie taught a variety of subjects including corn shuck dolls, non-fired pottery, lampshades, and surface design. In November of 1951, Flossie married Penland student Lester Perisho, a math professor from the Hampton Institute in Virginia, who had taken weaving classes in order to revive his own institution's program. After retirement the couple settled in a house on a hill halfway between the main part of Penland School and the Weaver's Cabin.[55]

By 1940, Penland—as both the weaving cooperative and a growing school—assumed a leadership role in regional craft promotion. Lucy Morgan helped found the Southern Highland Handicraft Guild and served on the Board of Directors. In the late summer of 1940, Penland held the Second National Conference on Handicrafts, during which Allen Eaton brought together craft organizers from twenty-five states plus the District of Columbia. The conference delegates discussed exhibitions and marketing strategies and outlined plans for building a national crafts organization. A keynote speaker discussed the Works Progress Administration's crafts programs and design documentation project.[56]

The Penland School of Handicrafts survived the gas rationing of the World War II years. During the war, occupational therapy gained importance as a discipline, and the school's curriculum met the need with classes. Veterans flocked to Penland as they did to other institutions of learning, with the program expanding to include formal instruction throughout the year. A class roster from the first summer session of 1940 listed forty-two students, with thirty-seven women and only five men, coming from twenty-one states and Canada. Seventeen of the participants worked in some form of education. Reflecting the school's expansion, ten years later the summer enrollment of 281 students consisted of 227 women and fifty-four men; included among this count were twenty-one married couples. Of the student body, nineteen of the students were identified as "G.I.," which included four women.[57]

Throughout the 1940s, weaving remained the central and most extensive course offered, with many distinguished weavers teaching, among them Mary Black, Margaret Bergman, and several teachers from Scandinavia. Classes in metal working, jewelry, and pottery also flourished. Shoemaking was one of the most unusual craft courses in the schedule. Lucy found the Mathews family—they were handcrafted shoemakers in Weymouth, Massachusetts—and convinced the son, Lincoln, to present a class at Penland. By the 1950s the Penland program had expanded into photography, enameling, other forms of jewelry, lamp shades, silkscreen printing, woodworking, and fireside or related crafts, which included just about anything from corn shuck chair seats to leather billfolds to braided belts. The school continued promoting the total mountain experience, offering a variety of the other activities for students during their stay. The class prospectus suggested that students prepare for the cultural experience by reading Sheppard's *Cabins in the Laurel* and Eaton's *Handicrafts of the Southern Highlands*.[58]

In the mid-1940s, Marian Heard of the University of Tennessee undertook a survey of crafts activities in the southeastern mountains for the General Education Board of the Rockefeller Foundation. The Southern Highland Handicraft Guild and the TVA's Southern Highlanders guided the survey, with Lucy Morgan serving on the study committee. In a letter to George Coggin of the North Carolina Department of Public Instruction, Lucy cited Clementine Douglas, who traveled as part of the research staff: "in the study they had made over all the mountains, two people out of three had gotten their start in crafts at Penland."[59]

As one result of the study, the Guild sponsored a series of workshops to be held at Penland. In putting together her first workshop proposal, Lucy sought suggestions from the other Southern Highland Guild board members. In response, Olive Dame Campbell cautioned her about the expansiveness of Penland's plans: "Now, dear Lucy, pull in your belt and let's talk about your budget." Always thinking big, Lucy had requested funds of about two-thirds of the total amount that the Guild was soliciting from the General Education Board. In 1945, Winogene Redding commented to Lucy Morgan that the first Guild workshop "was very good. We already are making plans for a better one next year."[60]

Penland profoundly affected many people's lives as they took part in and contributed to Lucy's dream for a comprehensive craft school. Major John Fishback first took weaving classes at Penland on the recommendation of an occupational therapist who had studied there herself. Fishback was in an army hospital recovering from a wound inflicted during World War II. The therapist met with little success in interesting him in projects until she suggested he weave something for his wife. He and his wife, Ellen, became regular fixtures at Penland. Fishback assisted in the weaving classes, while Ellen, acting as social director, organized sightseeing trips and served tea in the late afternoon. Because of his high standards of craftsmanship, Fishback was designated to be the weaver of green baize tablecloths for the newly renovated Independence Hall in Philadelphia. The project got underway in the mid-1950s, after the Park Service approached Penland about producing one hundred yards of fabric for fifteen tables. Since none of the original fabric had survived, a painting from the time is the only indication of what the cloth was like. A museum in England supplied a tiny historic swatch of green baize, and Penland tackled the many problems of reproducing it accurately.[61]

Irene Beaudin, a weaving teacher at the Ecole des Beaux Arts in Quebec, taught at Penland and directed the Penland Weavers and Potters. She brought several of her students from Canada to work as studio assistants. One of the young Canadians, Theresa LaFrance, first visited in 1947 and fell in love with the mountains and the school. She returned for many summers, first assisting in weaving and later teaching tapestry. On August 17, 1953, Theresa walked into the Roman Catholic Church in Spruce Pine on the arm of Colonel Fishback and exchanged marriage vows with Emma Conley's son John. The romance between John and Theresa began during her early visit to Penland, but she was not ready for marriage. After an industrial accident in Detroit, John returned home to Penland to recuperate, and this time he found Theresa receptive to commitment. Lucy Morgan had offered to pay for the reception of any "sweethearts" that had met at Penland. She not only fed 125 people at the wedding luncheon, she also arranged for the couple to honeymoon in the North Carolina mountain cabin near Franklin where she had been born.[62]

There are many Penland tales of close relationships formed and important life decisions made in this supportive and protective environment. Theresa, who had grown up in an orphanage in Canada, found both a real family and an extended community family at Penland. Theresa wrote personal comments on practically every page in her copy of *Gift from the Hills* and included snapshots of her own experiences. Newspaper journalist LeGette Blythe, who wrote the book, had tape-recorded Lucy Morgan's experiences in founding the weaving center and craft school at Penland. In the text Theresa underlined names of the people she knew and wrote comments of fact and affection. In the margin next to John Fishback's name, she wrote: "He gave me away at my wedding. I saw him this summer of 1973. He was 90 and still beautiful. I'll always love him."[63]

Theresa LaFrance married Emma Conley's son, John, with Colonel John Fishback presenting her at the altar. Lucy Morgan organized the wedding reception at the Pines and arranged for the couple to spend their honeymoon in her former home near Franklin, North Carolina.

Toni Ford produced publications that molded the school into a community. A daily mimeographed sheet called "The Grapevine" greeted students at breakfast and heralded school news—often including a mountain tale—and trumpeted a fair amount of friendly gossip about students and instructors. In 1932 Bonnie Ford began a booklet called *Mountain Milestone* in order to keep distant friends apprised of Penland news. Under Toni, the *Milestone* became a livelier publication, its frequency of appearance listed as "Now and Then," although it was usually written yearly. It tied together the greater community of those who at some time or in some way had passed through Penland, and served as a valuable publicity and fundraising tool.

The physical plant of the school continued to expand with the increased enrollment. An old farmhouse had served the school with dining facilities and provided some housing. After it burned in December 1944, former students rallied to Penland's need, contributing to the rebuilding after a Christmas letter was sent out to inform them of the tragedy. Major Fishback

After the Lily Loom House was built, Bonnie Willis Ford and Lucy Morgan ran the Penland Weavers and the Penland School from an office on the first floor.

wrote craft suppliers and local manufacturers soliciting contributions. In telling a friend about the fundraising efforts, Lucy said of his success: "He has been as amazed and pleased as the rest of us and says he has missed his calling, and is going into the advertising business."[64] The rebuilt Pines included a kitchen, lounge, and dining room on the first floor, with rooms on the upper two floors, including an apartment for Lucy Morgan.

The other major construction effort of the mid-1940s was named Lily Loom House in honor of the largest contributor to the building fund. The Lily Mills of Shelby, North Carolina, supplied most of the cotton yarns used at Penland, and the spinning factory was one of the regularly scheduled school excursions. In the early 1930s Lily began publishing "Lily Weaver's Worksheets," each containing a project using Lily yarns and written by a Penland faculty member.[65] This how-to concept continued in the expanded "Practical Weaving Suggestions," with contributions from Penland and other distinguished weaving teachers. After considerable negotiations involving Lily's owner, John Schenck, Toni Ford, and Lucy Morgan, Lily Mills donated $20,000 for the construction of a new weaving building larger than the Worst Craft House. As with all of Lucy's plans, her ambitions far outstripped the funds available. Thinking big as always, she refused to scale back and instead set about convincing people to trust her vision once again. Working in the unfinished building, the students proposed many innovative projects for raising money. Lily Mills even supplemented their original donation after another plea.[66] When the weaving moved to the Lily Loom House, the looms filled the entire second floor of the structure with related functions such as warp winding on the third floor and school administration offices on the first floor.

In the 1950s, Penland hosted many international visitors, usually sent by agencies of the federal government. Lucy proudly showed off her school to the world. In an eight-page report to the International Cooperation Administration, Mrs. Toshie Tsunematsu of Japan described her visits around the United States studying the farm extension service. She mentioned spending Christmas at Penland: "I can not forget the heartwarming and bright disposition of Miss Lucy Morgan. It was a gratifying experience for me to spend some time at the School of Handicrafts in the hills of North Carolina, doing handicrafts, having moments of introspection and peace of mind in the beautiful natural surroundings, and also participating in many gay programs with people from 19 countries. It was a wonderful experience." In 1949 Lucy and a group of Penland alumnae visited the school's European friends.[67] Other such trips followed.

Some of Penland's students became yearly fixtures, returning again and again for classes or work on special projects. Many students used their Penland-acquired skills to earn a living, either by producing crafts or teaching, while others investigated crafts for personal recreation and relaxation. Over the years discussions arose as to whether or not Penland would have had the same character if situated in a different place. Some followers argue that the spirit of Penland is vested in the people and centered on the crafts, while others—awed by the surrounding mountains—feel that the proximity to the beautiful natural setting contributes immeasurably to the experience.[68] Penland is a place for looking outward, while also looking within. Students have always sat on the porches or under the trees, absorbed in their own thoughts while regarding the mountains.

In 1962 the Board of Trustees of the Penland School offered the job of director to William J. Brown, a sculptor and graduate of the Cranbrook Academy of Art. At the time he had managed the Craft Center in Worcester, Massachusetts. Lucy wrote to Brown and his wife about their decision to move to the North Carolina mountains: "I find myself looking forward with less and less apprehension, and more and more satisfaction to the time when I will turn all the school's problems over to those with your wealth of understanding." With characteristic insight, she declared that she herself would be the "BIG problem. I have so thoroughly taken root here, that I am going to need all the help you can both give me in order to gracefully turn my duties over to another."[69] Later in the year, when the Browns arrived, a major celebration marked the transfer of the ceremonial Penland key to the new school manager. One of the current students, Naoma Powell, a recent Cranbrook graduate on her way to teaching at the Hindman Settlement School in Kentucky, composed an epic ballad for the occasion. In forty-eight stanzas she summarized the life of Lucy Morgan. The forty-seventh stanza reads:

> As Penland grew, it grows today.
> She is not done with dreams,
> But still awaits each coming day
> With ever-broad'ning schemes.[70]

Within a couple of years of the beginning of Bill Brown's administration, the craft school bought the Appalachian School property.[71] Public education, better roads, and other options for orphans made the need for a children's boarding school unnecessary. As with so many other mountain settlement ventures, the extensive physical plant of the Appalachian School was dedicated to a new purpose, but in this case with roots in the previous activities. Bill Brown brought new energy and professionalism to his tasks, attracted a new generation of young people to Penland, and solidified the school's reputation as a leader in craft education.

In 1962 Lucy Morgan retired from the mountain school she had built and nurtured. She left the Penland area with confidence in the new administration, although her relinquishing of her position took a little prodding, just as she had predicted. She lived her remaining years in the small community of Webster, North Carolina, a few miles north of her birthplace. In retirement, she continued to weave, clad in a handwoven dress topped by a store-bought sweater. Her great-niece assisted in putting the warps on her loom. In the summer of 1981, she was buried in a small cemetery shared by many other Morgan and Siler relatives; it is next to St. John's church, the early family place of worship that her brother Rufus had rebuilt.[72]

Penland developed along entirely different avenues than did either Berea or Gatlinburg. Even though strong personalities ran weaving operations in these other places, Penland owed its existence to one person. Although many people contributed a great deal to the development of Penland, without Lucy Morgan none of it would ever have happened. She conveyed her vision to others, and then let them know how significant and appreciated their efforts were. She seized possibilities and expanded her vision when people and opportunities presented themselves.

While Lucy Morgan's story has much in common with that of other women working for social betterment in the southern Appalachian Mountains, Penland stands out because of her success and her ability in attracting those who could see possibilities of their own. While many southern mountain workers came to the mountains from elsewhere, Lucy Morgan returned to the mountains after her college education and several years of teaching. She came back with the education, pretensions, and idealism of a mountain settlement worker, but confronted the people there not as outsiders but as kin.

6

the weavers of rabun

In a ranking of strong weaving personalities in the Southern Highlands, Mary Hambidge would be near the very top. As founder of the Weavers of Rabun in the northeastern mountains of Georgia, her operation did not conform to the patterns established by the other weaving centers. She struck out in a direction uniquely her own, largely because her education, environment, and inspiration were different than those of the leaders of the other craft ventures in the southern Appalachians. While no one could claim that she contributed the most or wielded the greatest influence, she accomplished much and inspired many. With her charming and flamboyant personality, she was able to get many people to help her in developing a weaving business and a series of other activities, all launched from her mountain home.

In the mid-1930s, Mary Hambidge created the Weavers of Rabun along Betty's Creek in the Rabun Gap area of the Georgia mountains. By 1937, Rabun Studios, her shop in New York City, was selling stoles, scarves, and yardage lengths woven in the mountains. Through a network of influential friends, aided by visibility in the largest city in the country, commissions arrived for large amounts of handwoven fabric intended for use in garments or interior furnishings. Unlike the other weaving centers, the Weavers of Rabun never produced guest towels or placemats or in any way catered to the impulse buyer.

Mary Hambidge did not come to either weaving or the mountains early in life. Born on December 20, 1885, Mary Crovatt grew up in a socially prominent family of Brunswick, Georgia. Her father, a lawyer, served in many civic capacities, including judge, mayor, and president of the local school board. When her mother, Mary Lee Slatter, married Alfred Hambidge, she was heralded as "one of Georgia's loveliest young women, gifted with many social graces."[1] Mary left the South at an early age to be educated in Cambridge, Massachusetts, and then continued living in the Northeast. In her twenties, Mary lived in New York City, aspiring to be an actress. When *Princess Bonnie,* an opera by Willard Spencer, was performed in Brunswick, Georgia, three separate reviews mentioned Mary among the excellent local talent: "Miss Mary Lee Crovatt, piquant and engaging in every movement and gesture, was another favorite who carried the house by storm with her sweet voice and realistic acting in the part of Kitty Clover."[2] A portfolio of Mary posing in a variety of costumes, dramatically expressing different emotions, suggested attempts to secure roles, but it included no glowing reviews of New York stage triumphs. She supported herself as an artist's model and as a professional whistler in an act with "Jimmy," a mockingbird.[3]

Mary's story is tied by many threads to that of Jay Hambidge, an illustrator for the popular periodical *Century.*[4] Hambidge evolved a system for ordering visual elements, which he named "Dynamic Symmetry," that he employed in both his commercial work and his paint-

Illustrator Jay Hambidge developed the theory of Dynamic Symmetry. He died in 1924, at the age of fifty-seven.

ing. His theory, which he believed was the foundation for all great art, outlined mathematical laws of proportion based on patterns of plant growth, known as phyllotaxis.[5] In 1918 he wrote Mary that an examination of a maple leaf caused him to see the link between art and nature. "All Greek art is summed up in a leaf, and anybody can see it when it is pointed out."[6] Hambidge believed that outstanding ancient art followed the laws of Dynamic Symmetry and that it worked in contemporary art as well.

In the fall of 1919, he delivered a lecture in London, in which he explained his theory of design types. "Static" design, as found in "crystals, cross-sections of seed-pods, and in natural mosaic forms" was set against "dynamic" design, represented by "man and the plant, the five regular solids of geometry, and Greek and Egyptian art, particularly the former." Jay used the word "symmetry," not in its usual sense of reflection along an axis, but rather "the proper or due proportion of the parts of a body or whole to one another in regard to size and form; excellence of proportion." Yale University Press published two of Hambidge's books, *Dynamic Symmetry and the Greek Vase* and *Dynamic Symmetry and the Parthenon*, both of which analyzed the respective subjects according to his system of proportions.[7]

Many prominent artists of the day, including Robert Henri, George Bellows, Lawrence Giles, Leon Kroll, Eugene Speicher, Christine Herter, Wilfred Konrow, and George Whittle, employed Hambidge's elements of Dynamic Symmetry in painting, crafts, and architecture. Several of these artists met regularly in the New York studio of Edward B. Edwards to hear Jay explain the application of Dynamic Symmetry in art. Dynamic Symmetry found acceptance in industry—for example, Tiffany artists employed the proportions in its jewelry and the Chrysler Corporation used the system in designing several of its cars.[8] In 1920 Yale University Press sponsored a trip to Greece so that Hambidge could corroborate the theory of Dynamic Symmetry through the use of on-site measurements of the Parthenon. While on this trip he communicated with his followers through *The Diagonal*, a magazine published by Yale.

Jay and Mary probably met through the artistic community and their relationship extended over a ten-year period, although much of that time was spent apart. Letters to Mary from Jay in the spring of 1914 open with a variety of pet names, "Lady Dainty," "Adorable Sight," and "My Own Darling."[9] Even though these first letters express the foolishness of a middle-aged man in love, later on the correspondence settled into the confidence of a strong shared belief system. In addition to the close affection they bore for one another, Jay also challenged Mary's intellect. He encouraged her to explore both the world of ideas and her own creative impulses.

Thirty-five-year-old Mary Crovatt accompanied her lover Jay to Greece. This 1920 trip altered the course of her life and formed the basis for her major accomplishments. Nearly thirty years later, Mary related her activities in Greece for a Voice of America broadcast to that country:

> It was while my husband was deeply engaged in his work on the Parthenon that I had leisure to wander about Athens, and one day came upon the Weaving Establishment on Amelia Avenue, started by the women of Athens for Greek peasants. My years of study with Mr. Hambidge had prepared me for what now happened. The moment I saw the looms and the Greek women at them, something deep within me, something that seemed to have been asleep in my subconscious, awakened, came to life. I knew that I had found the important thing for me. I had to learn to weave.[10]

Jay cut his study short and return to the United States to embark on a series of lectures defending Dynamic Symmetry. Mary remained in Greece, learning to spin and weave in the studio run by Kria Elene Avramea. While in Greece she also met Eva Palmer Sikelianos, an American married to the Greek poet Angelo Sikelianos. Eva researched Byzantine and Greek music and created performance pieces combining traditional music, dance, and poetry, which were enacted in garments she wove. In 1927 and 1930 Eva joined with others in recreating the Delphic Festivals in Greece. For Ted Shawn's production of *Prometheus Bound*, presented at both Festivals, Eva designed and wove all of the costumes.[11] Mary remained close friends with Eva, shared in her struggle for Greek independence, and provided a cabin for her when she was destitute near the end of her life.

In 1920 Mary Crovatt traveled with Jay Hambidge to Greece, where she studied weaving while he gathered data about the Parthenon.

During her yearlong stay in Greece, Mary corresponded with Muriel Noel, a weaving student at the Athens studio who had relocated to the outskirts of Cairo. They discussed yarns and the technical aspects of weaving, occasionally exchanging opinions on the position of weaving in an industrialized world. In one of her letters, Muriel commented: "I know that you and Mr. Hambidge don't altogether agree with me about that! But it is terrible to see the natives wearing nasty cheap turbans woven with the commonest Swedish designs! (evidently under the influence of the local 'Technical School') and I feel someone ought to study the lost weaving before it becomes a lost art."[12] Mary didn't share Muriel's belief that weaving should concentrate on retaining traditional patterns. From her first adventures in weaving, Mary prided herself in creating modern pieces utilizing an old craft and not merely repeating the past. Mary conducted herself as an artist, drawing inspiration and techniques from tradition, but not unduly bound by convention in producing new work.

During the spring of 1921, Muriel addressed all of these letters to "Mrs. Hambidge"—not to "Mary," as the friendly personal style of writing would suggest. Jay addressed his envelopes to "Mary Crovatt" during the same time period. Even though Mary traveled as his wife and assumed his name, Jay continued to refer to her by the name he had always known.

Within three years of their trip, Jay Hambidge died as a result of a stroke suffered while delivering a lecture. He was fifty-seven years old, and Mary almost forty. A *New York Times* article recording his demise mentions his wife, the former Cordelia Selina De Lorme of Council Bluffs, Iowa, and four children, but made no reference to Mary Lee Crovatt. Jay had lived apart from his wife and family for many years. Born in Simcoe, Canada, Edward Jay Hambidge became a naturalized US citizen in 1912, having spent his career working in the United States. In 1922 the state of Florida granted Jay's divorce from Cordelia, an event largely engineered by Mary's father.[13] Although there is no record of a legal marriage between Jay and Mary, he did provide for her in a will dated June 1920. He left Mary all his "property . . . in token of my love, esteem and affection for her and as a regard for her five (5) years of laborious service in difficult research work for me, which she carried on without compensation and at an actual expenditure on her part and from her own funds of Five thousand ($5,000) Dollars."[14] After Jay's death, Mary's correspondence, even from Jay's friends, is addressed to "Mary Crovatt Hambidge." The world viewed Mary and Jay as being married whether or not a ceremony actually took place

Even though born in Georgia, Mary first visited the mountains of her state after her fortieth birthday. After Jay's death, Mary attempted to eke out a living as a weaver, constantly seeking to lower her cost of living. During a two-year period from 1926 to 1928, Mary wove at a friend's summer home near Mountain City in Georgia's Rabun County.[15] While she went there seeking only an inexpensive lifestyle, she ended up falling in love with the mountains.

In Georgia, Mary "discovered" the Appalachian handweaving tradition. Prior to this she had naively supposed that hand textile production had long ago died out in the United States, and she planned on reintroducing weaving when she returned from Greece. Mary observed mountain women as follows: "They had kept their craft knowledge and their native integrity, but their looms had been relegated to the attics, or the woodpile, their spinning wheels put away to be used only now and them to spin a little thread for their men's socks."[16] Mary encouraged local women to spin wool yarn for her to weave.

After two years in the mountains, Mary returned to New York, where another major influence, Eleanor Steele, entered her life. Eleanor and her first husband, Hall Clovis, sang opera and toured together performing duets.[17] In 1930 Eleanor and Mary became friends

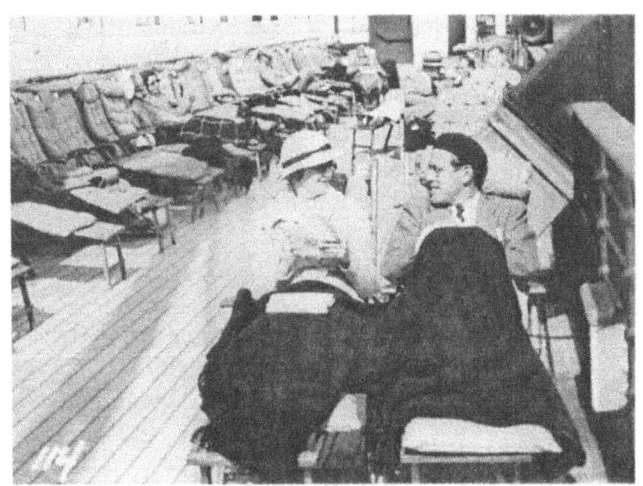

Eleanor Steele and Hall Clovis, husband and wife singers of opera duets, toured Europe performing in the early 1930s.

while working together on Bach's *The Contest Between Phoebus and Pan* produced by the Little Theater Opera Company of New York. Mary designed and wove all of the costumes for the opera production.

Mary Hambidge kept a notebook of detailed information on weaving fabric for the over forty costumes in "Phoebus and *Pan*.[18] Mary constructed the garments in two primary Greek styles: the short chlamys used by men and the longer version, the chiton, worn by both sexes. Simple straight panels formed the garments, with a braided cord belt tied at the waist to add form. The chorus wore robes woven in heavy cotton threads, while the ballet was clad in much finer cotton. For the apparel worn by the principal performers, designs resembling embroidery were inlaid by hand during the weaving. One set of costumes possessed a warm color scheme of yellows and oranges, while the other group used cooler greens, blues, and lavender.

Mary used Dynamic Symmetry in determining the proportions of each costume in relation to the body. In her notebook, an outline of a female figure is superimposed with a rectangle, the top corners of which fall at each elbow and the bottom corners at mid-calf. She also marked off the line at mid-hip. Measurements of each chorus member noted hip and calf length. While the width of all warps remained constant at forty-five inches, she customized the length for each garment. Since altering the width is difficult in weaving, she probably compensated for different sizes by hemming the sleeves and adjusting the side seam. Even though it would have been much easier to use the same rectangle for all of the costumes, Mary customized each one to its wearer. This method of adapting each costume to the exact proportions of the cast member was a departure from the customary practice of hemming all costumes a uniform number of inches from the floor, irrespective of the person's height.

Mary wove her own clothing during the thirties with a decidedly Grecian flair, having the look of costumes rather than everyday wear. The simply constructed garments often employed Jay Hambidge's design figures woven in an inlaid tapestry technique. For most of her dresses, she used a heavy silk warp with a finer silk weft, with the loose garment belted with a five-strand braid of multiple silk threads. The bottom edges ended in short fringe with a special finishing stitch to keep the ends from unraveling, rather than a hem. Even though most of the clothes used the basic rectangle, the necklines and armholes varied in design. Her two-piece outfits exhibited signs of professional dressmaker construction. Some ensembles consisted of a dress, cape, and hat, all with matching designs.[19]

During the early 1930s in New York, Mary envisioned a place in the Georgia mountains where crafts and agriculture could be practiced in an environment according to the principles developed by Jay. She expanded Dynamic Symmetry and imagined a self-sufficient lifestyle emerging from the practice of balance and proportion. Backed by her considerable family fortune, Eleanor Steele pledged support in helping Mary realize her dream. Eleanor gave with openhanded generosity—in one of her letters Eleanor admonished Mary, "don't worry so much about the money end. I know you are doing your best and we are all working towards the same end and it makes no difference who has money, just as there is some to help the cause along."[20]

Mary first rented space up the hill from Mountain City, Georgia, at Twin Tops, where she had lived during the late 1920s. In addition to having several women spin for her in their homes, she employed two recent high school graduates as weavers. The girls lived in one cabin, Mary in another, eating and weaving together in a large central building.[21]

The Rock House was one of the buildings on the property purchased by Mary Hambidge. She hired several men to run the farm.

However, Mary's plans needed more space, for both weaving and farming. She searched the area and found an ideal space along Betty's Creek in the Rabun Gap area. In 1938, after considerable negotiating, Hambidge purchased almost 800 acres, using Eleanor's $6,000.[22] She bought the land from a Mr. Latimer, who in turn had secured it from a group of Atlantans who were operating a hunting and fishing club on the site. They had built a large house of creek rocks and laid out the foundation for a much larger lodge before the combined circumstances of World War I and the breaking of their lake dam forced them to abandon their plans. The property consisted of both flat land near the creek and some mountain terrain. A gravel road wended its way from the small community of Dillard, starting at the boundary of the Rabun Gap School and meandering through the valley until it disappeared into North Carolina.

At age fifty Mary Hambidge had finally realized her dream of a place in the mountains. She recruited additional women as spinners and weavers and men as farm workers. Mary lived in a traditional dogtrot style log cabin, improved by the addition of a porch and a sunroom. This building sat on the hill behind the original Rock House, which housed the weaving studio and living quarters for some of the weavers. During Mary's almost forty years on the property, she built several more buildings to support the farming and weaving activities. The addition of a Weaving Shed, built with wormy chestnut logs cut on the property, centralized the looms and weaving. A retired Kentucky schoolteacher named Miss Leda Williams acted as chaperon to the young weavers who lived in the Rock House, developing "in the girls a sense of perfection in doing the practical things of every day life, training them in housekeeping, flower arrangement, proper hygiene, and the various graces of life in the home."[23]

In the mid-1930s, Mary sold weaving products during personal presentations before women's groups and gatherings of friends. Society newspaper accounts mentioned these speaking events: "Mrs. Hambidge pointed out that weaving teaches patience, satisfies a creative urge, pleases one's sense of rhythm, teaches one to like solitude and meditation. She believes that 'it does something to the soul' of the weaver."[24] The consistency of accounts spanning several years suggests that Mary had developed a workable sales approach. Mary spoke of learning about weaving in Greece, discovering the southern mountain craft activity, and the principles of Dynamic Symmetry. Wearing handwoven clothing, she extolled the virtues of natural fibers and of custom-made fabric for clothing, rugs, and curtains.

Within a couple of years the expansion of weaving production at Betty's Creek precipitated a bold new adventure in marketing. Sales trips in the North indicated a potential market for handwoven fabric among affluent consumers. In 1937 a shop called Rabun Studios opened at 810 Madison Avenue in New York City.[25] Eleanor Steele generously funded this attempt to reach a broader, more sophisticated, and wealthy clientele that would appreciate the one-of-a-kind quality of the fabric. Hall Clovis, Eleanor's husband, directed the shop, with Miss Josephine Kirpal serving as on-site manager. Rabun Studios continued operation for the next twenty years, with Miss Kirpal at the helm promoting Mary's handwoven fabric; eventually the store included a variety of other crafts.[26]

Faye Thompson, who became the weaving studio manager at Betty's Creek, wove the original sample books from which the customers selected fabrics to be woven, specifying certain widths and lengths. Buyers commissioned yardage for household interiors—draperies, upholstery, and bedspreads—or for garments to be constructed by their own tailors or seamstresses. Faye learned to weave from Mary Hambidge during the summer while she was still in high school. Starting at the age of eighteen, she worked for Mary full-time, continuing for twenty-two years until she married and moved out of the area.[27]

Young women working at the Weavers of Rabun pose on the Rock House steps in the late 1930s. Mary Hambidge is on the far right, next to Miss Leda Williams, housemother and retired schoolteacher from Kentucky.

Most of the weavers came to work for Mary at a very young age, as Faye had. Some learned to weave at the Tallulah Falls Industrial School in Tallulah Falls, Georgia, while others received instruction from Mary. Apprentices were required to assist with studio tasks before being allowed to weave on their own. The young women either lived in their own homes along Betty's Creek and its tributaries or stayed in the Rock House. Willie Mae Ramey, one of the first weavers to work for Mary at Twin Tops before the operation moved to Betty's Creek, helped dye yarn in a shed on the hill near Mary's cabin. After she was married, Willie continued to live in the Rock House, returning home on weekends, because her husband worked outside the mountains. Willie thought that her first child might be born on the Hambidge property because every time she tried to quit, Mary pleaded with her to continue working and she stayed a little longer.[28]

During the peak periods of operation, eight weavers worked at looms. Production ceased during the winter months, during which Mary usually visited New York. Women spun in their own homes, bringing yarn to the Weaving Shed. Dean Beasley, one of the weavers who resided along Betty's Creek for the rest of her life, specialized in scarves woven with angora on a silk warp and in woolen shawls. Dean survived as the last Rabun Studio weaver at the time of Mary's death, having put in a total of thirty-one years at the loom.[29]

A small pamphlet that accompanied the Weavers of Rabun products sold through the New York shop stated, "We are not repeating the old fashioned weaving of the Mountaineers. Our work is modern and based upon nature. We are attempting to bring out the simple beauty and quality inherent in nature's raw materials." This short statement of principles embodied Mary's other perspectives and hinted why weavers liked working for her: "Our work is created by human beings, not produced by machines. Our workers are never hurried. Our objects are—to bring out the natural beauty of the raw materials by simple, honest, hand process—to produce quality, not quantity—to give a living wage and a creative outlet to the worker and work of individuality to the individual."[30]

Rabun Studios carried woven fabric and offered books of swatches for yardage ordered in customized widths and lengths. The large woven samples, measuring about four and a half inches by eight and a half inches, gave the customer ample fabric to see and feel. One sample book contained forty wool samples, mostly of handspun yarn—over half of them were in natural sheep colors, white and browns. The remaining handspun and finer commercially spun wool fabrics were dyed reds, greens, and blues, all colors drawn from nature. Most of the fabric employed a very simple plain weave structure, while some others used twill or herringbone. A larger silk booklet contained over seventy samples, ranging from very fine to very heavyweight fabric, primarily in plain weave with a few twills. One very attractive series of silk materials used two heavy threads placed in stripes half an inch or more apart in a fine warp. The colors ranged the entire spectrum, but even the brightest hues were never garish. Mary's colors combined easily with one another, so the sample books were themselves small works of art.[31]

Accurate records survive of the yardage woven for most of the years that the Weavers of Rabun were in existence. Operating sales and production facilities so far apart—Georgia and New York—demanded an accurate system to track fabric woven for general sale and for commissions. Beginning with page 1, page numbers followed consecutively from late 1938, extending through the mid-twelve hundreds in 1957. Each page contained a fabric swatch about two inches by six inches and noted basic information plus width and length. Beginning in 1950, a concurrent numbering sequence was set up for yardage woven and sold at the Betty's Creek sales room added to the Weaving Shed in 1948.[32]

Almost all of the Weaver of Rabun yardage lengths from the late 1930s employed handspun wool yarns in both the warp and weft and, on average, measured thirty-two inches wide and seven yards long. Most production facilities put very long warps on the looms, spreading the preparation time over several pieces, but Mary Hambidge used short warps for each item. When starting a new piece, the weaver tied threads onto the previous warp and pulled yarns through the reed and the heddles, avoiding the laborious task of completely rethreading the loom, and thus saving time.

Although Weavers of Rabun fabrics in the natural wool colors of white, brown, and gray remained popular, after the first few years most yarns were dyed. Mary Hambidge mixed her own dyes and dyed yarn in an open-air pavilion adjacent to her cabin. She possessed an acute eye for color and was influenced by the colors of the mountains: flowers, leaves, and the red

In a dye shed near her cabin, Mary Hambidge mixed commercial synthetic dyes, duplicating colors she observed in the natural world.

Georgia soil. While working as an illustrator, Jay Hambidge had developed a system for mixing colors, which he imparted to Mary. As with most of Jay's ideas, in these colors she saw the balance and proportion of Dynamic Symmetry. Since the connection between her subtle colors and nature was so strong, many observers assumed that Mary used natural dyes, but this was not true. Her skill lay in observing the natural world and then mixing commercial dyes to approximate what she saw. Mary's vague answers to questions about her dye formulas were not an attempt at secrecy, but rather a result of her not exactly knowing what she had done.[33] She mixed dyes the way a good cook concocts a recipe—with a little of this and a pinch of that, letting her long experience guide the results.

In the mid-1940s, *Women's Wear Daily* described the operations of the Weavers of Rabun and pictured fabric swatches and the Weaving Shed with workers on the porch.[34] At the Rabun Studios in New York, "A wide variety of fabrics are offered in handsome patterns and rich-looking colors which are either natural, undyed shades from 'hand-picked' sheep, or mellow tones achieved by careful hand dyeing which is the result of a special color process." Clients paid from $7.50 to $9.00 a yard for this handwoven cloth that could not be found at other outlets in New York. "Fabrics are channeled only to the over-the-counter trade. Leading designers and notables of the stage and musical world are said to be among the shop's clientele."

During 1947, at the midpoint of the Rabun Studio's existence, wool still reigned as the most popular yardage fabric.[35] However, the demand for handspun fabrics from New York clients far outstripped the production capacity of the spinners, so that half of the yardage was commercially spun wool. The plain weave structure still predominated, with about one-fifth of the production employing either twill, or reverse twill herringbone. In 1947 a total of 744 yards came from the looms in 113 separate lengths. Two-thirds of the pieces used wool, and almost all of the remainder were silk, with fewer than ten lengths of cloth made from cotton or linen yarns. The most common production size was thirty-four inches wide by six yards long. In counseling buyers, the shop suggested seven yards for a man's suit, while a jacket required four and a half yards of fabric; a woman's suit or coat needed six yards. Prepared yardage stocked on the Rabun Studio's shelves accounted for just under half of the production. The other half came from clients ordering material from samples in a desired fiber, color, texture, and size. The commissioned pieces tended to be longer, with the longest measuring twenty-two and three-quarters yards. Special requests could be woven in widths of up to fifty-two inches.

The records of the regular numbered yardage do not tell the whole story for 1947, however, because another "Special Materials" notebook described other yardage lengths woven and order dates.[36] In that year, Yale University Press purchased sixty-five yards of linen as covers for a reprint of Jay Hambidge's book. The special materials notebook, which included another forty-two yards in five separate orders in 1947, suggested that these commissions were taken at the Weaving Shed in Georgia and did not come from the shop in New York. This notebook probably served as a precursor to the Betty's Creek records, which began in 1950.

The largest commission recorded at Betty's Creek came in 1945. A notebook with "Order for U.S. Navy" written across the top of each page contained specifications for fabrics used in converting the *Williamsburg* for use as the new presidential yacht. A newspaper article described the plans: "The 244–ft. 'Williamsburg' is a 14 year old, twin-skrew, diesel-powered ocean yacht. . . . President Truman will have two double staterooms on the boat deck. One will have gold draperies, oyster-white leather chairs, blue walls, the other will be done in beige and green."[37] The Weavers of Rabun wove cotton and silk into yellow, blue, green and blue-green fabric lengths designated for draperies, upholstery, cushions, and bedspreads. During August, September, and October in 1945, the weavers wove 250 yards of cloth in fifteen separate pieces to fill the order.

In addition to yardage lengths, the Weavers of Rabun produced scarves, shawls, blankets, and silk and wool neckties. After weaving, Mary vat-dyed the scarves and ties in a great array of colors. Dyeing articles after weaving them in white or natural yarn extended the palette by not having to thread many separate short warps. Also, dyeing could be postponed until sales indicated popular colors for the current season. The luxurious silk shawls contained intricate inlaid patterns using Jay Hambidge's designs. Most of Mary's own clothing and garment commissions from the 1920s and early 1930s incorporated Jay's Dynamic Symmetry design figures. The Rabun Studio also sold wool handspun and handknit socks, which Mary's patron Eleanor Reese regularly purchased as durable work socks for her husband. Mary wore heavy silk long stockings, knit in an open lace pattern, but these were not offered for sale.

Sales declined during the early 1950s as demand for yardage fell considerably. Now the spinners could again keep up with the production and most cloth was woven with handspun yarns, as had been the case in the early years of the business. As more employment opportunities were now available in the mountains, Mary found recruiting weavers more difficult. Helen Justice, who worked first as cook and later as a weaver, left the Weavers of Rabun after fourteen years. Because she never married and took care of her aged parents, Helen felt compelled to give up the weaving when a better-paying factory job became available at nearby Clayton Manufacturing. She liked weaving for Mrs. Hambidge very much and regretted having to leave.[38] The wages Mary Hambidge paid were low, but they were acceptable in the mountains during the earlier years of her business.[39] Even though she offered comfortable working conditions and an ample noon meal, hourly wage rates did not advance to keep pace with local competition.

In the late 1940s, a store was added to the Weaving Shed in Rabun Gap.

By the 1950s Mary had reached the age where most people retire to a rocking chair on the front porch. Now that she was nearing the age of 70, she finally received some long sought recognition for her work when several major museums exhibited weaving from Betty's Creek. The Museum of Modern Art in New York included a length of burgundy handspun handwoven suiting designed by Mary in the "Textiles USA" show of 1956. In 1958 the "Weavers of Rabun" exhibition appeared in the Rotunda of the Arts and Industries Building at the Smithsonian Institution in Washington, D.C. Over 150 items in the display depicted the best of Mary Hambidge's art in handwoven yardage lengths, scarves, and shawls dyed in her vibrant array of colors. Weavers and spinners from Georgia demonstrated during the opening days of the exhibition.[40] Always adept at securing publicity, Mary was the subject of a feature in the *Atlanta Journal and Constitution* Sunday color magazine supplement in the fall of 1957. Also, during these years articles about the Weavers of Rabun appeared in the *Georgia Review*, the Greek-American publication *Athene*, and *Handweaver and Craftsmen*.[41]

Soon after the inception of the New York shop, it expanded to carry other handcrafted products in addition to the weaving done by the Weavers of Rabun. Among the first craft objects added—one that consistently sold well—was pottery from Jugtown in Seagrove, North Carolina. Professional artists Jacques and Juliana Busbee revived and ran a ceramics business that had existed since colonial times in the Piedmont area of North Carolina. Mary Hambidge and Juliana became close friends. Mary used the Jugtown pottery in her home and Juliana wore clothes made from Mary's fabric.[42]

During the course of operation of the New York sales facility, manager Jo Kirpal reported regularly to Mary on finances. In 1948, Kirpal's monthly reports switched from a detailed account of income and expenses to "cost plus 40%" figures, which reflected a change in ac-

The Weavers of Rabun

counting procedures as a response to greater sales in the other crafts items. Jo kept up regular correspondence with Mary about orders and also related a fair amount of news about people and interesting events: "The Crosbys from Hollywood were here and brought pictures of that room you and Roy planned for them. They love it so and say it is the talk of Hollywood still." She mentioned a long visit Allen Eaton made to the shop; he admired the fabric and thought that there should be "Rabun Studios" in different parts of the country. In 1952 Jo inquired, "Have you ever heard of Bernard Leach and Shoji Hamada?" These two icons of contemporary production pottery had just returned from a visit to Black Mountain College in North Carolina. They invited Jo to a reception in their honor that evening. "At any rate they were greatly charmed with the kind of shop Rabun Studios is, and they were especially enchanted with your work. Mr. Leach says it is the finest he has seen in this country and he has been from coast to coast."[43]

Because of an increase in rent in 1956, the shop moved from 810 Madison Avenue to a new space on 67th Street. Only two years later, in the summer of 1958, the store advertised a "removal" sale, severing all relations with Hall Clovis and Mary Hambidge. After Clovis moved from New York to California, he lost all interest in the shop. Although the shop never made money, for twenty years it managed to cover its expenses by selling thousands of yards of handwoven fabric and other handcrafts. Miss Kirpal tried to continue the shop under the Rabun Studios name, but Mary objected, declaring that the name belonged to her. Jo wrote to Eleanor Reese, telling her side of the story and hoping for some subsidy to continue operations. "Mary has said for years that one cannot make money with the Crafts, and I never believed her. I still think that if we had a real business person in the shop instead of a person like myself, and that if a little bit of advertising could have been done, the shop could have broken even."[44] Since the shop relied almost entirely on word-of-mouth referrals and walk-in trade, even minimal advertising would likely have attracted new customers.

The weaving business continued along Betty's Creek after the New York shop closed. As

Mary Hambidge raised sheep on the farm at the Hambidge Foundation, although most of the wool for spinning was purchased.

late as 1963, fashion designer Laura Willis of New York, London, and Paris commissioned Rabun fabrics for a new line of clothing. The *Atlanta Constitution* described Willis's collection: "Her conceptions express a great simplicity and a classic restraint in these beautiful but difficult to handle fabrics. . . . Miss Laura, as she is called here, works like a sculptor—direct on the dress form or model."[45] The suits and coats used wool handspun yardage left primarily in natural colors, although some had been dyed the rust color of the Georgia soil. For blouses, eveningwear, and linings, the designer instructed her two local seamstresses to use silk. The heavier weight wool material worked well for coats and jackets, but it proved too bulky for the shaping and seamed detailing used in the world of haute couture.

The farm entered production at the same time that the weaving business developed. From her first vision of a community of workers in the mountains, Mary intended to achieve self-sufficiency. In the late 1940s the farm planted 130 acres of wheat and corn on the flatbottom land along Betty's Creek. A waterpowered gristmill on the property ground corn for grits and meal for Mary Hambidge and many of her neighbors. As many as sixty sheep, both black and white, provided wool for spinning. Ten cows supplied milk, cream, and butter. Four to six men worked the farm, depending on the season. The abundant noon dinner served in the Rock House to all workers and visitors came largely from the copious vegetable garden, either picked fresh or preserved.[46]

In 1944, the Jay Hambidge Art Foundation officially incorporated, with the professed belief that "Agriculture and the Handcrafts are the basis of a creative life." Eleanor Steel Reese's tax problems provided the impetus behind forming the foundation.[47] She deducted the $1000 per month she paid Mary from her taxes as a charitable contribution. In the early years after incorporation, very little changed; the weaving remained the central activity and the farming continued.

During the late 1950s and 1960s, literature published by the Jay Hambidge Art Foundation contained several references to founding a school, wavering between teaching crafts and promoting Greek culture. Mary never formally established a school, although a Junior Spinning club for young girls did exist in the late 1940s. The center conducted a crafts summer workshop for thirty women in 1951, and a few private students received weaving lessons in the 1960s.[48] Mary had remained enamored with Greece since her trip with Jay, and she planned a center for Hellenistic studies. In a hollow in the mountains, Mary saw a natural amphitheater where Greek plays might be produced. She proposed carrying out this vision with the help of actor and longtime friend Vassos Kanellos, who felt that "Greek drama springs from Mother Earth." A newspaper reporter quipped

Mary Hambidge hoped to produce Greek dramas in the Georgia mountains with the help of her longtime friend Vassos Kanellos.

that "the cows along Betty's Creek seem to like it," in an article about the Hambidge Foundation's expansion into Greek culture.[49]

Always generous, Mary invited many people to come live and work on her land at Betty's Creek. She outlined her desire to encourage creative people: "We never want this to be strictly an 'art colony' but a creative center for real workers. I hope to have a meeting house for conferences, and studios for artists and writers."[50] By the early 1960s most of Mary's energy was focused on encouraging creative people to build houses and workspaces that would be deeded to the foundation. In fact, the foundation only inherited one small house. Weaver Helen Justice expressed the sentiment felt by many along Betty's Creek when she observed that many people who came to the Hambidge property just took advantage of Mary's hospitality without contributing anything.[51] But Mary nurtured and challenged others, especially artists, writers, and musicians, who used their time profitably in the lovely mountain setting.

Mary invited several people to work with her in developing her foundation, among them Robert Marshall Shepherd. Bob, a young man with roots in Kentucky, had migrated to New York to seek his fortune in clothing design and merchandising. While recuperating from a World War II wound in Nashville, Tennessee, Bob learned of Mary from a mutual friend helping in the hospital. Bob and Mary often met during her trips to New York twice a year. They exchanged long letters for more than twenty years containing references to people they knew, books they had read, and generously sprinkled with bits of philosophy from Mary. He ended one of his letters with, "I wish so much that you were here for a talk with me now. You inspire me as no one else has ever done. I have never had the respect for any other person that I feel for you."[52] Mary's mysticism attracted him. Even though he visited Betty's Creek on several occasions, he declined Mary's offer to move to the Georgia mountains. He could not leave his steady job in New York for the financial uncertainties of managing a foundation with no guaranteed income.

Eliot Wigginton, of Foxfire fame, accepted Mary's invitation to live at the Hambidge Foundation. He first visited the retreat at Betty's Creek as a small boy with his father, landscape architect and professor at the University of Georgia, Brooks Wigginton. Eliot developed many happy memories of the mountains during his several visits, as the weavers fussed over the motherless little boy. Mary and Eliot became fast friends when he chose to do a senior project on Jay Hambidge's theory of Dynamic Symmetry at the private high school he attended. Eliot and Mary corresponded throughout his college years, with her encouraging him to come and help her at the foundation. After completing his education, Eliot moved to Betty's Creek, finished building a cottage on the property and lived there for six years. To support himself, Eliot taught English at the Rabun Gap-Nacoochee School, where his students published the *Foxfire* magazine that reported on local history and customs. In an essay composed shortly after Mary's death, he wrote, "Foxfire was born on her kitchen table, issue after issue came out of the little studio of mine, and when *The Foxfire Book* was published, I called her in the acknowledgments the 'most remarkable woman I have ever met.' I meant it."[53]

One of the primary distinguishing characteristics of Mary Hambidge's weaving operation that set it apart from all other mountain weaving establishments was the existence of a patron. In Eleanor Steele Reese, Mary had a benefactor who was generous and loving, and who never dictated terms. Eleanor's support came as close to a "free lunch" as can be imagined. Mary not only purchased the property on Betty's Creek with $6,000 from Eleanor, but she received also

$1,000 every month to carry out her vision. The stipend began in the mid-1930s and continued until Mary's death.

Mary and Eleanor wrote letters to each other for over thirty-five years.[54] By the early 1940s, Eleanor had divorced Hall Clovis and moved to Idaho to breed cattle with Emmet Reese, her second husband. The correspondence between the two friends spans the years 1938 through 1973. Although Mary saved over two hundred letters, this probably only represents half of the letters in the correspondence. A larger number of letters is supposed because in those instances when the established pattern of monthly letters was disrupted, the next surviving letters never started with an apology for not writing or an excuse of diverting activities. None of Mary's half of the correspondence survived, but she doubtless answered Eleanor with long, rambling chronicles of her daily life and thoughts on many subjects similar to those she wrote to others. Some of the topics Eleanor wrote about can readily be surmised: the weather, mutual friends, events of daily life, books, world events, and, in later years, health concerns. Other topics were of a more professional nature: the New York shop, legal matters with the Hambidge Foundation, and Hall Clovis in his capacity as manager of Rabun Studios. Eleanor mentioned her second husband, Emmet Reese, in most of her letters. Mary supplied Eleanor with woven items and wool socks for Emmet in great profusion. Whether Eleanor ordered these items or received them as gifts from Mary, she never paid extra for them.

Eleanor and Mary remained close friends in that inexplicable way that people without much in common sometimes can. They had great affection for one another. Eleanor was not mystical or reflective or analytical. She rarely spoke ill of others, except perhaps in allusions to difficulties during her marriage to Clovis. She attended both Methodist and Episcopal churches at different times during her residence in Idaho. She gave up her career as an opera singer for a life with Emmet on a cattle ranch, a decision she never regretted. She seldom offered advice, but wrote clearly and knowledgeably about legal and business matters. And she never made demands in exchange for her benevolence. Mary occasionally requested a raise in her stipend, and then Eleanor would gently explain that the original arrangement would remain in place. Rather remarkably, Eleanor never visited the property she financed and never saw Mary after moving to Idaho.

None of the publicity about Mary, the Weavers of Rabun, and the Rabun Studios ever mentioned Eleanor, apart from discreet references to "friends" supplying financial assistance. Thanks to Eleanor's backing, the development of the weaving business was allowed to follow a unique direction. She purchased the property in Georgia, underwrote the opening of the New York shop, and provided a continuing financial cushion for Mary's activities. Mary Hambidge never needed to sell directly to tourists or cooperate in marketing with other craft production centers.

Azoria Kanellos, daughter of Mary's friend Vassos Kanellos, described Mary, as a still-vibrant woman, then in her mid-seventies: "Yes, she was beautiful. . . . She colored her hair, used heavenly scents, a tiny bit of make-up, cared for her diet, was very feminine along with her famous dynamism, always extremely chic—in her own way. But her aura was strict, almost stern."[55] Unfortunately, when recognition finally came Mary's way in the late 1950s, the time when she could capitalize on it had passed. The foundation, which should have been the vehicle for continuing the work, never functioned properly. Mary dominated so completely that no one on the board could conceptually separate the foundation from Mary herself.

Mary Hambidge, who always wore handwoven clothing, surveys her property next to Betty's Creek in the mountains of northeastern Georgia.

Mary Creety Nikas, an interior designer and friend, assumed the running of the foundation in the last months of Mary's life. No formal plans existed for continuing activities after Mary's death. Mary could never quite imagine that she would cease to exist—and neither could most of her friends. However, on August 29, 1973, the inevitable happened, and Mary Hambidge died. The natural amphitheater where she had once hoped Greek plays would be performed became the place where friends scattered her ashes.

Mary Nikas formalized and put into practice many of the programs that Mary Hambidge had begun informally or only talked about. The weaving, which had dwindled to very little activity, finally ceased operations. Nikas investigated art colony management and established guidelines so that creative people could work at the Betty's Creek property for short periods of time. In 1974 the renamed Hambidge Center opened, offering residencies in the arts and sciences and a variety of workshops in crafts, writing, and nature study. The center also hosted exhibits, lectures, and concerts.

Aspasia Voulis, who had taken care of Mary in her final months, gathered many of Mary's papers, and the Hambidge Foundation published *Apprentice In Creation*. Mary had written long stream-of-consciousness letters and jotted down many stray thoughts on scraps of paper. Even though some of these reflections take the form of poetry, Mary probably never conceived of these random thoughts being compiled in book form.[56]

Every year writers, visual artists, craftsmen, composers, dancers, musicians, and scholars visit the Hambidge Center to pursue their own projects. While most of them know nothing of Mary Hambidge, they all owe a tremendous debt to her vision. They find peace for creative work in the beautiful surroundings that Mary knew stimulated and nurtured thought.

Mary Hambidge's goals and direction in life became clear after she discovered weaving at almost forty years of age. During her 1920s stay in the mountains, she formulated her future plans for a comprehensive community combining weaving and farming. She wrote long letters to Emily Hamblen, the friend in whose cabin she lived. Throughout the letters were frequent statements of trust in Providence: "I have such faith in God and Mr. Hambidge that I know they watch over me and whatever happens is right for me and the work."[57] The death of Jay Hambidge allowed Mary to follow her own direction without restraint, in ways that she could not have pursued had he lived. Clad in her handwoven garments, she accomplished a great deal from her home in the northeastern mountains of Georgia and dreamed of much more. Whatever interpretation is imposed on the events of Mary's life, her legacy will always be the weaving that she loved. Mary thought that during weaving, the weaver went right into the threads and became part of the piece—so, her identity is now in the threads she wove.[58]

7

other mountain weaving centers

Although Berea's Fireside Industries, Penland Weavers and Potters, and the Pi Beta Phi's Arrowcraft Weavers represent the largest and most influential weaving centers, dozens of other centers were born during the Appalachian Craft Revival. Because these centers served their immediate areas, the organizational structure and the experiences of their weavers were all very similar. Although they had much in common, these places sprinkled throughout the mountains each had their individual history. Since the Craft Revival movement remained unorganized until the inception of the Southern Highland Handicraft Guild in the early 1930s, each center invented itself in response to specific conditions of place, leadership, and financial support. Most followed the Fireside Industry model in both general organization and products, rather than veering off in some unique direction, as Mary Hambidge's Rabun weavers did.

The social settlement workers conceived the Craft Revival as economic development for women. Early mountain settlement workers started schools, but within a short time tackled other community problems in health and standards of living. Allanstand and Berea organized already practicing weavers and other crafts producers before they began teaching skills to new producers. Some of the early weaving programs started working with students in their schools, often expanding to include community women. By the 1920s, several organizers who had either worked in or studied settlement programs established independent weaving centers modeled on Fireside school programs. Throughout Appalachia there existed dozens of similar weaving programs: some in sponsored schools, some with both school and community components, and some entirely community-based. While a few centers drew leadership for the weaving program from their mountain communities, most weaving supervisors came from outside Appalachia.

School Weaving Programs

Mountain settlement schools served as the primary place for the development of weaving programs. In 1920 John C. Campbell compiled a list of southern Appalachian schools under the sponsorship of religious denominations or other agencies.[1] He identified over 150 schools along the ridges of the mountains, scattered throughout the several states intersecting in the Appalachian chain. Many of these schools taught weaving as industrial work offered for girls, along with other subjects such as sewing and cooking, while boys studied agriculture and woodworking. In the early part of the twentieth century, the Southern Industrial Education Association financed teachers for some school efforts and encouraged other schools through the promotion and sale of products created by their students.[2]

The largest weaving centers of the Appalachian Craft Revival combined school and community aspects, but many programs existed only within the schools. School programs usually emphasized weaving for home use and possible sale, rather than engaging in the operation of production centers. For the schools that produced salable items, the outside sponsors usually provided the market for their entire output. Of the five school-only programs that exhibited with the Southern Highland Handicraft Guild in 1933, three sent weaving products: Tallulah Falls Industrial School, Dorland-Bell School, and Asheville Normal and Associated Schools. Two others, the Blue Ridge Industrial School in Greene County, Virginia, and the John and Mary R. Markle School of Industrial Arts of Yancey County, North Carolina, taught weaving as part of their school programs, but contributed hooked rugs and baskets to the exhibition.[3]

The Berry Schools, which operated an early school based weaving program, exists today as a college, and continues to offer weaving. In the first decade of the twentieth century, Martha Berry charted the course for the Berry Schools near Rome, Georgia. The schools grew from a children's Sunday School near Martha's home into a series of small elementary schools, then to a boarding school for boys, and eventually into a coeducational school, finally expanding to the college level. In 1930 Ida Tarbell included Martha Berry on her list of fifty outstanding American women, joining Berea's Anna Ernberg as the only other mountain worker cited.[4] Like other wellborn southern women, Martha's family expected her to marry well and pursue the gentility of southern family life. Exhibiting great determination without teaching credentials, Martha Berry guided the development of her schools, demonstrating considerable skill in fundraising to keep them afloat. She secured money in northern cities, convincing wealthy patrons to support her cause based on the strength of her ideas and her engaging personality. Where many other mountain ventures had tried and failed, Martha succeeded in prying loose some of Henry Ford's millions for her schools.[5]

In 1902 Martha started the Boys Industrial School, with the name later changing to the Berry Schools, after the establishment of a separate campus for girls. The Berry Schools published a magazine, *The Southern Highlander*, primarily as a fundraising tool. Several different articles pictured students arriving at the school and then depicting them later as students. These before-and-after photos showed the young girls transformed into Berry students, with bobbed hair and wearing white school uniforms.[6]

Always on a tight budget, the Berry Schools depended considerably on student labor to build, maintain, and operate its facilities. Inez Wooten told of her bewildering arrival at the Berry High School in 1919, never dreaming that within a few years she would be selected and trained as Martha Berry's personal secretary. On one of her frequent fundraising trips up North, Martha sent a telegram summoning Inez to New York City with instructions to bring a spinning wheel. In her costume—complete with bonnet and apron—the young girl demonstrated spinning as a living exhibit among a display of weaving.[7] Crafts always made for good pictures—it was even better when those pictures could talk and deliver the message.

Willie Sue Cordell supervised the handicrafts, with Martha sending her to studios throughout the United States to improve her skills. Martha envied Berea's Fireside Industries' success and wanted her weaving program to rival that of the Kentucky school. However, weaving never grew beyond small student classes. The Berry Schools never joined the Southern Highlands Handicraft Guild, probably because they were able to secure a sufficient market among the school's patrons for the limited student production.

Like President Frost at Berea, Berry realized the importance of using weaving to demon-

Other Mountain Weaving Centers

strate the skills and character of mountain people. She turned her interest in traditional weaving and old patterns into a student recruitment tool. When visiting mountain homes, she would express admiration for the coverlets, which often led to a discussion of the school's weaving program, which in turn would lead to a mention of the opportunities that the schools offered for the children of the household.[8]

Tallulah Falls Industrial School, founded in 1909 by the Georgia Federation of Women's Clubs, followed the model of other industrial schools in teaching practical living skills to children from the foothills and mountains of northern Georgia. Mary Ann Lipscomb of Athens, Georgia, took an interest in the children living near her summer vacation spot at Tallulah Falls; she convinced the Women's Club to finance a school when she served as the state president.[9] Both day and boarding students attended the school.

Eliza Shirley, who learned to weave at Tallulah Falls Industrial School, later taught in its weaving program.

The situation at Tallulah Falls suggested that the work on crafts kept boarding students occupied during the hours after the day students returned home. The craft financial reports showed income and expenses holding amazingly constant, only once rising above $1,000.[10] The spectacular scenery of the Tallulah Falls Gorge drew tourists to the area, and they patronized the shop on the school grounds, buying the products of the weaving studio, furniture made of rhododendron branches, hooked rugs, and baskets, all made by the students. Some sales took place as a result of Southern Highlands Handicraft Guild membership, but the school did not sell through local chapters of the Georgia Women's Clubs. The limited production capacity curtailed the marketing. In addition to items for sale, the girls wove fabrics for school furnishings, making all of the curtains, rugs, bedcoverings, and table linens for the guest cottage.

The Tallulah Falls coverlets and household textiles included the standard array of mountain revival weaving, but there were some unusual items too. A folding screen with framed tapestry mountain scenes cannot be found in production at other centers. During 1927 Ester Carlson took a leave of absence from her teaching job in Upsala, Sweden, so that she could travel to Georgia to supervise the weaving at the thirty-one looms at Tallulah Falls.[11] She introduced several Scandinavian techniques, with a few incorporated into a table runner and other new products.

Lamar Trotti, editor of *The Georgian*, referred to the Tallulah Falls Industrial School as the "Light in the Mountains." The school gladly accepted this descriptive name, using it in various publicity efforts. Student Eliza Shirley embodied the theme on a poster—she was depicted carrying a child in one arm, a bright candle held high in the other, and leading a band of children. The industrial arts teacher realized Eliza Shirley's talents while she was serving as

Weaver Eliza Shirley served as the model for the poster of the Tallulah Falls Industrial School, with the motto *Light in the Mountains*.

class assistant, and took her to Lynchburg and New York City for added instruction in weaving and domestic science. In 1919 Miss Shirley returned to the Tallulah Falls School as teacher of weaving and industrial arts.

Commemorating the school's twenty-fifth year, Vera Connelly wrote an article about Tallulah Falls School for the July, 1943, issue of *Good Housekeeping Magazine,* in which she described the campus in between stories of eager children hungry for learning. In one of the two huge rooms of the crafts building filled with looms, she wrote, "Seated at these ancient contraptions are mountain girls as dainty and pretty as flowers, who are making the same exquisite rugs and coverlets and chair seats and table linens their great-great-great-grandmothers did. It is an unforgettable picture!"[12] The author related visiting a Tallulah Falls graduate at her home in the mountains. The young mother displayed a stack of items she had woven for her new frame home, still under construction. Very few of the Craft Revival weavers actually made items for themselves, even though Anna Ernberg and others envisioned products of the loom brightening and enriching modest dwellings.

Presbyterian-sponsored schools in North Carolina ran weaving programs for their students, the largest being Asheville Normal School and Dorland-Bell School in Hot Springs. The Asheville teacher training school added handicrafts to its curriculum in 1916; by 1935 the school reported sixty weavers at work.[13] Ten years after the Dorland and Bell Institutes merged in 1918—both schools were started in the late nineteenth century—Helen Hickman introduced weaving. Miss Hickman solicited women in the Hot Springs area to share their knowledge of old weaving patterns and natural dye formulas. The Presbyterian Church and the Southern Highland Handicraft Guild provided markets for the student weaving production.[14]

School and Community Weaving Programs

Aside from Berea College and the Pi Beta Phi School, many other mountain schools ran programs for both students and community women, most notably Hindman Settlement School and Pine Mountain Settlement School in Kentucky, the Pleasant Hill Academy in Tennessee, and the Weaving Room of Crossnore School and the J.C. Campbell Folk School in North Carolina.

Two Kentucky women, Katherine Pettit of Lexington and May Stone of Louisville, opened Hindman Settlement School in 1902 along Troublesome Creek after determining the need for a permanent settlement program in the state's eastern mountains. During the summers of 1899 to 1901, with assistance from a group of progressive young Kentucky women, Pettit and Stone ran social service programs in the Hazard area with sponsorship from the Kentucky Federation of Women's Clubs and, later, the Kentucky Women's Temperance Union. Writing in journals at the early summer camps, Katherine Pettit recorded her keen interest in textiles. Katherine related in great detail weaving her first piece of linen under the guidance of a local woman: "Mrs. Stacy says she knows we shall never learn to weave, for it will take a week to get the piece in and another week to weave it, that it would take a day to learn to tie the weaver's knot."[15]

For close to fifty years, Una Pigman supervised the weaving program at Hindman Settlement School, that a Hindman chronicler described as "the Fireside Industries which have brought much money into the homes in exchange for the 'pretty weaving' by the women of the region."[16] She came from a long line of mountain weavers, with several members of Pigman's immediate family weaving for Hindman. Una's sister, Winnie Day, an especially skilled weaver, produced tablecloths, guest towels, and many other items, which were marketed through several different centers—Hindman, Carr Creek, and Quicksand Crafts at Vest.[17]

In 1912 Katherine Pettit left the Hindman Settlement School and, with the help of Ethel de Long, established another settlement school on Pine Mountain in Harlan County, Kentucky. Pine Mountain Settlement School encouraged women to reproduce the old weaving patterns, raise sheep and spin wool, and especially seek old formulas from locally collected dyestuffs. In teaching weaving to children, the school emphasized the link with mountain traditions. Along with other Craft Revival weaving centers, Pine Mountain believed that the activity of weaving built "the children's character. They are having what is a rare experience in our life today, the joy of conducting all the processes in the creation of a lovely thing." The Southern Industrial Education Society supported the weaving program at Pine Mountain; after that organization disbanded, the Colonial Coverlet Guild of America helped pay the teacher's salary. One weaving manager had previously been a student at Pine Mountain, with several supervisors coming from Berea's Fireside Industries.[18]

The American Missionary Association founded Pleasant Hill Academy in Pleasant Hill, Tennessee, before the turn of the century, with Margaret Campbell introducing craft training into the school curriculum in 1930. She offered an extensive crafts course that included weaving, but she was particularly known for her skill in woodcarving. Independent of the school, Sarah Boyce conducted a community weaving program from her home during the years her husband served as administrator of Pleasant Hill Academy. Both Sarah and her husband had attended Berea College, where she learned to weave.[19]

In Avery County, North Carolina, Crossnore School developed a weaving program that continues to this day, still affiliated with the school and hiring local weavers. In December of 1911 Mary Martin Sloop and her husband, Eustace Sloop, arrived in Crossnore to establish their medical practice. As a young woman, Mary Martin had planned to be a missionary, but by the time she had completed her medical school training the church deemed her too old for the rigors of service abroad. After medical school and marriage, Mary fashioned her own mission work without any church backing in the North Carolina mountains, where her Piedmont family had spent their summer vacations.

In 1913 Mary rallied the community of Crossnore to replace their inadequate one-room school with a larger building with two classrooms. This launched her on a new career enhancing Crossnore's educational opportunities, which she continued throughout her life.[20] Mary Martin Sloop financed the ever-growing Crossnore School with a unique blend of private and public money. As a public school, Avery County educational funds supplied salaries for most of the teachers. To support the additional children who flocked to the school after it began taking boarding students, Sloop raised funds from friends, the sale of old clothes, and by securing the "approved school" designation for Crossnore from the Daughters of the American Revolution.

While funds for financing most independent mountain schools came from sources outside the mountains, Sloop found that money could be generated from within the area. When preparing to send a young girl to high school at Banner Elk, Mary requested used clothing from her cousins. The large trunk of mourning clothes that arrived—although not appropriate attire for a schoolgirl—attracted eager buyers among Crossnore area women.[21] By continuing clothing solicitations from friends and churches, the special sales days drew large crowds of customers from throughout the area, eventually settling into a permanent resale facility on Crossnore's main street.

On April 6, 1921, Nell Johnson recited her commencement address, "The Art of Handweaving," from memory at the first graduation of the Crossnore High School. Mary Martin Sloop summoned Nell back from the Berea Academy in Kentucky to be half of the first high school graduating class, assigning her this essay subject. Nell researched the topic in Berea College's library and based it on a domestic industries pamphlet by Art and Craft Movement designer Candace Wheeler.[22]

At the time that Nell gave her graduation speech, weaving instruction had been offered at Crossnore School for only one school year. Sloop modeled the weaving program after the Fireside Industries at Berea College, providing weaving instruction to both school children and women from the community. Crossnore assumed the role of marketing the items produced, as Berea had. The actual weaving started when money became available for teachers' salaries through the state-administered Smith-Hughes vocational education federal program. In the 1920–21 school year, Clara Lowrance and Zada Benfield initiated the program. A Texan educated at Presbyterian schools, Clara had taught at Crossnore for many years. Zada, a local Crossnore girl, assumed her duties after returning from Normal School at Berea. She left this position after only one year to get married, with Lowrance continuing until her retirement in 1926. Lowrance's assistant and former adult pupil, Lillie Johnson (Mrs. Newbern W. Johnson), known to all as "Aunt Newbie," guided the weaving program for the next thirty-five years.

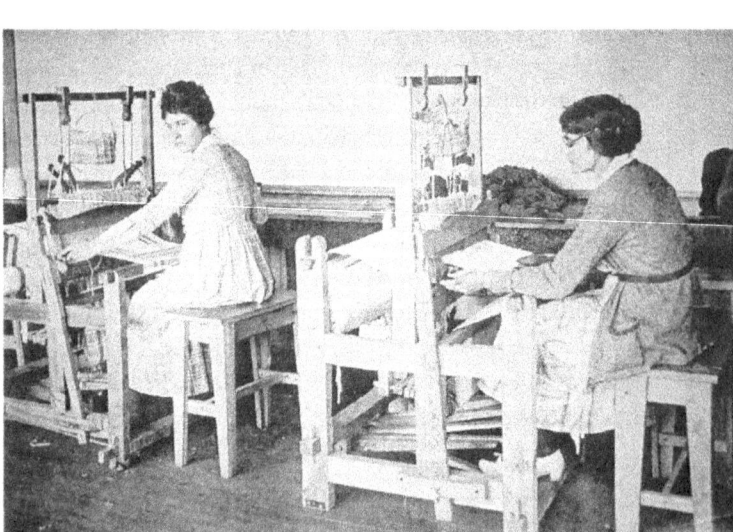

Marian Brown and Zada Benfield wove on Berea College looms in 1920, the first year of Crossnore Schools' weaving program.

In the early 1930s, the weaving, sewing, rug hooking, and sales areas at the Crossnore School were housed in two log structures that had been moved and combined into a single building.

Money came from the Southern Industrial Education Association to develop a community component to the weaving program. In the Association's newsletter for the fall of 1924, Mary Sloop reported on the effectiveness of the program: "It is not only a material help to them, but it makes a change in their attitude toward life, and for this reason we feel that the money given us by the Southern Industrial Education Association is bearing fruit in the lives of the women."[23] The 1922 report on the weaving class to the State Department of Public Instruction, Division of Trades and Industries, listed a program that was quite well developed after just two years of operation, with thirty young students and four married women.[24]

To accommodate the growing programs in weaving, rug hooking, and sewing, the school moved and combined two existing log structures on a piece of flat land along the main road through Crossnore. Because logging companies had depleted Avery County of timber at the turn of the century, the necessary materials for construction were not readily available, as they had been at Penland in adjacent Mitchell County. However, the larger, "recycled" building served the school only half a dozen years. The headline of *The Avery Advocate* for Thursday, October 10, 1935, heralded the news, "Weaving Building At Crossnore Burns With Heavy Loss." Unfortunately, the thirteen-year-old program had sustained damage estimated at $15,000 in materials and finished goods alone, not including the equipment and the building itself. While attending a D.A.R. meeting in West Virginia, Mary Martin Sloop and Aunt Newbie received the telegram informing them of the horrendous fire. They returned to Crossnore with $300 in donations collected from the D.A.R. and a determination to rebuild—but this time in stone. On the next Saturday, the Crossnore schoolchildren formed a human chain into the nearby river and relayed rocks out of the water. Construction proceeded through the winter; fires burning at night kept the cement from freezing.[25]

Aunt Newbie called in the few looms from women that wove at home and set them up in her living room. She had orders for weaving from the D.A.R. and she meant to fill them.

Ossie Phillips remembers the winter of 1935–1936 as very cold—and the weaving as cold work.[26] The looms moved into the new stone building when it was completed, and from then on Crossnore conducted one of the few programs where the weavers worked at a central location rather than in their homes.

When Aunt Newbie retired, she turned over the management of the Weaving Room to her assistant Ossie Phillips, who had started weaving when she was nine years old. Ossie spent over sixty years in Crossnore's weaving program, receiving the North Carolina Folk Heritage Award bestowed by the North Carolina Arts Council in 1998. She was recognized for her skill as a weaver and for her management of the weaving program. One Crossnore School director, lacking confidence in the weaving program, stripped the supervisor of authority for financial management and even for production. When this administrator wanted to completely close the weaving program, Ossie's response was to work for half salary to keep the Weaving Room open.[27]

The Weaving Room of Crossnore School, Inc., produced an array of products similar to that of other mountain weaving centers: guest towels, placemats, napkins, baby blankets, rugs, and scarves. A rug in the Lee Surrender overshot pattern was consistently popular with buyers. Coverlets always occupied several looms because D.A.R. members provided a large, constant market. Because Crossnore was an "approved school," the D.A.R. generously donated money for new construction and scholarships, and a D.A.R. member held a position on Crossnore's directing board.[28] At both national and state D.A.R. conventions, Crossnore's booth sold weaving and promoted the school. The D.A.R. also presented coverlets woven at Crossnore to a succession of First Ladies in the White House.

Crossnore relied on Smith-Hughes money to pay teachers' salaries just as Penland and the Pi Beta Phi School did. In North Carolina, it was George W. Coggin, State Supervisor of Trade and Industrial Education for the Department of Public Instruction, who administered the federal program. He provided financial assistance, encouraging the development of many community-based weaving centers in North Carolina. The handweaving centers were his pet projects.[29] After both became widowed, Mr. Coggin asked Aunt Newbie if she was interested in becoming his housekeeper. She accepted—but as his wife. They lived together in Raleigh until his death, only a little over a year after they took up residence together in the state capital. She returned to the mountains and is buried next to her first husband in the family cemetery in Crossnoe.[30]

The John C. Campbell Folk School in Brasstown, North Carolina, stands alone among mountain schools for its organizational structure, which was based on the Danish folk school model. The school arrived late on the scene in 1925, long after the establishment of most of the other major centers. The husband-and-wife team, John C. and Olive Dame Campbell, traveled throughout the mountains collecting information on education and social conditions as the representatives of the Southern Highland division of the Russell Sage Foundation. While immersed in studying the mountains, they talked of ways that problems could be addressed, deciding that a promising solution might lie in the system of rural education used in Denmark. After John's death, Olive teamed up with Marguerite Butler, a teacher at Pine Mountain Settlement School, to explore these possibilities. In 1922 the two women traveled to Denmark and other Scandinavian countries, spending over a year investigating the folk school movement. They liked the way that the Danish post-secondary folk schools focused on rural living skills and community-oriented development. Using these Danish ideas, they planned to establish an Appalachian folk school program aimed at young adults, rather than starting a school for children or an academic college. Writing in 1926, Olive projected that "the ultimate form which the John C. Campbell Folk School is to take must grow out of the community need and the consciousness of that need." On returning to the United States, they established criteria for the location of an experimental school; after investigating several sites, they decided on Brasstown, North Carolina, for their pragmatic educational experiment.[31]

The John C. Campbell Folk School concentrated its program on farming skills, crafts, and recreation. The folk school never gave grades or diplomas, but functioned as a social settlement center, perceiving needs and establishing programs in response. To address concerns within the community, the school established a credit union, a creamery, a farmers' cooperative, a club for homemakers, and an organization for craftsmen. Music, dances, lectures, and other recreational programs provided the school and its surrounding community with leisure activities.

Crafts had a prominent place in the school, viewed both as a way to supplement farm income and as a leisure pursuit. Margaret Campbell of Pleasant Hill Academy in Tennessee—no relation to either John or Olive—gave the first woodcarving workshop at the folk school. Olive speculated that with some direction the men whittling at the country store could turn their pastime into something more constructive. In 1935 an occupational therapist from Baltimore, Murrial Galt, coordinated the teaching of crafts and designed items for production. Murrial, known as Murray, married John Martin, a local farmer and the school's dairy manager, and continued the management of crafts teaching and production throughout her working life.[32] Although she had little knowledge of woodcarving, she worked with local men to come up with designs for subjects that they knew well—farm and woodland animals and birds. The carving group visited the barnyard to look carefully at a pig, taking special note of the location of the eyes in relation to the ears and snout. Different men—and, some time later, women—specialized in carving specific creatures. To fill customer requests, Murray designed St. Francis and crèche figures, which Helen Gibson, a second-generation carver, continues producing to this day.

The Campbell Folk School sent twenty-one carvings and fourteen pieces of weaving to the 1933 exhibit of the Southern Highland Handicraft Guild, suggesting a substantial program in textiles. Although hired primarily as a weaving teacher, Murray never raised textiles production to the prominence of carving. Louise Pitman, who ran the business side of the community crafts program, indulged a personal interest, becoming an expert on natural dyes. Other crafts specialties, including ceramics, basketry, jewelry, and especially blacksmithing, joined the school's curriculum over the years until crafts dominated the list of classes. As the crafts program grew in importance, the school's cooperative social activities became absorbed into the local economy of the nearby town of Murphy, North Carolina. The J.C. Campbell Folk School redirected its mission toward teaching adults, while still preserving some of the adapted Danish folk school ideas.

Today the J.C. Campbell Folk School offers crafts classes and a few other specialty courses to students from all over the country. The students live on campus in a variety of buildings and dine together in a central facility. A changing faculty of over 350 experts teaches over 450 single-week sessions throughout the year. Most of the teachers come from outside the mountains, although some live in the area—especially the carving instructors, many carrying on in the footsteps of a parent. The school also still provides recreation to the local community in the form of music, dance, and an annual craft festival.

Affiliated Community Weaving Programs

Agencies from outside the mountains sponsored weaving programs independent of schools. The Penland Weavers began as the Fireside Industry of the Appalachian School, but the school itself never offered weaving to the students. Although it soon stopped being dependent on Episcopal funding, Penland always relied on the church for sales outlets. In the early 1920s the Episcopal Church encouraged crafts at several of their missions in the mountains of Virginia, forming the Handicraft Guild of the Diocese of Southwestern Virginia. This guild sent carvings and furniture to the 1933 Mountain Handicrafts traveling exhibit, but did not include any of their production weaving.

Working loosely under Presbyterian blessing, Frances Goodrich brought to the mountains of western North Carolina the settlement house model of social development. Starting in the 1890s, she built a succession of houses around Asheville, where she and her fellow workers served as models for healthy Christian living while addressing community problems.[33] A 1909 Allanstand Cottage Industries brochure recounted one of Goodrich's missions: "In a nook of Buncomb County, N.C., many years ago, a settlement was formed with a day school as its nucleus. The two or three women who made a home together in the little cottage near the school-house found many avenues of approach to their neighbors, but a problem faced them such as meets every one who sets himself to social service, namely, how to bring material help to these neighbors without hampering them, or injuring their self-respect."[34] The gift of an old coverlet inspired Goodrich's inquiry into weaving methods and materials, a tradition that had almost died out in that area of North Carolina. "Our first coverlets were sold in a few weeks, and the demand for more was enough to justify at least a small start in business."

Frances Goodrich, a Presbyterian missionary, revived weaving and started Allanstand Cottage Industries to supplement the local subsistence farming near Asheville, North Carolina.

Based on this success, Goodrich promoted the home manufacture of several other crafts, establishing a shop at Allanstand, a drovers' station outside of Asheville.

Goodrich found weavers and dyers who were willing to share their skills with others. Three coverlets pictured in Hall's *A Book of Hand-Woven Coverlets* come from Allanstand; the weavers listed are Cumi Woody and Elmeda Walker. Born in 1837, Elmeda Walker would have been in her sixties when she met Goodrich and in her mid-seventies when she wove forty yards of upholstery fabric for the White House. First Lady Ellen Axson Wilson redecorated a bedroom in the White House with Appalachian-made crafts that she commissioned through the Southern Industrial Education Association.[35]

Goodrich skillfully publicized her revival of crafts. She relied for marketing first on her friends, then on church contacts, and eventually on supporters of the Arts and Crafts Movement and the Colonial Revival. The Presbyterian Church connection never meant direct financial support for her crafts development work, but Goodrich used the association as an avenue for marketing and fundraising initiatives. Even though a direct sales outlet existed throughout the history of Allanstand, substantial mail order business came through the women's network of church groups and arts organizations. Goodrich ran her operation from a log cabin at Allanstand, in 1908 expanding the business to a shop in the growing tourist city of Asheville.[36] Allanstand served as both inspiration and model for other mountain cooperatives. The system of central marketing for home-based production fit the limitations imposed by the mountains. During their 1911 journey into the mountains to find an appropriate site for their school, the Pi Beta Phi women stopped to visit Frances Goodrich. A page of Allanstand photographs in their newsletter accompanied the report to members.[37]

As she grew older, Frances Goodrich viewed the newly formed Southern Highland Handicraft Guild as a promising vehicle for the continuation of her work. She catapulted the fledgling Guild into direct retail crafts sales when she presented them with Allanstand Industries.

The federal government played a role in establishing mountain craft businesses, something that only came about because of the success of the denominational and private ventures. Most of these government programs developed in direct response to the Depression. Sometimes the Homemakers Clubs of the Extension Service and sometimes the Works Progress Administration or the National Youth Administration initiated projects. Most of these programs lasted only a few years.[38] The Southern Highlanders, Inc., a significant experiment on the part of the TVA in crafts marketing, was a notable exception to this rule, continuing for ten years and generating sales for dozens of craftspeople.

At least one Farm Bureau crafts project preceded the Depression. In 1920 Laura Copenhaver began Rosemont Industries in Marion, Virginia, as a way to use locally produced wool. She expanded the weaving and rug-hooking business in an old mill after the Farm Bureau left the area.[39]

Independent Weaving Programs

During the 1920s many small unaffiliated weaving centers came into being throughout Appalachia, most of them inspired by the success of the sponsored programs. Even though they were not directly affiliated with larger institutions, they embraced the same philanthropic spirit as the sponsored schools, religious missions, and service organizations. The impetus behind the founding of these independent centers was the same: providing work for local inhabitants and keeping alive the art of weaving. While some of the leaders started businesses within their home communities, most of them worked in mountain settlement schools before striking out on their own.

Some women—descendents of settlers of the Appalachian highlands—carried on the weaving heritage beyond family needs, selling commercially. The affiliated weaving centers discovered a few of these weavers and adopted them as icons and inspirations. The Walker sisters of Little Greenbrier, located within the Great Smoky Mountains National Park, continued life in their log cabin, rather like a living history display, long after the government bought up the land and moved the other residents out. One of the seven Walker sisters married and moved away, but the others—Margaret, Polly, Martha, Louisa, Sarah, and Hettie—refused to give up their mountain home. They sold illustrated poems, handweaving, and crafts to any tourists who made it to their door.[40]

At Valle Crucis in Watauga County of North Carolina, Allie Josephine Mast, usually referred to as either Josie Mast or Mrs. Finley Mast, descended from a long line of weavers and early pioneers of the area. "Like many another little girl, Mrs. Mast was taught to weave by her mother, and first made towels from flax grown in her father's own Watauga River meadows."[41]

Settlers moved into the Valle Crucis area during the late 1700s. A mid–nineteenth century Episcopalian missionary conferred the name of Valle Crucis to the small community that was situated at the intersection of two valleys. Even though the school he planned was not successful, the Episcopal Church sponsored the Mission School, which opened over fifty years later in 1902. Early in the twentieth century, the large Finley Mast frame house was opened to paying summer guests. Mrs. Mast fed her visitors plentifully—one guest commented, "Our party never sat down to a more bountiful or better prepared country dinner," and another recorded, "Once I counted 20 different dishes."[42]

The summer guests ordered weaving like the specimens they saw around the Mast farm. Josie appropriated a log cabin built in 1812 by an ancestor, David Mast, for her weaving production that was not far from the main house. She enlisted two of her sisters, Leona and Martha, to help in her weaving business. The 1934 survey conducted by the Women's Bureau indicated that Josie, then aged seventy-three, and one of her sisters, Aunt Lone, then seventy-nine, were still producing rugs, bags, and coverlets for sale. The researcher, Caroline Graves, added extensive notes to the interview form, commenting that Josie had exhibited her weaving at the Knoxville fairs of 1908 through 1910, and that First Lady Ellen Wilson had purchased a large rug for the White House. "These two sisters are far above the average mountain family. Have a lovely old home on a hard surface road."[43]

Josie Mast turned her family tradition of weaving into a business. She had skill both in weaving and in marketing. In 1930, she and two Tennessee women visited six north-

The Dougherty women ran a weaving business from a log cabin on their family property in Russellville, Tennessee.

ern cities, demonstrating weaving and spinning in large department stores on a promotional tour for the new Great Smoky Mountains National Park.[44]

In Tennessee's Greater Appalachian Valley at Russellville, the Dougherty sisters also continued the family weaving tradition by organizing the Shuttle Crafters. The Dougherty family traces back to Revolutionary War–era drummer boy Jean Adams, who settled in the fertile central valley between the ridges of the Appalachian Mountains. Among the family heirlooms is a draft of a weaving pattern called "Young Man's Fancy," dated April 16, 1833.[45]

From their large house and later from a reconstructed cabin nearby, Sarah Dougherty and her sister Ella Dougherty Wall coordinated several women who wove in their own homes. Their center, the Shuttle Crafters, joined the Southern Highland Handicraft Guild, which chose Russellville as its meeting site in 1934. The Guild held a reception "at the Dougherty home and at the log cabin work and exhibit rooms. Among the exhibits were shown examples of the weavings of five generations of the Dougherty family, the first being a bed sheet of linen spun and woven by Elizabeth Cable Mart, great-grandmother of Sarah Doughtery, and examples of coverlets woven by her grandmother, Betsy Flannery Adams, and her mother Leah Adams Doughtery, one by herself and one by her niece, Mary Doughtery."[46]

At the first Guild fair in 1948 in Gatlinburg, Sarah Doughtery took charge of the carding and spinning exhibit, arranging a display with "every step of the process of flax-growing through to the spun finished fabric." For visitors, Sarah also described dye plant cultivation and dye formulas that had been handed down through many generations of her family.[47]

Sarah Dougherty showed a flair for marketing, often dressing in period costumes while demonstrating flax spinning at sales events. Doris Ulmann's photograph of family matriarch Mrs. Leah Adams Dougherty appeared in Allen Eaton's book *Handicraft of the Southern Highlands*. In the picture, the elegantly dressed elderly woman is sitting very erect at her large old loom. When asked the circumstances of the photograph, the granddaughter, Mary Helms, replied, "Grandmother always wore black and lace," almost offended at the suggestion that the scene had been staged. The senior Dougherty, again dressed in black and lace, appeared in a film that Eaton made for the Department of Agriculture in the early 1940s. In the movie, her daughter Sarah shows an array of coverlet patterns woven under her direction.[48]

Unlike natives Mast and Dougherty, others came from outside the mountains to engage in crafts development. Both Wilmer Stone Viner and Clementine Douglas founded independent crafts centers after initial experiences in mountain settlement work. Both of the centers run by these women joined the Southern Highland Handicraft Guild as charter members, and the women assumed leadership roles within the organization.

Wilmer Stone grew up on a plantation in Louisiana, studied political science at Vassar College, and worked for six years at the Pine Mountain Settlement School in Kentucky. While working as a housemother, she developed a keen interest in natural dye plants and dye precesses, an interest the school's founder shared. Wilmer and her husband, H.E.S. Stone, later published *The Katherine Pettit Book of Vegetable Dyes*. In 1924 she opened the Weave Shop at Saluda, North Carolina. She continued her research on dyeing with native plants and created an extensive array of colors used in her weaving. Wilmer Stone Viner sold not only her own work in her shop, but also weaving done under her supervision by area women working in their own homes.[49]

For close to two decades, Clementine Douglas directed the Spinning Wheel, a weaving

During her tenure as art teacher in Kentucky, Clementine Douglas learned to weave and later opened her weaving business, The Spinning Wheel, just outside Asheville, North Carolina.

business and shop near Asheville, North Carolina. She began her mountain work teaching art during the summers in and around Smith, Kentucky. The Smith Community Life School tended to the educational, health, and social needs of part of Harlan County, and Douglas brought her art activities to many one-room schools. During her three summers in Kentucky, she became fascinated with the weaving she saw in homes, and found local people to teach her to weave and dye yarns with natural materials. In 1925 Douglas moved a log cabin to Beaver Lake, just outside of Asheville, to serve as her shop. An adjacent building combined her living quarters with a loom room where young women came to weave. Her biographer Bernice Stevens commented on Douglas's skill in designing for a public she knew: "Modern scarf and place-mats were based upon old drafts, changed and modernized by Clem's sure hand. But Clem did not draw all her weaving designs from the past. She studied the market, and designed things that contemporary-minded people would want to buy." In her later years, Douglas served as a U.S. government consultant in crafts development in Haiti, Hawaii, Costa Rica, and other countries.[50]

While most of the weaving centers started in new places in the mountains, which provided an untapped supply of women seeking employment, some began near the centers established already. In Gatlinburg, Tennessee, many shops sprouted up with the coming of the Great Smoky Mountains National Park. A steady stream of tourists, in ever-increasing numbers, flocked through Gatlinburg as the improved road led to the entrance of the largest national park in the eastern United States. Nella Cook worked in shipping for Arrowcraft and ran a weaving business with her sister. The Cooks lived just outside Gatlinburg and were educated at the Pi Beta Phi School. Nella dissolved her individual business when she took over the position of weaving designer and supervisor at Arrowcraft. Like Nella, most of the women who set up their own retail businesses learned the craft of weaving at Arrowcraft. They ventured out on their own because they felt they could make more money selling directly to consumers or providing items to other shops.[51]

The two most successful of the unaffiliated or independent weaving businesses—both in terms of sales and number of people employed—began in Berea, Kentucky. These businesses resulted from the inability of Berea College to respond gracefully to new ideas and work with people within the college community. Neither Matheny nor Churchill intended to develop businesses that competed directly with the Fireside Industries. They would have continued working within the college structure, but heavy-handed actions on the part of the college administration made it necessary for both to strike out on their own.

While espousing the common goals of the mountain revival weaving centers—providing employment and keeping alive the dying art of weaving—these independent establishments took radically different paths in pursuit of these objectives. Matheny followed the Fireside Industries model—weavers worked in their own homes and marketed through the women's network. Churchill brought workers into a central location and sold through established retail venues.

Part of Edith Matheny's success came from her generosity and warm personality. In 1926 Olive Dame Campbell wrote to President Hutchins of Berea College, informing him that she had asked Mrs. Matheny to be on the program of the March meeting of the Conference of Southern Mountain Workers. She also told him that she had invited Mrs. Ernberg to send an exhibit, even though she knew that the two women

> were not on good terms.... While I am on the subject, however, will you forgive me if I say that I have long felt that Berea ought to be the center to which all mountain workers could come for help in the line of fireside industries. So often I am asked where a worker can go to learn about weaving, dyeing etc.—go and pay for a regular course. The one person to whom I can refer for any help is Mrs. Matheny. It does seem as if one ought to be able to send such people directly to Berea's Weaving Department. I have done so in a number of instances in the past, and the people have ended up with Mrs. Matheny, because they could not get the help they needed from the Weaving Department.[52]

The college never committed the resources or restructured its operation to assume leadership in crafts education. Anna Ernberg held fast to her idea of apprentice learning and refused to tolerate anyone moving in on her turf. Hutchins had inherited the "weaving problem" between Matheny and Ernberg when he took over the presidency of Berea College from William Goodell Frost. Early in his tenure, Hutchins exchanged several letters with Frost in an attempt to understand the history and existing points of conflict in this long-standing antagonism.[53] Since the problems were rooted at the very core of Ernberg's beliefs, there was not any easy solution. Ernberg's feud with the administration endured, resurfacing in many forms over the years.

Edith Matheny first became fascinated with handweaving during a chance encounter with Edward Worst on a train trip through the South in 1911. Mrs. Matheny later described the event: "We were admiring the beautiful country known as the black belt, when our attention was directed to a small family within our car. The group was discussing an experience it had on this trip in recovering a stolen traveling bag. Mr. Matheny and I first became interested in the experience of the family, but soon became interested in the people themselves."[54]

The lost luggage led to other topics, with Worst talking of his manual training programs in the Chicago area public schools and especially of his love for handweaving.

The accidental meeting with Edward Worst and his wife and young daughter, and the ensuing discussion of weaving offered up an occupation to a woman much in need of one. In 1909 Edith's husband, Francis E. Matheny, shifted from teaching in the Berea Normal School to becoming dean of the Academy. In instituting a separate eating facility for the Academy, Dean Matheny "felt to give our dining room experiment the best chance to succeed we should board with our students to make them happy and give them care. In order to board with our students it was felt necessary that we send our one year old child to live with his grandparents in Ohio."[55] Berea College often exacted great sacrifices from the faculty and their families, placing the college mission above personal convenience or desire. Suddenly without her child and needing something to fill her time, Edith Matheny sought training from the Fireside Industries, developing her skills through home weaving projects.

Using several borrowed looms, Edith Matheny began offering weaving classes for Academy students in 1917. Fireside Industries weaving instruction occurred only in the context of production, with no emphasis on theory, design, or the variety of weave structures. The comprehensive Academy weaving class, which included plans that students "should weave furnishings for the Academy country home," counted as a credit towards graduation. As part of a Home Science course, students lived in a house and practiced home management skills. This house served as a model, both in architecture and interior furnishings, for an economical and comfortable mountain dwelling. As wife of the Dean, Edith Matheny received no pay for her services during the three years she taught in the Academy.[56]

Even though the Fireside Industries did not offer in-depth classes in weaving, Ernberg felt that Matheny was trespassing on her territory. In 1920 the Academy relinquished all weaving classes, and Dean Matheny conceded that "it is felt to be for the best we cheerfully discontinue our 'outlaw' and willingly give such aid as we may be able to the new plan." According to Edith Matheny, during its three years of operation, seventy-seven students took the Academy weaving class. Of that number, sixty-two were from the mountains, eleven from the North, three were faculty and one was a missionary.[57] Ultimately, Fireside Industries instituted actual weaving instruction through the Vocational Department, with other Berea divisions counting the class for credit.

After she left teaching, Edith Matheny wove household articles, collected old weaving patterns from area women, and experimented with natural dyes, never intending to start her own weaving business. Matheny credited Nellie, an eleven-year-old girl, with beginning the Matheny Weavers. Nellie came to Mrs. Matheny, declaring that she wanted to learn weaving and then to work for her. Matheny discouraged her because of her age, but the child persisted. Matheny finally relented, and Nellie proved an excellent student. Through Nellie, her mother and brother also took up the craft. Edith Matheny wrote about them: "Three years have gone; for the past two years this family has earned more than fifteen hundred dollars a year on hand looms in their home."[58] This would have been an exceptional family income for the mid-1920s, especially in eastern Kentucky.

Most of the Matheny Weavers wove in their own homes, but there was some central activity in the structure built for the business, adjacent to the Matheny home on Christmas Ridge outside of Berea. Ultimately fifty workers found employment in the weaving business during its most productive years. Reflecting many years later in a 1970 issue of *The Daily Record*, her hometown newspaper in Wooster, Ohio, Edith recalled that her weavers made between $42.50 and $80 a month at the time she left the business in 1936. She remarked with considerable pride that in their fifteen years of operation the weavers used the money earned to build a total of thirty-seven new homes.[59]

Allan Eaton referred to Edith Matheny as "an expert weaver, developing excellent color combinations and designs." Edward Worst, who originally inspired Edith to take up weaving, visited her often in Berea, where he researched local weaving and encouraged her efforts. In his 1926 book *How To Weave Linens*, the chapter "Old Kentucky Drafts" explained how he collected the designs: "The author was greatly assisted in obtaining these old drafts by Mrs. F.E. Matheny, who is probably the most successful worker in Kentucky among the girls and women of the hills."[60] The drafts consisted of five- and six-harness patterns in the one-shuttle weave structure Mary Megis Atwater would later call Bronson, after the New England weaver who had used it extensively.

A brochure from the Matheny Weavers offered coverlets in fifty patterns, as well as the possibility of reproducing colonial weaving from a photograph of an historic item provided by the purchaser. Table linens, curtains, rugs, dress goods, wool scarves and shawls, towels, dresser covers, cushions, handbags, and couch covers comprised the extensive list of items offered for sale. The final sentence of this brochure proclaimed, "This work is not connected with any church or school."[61] This brief sentence only hinted at the enmity felt by the college towards this upstart industry.

As in all such operations, marketing posed a major problem. Work was sold on consignment to colleges and churches, through private sales in homes, and through shops. While not a charter member of the Southern Highland Handicraft Guild, Matheny Weavers joined one year after the inception of the organization in 1931. In writing about her sales efforts, Matheny reflected the beliefs of many of the mountain crafts workers: "It is fair to say that up to the present much of the products have had in their sales the element of the need of the people in doing this work. While this is perfectly correct and the very best way of helping people, yet if the industry is to be permanent, the products must sell on their own merits and on no other basis."[62]

Berea College did not take this homegrown competition lightly. President Hutchins required that Mrs. Matheny's weaving business close as a condition of Dean Matheny's continued employment at the college.[63] Although other reasons also figured in the final decision, Francis Matheny resigned from the Academy in 1924, a few years after the President's ultimatum. He then actively participated in his wife's business.

In 1936, when the Mathenys decided to give up the weaving business and retire to Ohio, the *Berea Citizen* announced: "The College is to take over the entire properties of the industry, including all the equipment, the Matheny patterns, and the good will that has been built up by the Mathenys since the founding of the industry in 1921."[64] Edith's commercial venture had proven very successful, providing a living for her and her husband for over ten years. For her last year of operation, she estimated her gross sales at $80,000. Mrs. Matheny's employees gave her a surprise farewell party that they called a "Mother's Day Celebration," each wearing a red flower in honor of their "mother."[65]

Berea College seemed remarkably good at manufacturing competition for its own Fireside Industries. Where Matheny patterned her operation after the Fireside Industries, David

Weavers of the Southern Highlands

Churchill charted his own unique direction. Most aspects of Churchill Weavers have set them apart from the rest of the mountain weaving ventures, although the business still shared the basic goals of providing employment for local people and keeping weaving alive.

When William J. Hutchins assumed the presidency of the Berea College in 1920, he convinced D.C. Churchill, his boyhood neighbor from Oberlin, Ohio, to join him in the move to Kentucky. Churchill took over as physics professor and auto mechanics teacher with the prospect of developing an engineering department.

After growing up in an education-oriented family in Oberlin, D.C. Churchill received his higher education at the Massachusetts Institute of Technology. His father, a scientist, stressed the importance of understanding why things worked. At a young age, Carroll showed exceptional talents as an engineer and inventor, with many anticipating a brilliant scientific career for him. Instead, his mother and a young woman who later became his wife influenced him to dedicate his life to Christian service. As a Congregational missionary in India, he brought to bear all of his technical knowledge to found and administer the American Deccan Institute in Ahmednagar. The institute trained young men in marketable skills —among them carpentry, blacksmithing, and machine repair.[66]

While working in India, Churchill turned his attentions to an analysis of the handweaving industry, which employed more people than any other profession other than agriculture. In considering all aspects of the weaving trade, Churchill traveled to many countries, studying both household and small commercial handloom industries. He concluded that industrial mechanization and a consolidation of the domestic industries into factories would not benefit the workers. He proceeded on the premise that improving the efficiency of the small handloom operations offered the greatest flexibility as well as a fulfilling lifestyle for the weavers. Combining his careful analysis of weaving with his knowledge of mechanics, he redesigned the fly-shuttle loom, adding several innovations that allowed the weaver to significantly increase production. At the Industrial and Agricultural Exhibition of the India National Congress in Bombay in 1904, he won a gold medal in the open competition for his loom adaptations.[67]

Two years after the death of his first wife, Carroll married Anna Eleanor Franzen on May 5, 1914. This wedding took place in India, where Eleanor directed a boy's school. Born in Connecticut and the daughter of a Swedish Lutheran minister, Eleanor graduated from Wellesley College.[68] When World War I activities required a furlough from missionary work, D.C. and Eleanor Churchill returned to Ohio. Contrib-

Eleanor Churchill designed items for sale after her husband stopped teaching at Berea College; together they opened Churchill Weavers in Berea, Kentucky.

Other Mountain Weaving Centers

uting to the war effort, Churchill worked for the Garford Manufacturing Company of Elyria, Ohio, inventing retractable landing gear for airplanes, among other aviation improvements. The Churchill family had four children, two boys from the first marriage and two other children from the second. They all moved from Ohio to Kentucky in 1920, when Carroll became a teacher at Berea College.[69]

The final report that Churchill submitted to President Hutchins after two years of teaching at Berea detailed his frustrated attempts in dealing with students with little science background. He complained that his physics students preferred memorizing facts over attempting to understand basic concepts. He described his persistence in teaching: "I never willingly let a pupil go until he understands what I am driving at." Using his own tools, D.C. taught an automobile mechanics class in which he demanded so much of his students that only an ambitious few stuck with the course until the end.[70] Churchill's standards proved too high for most of the inadequately prepared mountain students.

When Churchill left Berea College in 1922, the official reason given was the failure of the school to commit resources for an engineering department. Although this was true, another complication factored very strongly into the decision. The Trustees Committee on Weaving issued a new policy: "We heartily endorse the attitude of the Prudential Committee in its refusal to permit any enterprise to be carried on by a commissioned worker for private profit during the school year. The manufacture of any product by a commissioned worker may be carried on only with the consent of the Prudential Committee. The Prudential Committee shall have authority to fix conditions of such manufacture, and the compensation if any." In this edict, the term "commissioned worker" was substituted for "Churchill" in the original draft version. The policy was intended to curtail Churchill's plans to manufacture the fly-shuttle loom he had designed during his service in India.[71] With this rather heavy-handed policy, the college both revoked the royalties paid to Anna Ernberg for her looms and forestalled Churchill's manufacture of his improved handloom. Even though the original employment agreement with D.C. Churchill permitted him to teach part-time while pursuing his scientific interests, in reality the college was not willing to tolerate divided loyalties.

At almost fifty years old, Carroll Churchill embarked on a new career. He never recorded his actual reasons for staying in Berea and starting a handloom weaving business. Confronted with the failure of teaching to offer sufficient scope for his talents, he could have sought

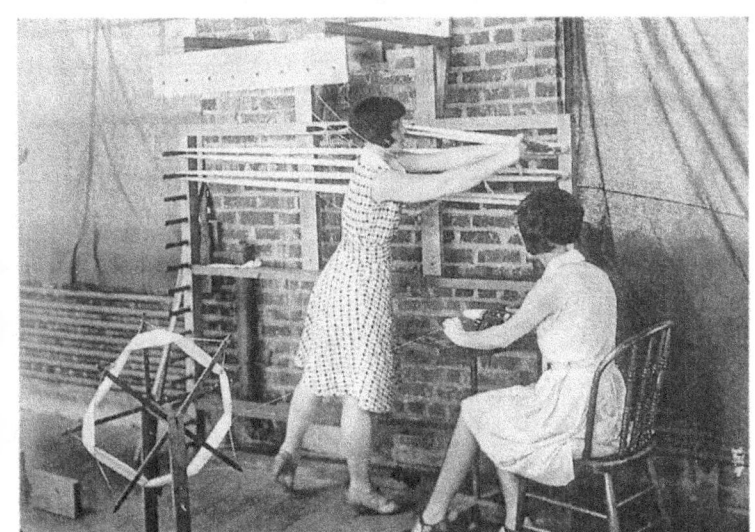

At Churchill Weavers, a woman winds a short warp for weaving samples.

employment in many industries where his scientific knowledge and problem-solving ability would have been welcome. No doubt Eleanor figured prominently into the decision to remain in Berea. Churchill had made a loom for his wife and she wove woolen scarves in their small college quarters.[72] She found personal enjoyment in weaving and showed a real flair for design. Weaving production combined the interests of both husband and wife. D.C. jumped from manufacturing looms for others to making looms for use in his own family industry. Drawing on their missionary background, they ascribed the benevolent desire of providing employment for this area of Kentucky as the rationale for their business venture.

Each of the Churchills soon developed a particular niche in the business. Given the opportunity, Eleanor exhibited remarkable management skills. D.C. evaluated jobs for efficiency, departmentalizing the weaving operations. Both men and women found employment as weavers, warpers, threaders, bobbin winders, mechanics, finishers, and packers. The weavers worked at fly-shuttle looms made by Carroll similar to the ones he had made in India. From his workroom in the basement of their building, D.C. worked incessantly, perfecting new devices to minimize stress on the worker while maximizing output in the many steps of the weaving process.[73]

Beginning with nothing in 1922, the business grew rapidly. From a very small shed on the edge of Berea, the Churchill Weavers building complex grew—as new wings were added, the center quickly became a large maze of activity. In 1948 the *Saturday Evening Post* romanticized Churchill's operations: "Here the flying shuttle of each loom follows the natural body rhythm of the weaver. Rhythm is the thing in hand weaving—rhythm not only of the hands but of the feet, for the loom has foot pedals much like those on a pipe organ. The whole coordinated series of movements becomes the pattern of the finished fabric. It is a process which leads readily into song, real mountain tunes, like Possum up a Gum Stump or Sugar in the Gourd." After twenty-five years, the business had expanded to a workforce of 150 people, grossing over $500,000 a year.[74] Most of the employees worked in the large rambling building, but some finished products at home.

In the early years of the business, the Churchills settled on lightweight woolens as their primary product. Scarves, baby blankets, and couch throws constituted the mainstays of their production line. In the late 1920s, Churchill Weavers offered yardage for women's clothing—some with border patterns—in wool, rayon, cotton, or combinations of fibers. In 1930 an elegantly produced 16-page catalog called "Churchill Hand-woven Covers" concentrated on the different types of blankets, throws, and baby blankets, some with added embroidered designs. A photograph of each piece accompanied a carefully worded description. One item, the Churchill "Kivverlet," depicted a small continuous over-shot pattern adapted from "the historic patterns of the Kentucky mountain weavers."[75] The large 75 x 108 inch spread, woven in one piece on a wide loom, avoided the sewing together of two sections, as was the case for traditional coverlets made on narrower looms.

By 1940 the Churchill Weavers no longer produced unfinished yardage lengths, concentrating instead on a wide selection of household fabrics, bed jackets, baby items, and men's neckties, which consistently sold well. Baby blankets persisted as a major item—the Churchills offered sixty different styles, not counting the color variations.[76] As a record of production, Eleanor saved one complete example of each item. Boxed separately with specific weaving information and colorways, these pieces stored in the basement are a design archive. Eleanor, who started out as the designer, later hired others for that position. However, she guided and approved all additions to the production line.[77]

From its start in 1922, Churchill Weavers grew very quickly, expanding operations and constructing additions to their building situated on the edge of Berea, Kentucky.

The Churchills marketed their weaving through gift shops and department stores. The fly-shuttle loom cut production time, enabling a competitive retail price, which included the seller's overhead. Churchill could deliver reliably and supply in sufficient quantities for larger outlets. Especially in the early years, Churchill Weavers did not try to compete in the placemat and finger towel market of Berea's Fireside Industries and the other mountain cooperatives. They sold through some gift shops with other weaving centers, but never through the women's club network. Churchill Weavers never relied entirely on the wholesale trade, but developed a lucrative retail catalog and operated their own stores. By the 1930s, Churchill owned retail shops in New York City, Los Angeles, Chicago, and, later, Detroit. In Berea, a sales area stood next to the production facilities where visitors could purchase woven goods at retail prices.

As Churchill grew, Berea College viewed this competition with concern. Anna Ernberg considered the Churchill establishment "a factory" and the products of the fly-shuttle loom not authentic handweaving. Ernberg described the pressure that the Fireside Industries felt in her 1926 final report to President Hutchins:

> One comparison will show the difference in cost of production. We are both weaving the kind of scarfs or shawls that women wear these days. On the Churchill looms a girl can make 40 to 50 in a day and she is paid ten cents apiece. One of our girls can make no more than one in two hours and it is only after a good deal of training that she can do it nice and evenly. She is paid 14 cents to 15 cents per hour. Their scarfs are, as a rule, more scanty than ours, but they sell them at as good a price as we ask and claim them to be handwoven.[78]

The college pulled its products from stores that also carried Churchill products. While the college may have felt that the two were competing for the same buyers, in reality each had found separate markets.

The criticism that the products from the fly-shuttle loom were not "handwoven" hurt both the Churchills' pride and the center's marketing strategies. They reacted to this accusation by including a detailed explanation of their weaving process in their brochures and by opening the Berea production facility to tours. In the early years of the business, Churchill protected operating secrets by not allowing others access to his innovations on the fly-shuttle loom. The tours took the public throughout their entire Berea establishment, presenting warp preparation, the actual weaving room, and the fabric finishing.[79] Cameras have never been allowed inside the weaving room.

The Southern Highland Handicraft Guild denied Churchill membership, but they were accepted into the Tennessee Valley Authority's Southern Highlanders. The two groups worked jointly on several promotional activities, and one of the Churchills' sons, Charles, who had joined the business, worked with the Guild on these projects. After several years of negotiations, in 1951 Southern Highlanders merged with the Southern Highlands Handicraft Guild, keeping the name of the latter and absorbing all their members. Even when the Southern Highland Handicraft Guild honored Eleanor Churchill with a life membership, she never quite forgave the earlier slight.[80]

The *Saturday Evening Post* article about the Churchill operation assessed the marketing of handweaving: "Do-gooders peddled the scanty output in cities much as they would solicit charitable contributions, painting a quaint picture of grandmaw weaving away in her backwoods shack. To Churchill, all this was sentimental nonsense. Unless hill people could sell their weaving on its merits and make a full-time living out of it, the art was doomed."[81] This harsh criticism pointed out the weakness of selling through the women's network, which avoided direct competition both in the art and commercial textile markets. To support the higher prices of handmade work, the mountain weaving centers regularly cited the social value of their work in weaving development.

This did not apply to the Churchills, who succeeded in building a specialty handweaving business that could hold its own in a world in which most textiles came from machines in factories. Churchill stands alone in many aspects of its operation. In Appalachian crafts development, women usually dominated, but at Churchill Weavers, D.C. and Eleanor shared management of equally important aspects of the business. Churchill chose to work with wool, while most other centers preferred cotton or linen. Workers came into a central location with departmentalized tasks; in other mountain areas, one weaver carried out all aspects of making the item, working alone in her home. Churchill Weavers followed a more standard business model than any of the mountain weaving centers.

8

weavers and managers

Weavers

Only women wove for the mountain weaving centers. The actual number of weavers employed at weaving centers was not large, because the social settlement workers established schools in small communities where they perceived need, rather than in the larger established towns of Appalachia. Only around one hundred community women worked at any one time for Berea or Arrowcraft, although their lists of potential weavers contained two to three times that number. At Berea, students needing campus jobs swelled the weaving ranks. Penland's weavers increased to sixty-four by 1930, but declined after that date. The majority of the other centers remained small operations, most with a dozen or fewer weavers.

Many of the Arrowcraft weavers lived some distance from the Pi Beta Phi School in Gatlinburg and transported supplies to weave in their homes.

An Arrowcraft record of production items over a nine-year period includes minimal information about the weavers. Josie Ogle, who batted out hundreds of Bouquet finger towels, appears in a list detailing the yearly earnings of over three hundred weavers. It gives Josie's wages for each of the nine years, totaling $896.79. The word "baby," written beside the 1937 figure, explains that year's low income. Under Arrowcraft's policy, women could not weave from two months before a baby's birth to two months after. Josie only regained her earlier weaving capacity in 1940. The ledger also notes an illness in 1944, and a star with "son" indicates that one of her children was in the military in 1945. In Winogene Redding's cryptic rating system, Josie Ogle received the letters "GS" beside her name, which the key defined as "Good, Slow"—with no indication whether "slow" meant a slow weaver or slow to deliver finished goods to the center.[1]

Scattered in the hills around Gatlinburg, the Arrowcraft weavers represented a cross-section of community women, coming from all of the major families in the area. Starting to weave as young women, many continued throughout their childrearing years. While many multi-generational families wove for Arrowcraft, the Carter family set the record, with sixteen employed family members.[2] Many weavers claimed kin through large extended families or through marriage. Initially women learned weaving from Winogene Redding, but later they acquired skills either at the Pi Beta Phi School or while assisting their mothers and other relatives. Many girls who became weavers received a decent basic education at the Pi Beta Phi School, and most of them considered their role in life to be a wife and mother. They wove not for recreation but for money.

As part of Bertha Nienburg's study of mountain crafts for the Women's Bureau of the Department of Labor, researchers gathered information about the families as well as crafts activities. During three days in June 1934, an interviewer contacted nineteen Gatlinburg households encompassing over thirty craft workers; fifteen of the families produced only weaving. Four entire families, including both parents and children, were engaged in other crafts, such as making baskets, fans, brooms, and chairs. Two-thirds of the households consisted of five to nine people, often including extended family members aside from children. While all of the families raised vegetables, over half raised almost all of their own food, including meat, eggs, and milk. All bought staples, defined as sugar, flour, lard, and coffee. Only one man, a barber, had full-time employment, while the rest worked for wages at part-time or odd jobs.[3]

Nienburg reported the average age among Arrowcraft weavers as early thirties. Weaving part-time since leaving high school, each weaver made around $100 a year. In three of the fifteen weaving households, one or more grown daughters also worked for Arrowcraft. The names of Clabo, McCarter, Ogle, and Reagan appeared several times, representing some of Gatlinburg's strongest extended families, with five Ogle households yielding nine weavers.

Because the population density was much lower around Penland than it was around Gatlinburg, Penland never employed as many weavers as Arrowcraft. Penland area men farmed, mined feldspar and mica, or cut timber. Women raised children and attended to household, garden, and farm chores. The Nienburg sample of thirteen Penland households showed that they provided for most of their food, with only one-third adding some meat to purchased staples. The study confirmed a similar pattern of food self-sufficiency for workers in other mountain centers.

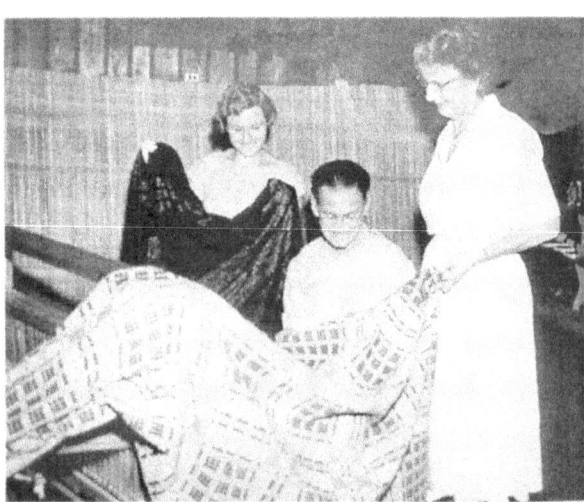

Winogene Redding, on the right, inspects a coverlet with Jean Carter, left, who had 16 family members weaving for Arrowcraft, and Izora Keener, still weaving at the age of seventy-eight. Keener was one of the first weavers recruited by Gene.

Weavers and Managers

In the southern mountain states, women wove because they could make "cash money," in what the Nienburg report confirmed as a subsistence economy. From the outset, both programs at Allanstand and Berea demonstrated that people outside the mountains would buy weaving. Most later weaving programs modeled themselves on these early centers, where makers received immediate payment and items were then resold to distant consumers. Even though independent entrepreneurs existed, most weavers worked for centers that coordinated activities and marketed the products. Reaching the urban middle-class customer would have been impossible for the isolated mountain weaver. The centers assumed the chores of making connections with potential buyers and handling the details of selling.

The weavers would have readily engaged in other occupations if choices had been available. One Nienburg survey question asked about work preferences, with most respondents indicating they would be happy to do anything. The Women's Bureau neglected to suggest other possible job opportunities. When asked if any family members would be willing to travel to a central location for work, most replied "none," but a few indicated that possibly a daughter or sister might be interested. Even when the Department of Labor representative hinted by her questions that other work would possibly be available at a central job site, most weavers expressed a desire to stay at home.

In the remote areas of the mountains, very few jobs that paid wages in currency presented themselves for either men or women. Even though the dollar amounts earned by women seem small, the money contributed significantly to each family's economy. According to the 1933 *Chattanooga Times:* "Workers Who Earned $86 a Year on Farm Now Paid Up to $540 for Weaving—Miss Morgan Founder." In a talk to the Tennessee Valley Authority, Lucy Morgan spoke about increasing economic opportunities in the TVA service area: "The most any weaver has made in one month was $104, the fruits of Mrs. Sadie Sparks' loom."[4] Morgan naturally focused on the most industrious weaver. The other two dozen Penland weavers only made between $50 and $150 per year.[5]

A Penland weaver works on a panel for an overshot coverlet.

The weavers at Arrowcraft, Penland, and most of the other weaving centers worked for piece rate, receiving a predetermined amount for each item completed. The amount earned differed greatly from person to person, depending entirely on how much work each weaver delivered to the center. The centers never required that weavers produce a set amount as a condition of continued employment. During the period around 1940, most Arrowcraft weavers earned from $50 to $200 per year.[6] Izora Keener, a top producer, consistently made $300 a year; her best year was 1940, when she made $459.26. A Women's Bureau interviewer who talked with Izora reported that the family raised most of their own food and had no other source of cash income. At the time of the interview in 1934, the forty-six-year-old Izora had woven for fourteen years. Her younger sister, living in the same household, had also woven for Arrowcraft for eight years.

During the early years of Crossnore's Smith-Hughes funded weaving classes, weavers reported earning 10 cents an hour for their labors.[7] Before the rebuilding of the Weaving Room after a fire, which precipitated the centralization of all weaving activity, home workers worked piece rate instead of an hourly rate. The payment for weaving sounds incredibly small—until one compares it to the other wages offered in the area. For example, one family returned to the mother's home in Crossnore during the Depression after her husband lost his job in the North. The father later told his children that he had never worked as hard in his life, before or since, as he did for the 12 cents an hour made laying rock during the construction of the Blue Ridge Parkway.[8]

By the 1940s, the federal government pressed Southern Highland Handicraft Guild members to comply with the new mandated minimum wage. The law regulating wages passed in the late thirties, but enforcement in marginal sectors like crafts lagged until after World War II. As an authority on crafts development, Allen Eaton wrote to the Department of Labor requesting an exemption for all rural handicrafts, arguing that paying a higher wage would hinder the social service objectives of the work. George Bent of Berea College, then secretary-treasurer of the Guild, summarized the moral conflict that many members felt: "Here we are supposedly a philanthropic organization working for the betterment and improvement of the mountains and then when the government comes along with a law that tries to make Wage & Hour rates decent it would be amazing if the Guild and its members who profess such high motives were the very first ones to oppose its application to themselves."[9]

The Guild failed to obtain an exemption from the wage laws for home-produced craftwork. In 1946 and 1947, under the direction of weaving supervisor Meta Schattschneider, Arrowcraft conducted a study of time and costs, which proved to government inspectors that their workers really earned more than the minimum wage. Since weavers were paid by the piece, it was necessary to calculate all the little bits of time required for preparation, the actual time spent throwing the shuttle, and finishing to ready the item for sale. Setting up the loom took many hours, but once done that could be amortized over the entire warp. Weavers kept detailed accounts of time spent winding the warp, tying on or threading, beaming, weaving, winding bobbins, and finishing. Arrowcraft calculated an hourly rate for each of the forty weavers in the study. The pay ranged from 24 cents to 72 cents, with most weavers averaging around 50 cents per hour. Before this study, Arrowcraft actually had raised its rates once Winogene Redding calculated the average hourly wage based on production time, which had indicated lower wages than the government recommended.[10] In 1945, when the government imposed a 40 cents per hour minimum wage, Arrowcraft again increased the piece rate to all weavers, bringing the lower-paid workers above the minimum wage.

The Arrowcraft wage study revealed a wide range of payment rates for comparable work. When setting the piece rate, the supervisor considered the degree of weaving difficulty for each item. While she might have erred in her determination of time required, comparison of seven different women weaving the exact same item, the Whig Rose Doily, showed a wide variation in the time spent and, therefore, in wages. Their hourly rate of pay varied from 24 cents to 51 cents, with most of the seven making around 45 cents. The speed of the weaver of course proved the differentiating factor, with faster weavers accomplishing more and thus able to earn more money.

The Women's Bureau of the Department of Labor advocated centralized craft production because compliance with laws could be more accurately monitored. At Crossnore, the one Appalachian weaving center where weavers worked at a central location, weavers first received an hourly wage, later switching to piece rate. Neinburg envisioned a regimented workforce, not the flexibility of Crossnore's Weaving Room, where weavers determined their own hours, adjusting weaving time to allow for their other responsibilities.

At Penland, Arrowcraft, Berea, and the other mountain centers, the weavers worked part-time, meaning both part of the week and part of the year. Childrearing and household duties dictated how much time women could devote to weaving. Appalachian Craft Revival leaders desired to increase the income of families, not restructure the household or the agrarian economy. The name "Fireside Industries" shared by many of these centers implied the home-based nature of the work. Both managers and weavers assumed that home and family came first.

In 1948 Beulah Moore made $373.97 weaving for Arrowcraft.

At the early weaving centers, the weavers themselves determined the amount of time they spent weaving, until lower product demand during the Depression forced rationing of work. As Arrowcraft distributed available work among weavers, Redding explained differences in the 1936 pay figures: "In dividing the work, we tried to give the neediest women the most work, that is why the higher brackets have less weavers as it was a sliding scale downward." She indicated that some women still exhibited discretion in choosing work hours: "The lower figures included those who had babies and the ones who did not want to weave steadily."[11]

In 1944 two young women, both with husbands in the army, requested weaving assignments from Redding, with one taking work and the other finally refusing. "She finally decided against taking the pot holders (it is their decision and not mine). She said she was too upset to weave." By the mid-1940s, demand for Arrowcraft weaving had increased enough to provide ample work for those who desired it. At Arrowcraft before World War II, one-third of the weavers made under $100 per year, with that portion increasing to half during the war. Of the 138 weavers in 1944, twenty-eight women took home over $300, while half of the weavers earned under $100. The large number of women in the lower group was a result of choice rather than lack of work, as confirmed by the ample number of high earners.[12]

The part-time nature of the work included choosing the part of the year for employment, with most Arrowcraft weavers drawing checks in four to nine months. Redding observed the ebb and flow of the year: "There are three seasons when the women are not able to weave so much, the planting season in the spring, corn-hoeing time in the late spring, canning season during the summer and the tobacco season in the fall."[13] Certainly the weaving manager also determined some of the part-time nature of the work, because sales of goods fluctuated with heavy demand during the summer tourist season, before the annual Pi Beta Phi convention, and alumnae bazaars around Christmas.

Arrowcraft alone among the weaving centers enforced a pregnancy rule restricting weaving activity. Redding explained her policy to Pi Beta Phi members: "My youngest weaver of 19 years who makes pot holders came in yesterday to tell me that she had just been to the doctor and paid him in advance for the baby, her first, that will soon be coming. She also wanted to tell me that he said she could weave some more before she gets into my ruling that no woman can weave two months previous or two months after the birth of a baby."[14] In Arrowcraft's records of individual wages, "baby" entered beside a figure explained the marked dip in yearly earnings.

At Penland product demand regulated the part-time work. In the early 1930s, about half of the forty weavers worked only one to three months, while the other half collected pay over a four- to six-month period.[15] Very few Penland weavers worked between January and May. When Gertrude Saylor and her husband's mother and sisters found they could weave in the winter, when their husbands left home for logging jobs. They requested weaving assignments from Lucy Morgan and agreed to deferred payment, receiving their wages when summer brought the return of tourist sales.[16]

Weaving met local needs most effectively as piecework done in the home. As in other home-based industries, the weavers bore many of the production costs, supplying space, incurring costs of heat and light, and traveling to the center to deliver finished goods. The Women's Bureau of the Department of Labor advocated hourly rates and campaigned vigorously against the piece-rate system, which could not be accurately measured or enforced when production took place in workers' homes. The Bureau documented poor home working conditions in cities among immigrant women and collected information on mountain craft workers in 1933 and 1934. In appendixes to her final report, Nienburg detailed abuses in the candlewicking and tufted bedspread and quilting industries. She only then generalized about the desirability of centralizing production for other crafts in the mountains.[17]

The supporters of the mountain weaving centers reflected the positive side of home production, although they did romanticize the situation a bit. "She [Edith Matheny] has established a hand-loom industry not in a central plant but in the homes of the people, where mothers and daughters may work by their own firesides in winter and under their own shade tree in summer; where they make their own labor schedules, and are able to look after the small children, raise chickens and fresh vegetables, and have opportunity to share in the social

Weavers and Managers

affairs of the neighborhood."[18] Even though the Women's Bureau of the Department of Labor considered work in the home to be largely negative, the weavers themselves preferred working on their own schedules at home. When the Bureau's interviewers questioned the weavers about working at a central location, less than half answered that someone in the family would be available to work outside the home.[19] The survey forms indicated a daughter's availability for such work—but not a housewife's. Additional costs for space and light appeared minimal when balanced against the very real expenses of acceptable work clothing, childcare, daily travel, and the other incidental costs of working in a distant location. Even delivering finished goods and picking up supplies, which the Women's Bureau saw in a negative light, turned into a social time for visiting friends and having refreshments.

After the establishment of the Great Smoky Mountains National Park provided other work options in Gatlinburg, a substantial number of women continued to weave for Arrowcraft. They gave three reasons for this. They liked working at home, they enjoyed the freedom to decide how much they wanted to work and when, and they did not want direct supervision by a boss. They felt that they possessed greater choice and dignity in working at home and they preferred weaving to other available jobs, such as waiting tables or clerking in stores. Their only complaint was that Arrowcraft failed to provide them with as much work as they desired.[20]

The ability to earn money meant added respect for women's labor, as was observed at Penland in 1925: "Now when the mother, by her weaving, receives checks varying from four to forty dollars, her time is too valuable to be spent in hoeing corn, and her husband, even though he 'can get no one else to do it so fast as she can,' looks for a man or a boy to take her place in the cornfield."[21] When given the choice, women preferred working inside at the loom rather than outside in the fields.

Women felt more self-worth as they earned money and controlled its distribution. When asked about her earnings, Arrowcraft weaver Cora Morton replied, "The money I made went

Chapel Hill photographer Bayard Wootten had the Penland Weavers pose in the Weaving Cabin for an illustration used in a 1928 brochure.

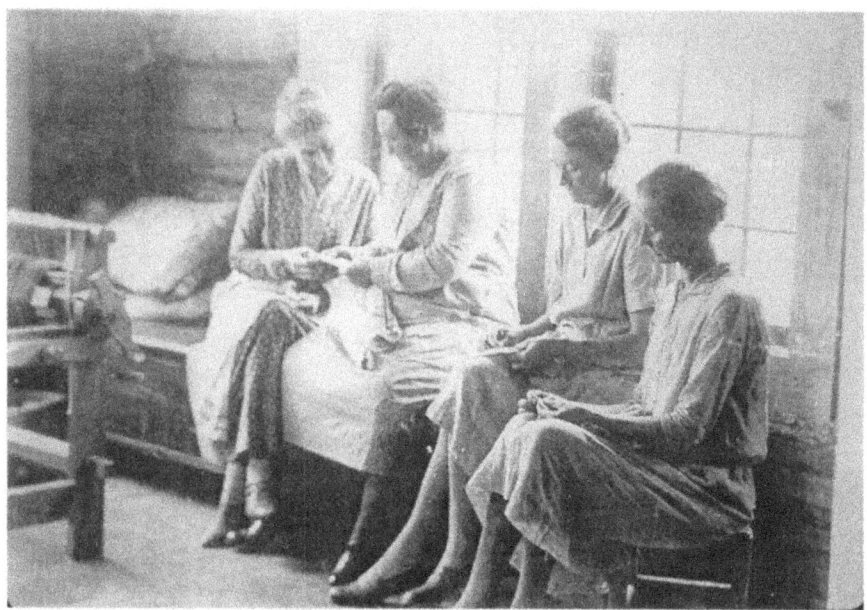

to buy clothes or something for the house. I spent it wisely."²² Shortly after assuming her duties in Berea, Anna Ernberg enumerated the benefits of weaving, ending with: "And how much will it mean for the mother of a family to have a resource of her very own for securing the money she so much desires for home comforts or the education of her children!" Weavers used their money for educating their children, for school clothes, or for luxury household items. "We have noticed in the past two years," wrote Winogene Redding, "that the children from these homes come to school better dressed; the homes are gradually becoming better furnished, especially in the matter of Victrolas; the women themselves wear winter coats instead of their sweaters; they have more pleasure than before because they now have money for an occasional trip to Sevierville and Knoxville." In addition to Victrolas, the weavers purchased gas-powered washing machines, which sat outside on their front porches, where neighbors could admire these new status symbols as they passed.²³

In a small booklet describing the growth of the Penland Weavers and Potters, Bonnie Willis Ford began with a tour of the weavers: "The first home we shall visit is a home which has been tastefully furnished largely with money which has been paid out of the treasury of the Penland Weavers and Potters. We find several children who have gone to school on money which they themselves have earned from the weaving or allied crafts. In the next we find that a daughter has gone to college, partly on money which her mother earned by work at the loom." As the journey continued into the Rabbit Hop community, "We would find there that one woman had bought herself some new false teeth, another a range stove, another a victrola, and so on all down the line of necessities and comforts."²⁴

The earnings of women went for quality-of-life purchases or children's educational expenses, while the men continued supporting basic family needs. The tales of how women spent their money never mentioned farm expenses, such as purchase of animals or equipment. Although one weaver from Penland told with pride of payments she had made on land, such expenditures

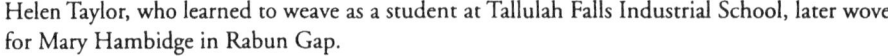

Helen Taylor, who learned to weave as a student at Tallulah Falls Industrial School, later wove for Mary Hambidge in Rabun Gap.

were rare. In an exception to the usual ways of spending money, the Mathenys encouraged their weavers to build homes, seeing "37 new homes during their tenure of service." Edith Matheny observed, "The husband can support the family, but cannot support the family and build a new home too. So, by the aid of the loom the new home is made possible."[25]

Among many students at Berea and other schools with labor programs, weaving served as a means of securing an education. Most Berea Fireside weavers wove only while in school. Students returning to their communities did not start home industries, as Candace Wheeler and Anna Ernberg had predicted. However, a few former students continued to weave as a hobby, making things for their own use rather than for sale. Lois Mason Whitfield learned to weave while attending high school at Tallulah Falls. She pursued a career in nursing, and in her leisure time wove an array of functional items for her home, family, and friends.[26]

At all the weaving centers, most workers learned their craft skills from a weaving supervisor. The Appalachian Craft Revival taught weaving for economic development to the grandchildren of people who had originally practiced it as a household art. Very few weavers came from families that had passed down weaving skills to younger generations. If an older weaver lived in an area, she usually served as a model or inspiration, rather than as a teacher. Since the weaver's instruction consisted of basic skills needed to complete an assigned task, very few weavers possessed comprehensive knowledge of weaving theory and design. Weavers started out with simple items, later acquiring more advanced techniques as they became required for more complex projects.

Anna Ernberg believed in the apprentice model of instruction, so Berea students learned to weave only as part of their labor experience. Ernberg strongly resisted teaching weaving in a classroom setting separate from the Fireside Industries, only relenting after Mrs. Matheny began weaving instruction in the Academy. In the early years of their centers, both Winogene Redding and Lucy Morgan traveled to weavers' homes offering basic instruction and introducing new skills when needed. At Penland, the Pi Beta Phi School, and Crossnore the state-administered federal Smith-Hughes vocational education programs supported weaving instruction. The Pi Phis and Crossnore offered weaving as a school subject, with many girls going on to work in community programs after graduation. Lucy Morgan received Smith-Hughes funds for her extension work with weavers and for the yearly Weaving Institute, which grew into the Penland School of Crafts. One of the conditions for receiving state funds was the introduction of tuition waivers for North Carolina residents. Aunt Newbie, the Weaving Room manager at Crossnore, regularly attended the Weaving Institute at Penland under this provision.

From Anna Ernberg to Mary Hambidge, the promoters of weaving claimed that the craft would be a creative outlet for women. Steeped in the tenets of the Arts and Crafts Movement, the leaders of the Appalachian Craft Revival believed the words of William Morris, who prophesied the coming of "a new art, a glorious art, made by the people for the people, as a happiness to the maker and the user."[27] In this spirit, Anna Ernberg declared, "An artistic product going forward in the family loom will be an educating and uplifting influence in the household." An early Penland brochure pointed out the benefits of crafts to the maker: "The revival of Colonial weaving . . . makes it possible for the people to stay in the mountain home with its high ideals, and to do there work which brings economic independence while at the same time satisfying a natural artistic taste and an inborn creative impulse." Mary Hambidge professed that "every American home" should contain a loom. "Weaving . . . is the perfect craft for women as it can be done in the home, gives creative ability full rein and results in something both beautiful and useful."[28] Even though they expressed the aesthetic benefits of weaving differently, they all agreed that the weaver did experience creative gratification in her labor.

Weaving can be a creative act, involving many unique choices. However, in production weaving, where a designer decides all the creative elements, the actual craftsperson replicates items rather than engaging in the creative process herself. For the weaving centers, a weaver produced objects identical to the sample given her by the weaving supervisor. Although reproduction might have required great skill, she neither improvised on the design nor included any of her own ideas in the final product. Even though the weaver might have experienced satisfaction in making beautiful things, this fulfillment was very different from a truly creative experience. While some might assume the maker to be engaged in creation because the items grew from the actions of her hands, when another person entirely directs the process, creativity is separated from creation. Only the designer reaped the rewards of creativity, since she made the dozens of choices required in developing a unique item, not the actual maker of each piece of production work.

While weavers might not have felt the joys of creativity, they felt the satisfaction of doing a job well. Even before the coming of the settlement workers, weavers valued craftsmanship. In *The Land of Saddle-Bags,* James Watt Raine related the story of a woman on her deathbed confiding to a neighbor: "I bin a-watchin' ye and I've noted that your perfession and your practice hits, so I'm going to give ye my six children." In a footnote, Raine explained that the term "hit" came from weaving, describing coverlet patterns matching at the central seam when woven in two panels.[29] Earlier in his 1904 report, Max West commented on the revival weaving not being up to previous craftsmanship standards and referred to Berea College's undertaking of "a revival in the quality as well as the quantity of the work."[30] Loosely based on fact, Lucy Furman's fictional account *The Glass Window* related the campaign of one woman for the installation of a window in her dark cabin. In the book Aunt Ailsie sets about convincing her husband that she needs extra light for her weaving because her eyes have failed over the years. With the "quare women" at the settlement school willing to pay $10 for a coverlet, the weaving gained in importance.[31]

Over the years that the Craft Revival weavers were in operation, working on successively more difficult projects, they developed excellent technical skills. They delivered straight edges with consistent beat, maintained the shuttle sequence in complex weaves, and followed patterns precisely. The weavers found gratification in the many points of fine craftsmanship exhibited in their work. Alice Green, who wove linen tablecloths for Penland, explained in detail the difficulties of working with linen and the hot hard pressing needed to finish the cloth. At the same time, she expressed satisfaction in a job well done and her pleasure in producing a beautiful item.[32] Many production weavers spoke with pride about both their technical skills and the beauty of their work. They did appreciate the aesthetic qualities of their production. While weavers experienced satisfaction from making distinctive and well-executed work, this differs from the joys of creative decision-making.

The weavers in larger centers like Arrowcraft and Penland determined the type of work they received. Most weavers specialized in a single item, such as Whig Rose placemats or Bouquet towels, but some preferred variety and were willing to accept any assignment from the manager. While some weavers felt they made more money batting out plain-weave placemats quickly, others preferred the slower and more complex pattern weaving, for which they received a larger piece rate per item. Each weaver's skill greatly determined the type of assignments she received. Beginning weavers started with simple plain weave items like potholders, and over time advanced to patterned articles like inlaid towels or overshot bags.

Nienburg's interviewers asked weavers whether they made articles for their own homes. Arrowcraft and Penland weavers overwhelmingly answered that they did weave items for themselves. The Gatlinburg group mentioned weaving curtains, while those from Penland wove garments. When she was a young woman, Crossnore weaver Ossie Phillips wove lavender material for a suit, which she constructed using only hand sewing, because she lacked access to a sewing machine. Ossie also related the story of a skirt she wore to a D.A.R. meeting where she sold Crossnore's handicrafts. When asked if the skirt came from Guatemala, Ossie replied with pride that she had woven it herself.[33]

The weavers from the mountain centers owned very few pieces of their own weaving because they could not afford them. Some weavers bought back their work from the center or kept seconds that did not meet size or quality standards. While they supplied the labor themselves, the cost of materials put most items beyond the budgets of the weavers. Even though merchandising sometimes showed placemats adorning tables in mountain cabins, the weavers themselves rarely used them.

Some weavers obtained celebrity status as a result of marketing publicity generated by the centers. Aunt Lizzie Reagan of Gatlinburg, with her deeply lined face and her attire from a past era, attracted the camera of noted photographer Lewis Hine during his 1933 visit to Gatlinburg. She also appeared as one of the few craftspeople named in the Southern Highlands issue of *House and Garden,* which appeared in June 1942.[34] Aunt Lizzie, who came to the Pi Phis as housekeeper and general informant on local customs and community kinship lines, wove on an old barn loom set up for her in a school residence.

Emma Conley of Penland also enjoyed star status, as in long dress and sunbonnet she demonstrated spinning or natural dyeing at the fairs of the Southern Highland Handicraft Guild. Publicity often focused on older women because they were respected figures in their communities, and because by their presence they formed the bridge between the self-sufficient mountain tradition and the current weavers. The centers seemed oblivious of the false impression they were sending when they featured their more revered members rather than the younger women, who after all were the majority of their workers. Only schools promoting student labor programs, such as Berea College, showed young people at looms, stressing that weaving enabled them to further their education.

Emma Conley, whose family settled along Conley Ridge adjacent to the Penland School, often demonstrated spinning at the Southern Highland Handicraft Guild fairs.

Managers

Managers of Appalachian Craft Revival weaving centers knew how to weave. A person knowledgeable about the craft would either start the industry or assume management of the operation, organizing and directing all aspects of weaving production. The supervisor, when asking a weaver to perform tasks, knew exactly the difficulty of the request. Weavers are, by nature, organizers; the craft demands attention to detail, an ability to see patterns, and deferment of gratification until a rigidly defined series of small actions add up to a whole greater than the sum of its parts. The same abilities required for weaving contribute to good management skills.

Clementine Douglas, Sarah Dougherty, Mary Hambidge, Edith Matheny, and Wilmer Stone Viner first learned to weave, then later developed their personal interest into businesses. Lucy Morgan, who envisioned weaving at Penland, sought instruction and acquired necessary skills in Berea, from both Anna Ernberg and Edith Matheny. Once schools decided to promote weaving seriously, they hired knowledgeable weavers to oversee the operation. Berea College hired Hettie Wright Graham, and later Anna Ernberg, to manage the Fireside Industries. When craft sales proved promising in Gatlinburg, Pi Beta Phi alumnae found Winogene Redding in Boston to direct the work.

Most weaving managers arrived in the mountains as part of the settlement movement, planning to work a year or two before returning home and taking up roles as wives and mothers. Winogene Redding, who thought she would give the Pi Phis a year of her life, ended up devoting her career to the cause of mountain crafts development. Anna Ernberg settled in New York City after completing her education in Sweden. When Fireside Industries considered her for the position of director, she wrote to a friend: "I can't tell you how much I would enjoy going there. I am so sick and tired of this terrible big city with all its rush and bustle and noise so a small place like Berea would seem almost like heaven to me."[35]

Lucy Morgan wove the curtains for her small apartment in the Pines. She used Summer and Winter weave structures and had a row of pine trees along the bottom of them.

Several weaving managers grew up in the South. Although Mary Hambidge had been born in Georgia, she lived in the New York area, first visiting the mountains after Jay's death in pursuit of inexpensive living. Although born in Louisiana and educated at Vassar, Wilmer Stone spent her girlhood summers in Saluda, North Carolina. She later chose to situate her weaving business near her summer home, following a stint at Pine Mountain Settlement School. Lucy Morgan, raised in far western North Carolina, described herself as follows: "I'm a pure blood unadulterated mountain gal."[36] She went to college in Michigan before finding her way back to the North Carolina mountains, although farther to the northeast of her family home. Lillie Johnson, a Crossnore resident, learned to weave in the program she later directed for most of her adult life. At Shuttle Crafters in Russellville, Sarah Dougherty continued the long line of weavers in her Tennessee family and provided jobs for her community.

No single personality type defined weaving managers: Ernberg was stern and intense, Redding definite and forthright, Morgan effusive and concerned, Hambidge flamboyant and visionary. However different they were from one another, these women shared the traits of perseverance, dedication to purpose, and a large capacity for hard work. None of them conformed to the female stereotypes of the time in which they lived. All of them fashioned their own livelihood out of their abiding interest in weaving, during an era when most middle-class women looked to men for support. Either they chose not to marry or shed a spouse early on, giving them the freedom to pursue their interests.

Not all supervisors possessed the same competence in weaving. Ernberg received her comprehensive knowledge of weaving in her native Sweden, developing proficiency in both drawloom and pattern weaving. Redding studied art and weaving in Boston, which made her an effective designer. Both managers of the two largest centers, acquired their training before coming to the mountains. Lucy Morgan's desire to learn weaving took her first to Berea and then to Chicago, where she sought additional skills in Edward Worst's studio. She began the Penland Weaving Institute in pursuit of more weaving knowledge for herself and her weavers. Mary Hambidge, who learned basic weaving in Greece, showed no interest in the many different types of pattern weaving, concentrating instead on color and texture.

Some early promoters of weaving sought instruction from mountain women. Frances Goodrich told of discovering weavers tucked back in the hills around Brittain's Cove and asking them to share their skills.[37] May Stone and Katherine Pettit learned to weave while operating their summer camps in eastern Kentucky. The Pettit journals reveal her admiration of coverlets: "Many of the women still spin and weave coverlids, blankets and cloth for their own use. We always asked to see these things and they take great pride in showing them." Later she recorded, "We have been looking forward for a chance to learn to weave for three years." When Katherine and May found a woman to teach them the mysteries of the loom, they eagerly took to the work: "Weaving has not stopped today, first one and then the other at the loom and Mrs. Stacy thinks it a marvel that we have woven a whole yard."[38]

Clementine Douglas collected coverlets and knowledge of woven textiles during her summer teaching in Smith, Kentucky. During the summers of 1920 and 1921, she set up a loom in her cottage and sought instruction: "Women who had woven in earlier days gave generously of their knowledge, and together they and Clem revived the craft of their grandmother's time."[39] Both Sarah Dougherty and Josie Mast came from families of weavers where skills were passed down over many generations.

All the weaving managers designed items for production, with some of them exhibiting more aptitude than others. Winogene Redding designed a variety of different items with more consistent quality than any other center supervisor. Designing for production weaving involved a blend of aesthetics and function. Redding related the difficulty in designing for a specific purpose: "One of the hardest problems I ever faced was when they told me to design a pot-holder for quantity production. I thought 'this is getting craft to about the lowest pitch you can get!' It had to be the right size, the right texture; heat-proof; flexible so it won't get in your way when you lift a hot pot. It's one of the most functional things you can make. There's quite a gap between designing a one-of-a-kind wall hanging and designing a handwoven pot-holder that will work."[40] Anna Ernberg's designs, more functional than aesthetic, took into account her student weavers, who wove only a short time each day and rarely continued in the industry for more than a year or two. Mary Hambidge, who emphasized color and texture in her products, preferred only simple weave structures. Edith Matheny, Sarah Dougherty, and Eleanor Churchill all received special notice for excellence in color and design.[41]

Lucy Morgan designed the earliest Penland products, readily adopting the good ideas generated by the students and the teachers at the Penland School. Many items in Penland's production line showed up in designs in the Lily Mills publication *Practical Weaving Suggestions.* Lily first published worksheets beginning in 1930, with detailed specifications for projects using the company's yarns; in the

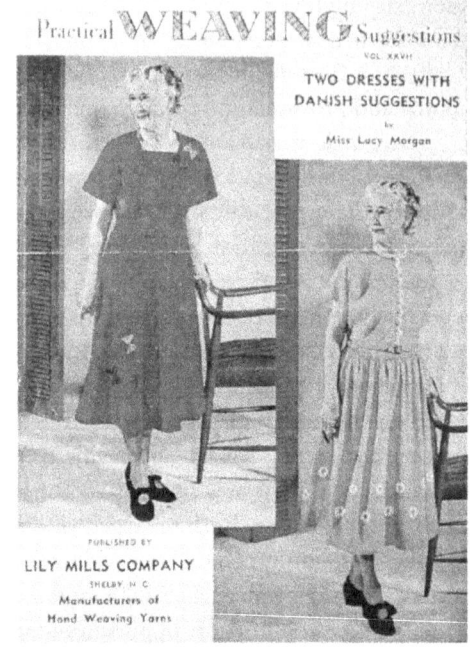

Lucy Morgan and several others weavers associated with Penland had projects published in Lily Mills' *Practical Weaving Suggestions.*

1950s they expanded into pamphlets. Lily prominently credited the designers of the projects. During the first thirty years of publication, Lucy Morgan and other Penland regulars—Edward Worst, Toni Ford, John Fishback, Ruppert Peters, Elizabeth Mattson, and Irene Beaudin—contributed over half the numbers.[42] Aunt Newbie, from Crossnore, adapted patterns she learned at the Weaving Institute at Penland into products for the Weaving Room.

The weaving centers freely borrowed both product ideas and designs from one another and from the wider weaving world. Lucy Morgan responded to Edward Worst when he questioned her about using an apron design: "To get back to the apron we sent you, you say you are not going to copy it, but why not? . . . We copied it from one someone brought that she had bought in Greece I think it was. And most of the things we make we have copied from things you have brought us."[43] Even though designers used product designs and weaving patterns borrowed from others, finished items presented individual interpretation of color and yarn choice. The identical idea for a piece could manifest itself in an amazing variety of products. For example, most centers produced a plain-weave linen or cotton towel with an inlaid design of a log cabin, usually with smoke coming from the chimney and a tree or two. Each center's rendition, however, possessed unique aspects; some cabins had doors and maybe a window, trees could either be pine or deciduous, and even the smoke curled differently.

Many weaving managers demonstrated their love of the traditional coverlet weaving of the mountains. Frances Goodrich, Anna Ernberg, Sarah Dougherty, and Clementine Douglas all collected old overshot pattern drafts. Shortly before her death, Katherine Pettit presented coverlets and blankets collected in eastern Kentucky to the John Bradford Club for their Lexington historical museum. All of the designers adapted mountain overshot patterns for use in items such as bags and rugs, or as borders on runners and aprons. Several centers actually wove coverlets, using both replications of traditional patterns and contemporary adaptations done in decorator colors. However, most centers dropped production of coverlets because the smaller items sold better and required less investment in time and materials. Only Crossnore continued making coverlets because they had a ready market through the D.A.R.[44]

In the mid-1930s, Allen Eaton observed, "Although much of the old-time weaving is still carried on, the more modern work constitutes the bulk of weaving in the Highlands today."[45] Many places expressed contemporary international influences in designs or techniques. Interest in the weaving of other countries emanated from a desire to learn more about the craft, rather than as a repudiation of local skills or designs. No conflict existed between respecting Appalachian weaving traditions and receptivity to international techniques and new design ideas. The weaving centers never functioned as historic preservation societies. In saving the art of weaving, they preserved the craft itself, rather than reproducing objects from the past. Penland School sought teachers, especially from the Scandinavian countries, so that they could learn unusual techniques and expand their knowledge of weaving. Although the designers drew on the mountain textile tradition for some of their inspiration, they remained open to good ideas from any source.

Even though Eaton claimed, "Swedish designs developed at Berea College," the Fireside Industries showed no Scandinavian type products.[46] Other than introducing some simple weaving structures that might be labeled Scandinavian, Anna Ernberg only used her homeland's techniques in her personal weaving and not in Berea's production. Throughout the long history of weaving, different cultures either developed similar techniques or shared them, making attribution extremely difficult. Ernberg never used design figures or a Swedish style in product development.

Tina McMorran attended a weaving workshop in Gatlinburg and was later hired by Pi Beta Phi to supervise Arrowcraft's weaving program.

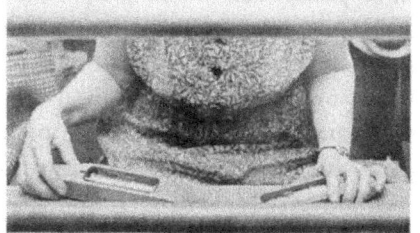

The designers strove to produce items that attracted customers. To achieve this goal, each designer decided on the type of item, the materials, the colors, and functional considerations. The designers understood the consumers, their middle-class lifestyle and the kind of homes they lived in. They also knew that woven goods purchased at a bazaar or church club meeting would be a casual or impulse purchase for most of the buyers. The decision would be in the hands of the woman and not a major acquisition discussed with her husband. The modest cost of most items fell within the limits of the household budget, usually controlled by the wife herself. A few guest towels could be picked up at a bazaar, or a scarf could be bought on an outing with a friend, or a set of placemats could be ordered from a catalog passed out at a civic meeting, without any risk of adversely affecting the family's finances. Even though helping mountain schools or women achieve some financial independence probably motivated the buyer, that incentive alone could not sell products—value and unique design were also essential.

Most weaving supervisors continued their personal involvement with weaving beyond their management and design duties. Winogene Redding and Sarah Dougherty frequently demonstrated weaving at shops and fairs. A dressed loom always sat in Mary Hambidge's cabin on the hill behind the Weavers of Rabun Weaving Shed.[47] After retiring from Arrowcraft, Tina McMorran joined the Twelve Designer Craftsmen's artists cooperative gallery in Gatlinburg, where she sold her wall hangings made from naturally dyed yarn. Lucy Morgan continued to weave projects in her retirement years, with a niece threading the loom.[48] Both Mary Hambidge and Lucy Morgan enjoyed wearing their own handwoven clothing throughout their lives.

These weaving supervisors assumed the multiple roles of designer, teacher, production manager, and marketing director. While they trained in weaving, they lacked preparation in most of the other functions they performed. Weaving education at that time usually included some knowledge of fibers, yarns, and even color, but rarely included art or design principles. Although educators recognized the need for the specific training of teachers, most people assumed that the only requirement for teaching was knowledge of a subject. The supervisors learned business management techniques as their ventures grew. Since most weavers have a knack for organization, the supervisors readily assumed the management challenges of coordinating materials, work assignments, inventory, personnel, and quality control. Marketing proved the hardest task for all the managers, with the centers producing many more goods than they could sell through their usual channels. They could have produced far more, had they explored other markets. They gravitated to the alternative market of the women's network because it was an avenue they understood. The women who ran the weaving industries learned the commercial end of their duties through trial and error—a common practice for most of the people venturing into craft sales.

All of the weaving centers declined after their major designer/managers left the enterprise. Most independent businesses failed after the loss of the founder—Weavers of Rabun, the Spinning Wheel, and the Shuttle Crafters all ceased operations. Bonnie Willis Ford carried on Penland Weavers for a few years after Lucy Morgan left Penland, but the school was clearly more important than the weaving. Some of the centers—Arrowcraft, Crossnore, and Berea—employed talented people at the helm, but the industries declined anyway, never regaining their former scope.

Times changed both in the mountains and in the homes of patrons. In 1967 Arrowcraft weaving supervisor Bess Mottern perceived problems in the product line that pointed to larger difficulties in the industry as a whole. "Are we limiting sales by catering to a lower income bracket by keeping our items under $5.00. By placing a few more expensive items such as area rugs of different techniques, wall hangings, more contemporary design, which will fit into today's modern homes, I am convinced would interest a larger percentage of people and a higher income bracket who will pay for more creative and exceptional work."[49] She was voicing a concern that Arrowcraft had not advanced with the commercial growth of Gatlinburg or risen to the height of competition within the modern craft world.

Weavers and Managers

The criticism Mottern leveled at Arrowcraft in 1967 could have included the rest of the weaving centers—and should have been delivered many years earlier. The centers essentially settled into producing and selling a line of small items that changed very little over time. Successive designers imitated their predecessors in style and in the kinds of items, rarely considering the consumer and never adapting to the changing market for crafts.

9

production

Weaving

When social settlement workers moved into the southern Appalachian Mountains in the early twentieth century, they chose weaving as the craft to promote among women. As a home-based industry, woven textiles combined many desirable characteristics: the skills were already known or could be easily taught, the raw materials were available locally or easily transported to the area, an extensive capital investment was not required, and work could be produced in the home without undue mess. The products displayed a uniqueness that found a ready market, and items shipped easily and inexpensively. Weaving also possessed some cultural and traditional ties to the area, coming out of the Appalachian household arts practiced by women in the not too distant past. While clay, metal, or wood crafts could have been encouraged, none met all of the criteria that weaving did, and none was considered "women's work."

Among the textile arts of basketry, quilting and other sewing crafts, lacemaking, and decorative needlework, weaving appeared to be the most desirable. Although many of the early craft centers offered baskets, they sold for little, presented storage and shipping problems, and had limited use in the contemporary home. Quilting enjoyed popularity as a leisure pursuit among women all over the country.[1] The sewing crafts, in general, offered little sales potential because of the wide availability of products and because many women sewed at home. Elias Howe's invention of the sewing machine in 1846, combined with the Singer Sewing Machine Company's astute marketing, revolutionized home sewing and transformed the manufactured clothing and home textile products industries.[2]

In the nineteenth century, weavers in Appalachia used large barn looms with four harnesses and a counterbalance mechanism.

Production

Large companies employed jobbers who traveled in the mountains recruiting young women to work the needlecrafts of tufting and candlewicking for bedspreads, an industry that flourished during the Depression. The mountain settlement workers failed to anticipate the popularity of this craft, which grew in fashion after most of the weaving establishments had begun. Mountain women lacked a lacemaking tradition, which would have been practiced more by newly arrived European immigrants. In the early part of the twentieth century, fashions changed, greatly decreasing the use of lace in clothing and home decoration. Early test marketing by Frances Goodrich and William Goodell Frost suggested a sales potential for handwoven coverlets, which they pursued without even considering possible alternatives.

The act of weaving is both easy and hard, because many small steps contribute to a complex operation. Handweaving revivalist Mary Megis Atwater started her comprehensive book, *The Shuttle-Craft Book of American Hand-Weaving*, with the words "Weaving is essentially a simple matter, requiring no special talents, no lofty intellect or high degree of manual skill for its accomplishment. It is made up of a number of separate processes, each easy in itself but each requiring care and accuracy in its performance." Through her book and the correspondence course she offered through her Shuttle-Craft Guild, which began in 1924, Atwater initiated the hobbyist into the world of weaving. While the basic steps of weaving are not difficult to perform, they require precision, with skill developing over time. Atwater commented, "Each age and each country has its own weaves and patterns and nobody could possibly know and follow them all."[3] Weavers often specialized in one type of weaving, with a comprehensive knowledge of the craft taking years of study.

A basic definition of weaving is the interlacement of two elements crossing at right angles. The warp forms the vertical threads that are placed on the loom before the weaving process begins. The weft consists of horizontal threads that interlace with the warp to form a piece of fabric. Although weaving can be as simple as an over-one-thread/under-one-thread sequence, other interlacement patterns create a great variety of interesting patterns.

In the Appalachian mountains, weavers used four-harness looms built by the man of the household or a local carpenter. Looms come in many varieties, but all serve the same basic function of maintaining equal tension on the warp threads. The weavers of the southern Appalachian Mountains used foot-powered looms employing a counterbalance harness-raising mechanism. Although they were large, the nineteenth-century looms disassembled for storage easily. In busy farm households, weaving occupied the winter months, while during the growing season the loom resided in the barn, broken down into pieces. Weaving often took place on a porch or in a separate outbuilding.[4] The weaving centers of the Craft Revival introduced smaller looms with the same counterbalance mechanism as the so-called "barn looms," but with more precise engineering to better withstand the tension of the warp. Anna Ernberg designed an efficient loom, later manufactured by Berea College's Woodworking Department, which was used by many other weaving centers. A competent woodworker can build a loom, but either a precise plan or a thorough understanding of the weaving process is needed. The operation of a loom requires exact ratios between the many parts to perform satisfactorily.

With a foot-powered loom, as the name implies, the weaver's muscles provide the mechanical force needed to operate the loom by stepping on a treadle or pedal underneath the loom. The treadles control harnesses, each carrying hundreds of heddles with a single thread passing through the central eye of each heddle. After the weaver depresses a treadle raising one

Anna Ernberg designed a small four-harness counterbalance loom that was manufactured in the Berea College woodshop.

or more harnesses, she throws the shuttle through the shed, the open space created between the activated threads. The shuttle carries the weft thread, which is wound onto a quill, or bobbin. After throwing the shuttle with one hand and catching it with the other, the weaver beats the weft into position. She then advances to the next line of her pattern, repeating the sequence again of raising the harnesses, throwing the shuttle, and beating. Weavers learn to judge the exact tension on the yarn as it comes from the shuttle, the amount of pressure of the beat against the already completed cloth, and the speed of the consecutive repeated actions of weaving. To most people, the term "weaving" means the act of throwing the shuttle, although the broader definition of the word actually encompasses the entire process, from planning through loom preparation, including weft placement.

The fly-shuttle loom used by D.C. Churchill and the Mountain Weaver Boys in Berea, and the Biltmore Weavers in Asheville, North Carolina, was operated by foot-power and shared the same counterbalance operation as other mountain looms. However, a fly-shuttle mechanism, activated by the weaver pulling an overhead cord, propelled the shuttle though the open shed with a spring device instead of the weaver throwing it. All other weaving operations proceeded in the same manner, although Churchill added some innovations that reduced stress on the weaver. The fly-shuttle greatly increased weaving efficiency, thus prompting criticism from other centers that the speed of weaving sacrificed control.

La Delle Allen of Arrowcraft tried to explain the differences in fly-shuttle weaving: "Standardization in weaving tends to give inferior products. . . . There is a lack of feeling in fly shuttle weaving, that indefinable something called art, which can be produced only by the real artist and craftsman."[5] With these subtle distinctions, she placed the burden of discerning differences on the consumer: "There is a difference in the two kinds of weaving which one with an appreciation of art and a discriminating taste recognizes." Arrowcraft and Berea College successfully kept Churchill Weavers from joining the Southern Highland Handicraft Guild based on this presumed inferiority of their products. Actually the fly-shuttle lends itself to one shuttle weave structures with few weft changes. Therefore, the real difference in weaving was seen in the type of products, rather than in any discernable difference in quality. Biltmore and the Mountain Weaver Boys produced yardage for men's clothing and Churchill achieved distinction in throws, baby blankets, shawls, and scarves.

Warp preparation, called "dressing the loom," consisted of many steps, beginning with measuring warp length. In the most common method for determining equal length, the mountain weaver wound the thread around warping bars. Parallel rows of stout pegs fit either into the outside wall of a cabin or onto a frame to form the warping apparatus. The placement of

Production

Weavers wound warps using large frames in which they followed a path around pegs to produce warp threads of the same length.

peg rows may be as close as one yard, but in the mountains they were often positioned several yards apart. Even the narrow width of a towel required two hundred threads, which the weaver wound continuously around the pegs until reaching that number. At one end, and sometimes at both ends of the warping frame, two or more pegs about six inches apart allowed for the cross. Crossing threads in sequence kept them from knotting around each other when they were removed from the warping frame, creating a large crocheted chain.

Mary Hambidge put on very short warps of between three to ten yards for most of her wool and silk yardage lengths. In Gatlinburg the weavers routinely put on 110 yards and, at Crossnore, the supervisor felt 50 yards was the best length.[6] Not all weavers owned their own apparatus for winding warps, so they either prepared the warp at the weaving center or used the warping frame of a relative or neighbor.

After the warp is wound, the loom can then be warped or dressed using one of several methods. The end result is the same: threads separated through the reed pass one at a time through eyes in heddles that hang on the harnesses and are stored on the back, or warp beam, of the loom. Just as in a recipe, the weaving draft noted the order of thread placement in the heddles, which determined the weave structure and pattern. As the weaver tied the warp to the cloth beam at the front of the loom, she adjusted the tension on the threads. Loom preparation included tying up the foot pedals in the proper sequence and harness combinations for the desired pattern. The common overshot weave structure required tying six treadles.

After accurately describing the long process of warping a loom in *Spirit of the Mountains*, Emma Bell Miles exclaimed, "'Now at last you go to weaving,' I said. But she only smiled and showed me how even now all was not in working order. A few moments' trial brought notice a loose thread or two, several twists, a 'flat,' and a broken thread to be coaxed into harmony

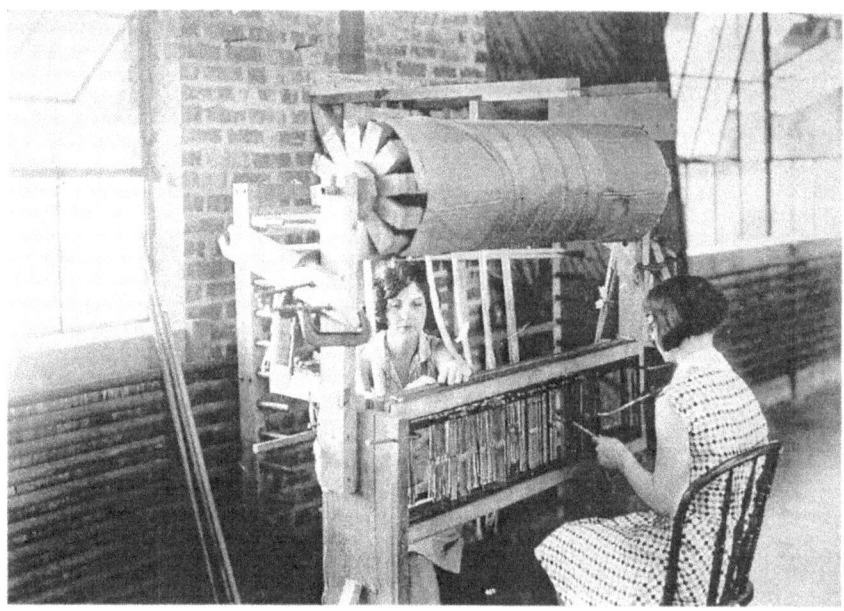

At Churchill Weavers, D.C. Churchill analyzed the task of weaving, reorganizing it for greater efficiency. The warp was wound onto a removable back beam and then threaded through the heddles on harnesses that were later dropped back into the loom frame.

with the rest. At last, in the fading light, Aunt Genevy proudly descended the stairs to finish the supper I had set on the fire, and announced that she would begin weaving Monday morning."[7] Mistakes in threading, if uncorrected, resulted in visibly defective stripes, evident in the whole length of the fabric. All threads required correct positioning and equal tension before weaving commenced.

Weavers checked frequently during the warping process for mistakes, gaining proficiency as they repeated the process. Family members often shared in tasks—perhaps a child would be asked to hand yarns in order to the threader. Whenever possible, the weaver tied a new warp to the old one and pulled it through the reed and heddles. By specializing in only a single production item, the weaver cut the preparation time and eliminated mistakes in threading by tying onto the previous warp.

Arrowcraft recorded the exact amount of time required for warping. For an apron with the warp total of 814 threads, set at twenty-four threads per inch, and sleyed, or put two to a dent, in a twelve-dent reed, the weaver took seven hours and ten minutes to dress the loom. (The reed resided in the loom's beater, separating threads and regulating the density of the fabric by spacing the threads.) The figures indicate that she spent two hours and forty minutes winding the seventy-eight yards of warp, three hours and forty minutes tying on to the previous warp, and fifty minutes beaming.[8] Another four to five hours would have been needed to thread the reed and heddles individually instead of tying onto the previous project. In the best-case scenario, most of Arrowcraft's small items took between seven to ten hours to warp the loom, with extra time for correcting mistakes, if needed.

In weaving on a floor loom, the repeated motions set up a rhythm that most weavers find physically satisfying. With production weaving, where the weaver performs the action sequence of raising harnesses, throwing the shuttle, and beating over and over again, the physical rather than the conscious part of the mind controls the process. The weaver feels any disruption in the pattern of movements, with her body perceiving a mistake rather than her eyes seeing it. When weavers say they like weaving, they're talking about this process of throwing the shuttle.

Bishop Junius Horner, head of the Western North Carolina Episcopal Diocese, the sponsor of the Appalachian School at Penland, strongly objected to Lucy Morgan's proposal of weaving as a suitable occupation for women. Remembering the large cumbersome looms and the women's complaints about the chore of weaving for necessity, he thought the work too hard. Lucy countered, noting the ease of operating the modern streamlined looms. The Bishop agreed to change his position if petite Lucy could weave for eight hours in a single day.[9] She demonstrated her endurance, and he assented to her plans for introducing weaving.

During the weaving process, the weaver utilizes her whole body, moving both arms and both legs in a sequence of movements. During the middle part of the twentieth century, weaving held great favor among occupational therapists, with such well-known weavers as Mary Atwater and Mary Black coming out of an occupational therapy background.[10] Although good for building up muscles, the process of weaving did cause some stress on the body. Weavers complained of back problems, but the major stress to the back occurs during threading the loom rather than in the act of throwing the shuttle. Good posture at the loom prevents most back problems. Another common complaint, "weaver's bottom," results from sitting on a hard bench that cuts off circulation to the legs. A padded bench of the proper height, with the top angled slightly towards the loom, alleviates this problem.

When asked by the Women's Bureau of the Department of Labor in its 1934 study, several of the weavers declared that they worked hard.[11] A weaver speaking with a non-weaver tended to impress her audience with the exacting nature and the many steps involved in her craft. Presenting weaving as difficult enhanced the maker as a master of complex skills and justified the high price of her product. The Bureau's interviewer recorded the conversation with Mrs. Nolan of the Pine Mountain Settlement School: "Has taught daughters the simple patterns, but thinks the 12 treadle is too hard, doesn't care whether they learn it or not." Even in the mountains, work with the head was viewed as having greater value than that with the hands. As early as 1900, Berea College encountered "a feeling among the people that these noble industries were old-fashioned and something rather to be ashamed of."[12] The weavers desired a better life for their children, something that would be achieved through education and the elimination of physical labor.

Plain weaving, the simple over-and-under thread structure, proceeded faster than any other type of weaving. Colored and textured yarns added interest without substantially increasing the time required. Although introducing a pattern into woven goods greatly increased the length of weaving time, it also added considerably to the value of the finished product. The birds, flowers, and other recognizable figures that adorned small towels and baby bibs employed a hand-manipulated inlaid technique. Often mistaken for embroidery, the figure emerged row by row together with the background as the weaving progressed.

Although the Appalachian weaver used some hand-manipulated techniques, the mechanism of the loom created most of the patterns in which the structure or pattern was threaded onto the loom. Drafts recorded the exact distribution of threads put through heddles on

In the first decade of the twentieth century, Berea College offered coverlets in a variety of popular patterns.

designated harnesses, much in the same way that musical notation identifies individual notes. The drafting system used in the mountains even resembled music, with small slash marks, each indicating a thread, distributed over four long lines representing the four harnesses on the loom. Even after threading a pattern onto the loom, the weaver controlled many different design options within the treadling sequence. Early weaving centers collected the drafts written on long narrow strips of paper that many mountain families saved even after weaving ceased.

Although by no means exclusive to the southern Appalachian Mountains, the overshot weave structure and coverlet weaving symbolized Appalachian weaving to many people. In overshot, the pattern is formed on a plain-weave ground with weft threads skipping over several warp threads. In the typical coverlet, the wool weft, in either indigo blue or madder red, offered a striking contrast in the large bold designs to the plain-weave white cotton ground. Their early acquaintance with attractive overshot coverlets drew both Frances Goodrich and President William Goodell Frost of Berea College into promoting weaving among mountain women.

Some weavers created unique patterns, but most borrowed patterns from their neighbors, often combining elements from different designs. They named their patterns after things, places, or events, such as Catalpa Flower, Kaintuck Beauty, and Bonaparte's March; sometimes the names were simply descriptive, as in Sixteen Snowballs. Eliza Calvert Hall commented on the confusion of identifying coverlets by their names: "Sometimes one name does duty for two or three dissimilar designs, and a design may have one name in North Carolina, another in Kentucky, another in Tennessee, and still another in Virginia, as if it were a criminal fleeing from justice."[13] For Crossnore's popular "Lee's Surrender" overshot rug, an explanation of the pattern related design figures to specific features in the Civil War occasion at the Appomattox courthouse. Whether true or not, the story of a Confederate mother creating the design in memory of her lost son illustrated the desire of both the weaver and the consumer to identify with the pattern.[14]

Production

Edward Worst presented another weave structure, identified in "Old Kentucky Drafts," the last chapter of *How To Weave Linens*.[15] He featured large designs in a structure that contrasted grouped thread textured areas with plain-weave sections, with both the warp and weft of the same weight and color of thread. Mary Atwater named the structure after New England professional handweavers J. and R. Bronson, but home weavers used this structure as well.[16] Worst, who does not give this structure a name (other than "five-harness drafts"), explained that the use of this type of weaving was not widespread because of the difficulty of tying up the loom. But, "Mrs. Matheny, one of the most effective workers among the mountain folk, has her workers operate these five-harness looms in a most successful way. As a result they produce many of the old-time patterns." Most of the weaving centers produced tablecloths and towels in the Bronson weave structure, but failed to mention any connection with traditional mountain weaving in their promotional materials, as they had with overshot coverlets.

The weaving centers only sold other nineteenth-century Appalachian household textiles—jeans, linsey-woolsey, and flannel—during their very early years. No market existed for these durable modest fabrics, at least at the high price forced by the slow pace of the handloom. At Allanstand Cottage Industries and Berea College, these household fabrics, bought from weavers and then resold, appeared in very early sales brochures.[17] When designers controlled production, the poor-selling utilitarian fabrics were dropped from the line. However, Aunt Lizzie Reagan from Arrowcraft produced some novelty items in linsey-woolsey.

Other than overshot and Bronson, which had historical ties to the area, the Appalachian centers used weave structures reflecting the type of weaving done by hobbyist handweavers throughout the country. Being educated women, the designer-managers of the weaving centers naturally gathered information about weaving from written sources. Handweaving as a leisure pursuit for American middle-class women emerged in the early twentieth century, with fancy needlework and lacemaking having consumed the idle hours of many a creative woman in previous decades. Because of the equipment and skill required, weaving never reached the popularity among hobbyists that knitting, crochet, sewing, and quiltmaking achieved. In 1918 Edward Worst published his first weaving book. Mary Megis Atwater began experimenting with a correspondence course for handweavers in 1922, needing to support two children after the early death of her husband. "I had heard of the handweaving industries in Berea, Kentucky, and in one or two other places in the South, and it seemed to me that a similar project would meet our needs." Finding her gift in teaching others about weaving rather than producing weaving herself, Atwater's pattern book first came out in 1928.[18]

During the Appalachian Craft Revival, the designers demonstrated their knowledge of pattern weaving and employed many loom-controlled weave structures. Although they used some of the weave structures seen previously in Appalachia, designers drew on many different weave structures, or methods of interlacing the fiber elements, each of which affected the fabric's look, density, and surface. Armed with many weave structures, the designer suited the cloth type to the function of the item.

Despite various influences—among them the Swedish background of Anna Ernberg at Berea, the importation of Scandinavian teachers at Penland, and the widespread availability of Scandinavian weaving books and magazine articles—the weaving centers did not adopt weave structures commonly used in Scandinavian countries, such as bound weave, rya knotting, or drawloom techniques.[19] The managers even rejected the highly patterned Scandinavian folk styles in their designs, showing a preference for accents rather than all-over patterning. Even at Tallulah Falls Industrial School, where Ester Carlson, from Upsala, Sweden, taught weaving in 1926, only a few products showed a Scandinavian influence.[20]

Early settlement workers venturing into the mountains found overshot coverlets woven with linen or cotton handspun yarns for the warp and with handspun wool for the pattern weft. Although local agriculture supplied the raw materials for early coverlets, by the late nineteenth century country stores or traveling peddlers furnished mountain weavers with commercially spun cotton yarn.[21] Although the managers introduced design innovations, they usually kept the basic form of the coverlets much the same, utilizing commercial cotton warp and handspun wool weft yarns, only switching to commercially spun wool weft when demand outstripped the ability of the local spinners to supply the yarn.

Mary Hambidge delighted in finding spinning wheels during her stay in the Georgia mountains in 1928, and she commissioned women to produce handspun wool yarn for her.[22] Berea, Gatlinburg, Penland, and other weaving centers encouraged handspinning in their early years, but they eventually found the process too time-consuming to meet the demands of production weaving. The mountain spinner preferred the great or walking wheel, where the spinner turned the wheel with her hand, drawing out the fibers, letting them twist from the tip of the spindle, and winding up the thread, all in a three-part motion. When using the smaller foot-treadle wheel, the spinner sat on a low stool, leaving both hands free to control the fibers. The increased labor costs for handspun yarns added to the price of the final products, with the consumer rarely appreciating the additional effort. Mary Hambidge tried very hard to carry on her business weaving with handspun wool only, but found that the local spinners could not keep up the supply.

In her 1909 book, *Old Andy, the Moonshiner,* Martha Gielow tells of the proud mountain grandmother preparing to send her young granddaughter off to boarding school, "and the new frock she had just finished weaving for Sal was dyed red with pokeberry juice."[23] Because of her greater acquaintance with Appalachian crafts through the Southern Industrial Education Association, Gielow dressed her damsel in a brightly colored dress using an unusual dyestuff, rather than the more commonly used madder for red.

Indigo and madder appear most frequently in traditional Appalachian coverlets, greatly outnumbering other dyes from natural sources. Although the dyer might have collected wild indigo or grown madder, she probably purchased both dye substances from the local store. Very early weaving centers discouraged the use of commercial dyes in coverlets, believing them fugitive or not colorfast. Along with everything else, the settlement workers sought the secrets of mountain plants

At the Penland School, Meta Lewis helped Emma Conley record many of the dye formulas using natural dyestuffs.

for their healing properties and dyes, systematically recording the knowledge that had been passed down through generations of women. Most of the knowledge of natural dyes used in historical Appalachia came from the work of Louise Pitman at the John C. Campbell Folk School, Katherine Pettit and Wilmer Stone Viner at Pine Mountain Settlement School, and Emma Conley and Meta Lewis at Penland.[24]

The mysteries of the indigo dyepot intrigued several of the early mountain settlement workers, among them Lucy Morgan, who published a pamphlet on producing varying shades of blue through fermentation and the many delicate steps of processing the indigo plant. Eaton also reported this fascination with indigo: "Sarah Dougherty knows of one pot that has been in continuous use for ninety-four years; and it is said that Mrs. Gretchen Bayne started her indigo dye from a pot that had been in use since 1797."[25] Once the chemical reaction took place, the indigo produced a durable blue color, which wool took especially well.

At the Homespun Fair held annually at Berea College around the turn of the twentieth century, a Cincinnati cotton manufacturer awarded premiums for yarn using natural dyes. Cash prizes ranged from $3 for first place to $1 for fifth, with seven different color categories. At that same fair, the top prize-winning coverlet received only $2, which suggests the value placed on obtaining the exact dye recipes, which had to be supplied with each entry.[26] Although this manufacturer might have been interested in supporting the college's work, he more likely desired knowledge of the dye formulas and reactive agents used in the mountains. Because Germany dominated the commercial dye industry at this time, American businesses sought independence though a better understanding of dye chemistry.[27]

Although the natural dyes fascinated many early mountain workers, very few of these dyes appeared in the products of the weaving centers, aside from the early use of indigo, madder, and shades of yellow and brown from other plant sources. Many centers tried to revive interest in natural dyeing, but the long and involved dye processes raised the price beyond acceptable levels. Without higher prices, natural dyes were not cost effective for production items. Dyes from plant materials required extensive knowledge of sources and sensitive formulas for the dye bath. Collecting extremely large quantities of dye materials at specific times of the year also presented problems. Gatlinburg dyer Mary Frances Davidson gave directions for gathering the dyestuffs required for one pound of wool: "Barks—one peck finely chopped. Flowers—one and one-half quarts, dried flower heads; one and one-half pecks fresh flower heads." Arrowcraft produced some items under Tina McMorran's supervision that used yarns dyed with natural dyestuffs. After retirement McMorran continued living in Gatlinburg, weaving wall hangings featuring "veg-

The Homespun Fair, held during commencement at Berea College, offered prizes in many categories, including dye formulas.

etable" dyed yarns.[28] Although many people assumed that Mary Hambidge used natural dyes, she actually mixed commercial synthetic dyes to match colors she saw in nature.[29]

The natural dyes proved much better as a publicity tool than for actual use—Emma Conley and her dyepot graced many a Southern Highland Guild Fair. In her sunbonnet she offered picturesque photo opportunities, becoming quite a celebrity.[30]

Amount of Production

From 1936 to 1944, Arrowcraft weavers produced 6,328 Bouquet finger towels. During these nine years, a total of 31,571 finger towels of all types rolled off the Gatlinburg looms, in addition to a substantial number of larger guest towels. While the Bouquet motif was not Arrowcraft's most popular design, it had the distinction of continuous production over the entire nine-year span. The Morning Glory finger towel, which topped production at 7,705, was only introduced in 1938.[31]

For a Bouquet finger towel, Arrowcraft weaver Josie Ogle took three hours and ten minutes to wind the warp and dress her loom, tying on the warp to the previous threading. These calculations, from April 1941, stated that the actual weaving of one towel took forty-five minutes, with hemming and pressing taking another seventeen minutes. According to her, winding bobbins took one minute, making the total production time sixty-three minutes. In June of 1936, the Bouquet finger towel offered in white and pastel, and in linen and cotton, sold for 40 cents, with its price increasing to 50 cents by 1941.

Although each center developed its own procedures, all modeled their basic structures on Allanstand and Berea College, the earliest centers. Centers began by taking in work brought to them by the makers and then reselling it, gradually changing over to requesting specific items. As the market for handwoven work expanded, Berea College warned consumers about the availability of items: "It should be understood that these are hand-products, not machine-made, and consequently the supply is precarious. Sometimes a good weaver is stopped by a disease among the sheep, or her weaving detained at home by the rising of a mountain stream!"[32]

All the weaving centers employing home workers functioned similarly: the manager designed pieces, assigned them to weavers, checked out sufficient yarn for the project, and received finished goods. The centers purchased yarn from suppliers at bulk discounts, guaranteeing standardized quality. The weaver wove at home at her own pace, hemmed or finished the work, washed and pressed items, then returned them to the center. All work was delivered ready for the sales shop or to be sent to a customer. She either received immediate payment or was paid within the month. The center sold the work, assuming financial responsibility for management and marketing.

Even though the Pi Beta Phis first hoped to take work on consignment with payment to the maker when items sold, they found people would not produce on the promise of future sales. They interpreted this reluctance as lack of incentive: "They do not seem to care enough about having those comforts of which they know not, which their work would eventually bring to them, to work and wait for its sale." Showing greater sensitivity to the workers, Anna Ernberg declared that they could neither finance materials nor wait for remuneration for their labor.[33]

A very few of the early weavers learned skills passed down from family members, but most women needed instruction in weaving. Many school-based weaving programs taught skills to children enrolled in the school and also to women who worked in their homes.

Production

Centers receiving Smith-Hughes vocational education money provided instruction at a central location for the home weavers. The program at Penland constructed the Weavers' Cabin in fulfillment of this requirement and turned the assigning of work into a social function: "It is a day which is looked forward to by these 'weaver-mothers' because it is a day when they can leave their homes and meet their friends and neighbors for a common day of work and comradeship."[34] At Gatlinburg, delivering money directly into the weaver's hands sparked the Weavers' Day, although it turned into an educational and social occasion.[35] Even though the Women's Bureau of the Department of Labor elicited help from the Southern Highland Handicraft Guild in encouraging central production facilities, the centers continued their home-based methods of operation. The exception, Crossnore, centralized weaving when Aunt Newbie called in looms from home weavers after the school's weaving building burned down. Pressure came from the urgent need to fill orders for the D.A.R., rather than compliance with federal guidelines. Although women wove in Crossnore's new stone building rather than at home, the workers chose their own hours and received piece-rate pay.[36]

The Woman's Exchange Movement sold unregulated stock on consignment, with individual makers reproducing those items that sold consistently.[37] Even in the very early days of selling through the Southern Industrial Education Association, the mountain centers realized the need to dictate the items produced and the need to ensure quality. The settlement workers, who understood the standards and tastes of middle-class consumers, mediated between the producers and the distant market. When the mountain settlement schools hired weaving managers, the buying of unsupervised products declined, with design, production, and marketing falling under their direct control.

On assuming their duties, Redding and Ernberg continued marketing coverlets and traditional items, but they soon realized better sales with smaller items. An important shift in production took place during the late 1920s and early 1930s, when the emphasis moved from coverlets, yardage, and larger items to guest towels, runners, and smaller pieces. Several factors contributed to this concentration of production on lower-priced items. Those selling through

The Georgia Federation of Women's Clubs sponsored the Tallulah Falls Industrial School and bought crafts items made at the school.

women's clubs or special sales events organized by women, such as the Pi Phis and Penland, discovered that their customers used limited personal discretionary money for their purchases. A modestly priced set of placemats or a guest towel could be bought by dipping into household funds, where a more costly coverlet or rug required working within the larger family budget, often controlled by the husband. A socially conscious woman could dispense some small charitable giving within the family budget and could buy herself a scarf or a bag to help a good cause.[38] Near-total reliance on the women's network for marketing meant gearing production towards the type of items that appealed to this group, and keeping within their budget.

At Berea, Ernberg expanded the weaving program, including larger numbers of students in the college's labor program, which resulted in higher production of small items. Students in their short weaving shifts lacked both the time to complete larger projects and the time to develop skills. Home workers with years of experience gradually decreased during the Depression, as Ernberg gave preference to providing work for students out of loyalty to the college.

Placemats ranked as the all-time best-seller at Arrowcraft. At any one time the product line carried between eight to twelve designs of placemats, with many offered in a variety of colors. Among placemats, Whig Rose, the indisputable favorite, led placemat production; 16,332 were made between 1936 and 1944, not including the longer Whig Rose runners. Cora Morton wove Whig Rose for thirty-seven of the forty-seven years she threw a shuttle for Arrowcraft, and her daughter Jane continued in the path charted by her mother, also specializing in Whig Rose.[39]

Detailed records, such as the ones compiled by Winogene Redding for the nine-year period between 1936 and 1944, have not survived for most of the weaving centers. Therefore, the 1933 Southern Highland Handicraft Guild exhibition of mountain handicrafts circulated by the American Federation of Arts offers a rare opportunity to compare the types and prices of objects produced by the centers. Of the approximately six hundred pieces in the exhibit, half came from ten different weaving establishments.[40]

With fifty-two woven items, the Spinning Wheel, of Asheville, North Carolina, contributed more than any other center. Arrowcraft followed closely with fifty-one, and Matheny Weavers sent thirty-eight pieces. Penland, Crossnore, and the Fireside Industries from Berea each submitted around twenty works. This show featured all small home or personal accessories that could conceivably be made of fabric, with the exception of clothing, which posed problems in sizing, construction, and changing fashions. Fifty object names described the items, with some terms covering different but similar pieces. Because of the large and uneven number of submissions, the centers decided what to include individually, rather than a curator assigning a certain quantity to each participant. If directed by a curator, the item identification would surely have used consistent terms.

The centers showed great diversity in the merchandise they exhibited, with Matheny, Arrowcraft, and the Spinning Wheel sending items in twenty different categories. All centers contributed towels, runners, and bags and purses. Towels, both large and small, comprised the largest single group. The profusion of runners, in both contemporary patterns and traditional overshot designs, appealed to the older conscientious housewife who would not consider leaving any flat surface in her home unadorned. The centers favored items like towels and runners, for which most of the production time was spent weaving rather than finishing. With these two items, the processes of handsewing hems or knotting fringe completed the products once they were cut from the loom. Bags and purses required more extensive construction.

Production

The second largest group of items in the exhibition consisted of tablecloths, napkins, potholders, pillow tops, scarves, rugs, and bibs and other baby articles. A few centers included lengths of fabric, labeled as skirting, curtain material, or yardage. Some exhibitors showed considerable ingenuity in devising small special purpose fabric items, including handkerchief cases, hot mats, pin cushions, scrapbooks, neckties, traveling cases, and vase mats. Only Crossnore sent placemats, suggesting that placemats as a home fashion item gained popularity sometime after 1933. By the mid-1930s, Arrowcraft showed the increased importance of placemats by adding additional designs and rapidly accelerating production. However, they referred to the small fabric rectangles used to demarcate place settings on a bare table as "doilies." The Weave Shop of Saluda, North Carolina, sent the only decorative wall hanging. At this time Appalachian Craft Revival weaving stressed functionality, offering very few purely artistic products.

Coverlets formed the more visually exciting part of the exhibit, with over half of the eleven coverlets submitted coming from Allanstand. Notable in the display, and practically the only item not for sale, was a Double Chariot Wheel indigo coverlet identified as having been woven by Mrs. Elmeda Walker for the mountain room in the Wilson White House. In addition to a variety of large bed-sized coverlets, both Berea and Arrowcraft exhibited miniature overshot coverlets for doll beds. The amazing diversity of names assigned to finished lengths of fabric included: couch throw, couch cover, afghan, steamer throw, driver's robe, motor blanket. Only one piece from the Pine Mountain Settlement School was simply identified as a blanket.

In addition to the Southern Highland Handicraft Guild exhibition catalog, the Southern Highlanders' catalog offers another comparison of production from slightly later in the 1930s.[41] This catalog pictured items, described them briefly, and listed prices, but lacked specific production center designations, only listing the general membership at the end. Among the textiles featured were baby items such as bibs and blankets with matching sacque, bags ranging from large carryalls to small coin purses, potholders, scarves, mufflers, shawls, and men's neckties; under the heading of "linens" were placemats, napkins, and towels in a variety of sizes. (In the

Churchill Weavers encouraged visitors to tour their facilities and watch the fabric being woven by hand, not machines.

usage of the time, a "scarf" adorned females, while a similar length of fabric made for males appeared under "muffler.") In all, the Southern Highlanders catalog depicted sixteen item categories with eighty-two different designs, a similar diversity to that shown in the Southern Highland Handicraft Guild exhibition. As the subheading "Handmade Gifts of Unusual Beauty" indicated, the catalog was aimed at the gift market, featuring mostly small and relatively inexpensive pieces. The other crafts depicted also tended to be small and within the moderate price range, with only a few chairs and small tables at the high end of the collection.

The Southern Highlander catalog showed proportionally more baby blankets, small throws, and scarves than were included in the Southern Highland Handicraft Guild exhibition; this was because Churchill Weavers supplied many wool goods. Churchill created a niche not filled by the other weaving centers by offering the wool items their fly-shuttle weaving produced with great efficiency. Churchill designed items with few color changes in the weft and minimal finishing after being cut from the loom.

Mary Hambidge's studio stood alone in weaving yardage, with over half of its production in wool and the remainder in silk, cotton, and linen, all done in very simple weave structures using either natural colored wools or the rich palette of Mary's dyes. With assistance from a tailor, dressmaker, or interior coordinator, the consumer converted the fabric to its final use in clothing or household furnishings. Because Hambidge controlled a dedicated New York sales outlet subsidized by her patron, she did not have to appeal to the casual buyer with small inexpensive items.

Although several weaving centers manufactured rugs with fabric strip weft during their developmental years, rag rugs quickly disappeared from production lines. The centers continued weaving a limited number of rugs, but these were patterned and made with heavy yarn, like the Lee's Surrender rug produced at Crossnore. From the earliest years, each mountain weaving center sought its particular market niche, naturally continuing to produce those items that sold the best. Rag rugs represented an area where the centers, in marketing their work throughout the country, competed with locally handwoven products. In the latter part of the nineteenth century, loom manufacturing companies advertising in women's magazines promoted rag rug weaving as a means of augmenting farm income. The Newcomb, Deen, and Eureka Loom Companies sold looms with fly-shuttles or other automated devices that turned out work faster and, therefore, cheaper.[42] Rag rug weaving flourished on Midwestern farms supplying local needs, often with the buyer supplying the cut fabric strips. These weavers rarely attempted more complex weaving products.

Most Appalachian weaving centers produced very similar work. Where sewn-in labels are not included, attributing specific pieces to their places of origin can be extremely difficult. Some centers attached labels with the center's name, but not consistently. In the early twentieth century, Berea used an elaborate woven label with a weaver seated at a loom, with "Fireside Industries" in large letters across the top and "of Berea College, Berea, Kentucky" at the bottom. In the late 1920s, Berea College considered using a single label for the entire student labor program, but Ernberg persisted with a separate "Fireside Industries" label because community women wove some products, not exclusively students.[43] Long before the government required labels identifying country of origin and fiber content on textiles, labels served an important marketing purpose. Since most of these centers operated with precarious finances, labels were sewn on items when they were available. Often label orders waited until the center could afford to pay for a new shipment.

Production

The early weaving centers liberally copied designs from one another, differing only in colors and yarn selection. Some places established a few signature pieces that were respected by other venues, like Berea's towel with a cardinal, or Penland's towel with overshot border pattern on both ends and a narrow central band. Towel design usually placed a colored decorative strip at one or both ends of a white plain-weave body. Another common towel type featured an inlaid design, such as flowers or a log cabin, with each center slightly varying the cabin, altering the smoke rising from the chimney or perhaps adding a tree.

Each Appalachian weaving center produced a large number of different products. In 1936 Arrowcraft weavers wove twenty different types of items in fifty-five designs, not including additional color variations. In approximately the same period, Berea produced about twenty categories of objects in almost one hundred distinct design units.[44] By 1943 Arrowcraft had added several more types, offering over seventy design choices. Other centers engaged in similar product diversity.

Arrowcraft and the Fireside Industries of Berea led in production among the Appalachian weaving centers. During the fall of 1935 and into the winter of 1936, the student looms at Berea Fireside Industries manufactured over 2,500 finger towels. In 1936, over a slightly longer period, the Arrowcraft weavers produced 2,000 more small towels, for a total of 4,500. But in larger guest towels, Berea made slightly over 2,000 while the Arrowcraft weavers produced about 200 fewer. During this particular period in the mid-1930s, Arrowcraft led in production, with over 30,000 pieces, while Berea weighed in at half that number, with around 15,000. Berea had 8,500 student labor items and 6,500 from community women, although

Arrowcraft displayed items for sale in a home-like setting to the tourists passing through Gatlinburg on the way to explore the Great Smokey Mountains National Park.

the community figure probably included baskets and other non-woven textiles. While exact comparisons cannot be made, more looms around Gatlinburg were kept busy than in Berea, although both centers produced thousands of items. After Anna Ernberg retired, Berea's production declined, while Arrowcraft's output steadily increased. By 1943, less than ten years later, Arrowcraft weavers had almost doubled their production, to over 55,000 items.

In the earlier growth years of the Appalachian handweaving industry, the centers produced at or near their capacity. Later when sales revenues dropped, the supervisors cut production by not hiring new weavers as older ones retired. Only Arrowcraft made it through the Depression with higher production rates than when it started. While surviving the Depression, when other businesses throughout the country failed by the thousands, most centers never regained their former size. Arrowcraft continued introducing both new and redesigned items in an effort to broaden product appeal to Gatlinburg's growing tourist market, while at the same time introducing special pieces appealing to their Phi Beta Phi sponsors. Other centers only reproduced good sellers, sadly neglecting new designs and never seriously seeking expansion. As the women's network sales weakened, they failed to analyze the changing market. Women still wanted to weave and the centers could have continued and even increased their production levels if they had better understood the market for handcrafted goods.

10

financing and fulfilling a mission

Pricing

In pricing handmade products, the maker always had the significant problem of covering the costs of materials and labor while staying under the limit of what a consumer might be expected to pay for an item. The individual craftsperson usually undervalued her labor, and attached no monetary value to the many extra processes performed by her and her family. In addition, she usually ignored the overhead of workplace and equipment required for production. When a craftsperson progressed from constructing pieces for friends and family to selling the items, she invariably figured the price based on the cost of materials, with a small addition for her time. Also, the settlement workers who took on the responsibility of marketing crafts were well acquainted with the low-priced handcrafted merchandise available through Women's Exchanges in most cities in the United States.[1]

Marketing, which emphasized craftsmanship, quality of materials, rarity of technique, unique designs, and the needy circumstances of the maker, was used to extend the prices into a higher range. In the early years of the Appalachian Craft Revival, the brochures concentrated on the help extended to the maker that buying the products would provide. Appeals contained extensive mission statements of the craft development centers; the items and their prices were added almost as an afterthought.

In the first decade of the twentieth century, Allanstand Industries and the Fireside Industries of Berea College sold items ranging in price from $1 to $10, with coverlets the most expensive item at both centers. By the early 1920s, after Anna Ernberg had assumed management of Berea's weaving program, coverlet prices rose to $25 and $30.[2] The steep price increase suggests a more accurate evaluation of production expenses, coupled with a knowledge of how much a typical middle-class consumer in the North would pay.

In the 1920s, Penland, Crossnore, and several other weaving centers began operations, and the Pi Phis hired Winogene Redding to expand their weaving program. Following Berea's lead, all of these places charged $25 for a coverlet.[3] The centers knew of one another's work because their school representatives met annually at the Conference of Southern Mountain Workers every March in Knoxville. Also, Penland and Crossnore were directly linked to Berea since their teachers received training there.

The 1933 Southern Highland Handicraft Guild exhibition catalog presented more variation in prices than one might have expected from retailers in a specific geographic area and in touch with each other.[4] Even at a single center, prices of similar items varied, suggesting that price was decided by the actual costs of time and materials, rather than by any predetermined

In the early 1930s, the Fireside Industries of Berea College offered a large variety of bags and purses.

product category rates. Allanstand showed seven of the eleven coverlets in the exhibit, with prices ranging from $12.40 to $50, according to size. Two of Crossnore's three "spreads"—rather than coverlets—in Martha Washington overshot designs cost $22.50 and $25, depending on size.

In the 1933 exhibit, "runners" and "bags" covered a wide range of sizes and weaving complexity; difficulty of bag construction was also a factor. Both items sold at prices ranging from $1 to $9.50, with most of them in the range of $2 to $5. Bags from the Spinning Wheel were higher, at $9.50, because of the addition of tops, either carved or amber. Finger towels, although more standardized in size, fiber content, and decorative elements, still varied significantly in price, from Penland's $.40 to the Spinning Wheel's $.95.

Churchill Weavers sold their products independently of the Southern Highland Handicraft Guild, which had denied them membership. A Churchill Weavers 1928 "Trade Price List" indicates that scarves were priced between $1.50 and $2.40. With the standard retail markup, the scarves would have sold for between $3 and $4.80. The Southern Highland Handicraft Guild members' scarves ranged between $.60 and $3, disproving Anna Ernberg's assertion that Churchill undercut the prices of the mountain weaving centers. Five different centers sent baby blankets to the 1933 show, ranging from $5 to $8.50. During that same period, Churchill Weavers retailed a plain baby blanket for $2.75, larger and more elaborate ones for as much as $7.75, and the top of the line with embroidered designs for $10.[5] Even when selling through shops, which cut into their profits, Churchill competed within a comparable price range, not substantially lower than the weaving centers.

When determining prices for items, the weaving centers took into account the costs of labor and materials. The weaving times for a guest towel with simple colored stripes and a comparable towel with inlaid figures were quite different. At Arrowcraft, three similar designs for small finger towels all took between twenty-eight and thirty-two minutes for weaving, hemming, and pressing. However, weaver Josie Ogle spent a total of sixty-three minutes making one of her more expensive inlaid Bouquet finger towels. In 1941 the Bouquet finger towel sold for $.50, ten cents more than an overshot border towel that took considerably less time to weave.[6] In the 1940s, Penland Weavers and Potters sold a cotton warp and linen weft guest towel with border designs for $1, and a similar all-linen towel for $2. Linen in the warp constituted the only difference between the $1 and $2 items, reflecting the difficulty of working with a linen warp. A towel having an inlaid log cabin in cotton and linen was priced at $1.75, even though it took longer to weave, confirming the value of 100 percent linen.

Upon her arrival at Berea's Fireside Industries, Anna Ernberg more than doubled prices after analyzing costs. Even though this increase brought in more income, it covered only

Berea's direct management expenses. The prices that Berea charged allowed no margin for wholesale sales. Ernberg turned the undervaluing into a virtue: "We do not send consignments to shops, but are grateful for orders direct from friends who are interested in our cause, thus saving the middleman's profit."[7] Although Ernberg realized that she was offering reduced price, consumers accepted the lower figure without really understanding the bargain they were getting. Maybe Ernberg thought that people would not have paid the higher prices. Unfortunately, these lower prices became the expected standard for handweaving.

While those acquainted with hand production might view prices as low because they understand the amount of work involved, most consumers would know little about the process. Comparing the prices of handmade items to commercially manufactured goods, the buyer would consider the handcrafts to be expensive. The Pi Phis straightforwardly tackled this perception of high prices: "While the true value of any work of art is not to be measured by monetary standards but by the wholesome enjoyment it yields to those who behold it, the laborer should feel that he is worthy of his hire. By encouraging the best work from our little mountain community let us, one and all, as loyal Pi Beta Phi's uphold the standard of prices for the work that means so much to every inhabitant of Gatlinburg."[8]

Under Winogene Redding, Arrowcraft calculated retail prices following this procedure: "We took 50% of the total cost of labor plus materials for our overhead, then 25% of that to reach a retail price. . . . For instance, an article whose labor plus material cost was 80 cents would be sold at $1.50, never less."[9] After Meta Schattschneider took over Arrowcraft management, she adopted a similar system for calculating prices. Adding together the cost of material, weaver payments, and—sometimes—sewer payments, she came up with a final production cost. Schattschneider then made a judgment call as to whether that figure should be adjusted upwards or downwards, doubling that result to arrive at the sales price, rounded to the nearest 25 cents.[10] While at first glance this method paralleled practices followed by most businesses in estimating management overhead expenses and profit, the formula neglected retail expenses entirely. The result determined should have been the wholesale price—doubling *that* price would produce the retail sale price. Schattschneider's calculations led to Arrowcraft's retail price, in effect giving all consumers the wholesale price for their purchases.

Without prior business experience, the weaving centers failed to understand the usual practices for establishing wholesale and retail prices. While Arrowcraft knew that prices should include costs for management, overhead, and marketing, they neglected to account for retail sales expenses. The grim reality of any manufacturing business is that it takes as much effort to sell an item as it does to make the thing in the first place.

This practice of underestimating expenses—leading to artificially low prices—has a long history in handicrafts. While not including a realistic estimate of Arrowcraft's expenses, both Redding and Schattschneider did systematically determine costs, establishing prices proportional to one another based on time and materials. Although they did not include realistic evaluation of all of the costs, they based their numbers on expenses, rather than on some arbitrary idea of what consumers might pay. At other weaving centers, the variations in pricing, especially for similar products, suggest that they also used set criteria for determining costs and setting prices. But since prices were similar to those at Arrowcraft, and since all of the centers paid similar labor and materials costs, the inescapable conclusion is that they all made the same error in computing retail sales figures. While Ernberg realized that she was passing along wholesale prices to the consumer, other weaving centers might not have been aware of the generosity of their miscalculations.

In addition to covering costs for weavers, yarn, managers, and overhead on facilities, all of the centers took on the marketing costs as well. In the price structure used by most businesses, selling costs would have been half of the retail price. Remarkably, the centers managed to carry on all production, supervision, and marketing functions even on this minimized income. If they had used more common business practice, the price structure would have allowed profit margins at both retail and wholesale levels. Because of their sense of mission, the centers operated within tight financial constraints and reinvested any surpluses back into expanding the business.

The system the centers followed only worked because they marketed directly to the consumer. First selling to friends and then through the women's network, most then developed sales rooms at their centers for tourists. All of the centers expected their supervisors to market production as a part of their duties. Eventually places like Berea College and the Pi Beta Phi School realized that managing a store and direct sales constituted a separate activity, and relieved their weaving coordinators from these responsibilities. However, no increase in price accompanied their reorganization, and the shops continued to operate within the established income margin.

In effect, the weaving centers created a box for themselves, only realizing their predicament when they attempted sales through standard commercial outlets. The prices for handweaving that the centers offered became the standard that middle-class women expected to pay for such work. No one remembered Ernberg's statement about cutting out the middleman. If centers sold direct at one price and then through shops or other outlets at a higher price, they would be competing with themselves and undercutting the very merchants that were trying to promote their products to a wider audience. Only Churchill Weavers factored into their prices a margin for retail sales and successfully sold through gift shops and department stores.

Louise Pitman, who worked at John C. Campbell Folk School for seventeen years before assuming the directorship of the Southern Highland Handicraft Guild, argued against wholesaling crafts: "It is to our advantage then to reach the customer with as few intermediate hands as possible. That is one reason why I oppose wholesale for most handicrafts—they can not stand the added percentages." She was afraid that higher prices would scare off customers, and

Louise Pitman, standing, discusses John C. Campbell Folk School business with Olive Dame Campbell.

Financing and Fulfilling a Mission

she knew that it was impossible for craft workers to lower their labor costs. In most wholesale production, higher volume results in manufacturers making more money, even if they take in less per item. Crafts pricing presented no such allowance for a reasonable discount for wholesale business. Wholesaling crafts rarely resulted in higher profits, because the original pricing structure failed to include all of the real costs, especially undervaluing manual labor and the workers' hidden costs of equipment and overhead. In meeting the increased demand created by wholesaling, the craftspeople traded a higher price per item for increased volume and hours. Since labor constituted the craft workers' commodity, they earned more money by producing greater quantities; but in wholesaling they worked longer hours, receiving less per unit for their labor. Pitman observed the effect of increasing production for wholesale on the woodworkers at Brasstown: "It kills the creative skill of the carver, takes away his pleasure and his ability to do continued fine work; hence the article suffers."[11] The worker preferred having the work valued at more money per item, thus selling less, than receiving a larger total return for a greater amount of production, but at a lower individual price.

Marketing Hand Production

The social settlement workers first began selling the limited production of their school craft programs and community women's projects to their personal friends and then rapidly expanded sales through the women's network. The sponsoring organizations of the early centers constituted a willing group of consumers already primed to do their duty to help the less fortunate. Products made in the mountains sold through special exhibits or sales mounted by individual supporters, church groups, art clubs, and social service organizations. The coordinating body absorbed all the presentation costs as their contribution to the worthy endeavor.

Each of the weaving centers possessed its own avenues for selling through its sponsoring institution. While these larger organizations rarely supported the weaving program directly, they served the important function of providing customers for the handcrafted work. Berea College developed a vast support system for their educational programs, which bought the craft production of the college-run Fireside Industries. The Pi Beta Phi Fraternity college chapters and alumnae clubs, already contributing to their mountain school, bought baskets, weaving, and chairs as additional help to the area people. The Episcopal Church that supported the Appalachian School extended additional help to Penland Weavers and Potters through women's club sales and exhibits at its annual conventions. Although not directly affiliated with either institution, Crossnore School relied on sales opportu-

Ossis Phillips, wearing glasses with dark frames, shows members of the Daughter of the American Revolution some of the weaving produced at Crossnore.

nities courtesy of the Daughters of the American Revolution and the Presbyterian Church. Even Mary Hambidge sold her earliest work by speaking to women's clubs.

Because the consumers for handweaving lived at a distance from the production, the sellers communicated with the buyers through several channels. In the *Berea Quarterly* and *The Arrow*, the Fireside Industries and the Pi Phis provided information about the development of their weaving programs, the significance of the work for mountain women, and interesting facts about the craft. Several other centers, such as Crossnore and the Berry Schools, kept in touch with supporters through regular newsletters. Most centers produced a small catalog outlining the center's purpose and offering merchandise; the sponsoring organization would then share the catalog with its members. Often traveling with products of the weaving industry, the weaving supervisors presented programs to women's groups. However the weaving centers distributed their stories, they believed that information about their mission and the craft of weaving helped sell their products.

In their communications with potential buyers, most institutions appealed to the charitable nature of the work. Penland put forward a typical entreaty: "HELP THOSE THAT ARE WILLING TO HELP THEMSELVES. . . . Without the chance to sell the goods it is impossible for the mountain women to find gainful occupation."[12] While appealing to altruistic feelings in consumers, the centers believed their products worthy of the price, extolling the virtues of the products at great length. Additional reasons for buying the weaving included good design, excellent workmanship, the uniqueness of the work, and the historical links to past traditions.

Sales publications highlighted quality, as Josephine Robinson wrote in the *Berea Quarterly*: "The cotton counterpanes are often beautifully woven. . . . The linsey is an extremely durable fabric." Like writers after her, Robinson felt comfortable pointing out the unique designs: "The variety of patterns of weaving is bewildering, and the names of these patterns show a great liveliness of imagination."[13] A later Berea brochure emphasized the quality of the Mountain Weaver Boys' work: "These genuine hand-loomed homespuns, for men, in our judgment represent the best values to be had in this type of material. They are made from the finest new wool, hold their shape and crease, and wear almost indefinitely."[14]

Occasionally articles profiled a particular weaver, such as Arrowcraft weaver Mollie Moore: "She lives almost at the head of Baskins Creek and trudges a rough mountain road which crosses a creek seventeen times—there are foot logs—between school and her home." In nine months Mollie wove 771 intricate Washington diamond ring runners with help from her daughters. Mollie "says she 'would a sight on earth' rather weave a pattern than just plain weaving, it's more interesting."[15] The stories about the weavers drew attention to their skill, while personalizing their work.

All of the weaving centers placed high value on their historical connections to people and places in the mountains. Some stories grew into legends, as retelling reinforced and sharpened connections. Frances Goodrich credited a gift of a Double Bowknot coverlet with inspiring the process of using weaving to help the local economy. Marguerite Butler of the John C. Campbell Folk School, like many others, repeated the coverlet story: "The gift of one golden-brown treasure dyed with chestnut oak started the revival of the old mountain crafts which have brought joy through all these years, not only to the creators in the mountains, but to the larger world outside."[16] Through repetition, the romantic story of the coverlet gift, linking

Mollie Moore wove for Arrowcraft for over forty years, especially fond of the intricate overshot patterns.

crafts development to the mountain heritage of handweaving, became the accepted origin of the Appalachian Craft Revival.

Even Mary Hambidge, who prided herself on producing modern weaving, promoted history and a sense of place in selling her work. "Here they had continued to practice their skills in carding, spinning and weaving, which they had always used in their daily life. They still clung to the early American pattern of living, close to Nature, with Agriculture as their chief means of livelihood."[17] Other centers, however, were candid about reviving the mountain art of weaving, as opposed to participating in a continuous tradition.

Often the historical connections named people who preceded the current weaving operations. The Pi Phis profiled women like Aunt Lydia Whatley, Aunt Lizzie Reagan, and Aunt Sabrina, the latter of whom "considers herself an authority on most domestic subjects. Although the need for handmade cloth has passed, on King's Branch, as in other mountain communities, her hands have not forgotten their skill in the old arts of carding and spinning."[18] After lamenting the loss of old looms to a kindling woodpile or for use as a chicken roost, Penland claimed its identification with traditional mountain weaving: "Miss Amanda is still here, now 83 years of age, to tell of the 'stints' for winter days and winter nights, the carding of the wool and the spinning of the wool or flax of a night, together with the weaving of 3 to 5 yards of cloth of a day to outfit their family of seven for the year."[19]

Publicity and sales brochures published by the weaving centers described the revival of the art of weaving, which was part of the mountain heritage. They never suggested that they were offering authentic reproductions or implied that their placemats had actually graced tables in mountain cabins. References to Appalachian design origins described only the coverlets that were woven with overshot patterns based on old drafts collected in the mountains. However subtle the distinction, centers carefully marketed pieces as woven by Appalachian women, not as Appalachian weaving. Even though many publicity writers romanticized their stories about the people and process, they never intentionally misrepresented the products or the method of production. The centers believed that they offered good value for the price, and their tales added other compelling reasons for purchase.

For the most part, the weaving supervisor or another person knowledgeable about the craft made the sales pitch, so inaccuracies were rare. Sometimes the seller exaggerated for effect: "Handmade quilts with the quaint design and staunch workmanship of our great grandparents; kivers, which represent the toil of scores of mountain mothers, sent to pay a child's way through college; hooked rugs, runners, scarfs, bags, pillow-covers, made by girls who work two or four hours a day upon their hand looms to help pay for book 'larnin.'"[20] The writer of this catalog piece came from Berea's craft marketing division rather than from the production department. These exaggerations and attempts at local dialect were exceptions rather than common practice.

In the earliest years of the weaving operations, direct sales only occurred when teachers needed gifts for friends, when supporters of the sponsoring institution visited, or when an adventurous tourist found the place. As sales increased, centers set up small displays, and then eventually designated separate areas as shops. In Clover Bottom cabin at Berea, which served as Fireside Industries headquarters starting in 1902, Hettie Wright Graham utilized handwoven textiles in the interior decoration, showing ways of using fabrics in contemporary homes. Earlier, Josephine Robinson, assisted by Mrs. Frank Hayes, bought, resold, and shipped weaving from Stapp House on Berea's campus.[21] Anna Ernberg included a display area in the plans for her Log Palace. Years later, as work pressures mounted, the college took the shop from Ernberg's direct control, expanding it as a separate facility from the Fireside Industries, although still situated in the Log House.

In 1899 Frances Goodrich held her first exhibit at the Allanstand log cabin, which turned into a salesroom by 1902. "The business of marketing our products was for some years carried on from Allanstand with the aid of an annual exhibition in Asheville. In 1908 we felt justified in opening a shop in Asheville, and in 1917 the business was incorporated."[22] During their "trip of investigation" in 1911 to find an appropriate site for their settlement school, the Pi Phis visited Allanstand, which planted the seed for later commercial craft sales ventures. After selling $1000 worth of crafts in the first month after opening their Gatlinburg shop in 1926, Arrowcraft moved into much larger facilities beside the main road through town only three years later.[23] The Pi Phis realized that an increasing number of tourists would be drawn to Gatlinburg as the gateway to the newly proposed national park in the Smoky Mountains.

A shop on the grounds of the Tallulah Falls School sold students' handcrafted items to Tallulah Gorge tourists and to visiting members of their sponsor, the Georgia Federation of Women's Clubs. Penland established a sales display area in the Edward Worst Craft House for the convenience of both Weaving Institute

In 1926 two Pi Beta Phi alumnae opened the Arrow Craft Shop in Gatlinburg—within a year promising sales led to keeping the shop open throughout the entire year, instead of just summers.

students and tourists who found their way up the mountain to the school. The log weaving room at Crossnore School sat beside the main road through town, its sign welcoming tourists. After that building burned down, a small Homespun House replica directed visitors to the site of their new stone salesroom and weaving operation.[24] The weaving centers absorbed the overhead costs of the shops as part of their larger operations without increasing prices to cover the new functions.

From its inception, Churchill Weavers used a different marketing tactic when Eleanor Churchill, armed with a suitcase filled with her weaving, knocked on the doors of big city department store buyers. Churchill Weavers also developed its own on-site shop, but for a slightly different reason. To counteract the criticism that "fabrics were not really handwoven," Churchill Weavers responded by "keeping the Loom Room open to the public and invited visitors to watch the work being done." After first selling retail to participants touring their facilities, Churchill Weavers opened direct sales stores in Chicago, Detroit, New York, and Los Angeles. Churchill's cost structure calculated expenses and profit for wholesale prices that allowed a standard markup for retail, making marketing to gift shops and department stores feasible. Eleanor Churchill chose Lila and Richard Bellando to carry on the business. Lila attributed the survival of Churchill Weavers to a mixture of retail and wholesale merchandising.[25]

Mary Hambidge and her patron Eleanor Steele Reese conceived an ambitious marketing strategy of establishing a center in New York City, which brought unique handwoven fabrics directly into the home territory of their upper-class customers. Previously, Hambidge sold her work through women's organizations and groups of friends. Using Eleanor Steele's capital—something in very short supply at the other weaving centers—the Rabun Studios opened a small storefront at 810 Madison Avenue. Unlike at the other centers, on-site sales at Rabun Gap started many years later. In 1948 the shop built onto the Weaving Shed on the Hambidge Foundation property opened, catering to the few tourists who wandered down Betty's Creek road.

Mary Hambidge turned down an offer to sell through a fashionable department store, amazing her friend Robert Marshall Shepherd: "I took Mary to dinner one New York evening to the River House apartment of my bosses, Pauline and Walter Hoving, and Walter offered to take everything the Weavers of Rabun could produce to sell at Bonwit Teller (which he owned and was president of at the time.) It took me years to understand Mary's refusal. It didn't interest her. It was just too commercial!"[26] With the security of Eleanor Steele Reese's generosity, Hambidge charted a different course for her weavers. Another person without Mary's sense of commitment to the simple agrarian lifestyle might have eagerly seized the opportunity, hiring more weavers and adopting production techniques.

Appalachian Craft Revival marketing managers always assumed that their buying public lived outside the mountains, primarily in northern and Midwestern cities. The women's network provided access to these consumers, usually through a sponsoring agency or the personal contacts of organizers. Several groups formed to help market southern mountain crafts, offering the work of several centers jointly, instead of the more common exclusive presentation before individual women's groups. Martha Gielow formed the first such organization, the Southern Industrial Education Association, in 1905.[27]

Built on the model of the Women's Exchanges founded in many American cities to help distressed gentlewomen after the Civil War, the Southern Industrial Education Association promoted Appalachian handicrafts and supported agriculture and home arts teachers and programs at mountain schools. It centered its activities in Washington, D.C., with auxiliaries in several other American cities, many of which survived the 1925 demise of the parent organization.

The organization's commercial activities took several different forms, including displaying items for sale at its headquarters in Washington, sponsoring short-term exhibitions, and supplying merchandise to shops in other parts of the country. In Washington, the association sponsored an annual bazaar, which featured the current First Lady as honorary chairwoman. In 1919 the exchange sales totaled $13,183.52, with the association keeping approximately one-third for expenses and remitting $8,912.33 to mountain producers. The Association declared that its sales activities "bless both the giver and the receiver. Through it the producer of the highland craft finds a market for her wares, for which there was not demand before and receives a price therefore which she fixes herself, and the Association benefit comes not from the producer but from the increased price over that fixed by the producer for which the articles are sold."[28]

In the mid-1920s, Olive Dame Campbell, recently returned from her Scandinavian excursion, decided that crafts should be explored as an economic development tool in Appalachia. She envisioned some type of organization uniting the many small crafts efforts in the mountains. With Allen Eaton and Edward Worst as speakers, she scheduled round tables on the subject of Fireside Industries at several Conference of Southern Mountain Workers meetings in Knoxville. Although the various schools and craft centers had contemplated organizing for several years, they finally allied themselves for joint education and promotion in 1930. Early the next year, Frances Goodrich gave her Allanstand Cottage Industries store in Asheville to the new Guild, thus establishing direct retail sales as a primary function of the organization. Allanstand sold the work of fifteen craft producers in its first year of operation under Guild management, expanding to represent twenty-three members by the end of the decade. During the 1930s, fifty-three individual makers and centers displayed their production: Berea College, John C. Campbell Folk School, Ralph Morgan (a nephew of Lucy Morgan who worked pewter), Penland Weavers, Arrowcraft, and the Spinning Wheel made the most money.[29]

Guild members, primarily the larger craft production centers, established priorities and directions for the young organization. Cautiously reaffirming the commitment to retail sales, the Guild opened a shop during the summer months at Big Meadows, Virginia, on the Skyline Parkway. Faced with many problems, Guild President Winogene Redding expressed her frustration: "One of our greatest stumbling blocks at present is the merchandizing of the crafts. Our individual members do not understand why Allanstand has to have a discount in order to operate, at least many of them."[30] While the shop's manager and salespeople received pay, the officers of the Southern Highland Handicraft Guild performed numerous organizational tasks without compensation.[31] Like the individual centers, the Guild kept prices artificially low by absorbing expenses and functioning on a meager overhead.

The Guild codified its sales policy in 1942 after a customer challenged Allanstand's new manager, Esther Bloxton, alleging that he had previously received a discount. Bloxton explained to the head of the Allanstand's Managing Committee, George Bent of Berea College, how she handled the difficulty, and requested a written policy statement to produce in future situations. He promptly responded, clearly explaining Allanstand's three major policy points: 1) all sales must be cash, 2) no discounts to anyone, and 3) no exchanges or returns.[32]

In the survey report conducted for the General Education Board of the Rockefeller Foundation, Marian Heard summarized the importance of the Allanstand shop, indicating the almost $300,000 in sales generated in the slightly more than ten years of operation. Desiring funding for workshops, she stressed the educational aspects of the Guild sales operation: "The shop furnished to members a much-needed testing-ground for their products as well as practical lessons in how to price, and an understanding of costs and other phases of marketing."[33] The Guild only started taking standard markups, covering retailing costs more adequately, and paying the administrative staff in the 1950s.[34]

The Southern Highlanders, which started in 1935 as one of the Tennessee Valley Authority's economic development programs, ran several retail outlets and produced a catalog. Southern Highlanders served both the mountains and TVA territory extending into western Tennessee and Kentucky. Most Southern Highland Handicraft Guild members also joined the new marketing venture.

Cora Morton demonstrates weaving at the Southern Highland Handicraft Guild Fair, which showed the complexity of the craft.

During its first two years of operation, the TVA subsidized Southern Highlanders as one of its economic development demonstration projects. Southern Highlanders, operating as a corporation, sold stock to craft producers, with TVA retaining the largest holdings. The stock actually paid modest dividends during the life of the corporation. For the most part, the largest stockholders also sold the most items: Allanstand Cottage Industries, Arrowcraft, Berea College, J.C. Campbell Folk School, Churchill Weavers, Markel School of Handicrafts in Yancey County, North Carolina, and The Spinning Wheel.[35]

Southern Highlanders purchased items from their shareholders and then sold them through a catalog or in their own retail shops. Sales proved promising from the beginning: starting at $8,696 in 1935, the figures more than doubled in 1936 to almost $20,000, and doubling again to over $40,000 in 1937.[36] Still in its early years, Southern Highlanders quickly pared down their several retail operations to two stores: their first shop, at the dam site in Norris, Tennessee, and the one at Rockefeller Center in New York City. Other shops, located in the Patten Hotel in Chattanooga, at the Chickamunga Dam site, and in the Palmer House in Chicago, closed when sales failed to meet expectations. By the mid-1940s sales for the two remaining shops came to over $100,000, with the New York location generating over two and a half times the business of Norris.[37] The governing board raised the markup on the items sold to reflect the higher cost of doing business in New York. Norris added one-third more to its purchase price, while the New York shop doubled its cost for the retail price.

In 1938 Southern Highlanders bought over $40,000 worth of merchandise from 179 producers, placing the largest orders with Arrowcraft, Berea College, J.C. Campbell Folk School, Churchill Weavers, jeweler Stuart N. Nye, the Spinning Wheel, and Woodcrafters and Carvers, which was run by O.J. Matill, a former employee of the Pi Beta Phi School. Four of these seven organizations produced primarily woven goods; of the four, three also were major suppliers of crafts to the Southern Highland Handicraft Guild shops. Churchill Weavers, which had been denied Southern Highland Handicraft Guild membership, provided almost 15 percent of the total merchandise sold by Southern Highlanders.[38]

After Southern Highlanders merged with the Southern Highland Handicraft Guild, the Guild inherited the shop in Rockefeller Center. Robert Hart, the shop manager in the early 1950s, described the procedures for acquiring stock: "All merchandise is purchased for cash at the risk of the shop." He pointed out that the craftsmen preferred direct sales, rather than placing their work on consignment, whereby they would receive money only when the item sold. Quality and price were major selling points: "It is still true that many articles within the range of the family budget can be made by hand for home use which are superior in quality to machine made articles."[39]

Finances of Weaving Centers

In comparing the weaving centers' finances, differences in their structure and operations become very obvious. While most of them produced similar products and espoused the same general goals, their businesses developed in distinctive ways with many factors specific to location contributing to their structure. Even with shared missions and similar problems, each center followed a slightly different path, directed by its individual sponsoring institution and strong leader. The Appalachian Craft Revival only appears cohesive from the vantage point of fifty to seventy-five years later.

For the weaving centers, success was defined as survival—and many lasted through both difficult and drastically changing circumstances. The Arrowcraft shop continued for over sixty-five years, with the weaving activity predating the opening of the sales area. Penland Weavers produced weaving and metal work for fifty years. Even Mary Hambidge's operation survived for over thirty-five years. These centers never lacked women willing to weave for them. Even as conditions changed in the mountains, with better transportation and the increasing availability of other types of work, some women still chose to weave in their homes. Three weaving centers continued to operate through the end of the twentieth century: Berea College's Fireside Industries, existing as a student labor program; the Weaving Room of Crossnore School, hiring only community women instead of students; and Churchill Weavers. All three places changed and adapted, surviving the Depression, the retirement of their early leaders, and major changes within the mountain area.

At many of the weaving centers, other institutional functions increased, gradually eclipsing the weaving itself. Through the years, even though the Arrowcraft weaving program continued, the Pi Beta Phi Fraternity concentrated more on Arrowmont, their crafts school in Gatlinburg. The Penland Weavers dwindled considerably, but the Penland School, begun as the Weaving Institute but expanding into many areas of crafts education, grew to dominate staff time and resources. Although the Weavers of Rabun ended with the death of Mary Hambidge, the Hambidge Foundation continued as an artists' colony on the property in northeastern Georgia.

Did the weaving centers make money? For most of them, the answer is yes. The weaving businesses provided work for women in small rural communities by generating large amounts of gross sales. Although the figures might not seem big by today's standards, they brought money to women in rural communities that could not be gotten through other sources. During her time at Berea, Anna Ernberg produced the highest income of all of the weaving centers, with Arrowcraft assuming the lead by the 1940s. The Penland Weavers and Potters, the Weaving Room of Crossnore School, the Spinning Wheel, the Dougherty's Shuttle Crafters, and the other centers played in a smaller league than the big teams of Berea and Arrowcraft. Mary Hambidge, who sold to many distinguished people through the New York shop, consistently sold her production, although she never expanded her operation.

Allanstand under Frances Goodrich reported making $10,000 in sales in 1918 from a variety of crafts items, including coverlets, table-runners, cushion covers, baskets, brooms, shuck hats, toys, and tufted and knotted spreads.[40] None of the other centers brought in such amounts of money so early in the century.

Detailed accounting of the Fireside Industries at Berea starts in 1907 with close to $1,500 in gross sales, a figure that remained relatively constant throughout Jennie Lester Hill's management years. Sales rapidly increased under the supervision of Anna Ernberg, peaking in 1928 with close to $36,000 and then declining with the Depression. The gross sales numbers continued downward after Ernberg's retirement, largely reflecting a leadership void at Fireside Industries.[41]

Arrowcraft figures showed a more or less steady rise in gross sales except for a dip during the Depression. From 1922 through 1924, consistent sales of over $2,000 indicated a sufficient market to warrant employing a weaving manager. By the end of the 1920s, Arrowcraft receipts grew to over $20,000 per year because of Redding's expansion and supervision of the weaving. In the 1930s income leveled off because of the Depression. Arrowcraft's earnings increased to over $100,000, by the mid-1940s, jumping during that decade from a little over $40,000 to over $140,000. Although Arrowcraft sales represented several kinds of crafts, weaving generated about 75 percent of the income. The dedication of the Great Smoky Mountains National Park in 1940 sparked an invasion of tourists to Gatlinburg. Even during the early 1940s, with wartime travel restrictions, Arrowcraft grossed over $50,000.[42]

Tallulah Falls Industrial School only topped $1,000 once, in 1929. While most centers showed steady increases in gross sales over time, falling only during the early Depression years, Tallulah Falls showed a very uneven earning pattern. From 1924 to 1946 the entire crafts operation, including baskets, rhododendron furniture, and weaving, grossed not much over $10,000.[43]

Arrowcraft developed a large mail-order business, which eventually accounted for about one-third of its total sales.

The objective for the crafts program obviously had more to do with keeping boarding students occupied than it did with making money.

It took several years for the gross sales of the Rabun Studios shop at 810 Madison Avenue in New York to climb to the $5,000 plateau, which it did in 1943. In 1949 the shop changed its accounting system, reflecting more sales in handcrafted items other than woven fabric. Yearly sales for the Rabun weavers' yardage, scarves and shawls, and knitted items hovered around the $3,000 mark until the mid-1950s, when the shop closed.[44]

While the weaving centers were selling their production, did they cover their expenses? Did any of them make a profit? The institutions and individuals that generated the weaving centers thought of themselves as non-profit entities, functioning for the benefit of the women they employed. Even the Spinning Wheel and the Weave Shop, which Nienburg classified as commercial businesses, were conceived as service organizations rather than profit-making enterprises. While parent institutions assumed some nominal costs in the beginning stages, all expected the weaving operations to cover their own expenses. Some institutions, such as Penland and Crossnore, even hoped that the weaving would make their sponsors money. Since weaving functioned as an adjunct to the main educational mission, the institutions devoted very few resources to developing the craft industries. Like most crafts businesses the world over, the weaving business grew only at the rate that it generated capital through sales that it could reinvest in operations.

Berea's Fireside Industries yearly financial summary detailed weaving production and sales expenses.[45] Community women workers, student labor, and management salaries comprised personnel expenses. Direct production expenses consisted of supplies, repairs and replacements, and laundry. Heat, light, water, insurance, and office supplies were the overhead costs of maintaining the building and operations. Advertising, field expenses (travel), livery, and freight made up the marketing expenses. Ernberg raised the money to build both the Log House and Ballard Cottage, which might partially explain the lack of a charge for space rental in the accounting. However, the records for the Mountain Weaver Boys also show no assessment for space, so the college probably provided space, requiring the industries to assume all other operational costs.

Weaving at Berea functioned in the black from the earliest surviving financial records in 1907; dipped to a loss in 1912, Ernberg's first full year; recorded another loss in 1926; and then maintained gains until the Depression losses from 1932 to 1939. Before Ernberg took over Fireside Industries, both income and expenses hovered around $1,500, showing gains of a few hundred dollars. In a more or less steady increase during Ernberg's first ten years, gross income figures grew to over $10,000 with income over expenses. In Ernberg's next decade the numbers soared to $20,000 and then over $30,000. A downturn in income, with accompanying losses, started in 1932, due to the Depression and Ernberg's increasingly poor health. Income lagged behind expenses until the 1940s, when Berea College scaled back the Fireside Industries into a much smaller business.

In evaluating Fireside Industries' reported gain and loss figures, a standard accounting practice skewed the bottom line. Gains in inventory counted on the plus side of the ledger. All unsold merchandise represented income to the accountants, but many administrators at the college understandably viewed it as a liability. This explained why Ernberg was able to claim that she made money, while others in college management talked about the heavy losses in weaving. President Hutchins defended Ernberg while acknowledging her deficits, feeling that no other college employee showed better potential for conducting the operations of the Fireside Industries.[46] In calculating only expenditures against income—excluding unsold inventory—there are only slight losses for most of the Ernberg years. Even though Fireside Industries incurred some losses, Ernberg's management produced steady income growth for the first twenty years of her reign.

When Ernberg retired, Berea College employed outside consultants to recommend changes in the Fireside and Woodworking Industries.[47] Their detailed examination of Fireside noted the dismal accounting practices that lumped manufacturing and merchandising expenses together. The consultants found the looms underutilized and suggested longer warps, tying new warps to old warps, and similar production efficiencies. According to their analysis of expenses, most of the items were priced too low, often set below production costs. They recommended paying students on a piece-rate system instead of an hourly wage. While most weaving centers, including Berea, paid women who worked in their homes a piece-rate, Berea paid students by the hour.

While her retirement offered an opportunity for necessary reorganization, Fireside never again attained the size of operations or the gross sales experienced under Ernberg. Student labor imposed operating schedules no profitable business would tolerate, with employees working for short periods of time during the day. Even at the beginning of the twenty-first century, Berea College balances the contradictory goals of providing work for students and covering costs of the commercial craft production.[48]

Early in their history, the Pi Beta Phi Settlement School teachers thought that selling items to their friends would make some much-needed money for the local people. The 1916 financial report explained an unanticipated expense not balanced by income as payment to weavers and other craft workers. The teachers had planned to serve as agents, paying the makers when they received payment from the buyers.[49] When craft producers rejected this idea, demanding cash as soon as items left their hands, the Pi Phis found themselves managing a business.

Arrowcraft managed the weaving and marketed directly to the alumnae clubs, through their catalog, and from the shop. Within a year of hiring Winogene Redding to expand the weaving program, the Pi Phis separated the functions of manufacturing and marketing with the creation of the Arrow Craft Shop (soon condensed into Arrowcraft). While Arrowcraft did purchase many different crafts items directly from makers, the weaving business, which it totally directed, generated two-thirds to three-quarters of the total income. It took a few years for Redding to build up the weaving program such that sales completely covered payments to weavers and other costs, and all through the lean years of the Depression the sales outstripped the expenses. In the 1940s, Arrowcraft paid roughly one-third of the income from weaving to the weavers.[50] The price structure assumed that all of the costs of managing both the weaving program and the Arrowcraft shop came out of the same markup.

Both Berea College and the Pi Beta Phi Settlement School supplied small developmental costs and covered some losses, but the weaving programs functioned as auxiliaries to the schools' main educational missions. The institutions never intended to invest much money in these industries, viewing them as income generators, rather than operations requiring capital. These sponsors allowed the weaving programs to grow, but only in direct proportion to the income they generated from their own activities.

From the mid-1920s to the mid-1940s, the Tallulah Falls Industrial School usually made

The Tallulah Falls Industrial School, which was sponsored by the Georgia Federation of Women's Clubs, never had a large weaving program, although they produced a variety of items.

a modest profit. The program showed more vitality in the 1930s than at any time before or after, with income averaging around $800 and expenses averaging around $500. The stability of income and expenses during the 1930s—when other institutions were experiencing downturns—suggests that the crafts program was meeting primarily educational goals at this constant level, always paying for itself. During the 1940s, when most craft business experienced an increase in income, sales at Tallulah Falls dropped, actually showing losses.[51] The school had put other priorities above the crafts program.

At the smaller institutions, such as the Appalachian School at Penland, North Carolina, no capital existed to fund additional programs. Lucy Morgan financed the weaving out of her personal funds. In the early years of the Depression, she petitioned the Episcopal Diocese's committee of education to assume operating losses: "You know, if you have observed, that twice during the life of the weaving, I have risked all I possessed, and all the strength of my body and soul, to make this work go."[52] Although the church refused her request to cover expenses, it separated the Penland Weavers and Potters accounting from that of the Appalachian School. Operating, management, wages, supplies, and payment to the weavers averaged around $13,000 for the remainder of the 1930s, after those early dark years of the Depression. Lucy deferred payments to herself and other creditors when receipts did not equal expenses, because there was no operating capital. She owned the land for the Edward Worst Craft House, and she advanced operating capital during the early years of the school.[53]

Although the weaving centers initially received small amounts of funding from their sponsoring institutions, only Mary Hambidge had a patron throughout her life. Because of the subsidy from Eleanor Steele Reese, Mary Hambidge lived in a protected environment, sheltered from harsh economic realities. Eleanor saw her contributions as seed money for a venture she assumed would become self-sustaining. Even though the shop and the custom weaving business consistently failed to cover expenses, Eleanor's early commitment of $1,000 a month continued throughout Mary's life.[54]

For the Rabun Studios in New York City, receipts from sales exceeded expenses for the first time in 1943.[55] During the shop's first few years, money from either Hall Clovis or Mary Hambidge defrayed expenses. In 1943 and 1944, the shop managed to cover its expenses, and by 1945 Mary Hambidge received payments for the goods she supplied to the shop. Before 1945, Hambidge supplied goods to the shop in New York without any money flowing back to her in Georgia, other than her monthly stipend. The detailed monthly accounts showed major expenses for rent and the salary of shop manager Josephine Kirpal and various small expenditures, but no figure for the wholesale cost of merchandise except an occasional check to Juliana Busbee for the Jugtown pottery.

In December 1945, Rabun Studios' records indicated the large lump sum of $2,000 paid to Mrs. Hambidge, with smaller payments occurring monthly in 1946, totaling $5,883.96. In the middle of 1947 the shop's accounting system changed, reflecting its new policy of placing goods on consignment, with Hambidge receiving the cost plus 40 percent when items sold. She fared well under this system, regularly selling several hundreds of dollars' worth of goods each month, averaging $3,000 per year through the mid-1950s. During the last decade of Rabun Studios, the other craft items sold much better than the yardage produced by Rabun weavers.

Many independent weaving businesses existed without affiliation with a larger institution, such as Clementine Douglas's Spinning Wheel, the Dougherty's Shuttle Crafters, Wilmer Stone Viner's Weave Shop, the Matheny Weavers, and Churchill Weavers. Individually, their many years in business attested to their ability to cover expenses. Matheny and Churchill even claimed real financial success, providing a decent living for their owners.[56]

Government Assessment of Handicrafts

Over the years, the federal government produced a few independent assessments of handicraft work in the southern Appalachian Mountains. In 1904 Max West evaluated the Arts and Crafts Movement for the Department of Labor. In a section on the revival of handweaving, he mentioned work at Allanstand, Berea, and Hindman. West concluded: "While the articles produced by handicraft in the United States are of small value compared with the products of machinery, and can not be expected to increase to such an extent as to diminish noticeably the demand for factory products, the revival of handicrafts is of not little importance to a considerable number of persons." He noted both the benefits to the worker in providing "a means of livelihood and a new interest in life" and to the consumer by bringing "increased pleasure in the things of daily household use and ornament." As an indirect result, handicrafts established "standards of durability and taste," which West predicted would positively influence "factory-made goods."[57] While not attributing great economic significance to the crafts revival, West nevertheless ascribed value to both makers and consumers.

In 1930 the Department of Agriculture chose Knott County, Kentucky, as the site for a study of rural economy, written by Wayne Nason; the study would include a special section on rural industries. As home-based or Fireside Industries, weaving and other textile work were scrutinized, along with basketmaking and furniture making. "Other Rural Industries" reported on sawmilling, grist milling, coal mining, blacksmithing, and stone quarrying as possible sources of supplementary incomes to the predominantly farming economy. Concluding that depressed markets and problems in transportation deterred expansion of the extractive industries, Nason perceived more potential income generation in the skilled crafts. He recommended hiring a supervisor and possibly a marketing agent for the Fireside Industries, expanding programs similar to those established by the settlement schools, consolidating workers into centers, and adding craft books to school libraries for public use. The report advocated governmental involvement in crafts promotion and education at all levels, as had been done in Europe: "It might also be well to consider the formation of a national association for the preservation and development of the rural handicrafts."[58]

Later in the Depression, another branch of the federal government, the Department of Labor, studied crafts as economic development. In her 1935 report, "Potential Earning Power of Southern Mountaineer Handicraft," Bertha Nienburg primarily promoted the centralization of production and drew attention to worker abuses in the candlewicking, quilting, and chair caning industries. Although she advanced the Women's Bureau's agenda of abolishing home-based labor and documented worker subjugation in several hand-labor industries during the early Depression, she neglected to fulfill the study's original mission of assessing the economic potential of existing crafts in the southern mountains. By designating business operation categories not reflective of actual situations and overextending the geographic area, she skewed the results, minimizing the importance of hand production in the established Appalachia craft centers.[59] When venturing into the crafts marketing arena, the Tennessee Valley Authority followed advice from the Southern Highland Handicraft Guild, rather than adopting Nienburg's recommendations.

Nienburg mistakenly assumed that women preferred full-time employment over part-time work such as that supplied by the weaving centers. In citing the women's low average yearly incomes, she implied that they would choose full-time work for its larger salary, failing to consider the workers' own desire to maintain their rural lifestyles and their preference of home-based work. Even to government representatives, who implied that there would be better-paying and more steady work at central locations, less than half of the people questioned responded that a family member was available who could work away from home. Significantly, unmarried young women formed three-quarters of that group. Almost none of the married women responded that they would willingly travel to a center for a regular job.

In 1938 and 1939 the Department of Agriculture surveyed the status of arts and handicrafts throughout rural United States, collecting data through Extension Service representatives on a form prepared by Allen Eaton.[60] Although it was not specifically a study of southern mountain crafts, the report confirmed the importance rural Americans placed on handicrafts of all types. About half of the respondents made things primarily for their own use, with only one-fifth receiving income from their production.

Fulfillment of Mission

All Appalachian Craft Revival weaving centers stated two main reasons for promoting weaving among women: 1) to save the art of weaving and 2) to provide employment for women. Since they intended to provide this employment by encouraging women to weave, the second goal facilitated the first. While Anna Ernberg and others envisioned women weaving household textiles for their own use and starting small home-based industries, this rarely happened.

Weavers produced thousands of guest towels and placemats for the established centers, but they had no way to reach the consumer on their own. While Frances Goodrich, Edith Matheny, and other organizers collected old overshot pattern drafts and dye formulas, which saved some of the southern mountain weavers' textile heritage, most center supervisors designed primarily contemporary items that appealed to their urban customers. In the end, weaving continued because women could make money doing it.

The centers took credit for fulfilling their mission in media pieces generated by people connected with their operations. Both before and after she married vocational educator and former Appalachian School teacher Toni Ford, Bonnie Willis wrote many articles extolling Penland's successes. In her capacity as Lucy Morgan's assistant, she commented on providing employment in an article for *Mountain Life and Work*: "These women, who ten years ago had no money which they could call their own, and who today are economically independent of their husbands, are unceasing in their praise of what weaving has done for them."[61]

From her very early years in Gatlinburg, Winogene Redding kept the Pi Beta Phi members informed of the progress of the weaving program through regular articles in *The Arrow*. She always included mention of the economic benefits, such as in this wartime account: "One of the weaving families, a mother and two daughters (the son is in the army) told me that they must depend entirely upon their weaving this year because plowing is too hard for Minnie, . . . the eighteen year old daughter."[62] In the mid-1940s, Meta Schattschneider commented in *Design*, a national arts magazine, on skills originally providing family necessities finding new usefulness: "The basic purpose for weaving has been transferred from clothing to cash." She described Arrowcraft's development: "It has grown into a business supplying between 80 to 125 weavers with all the work they can possibly do."[63]

Sam Stahl, Director of Public Relations for Berea College, in 1968 wrote the history of the Fireside Industries for the weaving magazine *Handweaver & Craftsman*. He stressed weaving's traditional roots and its development into a business that employed first community women and later students.[64] Stahl's article, like most of the publicity pieces generated by the institutions themselves, straightforwardly described the place and the products, avoiding exaggerations.

In the early Appalachian Craft Revival, women who reported on the arts and on social concerns wrote about the weaving centers for national magazines. In these pieces the writers confirmed adherence to the center's stated goals, described the weaving, and mentioned the economic importance of the work. In her 1902 article for *The House Beautiful*, Katherine Louise Smith outlined the mountain domestic industry of weaving and explained Berea College's role in providing markets for products. "The mountain women . . . are glad to get the seven and a half dollars for which the average coverlet sells, for they know it means a little learning for the boy or girl."[65] Also, in *The House Beautiful*, Mabel Tuke Priestman, who wrote extensively on the Arts and Crafts Movement, mentioned weaving done by Acadians in Louisiana and by Appalachian women at Berea and Allanstand: "The revival of domestic weaving is a very important step in the labor movement, as it gives employment to those living in rural districts, who have few interests in their monotonous lives, and saves from oblivion a beautiful craft, distinctly American in its concept."[66]

Social commentator Mabel Potter Daggett wrote a piece for *The Designer*, "Turning Grandma's Quilts Into Money," with the subtitle, "The Story of American Women Who Are Weaving Quaint Patterns into Steady Incomes." Daggett told of a woman who received a commission for a coverlet: "Since then, by the aid of her loom, she has raised and educated six

At Berea College, one of the two buildings assigned to the weaving in the very early twentieth century, Clover Bottom Cabin, served as a display area for use of textiles in the home.

children and purchased the rose-covered cottage in Asheville where she now lives." She also chronicled the tale of a young girl going to school at Berea—upon observing how handwoven fabric decorated special places for distinguished campus visitors, she returned home desiring to learn weaving from her grandmother.[67]

The Appalachian Craft Revival did succeed in keeping weaving alive and in providing income for women, as evaluated by the weaving centers and a few other observers. From the vantage point of today, it would be easy to explain how centers could have fulfilled their mission better. All of these places could have benefited from more extensive knowledge of business practices, especially when it came to pricing. Their product lines could have included more expensive and more artistic items, emphasizing creativity. They could have sought broader markets through wholesale outlets. The products could have been presented in paid advertisements, instead of relying mostly on unpaid publicity. The workforce could have been regimented, tying the weavers to set schedules or demanding participation at central locations, where production could have been more tightly controlled.

If the weaving centers had sought professional advice when they started out, no prudent business consultant would have encouraged developing a business—with no capital—which would grow unevenly and slowly, forever depending on the reinvestment of meager profits. In starting the weaving centers, the women organizers were more idealistic than practical. The businesses they built were based on the goodwill of others. They wanted to help the rural

Financing and Fulfilling a Mission

women in the mountains by providing a small income, so they adapted to workers' priorities when necessary.

The weaving centers survived the Depression and continued through many later changes in the mountains. The Weaving Room of Crossnore School, Churchill Weavers, and the Fireside Industries of Berea College still supply placemats, baby blankets, and a variety of other handwoven goods to consumers. The Southern Highland Handicraft Guild, with its Allanstand sales outlet, continues to be a strong force promoting crafts in Appalachia. The Penland School of Crafts, the Arrowmont School of Arts and Crafts, the John C. Campbell Folk School, the Hambidge Center, Hindman Settlement School, and the Pine Mountain Settlement School redirected their missions, but all still serve as vital educational institutions in Appalachia. Many other centers have changed so much that only a few old-timers still remember the looms or the weaving.

Now very old women, the weavers speak of the weaving and the managers with affection. Weaving provided a job where no others were available. The women still reflected pride in their work, often remembering very minute details of construction even decades after they stopped weaving. They complained only that they would have liked more work. Although the weaving progressed as a business, the organizers conceived of it first and foremost as a social program providing a needed service to their workers. In the words of Arrowcraft's Tina McMorran: "This is more than a story about weaving. It is the story of vision and foresight. The revival of this native craft has preserved an American tradition, and helped the people of Gatlinburg to help themselves." [68]

In 1935 the Weaving Institute moved into the unfinished Edward Worst Craft House, where weavers hard at work often lined the porch.

appendix
oral history interviews conducted by philis alvic

Tapes of the interviews only are available at Special Collections, Berea College. The tapes on Penland and Crossnore are available at the Southern Folklife Collection, University of North Carolina–Chapel Hill.

Interviewee	Center	Dates
Effie Anglin	Berea College	4/13/95
Renee Banner	Crossnore	8/25/98
Garry Barker	Berea College	5/20/93, 5/14/91
Lila Bellando	Churchill Weavers	5/15/93, 5/17/93
Sandra Blain	Arrowmont	6/13/91
Minerva Bobbitt	Berea College	5/7/93
Robert Boyce	Berea College	5/17/93
Iris Brandt	Crossnore	8/25/98
Dorothy Brockman	Brockman Weavers	6/17/93
Jane Brown	Penland	7/18/93
Nell Johnson Buchanan	Crossnore	11/30/95
Ona Buchanan	Crossnore	8/6/98
Katharine Califf	Penland	7/15/92, 7/15/93
Adelaid Chase	Penland	7/22/93
Sheila Clark	Crossnore	8/15/98
Virginia Coffey	Crossnore	8/26/98
Neil Colmer	Berea College	5/5/93
Kathryn (Kat) Conley	Penland	7/26/92
Theresa LaFrance Conley	Penland	7/14/92
Winnie Pigman Day	Hindman	6/22/95
Ellen Evans	Berea College	4/12/95
Bartlett Farmer	Crossnore	8/21/98
Emma Sloop Fink	Crossnore	6/13/95, 8/26/98
William (Bill) Ford	Penland	7/21/92
J. G. Fortner	Penland	7/13/92
Frances Fox	Gatlinburg	7/94

Appendix

Interviewee	Center	Dates
Virginia Foxx	Crossnore	9/2/98
Alice Green	Penland	7/16/92
Virginia Hartley	Crossnore	6/20/95, 8/27/98, 8/14/96
Marian Heard	Arrowcraft	6/18/91, 11/27/95
Mary Helms	Shuttle Crafters	6/91
Nella Cook Hill	Arrowcraft	6/4/91
Eleanor Hjemmet	Crossnore	8/26/98, 8/17/96
Laurence Holden	Hambidge Center	5/10/95
Ava Hoskins	Churchill Weavers	4/20/95
Cora Johnson	Crossnore	8/25/98
Mary Johnson	Crossnore	8/19/98
Loyal Jones	Berea College	6/16/93, 5/15/91
Daisy Justice	Hambidge Center	5/21/95, 9/26/96, 10/8/97
Helen Justice	Hambidge Center	5/24/95
Etta Kelley	Berea	5/11/93
Sally Kesler	Penland	8/25/92
Susan Morgan Leveille	Penland	8/24/92
Douglas Long	Penland	6/16/92
Helen Luce	Crossnore	6/20/95, 8/27/98, 8/15/96
Murray Martin	John C. Campbell	5/19/95, 7/1/95, 1/17/97
Robert Martin	Crossnore	8/17/98
Jessie Morgan McKinney	Penland	6/17/92, 6/17/92, 8/16/96
Veryl Cook Monhollen	Arrowcraft	6/18/91
Ralph Morgan	Penland	8/25/92
Louise Morgan	Penland	10/24/92
Betty Morgan	Penland	7/7/92
Cora Morton	Arrowcraft	6/12/91
Mary Nash	Berea College	5/16/93
Sue Ogle	Arrowcraft	6/7/91
Margaret Orr	Crossnore	6/21/95, 8/5/98
Mabel Owens	Crossnore	8/21/98
Flossie Willis Perisho	Penland	6/14/92, 2/21/93, 12/1/95
Doris Phillips	Arrowcraft	7/6/91
Ossie Clark Philllips	Crossnore	6/13/95, 6/19/95, 8/15/96
Virginia Piland	Berea College	5/7/98
Naoma Powell	Quicksand Crafts	5/26/96
Willie Mae Ramey	Hambidge Center	5/18/95, 9/24/96, 9/26/96
John Ramsey	Berea College	5/10/93
Bonnie Rash	Crossnore	6/16/95
Maggie Robinson	Penland	7/12/92
Gertrude Saylor	Penland	7/23/93
Bob Shepherd	Hambidge Center	4/17/95

Appendix

Interviewee	Center	Dates
Julia Woodfin Smith	Berea College	4/18/95
Julie Sowell	Berea College	6/93
Anne Johnson Stanley	Crossnore	8/12/98
Bernice Stevens	Arrowcraft	6/5/91, 7/21/94
Patsy Storla	Crossnore	8/13/98
Katherine Styles	Penland	6/16/92
Jennie Clark Vance	Crossnore	8/24/98
Lois Whitfield	Tallulah Falls	5/23/95
Shannon Wilson	Berea College	5/16/91
Jerry Workman	Berea College	4/12/93
Estella Young	Penland	7/23/92

notes

1. Foundations of the Appalachian Craft Revival

1. Allen Eaton, *Handicrafts of the Southern Highlands*, 92.
2. Caroline McKnight Hughes, "Our Industrial Work at the Settlement School," 444.
3. Emma Bell Miles, *The Spirit of the Mountains*, 36–70.
4. Robert R. Madden and T. Russell Jones, *Mountain Home: The Walker Family Homestead*.
5. Jake Carpenter, "Anthology of Death on Three Mile Creek."
6. Margaret W. Morley, *The Carolina Mountains*, 194.
7. Frances Goodrich, *Mountain Homespun*, 21–26; and Eliza Calvert Hall, *A Book of Hand-Woven Coverlets*.
8. Lucy Morgan with LeGette Blythe, *Gift from the Hills*, 9–10.
9. Katherine Pettit, "The Daily Record of the Social Settlement at Sassafras, Kentucky," entry for June 27.
10. Effie Anglin, interview by the author, tape recording, Berea, Ky., 15 May 1995.
11. Allen Eaton, *Handicrafts of the Southern Highlands*, 68.
12. Harriet Goodsell Rauch, ed., "News from Little Pigeon, Craftsman's Fair of the Southern Highlands," 284.
13. Wilma P. Elkins, *Winnie the Weaver*, 4, 6–7.
14. John C. Campbell, *Southern Highland Schools Maintained by Denominational or Private Agencies*.
15. Allen F. Davis, *Spearheads for Reform*, 6–7.
16. Jennie Lester Hill, *Fireside Industries at Berea College*; [Mary Sloop], *Weaving Department*; and [Amy Burt?], *The Appalachian School* (1924).
17. [Frances Goodrich], *Allanstand Cottage Industries*, 8; [Mary Sloop], *Weaving Department*, 2; and Winogene Redding, "An Old Art Modernized," 309.
18. [Mary Hambidge], *The Jay Hambidge Art Foundation*, 2.
19. [Frances Goodrich], *Allanstand Cottage Industries*, 3.
20. Jennie Lester Hill, *Fireside Industries at Berea College*, 3; and [Anna Ernberg], "The Hand-Loom," 13.
21. [Mary Sloop], *Weaving Department*, 5.
22. [Amy Burt?], *The Appalachian School* (1925), 6; and Bonnie Willis Ford, *The Story of the Penland Weavers*, 11–12.
23. Winogene Redding, "News from Little Pigeon," 921.
24. [Frances Goodrich], *Allanstand Cottage Industries*, 11; and *Mountain Homespun*, 25.
25. [Anna Ernberg], "The Hand-Loom," 13.
26. [Amy Burt?], *The Appalachian School* (1924), 14; [Mary Sloop], *Weaving Department*, 5; and Mary Hambidge, *The Jay Hambidge Art Foundation*, 2.
27. Allen Eaton, *Handicrafts of the Southern Highlands*, 59.
28. On the art and social movement: Mina Carson, *Settlement Folk*; Robert M. Crunden, *Ministers of Reform*; Kathleen Waters Sander, *The Business of Charity*; Wendy Kaplan, *"The Art that is Life"*; Anthea Callen,

Women Artists of the Arts and Crafts Movement; Mabel Carney, *Country Life and the Country School*; Walter Rauschenbusch, *Selected Writings*; and Jacob Henry Dorn, *Washington Gladden*. On the women of the Progressive Era: Carl J. Schneider and Dorothy Schneider, *American Women in the Progressive Era, 1900–1920*; Allen F. Davis, *Spearheads for Reform*; and Jeanne Madeline Weimann, *The Fair Women*.

29. John C. Campbell, *Southern Highland Schools Maintained by Denominational or Private Agencies*.

30. Kathleen D. McCarthy, *Women's Culture*; and Lori D. Ginzberg, *Women and the Work of Benevolence*.

31. Olive Dame Campbell, "Flame of a New Future for the Highlands," 9.

32. Donald Alvic, "Settlement Schools" map.

33. Berea College, *Annual Circular*, 5.

34. Elizabeth Allen Clarke Helmick, "Pioneering in Gatlinburg," 254.

35. Winogene Redding, "Weaving Department Report, September 1925–May 1945," 44, 46.

36. Muriel Earley Sheppard, "Mountain People Aided by Appalachian School," n.p.

37. Lucy Morgan with LeGette Blythe, *Gift from the Hills*, 5, 60.

38. Muriel Earley Sheppard, *Cabins in the Laurel*, ix; and Katherine Styles, interview by the author, tape recording, Mitchell County, N.C., 16 June 1992.

39. Mary Sloop with LeGette Blythe, *Miracle in the Hills*, 46.

40. Wylly Folk St. John, "Weavers of Rabun," 20.

2. Common Threads

1. Allen Eaton, *Handicrafts of the Southern Highlands*, 90–91.

2. Kathleen Waters Sander, *The Business of Charity*.

3. Southern Industrial Educational Association, *Southern Industrial Education Quarterly*, March and June 1918.

4. Kathleen Curtis Wilson, *American Homespun for the President's House*.

5. Southern Industrial Educational Association, *Southern Industrial Education Quarterly*, September and December 1919.

6. Southern Industrial Educational Association, *Southern Industrial Education Quarterly*, September and December 1919.

7. Allen Eaton, *Handicrafts of the Southern Highlands*, 90–91.

8. Isaac Messler, "Our Co-Worker," 8.

9. John Mark Glenn, Lilian Brandt, and F. Emerson Andrews, *Russell Sage Foundation, 1907–1946*, 11.

10. Oliver Dame Campbell, *The Life and Work of John Charles Campbell*, 104, 117; and John Mark Glenn, "Resolutions for Executive Committee," 20 June 1908. Russell Sage Foundation, Campbell Papers, Southern Historical Collection, University of North Carolina–Chapel Hill.

11. John C. Campbell, *The Southern Highlander and His Homeland*, xvi.

12. Olive Dame Campbell, *The Life and Work of John Charles Campbell*, 264.

13. "Conference 1930 [Southern Mountain Workers]," March 1930. Special Collections, Berea College.

14. William J. Hutchins, "Introduction," 1.

15. Cecil J. Sharp and Olive Dame Campbell, *English Folk Songs from the Southern Appalachians*.

16. Olive Dame Campbell, *The Danish Folk School*.

17. Olive Dame Campbell, Appalachian Settlement School Project, [1940?]. Special Collections, Berea College.

18. John Mark Glenn, Lilian Brandt and F. Emerson Andrews, *Russell Sage Foundation, 1907–1946*, 584.

19. David B. Van Dommelen, "Allen Eaton: In Quest of Beauty," 35–36.

20. Allen Eaton, *Handicrafts of the Southern Highlands*.

21. Edward F. Worst, *Foot-Powered Loom Weaving*.

22. Olivia Mahoney, *Edward F. Worst*.

23. "Program: Fourteenth Annual Conference of Southern Mountain Workers," 1926; "Fifteenth Annual Conference of Southern Mountain Workers," 1927; "Program: Sixteenth Annual Conference of Southern Mountain Workers," 1928; and "Program: Eighteenth Annual Conference of Southern Mountain Workers," 1930. Knoxville, Tenn.: Conference of Southern Mountain Workers, Special Collections, Berea College.

24. [Olive Dame Campbell] "Adjourned Session [Conference of Southern Mountain Workers]," *Mountain Life and Work* (July, 1926): 23–24.

25. Allen Eaton, *Handicrafts of the Southern Highlands*, 241.

26. "Constitution: Southern Mountain Handicraft Guild," Southern Highland Handicraft Guild Archives, Montreat College.

27. "Southern Mountain Handicraft Guild Membership List," 27 March 1930 and "Southern Mountain Handicraft Guild [Membership List]," 5 October 1933. Southern Highland Handicraft Guild Archives, Montreat College.

28. *Frances Louisa Goodrich, 1856–1944*, 37.

29. Katherine Caldwell, *From Mountain Hands*, 12.

30. Helen Bullard, *Crafts and Craftsmen of the Tennessee Mountains*, 6–7.

31. Lucy Morgan, "Minutes of the Annual Meeting," 26–17 October 1934. Southern Highland Handicraft Guild Archives, Montreat College.

32. Philip Selznick, *TVA and the Grass Roots*, 228.

33. "Holders of Common Stock," 1938; "Merchandise Purchases," 1938; and "Certificate of Common Stock," 1935. Norris, Tenn.: The Southern Highlanders, Inc., and A.E. Morgan Papers–TVA Project, SE/RG 142, #19, National Archives.

34. "Tennessee Valley Associated Cooperatives, Inc.: Report of Relief Benefits During the Year 1936," [1937], and A.E. Morgan Papers–TVA Project, SE/RG 142, #19, National Archives.

35. Southern Highlanders, *The Southern Highlanders Incorporated: Handmade Gifts of Unusual Beauty*, 1–24.

36. Garry Barker, *The Handcraft Revival in Southern Appalachia, 1930–1990*, 47–49.

37. Southern Industrial Educational Association, *Quarterly Magazine of the Southern Industrial Education Association*, March 1917, 2.

38. Allen Eaton, *Handicrafts of the Southern Highlands*, 243–44.

39. Allen Eaton, *Handicrafts of the Southern Highlands*, 253–54; and "The Brooklyn Museum Exhibits Handicraft of the Southern Mountaineer," 138.

40. Erwin Christensen, The American Federation of the Arts, to Miss Jean Thomas, 24 November 1933. Special Collections, Berea College.

41. Southern Highland Handicraft Guild, *A Catalogue of Mountain Handicrafts*, 1–30.

42. Southern Highland Handicraft Guild, *A Catalogue of Mountain Handicrafts*, 11.

43. Allen Eaton and Lucinda Crile, *Rural Handicrafts in the United States*, 9.

44. Allen Eaton, "To Friends of the Rural Arts Exhibition," 25 March 1938. Special Collections, Berea College.

45. Clementine Douglas, "The Rural Arts Exhibition," 8.

46. [Allen Eaton], "Rural Arts Exhibition, Check List," 1937. Southern Highland Handicraft Guild Archives, Montreat College.

47. Allen Eaton, *An Exhibition of the Rural Arts*.

48. Allen Eaton, "To Friends of the Rural Arts Exhibition," 25 March 1938. Special Collections, Berea College.

49. Olive Dame Campbell to John Mark Glenn, Russell Sage Foundation, 7 March 1928. Campbell Papers, Southern Historical Collection, University of North Carolina–Chapel Hill.

50. [Allen Eaton], *Old Crafts: New Horizons*.

51. "Southern Highlands Issue," *House and Garden*, 15.

52. George W. Coggin, "Trade Extension Textile Classes in North Carolina," [1937]. Coggin Papers.

53. Louise Moore, "'Arts and Crafts' Programs Reimbursed," 1941. Coggin Papers, North Carolina State Archives.

54. Bertha M. Nienburg, Louise R. Foeste, Rebecca G. Smaltz, and Carrie W. Graves, "The Potential Earning Power of Southern Mountaineers—Survey Forms," 1934–35. Women's Bureau, Department of Labor, 530, 44:416/Box 232, National Archives; and Bertha M. Nienburg, "Potential Earning Power of Southern Mountaineer Handicraft."

55. Catharine R. Belville, "The Commercialization of the Home Through Industrial Home Work."

56. Philis Alvic, "Potential Earning Power of Southern Mountaineer Handicraft."

57. Bertha M. Nienburg, "Potential Earning Power of Southern Mountaineer Handicraft," 2.

58. "Minutes for Guild Meeting, Oct. 16–17, 1934." Southern Highland Handicraft Guild Archives, Montreat College.

59. Meta Schattschneider, "Wage-Hour Studies," 1947. Arrowcraft, Pi Beta Phi Archives, Arrowmont School.

60. Mary S. Hoffschwelle, *Rebuilding the Rural Southern Community*, 33, 124.

61. Allen Eaton and Lucinda Crile, *Rural Handicrafts in the United States*.

62. Olive Dame Campbell, Letter to Tax Exemption Board, [1946]. Southern Highland Handicraft Guild Archives, Montreat College.

63. Marian Heard, "Report of an Exploratory Study"; and Marian Heard, "A Five-Year Plan."

64. Garry Barker, *The Handcraft Revival in Southern Appalachia, 1930–1990*, 40–42.

65. Marian Heard, interview by the author, tape recording, Knoxville, Tenn., 18 June 1991.

3. Berea College and Fireside Industries

1. Allen Eaton, *Handicrafts of the Southern Highlands*, 60.

2. Elisabeth S. Peck, *Berea's First 125 Years, 1855–1980*, 2–7, 49–62.

3. William G. Frost, "Our Contemporary Ancestors in the Southern Mountains," 313.

4. Anna Ernberg, "History of Fireside Industries," 13.

5. Berea College to Friends, 27 November 1897. Special Collections, Berea College.

6. Max West, "The Revival of Handicrafts in America," 1580.

7. K.U. Putman, "Annual Report to President Frost," 1909. Special Collections, Berea College.

8. Allen Eaton, *Handicrafts of the Southern Highlands*, 62.

9. Josephine A. Robinson, "Report of the Principal of the Women's Department," 1902; and Josephine A. Robinson, "Report of the Ladies Department," 1901: 6. Special Collections, Berea College.

10. William Goodell Frost, "University Extension in the Southern Mountains," 9; Allen Eaton, *Handicrafts of the Southern Highlands*, 63; and Berea College, "The Age of Homespun," 27.

11. Josephine A. Robinson, "Report of the Principal of the Women's Department," 1902: 6. Special Collections, Berea College. Josephine A. Robinson, "Homespun 'Bed-Kivers,'" 28–29.

12. Candace Wheeler, *Home Industries and Domestic Weavings*, 15. A later publication entitled *How To Make Rugs* was published by Doubleday, Page and Company in 1902. Since the text is almost identical in the Doubleday booklet—except for an appeal to the Federation of Women's Clubs to sponsor home industries—I assume the targeted pamphlet was deemed wothy of publication.

13. Eleanor Frost, "Honor to Whom Honor Is Due."

14. Berea College, "Clover Bottom Cabin," 5–7.

15. Max West, "The Revival of Handicrafts in America," 1581–1582.

16. Hettie Wright Graham to President Frost, 27 January 1902. Special Collections, Berea College.

17. H.A.P., "Berea College," 459–60.

18. Hettie Wright Graham to President Frost, [1904]. Berea College, Special Collections.

19. Faculty file on Jennie Lester Hill; and Jennie Lester Hill, "Annual Report," June 1907. Special Collections, Berea College.

20. Jennie Lester Hill, *Fireside Industries at Berea College*, 3.
21. Jennie Lester Hill, "Our Fireside Industries," 22, 21.
22. William Goodell Frost to Anna Ernberg, 18 April 1911. Special Collections, Berea College.
23. Eliza Calvert Hall, *A Book of Hand-Woven Coverlets*, 281.
24. William Wade to President Frost, 24 Feburary 1911; Anna Ernberg to William Wade. 22 February 1911; and William Wade to President Frost, 10 May 1911. Special Collections, Berea College.
25. "Death Claims Mrs. Ernberg, Famed Berean."
26. Anna Ernberg, "Ruskin's Ideal for Humble Homes."
27. Anna Ernberg, *Fireside Industries at Berea College*, 5.
28. Anna Ernberg, *An Appeal to the Women of America*.
29. "Corner Stone Laying, The Sunshine Ballard Cabin," 1921. Special Collections, Berea College.
30. Anna Ernberg, "Fireside Industries Report," 1921: 4. Special Collections, Berea College.
31. Eleanor C. Stockin, "Report of Assistant of Fireside Industries," 1926. Special Collections, Berea College.
32. "Revives Colonial Industry in Mountains of Kentucky"; Anne Weiss, "Tales of Southern Mountain Life Are Strange As Fiction"; and Berea College, "Workers at Berea Tell About School Affairs."
33. Anna Ernberg, "They have eyes and see not, and ears and hear not," 6, Special Collections, Berea College.
34. "Memo to President Hutchins," [1921]. Special Collections, Berea College.
35. "Berea College—Worker's Commission," contacts for service from President Frost. Special Collections, Berea College.
36. William J. Hutchins to President and Mrs. Frost, 27 June 1920; and William Goodell Frost to William J. Hutchins, 9 July 1920. Special Collections, Berea College.
37. Anna Ernberg to William J. Hutchins, Sat. p. m. [1920]; and Anna Ernberg to President Hutchins, 14 November 1922. Special Collections, Berea College.
38. William J. Hutchins to Anna Ernberg, 22 August 1922; and William J. Hutchins, "Report of Trustees' Committee on Weaving" (handwritten changes), [1922]. Special Collections, Berea College.
39. Anna Ernberg, Annual Report, [1913]. Special Collections, Berea College.
40. Ida M. Tarbell, "Novelist Picks Nation's Fifty Foremost Women" and "Berea Woman Called One of 50 Outstanding Women." On Tarbell's accomplishments, see Phyllis J. Read and Bernard L. Witlieb, *The Book of Women's Firsts*, and Kathleen Brady, *Ida Tarbell: Portrait of a Muckraker*.
41. William J. Hutchins to Members of the Prudential Committee, 15 February 1932. Special Collections, Berea College.
42. Anna Ernberg, "Annual Report to President Hutchins," [1925]. Special Collections, Berea College.
43. Treasurer's Reports. Berea College, 1911–1946; and data forms for each year from the Fireside Industries. Special Collections, Berea College.
44. Fireside Industries Accounting Forms, 1911–1946. Special Collections, Berea College.
45. Four typed pages of item lists, made, sold, price, and sales, "August 1935 March 1936." Special Collections, Berea College.
46. Anna Ernberg, "Annual Report to President Hutchins," [1931], 3. Special Collections, Berea College.
47. Anna L. Walker, "Annual Report to President Hutchins," 1934. Special Collections, Berea College.
48. Robert Boyce, interview by the author, tape recording, Berea, Ky., 17 April 1993; Philis Alvic. *The Weaving Room of Crossnore School, Inc.*; and Alice Davidson, interview by the author, Louisville, Ky., 1 August 1999.
49. M.E. Vaughn to William J. Hutchins, 20 January 1923. Special Collections, Berea College.
50. Louise Bradley, "Marguerite Porter Davison, Interview with John Davison"; Marguerite Porter Davison. *A Handweaver's Source Book*; and Marguerite Porter Davison, *A Handweaver's Pattern Book*.
51. "Death Claims Mrs. Ernberg, Famed Berean." Special Collections, Berea College.
52. Anna Ernberg Tombstone, Berea Cemetery, 1940.

53. William J. Hutchins to Edward F. Worst, 1 November 1922; and Edward F. Worst to William J. Hutchins, 8 November 1922. Special Collections, Berea College.

54. "Men's Weaving, Accounting Forms," 1928–1947; Berea College, "Mountain Weaver Boys," [1943]; and Edward F. Worst to Mr. Taylor, 28 February 1929. Special Collections, Berea College.

55. Elizabeth Chesley Baity, *Man Is a Weaver,* 239–41.

56. Berea College, "Mountain Weaver Boys," [1929].

57. George R. Bent, "Annual Report of Mountain Weaver Boys," 28 July 1930. Special Collections, Berea College.

58. George R. Bent, "Annual Report on the Mountain Weaver Boys," 27 July 1932; and "Men's Weaving—Accounting Forms," 1928–1947. Special Collections, Berea College.

59. Bess Ledford, "Annual Report of the Mountain Weaver Boys," 1934. Special Collections, Berea College.

60. Berea College, *Chimes.*

61. Bess Ledford, "Annual Report of the Mountain Weaver Boys," 1934. Special Collections, Berea College.

62. Bess Ledford, "Annual Report on the Mountain Weaver Boys," 1941. Special Collections, Berea College.

63. Comparison of accounting forms from Fireside Industries, 1911–1946, and Men's Weaving, 1928–1947. Special Collections, Berea College.

64. Lewis K. Urquhart, "Berea's Labor Day," 52.

65. Berea College, *Berea College Work Study Program, Centennial Celebration.*

66. F. Boone Dundee, "A Labor Field Day," 7.

67. Wilson Evans, "Increasing the Educational Value of the Berea College Work Program."

4. Pi Beta Phi Settlement School and Arrowcraft

1. Caroline McKnight Hughes, "Our Industrial Work at the Settlement School," 444.
2. Sarah G. Pomeroy, "The Business Side of the Convention," 334.
3. Elizabeth Allen Clarke Helmick, *The History of Phi Beta Phi Fraternity,* 19–21.
4. May L. Keller, "A Trip of Investigation to Gatlinburg," 183.
5. Anna F.T. Pettit, "A Trip of Investigation," 54.
6. Alice Matthews, "Reading List on the Southern Mountaineers."
7. Thomas R. Dawley Jr., "Our Southern Mountaineers," 12714.
8. Pi Beta Phi, *Pi Beta Phi Settlement School in the Southern Mountains,* 3.
9. Edna L. Stone, "The Pi Beta Phi Settlement School," 289.
10. Elizabeth Allen Clarke Helmick, "Pioneering in Gatlinburg," 254.
11. Hennrietta McCutchan Huff, "Memoirs of Settlement School," 9.
12. Mary O. Pollard, "Good News from Little Pigeon," 393.
13. Pi Beta Phi, "Report of the Pi Beta Phi Settlement School, 1912–1915," 73.
14. Elizabeth Allen Clarke Helmick, "News from Little Pigeon," December 1915, n.p.
15. Caroline McKnight Hughes, "Our Industrial Work at the Settlement School," 444.
16. Elizabeth Allen Clarke Helmick, "News from Little Pigeon," March 1916, 440.
17. Elizabeth Allen Clarke Helmick, Mrs. Richardson, and Abbie B. Lanfmaid, "A Brief History of the Settlement School," 461–63.
18. Pi Beta Phi, "Mattie Huff Pledge," 333; Pi Beta Phi, "Blanche Huff Pledged by Iowa Gamma," 477; and Hennrietta McCutchan Huff, "Memoirs of Settlement School," 10.
19. Pi Beta Phi, "Report of Officers: Smith Hughes Department—Weaving," 63; and Pi Beta Phi, *A Century of Friendship in Pi Beta Phi,* 198.
20. Marion Webb Mueller, "Settlement School Panorama—1945–1967," 13.

21. Nita Hill Stark, "Report of the Chairman of Settlement School Committee," 39, 43.

22. Betty Driscoll Mayo, "Old Barn Becomes Craft Center," n.p.

23. Winogene Redding, "Weaving Department Report, September 1925–May 1945," 43; and Winogene Redding, "News from Little Pigeon," 918–22.

24. Nella Hill, interview by the author, tape recording, Gatlinburg, Tenn., 4 June 1991; Doris Phillips, interview by the author, tape recording, Pigeon Forge, Tenn., 7 June 1991; and Sue Ogle, interview by the author, tape recording, Pigeon Forge, Tenn., 7 June 1991.

25. Winogene Redding, "Weaving Department Report, September 1925–May 1945," 43. Pi Beta Phi Archives, Arrowmont.

26. Pi Beta Phi, "Settlement School Reports," 38; and Pi Beta Phi, "Report of Director of Settlement School," 32–35.

27. Agnes Miller Turner, ed., "News from Little Pigeon, A Visitor's Impression," 183.

28. Veryl Monhollen, interview by the author, tape recording, Gatlinburg, Tenn., 18 June 1991.

29. Winogene Redding, "Weaving at Gatlinburg," 872.

30. Michael Frome, *Strangers in High Places*, 173.

31. William S. Taylor, "Recommendations—The Arrowcraft Program," 164.

32. Allen Eaton, *Handicrafts of the Southern Highlands*, 106.

33. Winogene Redding, "Record Book, 1936–1949." This book contains production records, payment to weavers, and production time studies. Pi Beta Phi Archives, Arrowmont. Cora Morton, interview by the author, tape recording, Gatlinburg, Tenn., 12 June 1991.

34. Jerome Eric Dobson, "The Changing Control of Economic Activity in the Gatlinburg, Tennessee Area, 1930–1973," 14.

35. Winogene Redding, "Record Book, 1936–1949."

36. Winogene Redding, "Something About Our Weavers (draft)," 2.

37. Winogene Redding, "Summary of the Weaving Department for 1944," 1; Doris Phillips, interview by the author, tape recording, Pigeon Forge, Tenn., 7 June 1991; and Sue Ogle, interview by the author, tape recording, Pigeon Forge, Tenn., 7 June 1991.

38. Bertha M. Nienburg, "Potential Earning Power of Southern Mountaineer Handicraft"; and Bertha M. Nienburg, "The Potential Earning Power of Southern Mountaineers—Survey Forms," 1934–35. Box 232: Women's Bureau, Department of Labor, National Archives.

39. Winogene Redding, "Annual Report—Weaving Department 1940–1941," 1.

40. Allen Eaton to Mr. Gustav Peck, U.S. Department of Labor, 16 July 1941. Southern Highland Handicraft Guild Archives, Montreat College.

41. Meta Schattschneider, "Annual Report 1946–1947—Weaving Department," 1947. Pi Beta Phi Archives, Arrowmont.

42. Meta Schattschneider, "Wage-Hour Studies," 1946–1947. Pi Beta Phi Archives, Arrowmont.

43. Winogene Redding, "Weaving Department Report, September 1925–May 1945," 46; and Winogene Redding, "Record Book, 1936–1949."

44. Meta Schattschneider, "Wage-Hour Studies," 1947. Pi Beta Phi Archives, Arrowmont.

45. "Statement of Expenses and Losses," *The Arrow*, 1930, 1940, 1950; and "Comparative Statement of Operations—Arrowcraft Shop," 81.

46. Winogene Redding, "Weaving Department Report, September 1925–May 1945," 44; and Winogene Redding, "Weaving Department Report, July 1937–June 1938," Pi Beta Phi Archives, Arrowmont.

47. Winogene Redding, "Annual Report—Weaving Department 1940–1941," Pi Beta Phi Archives, Arrowmont.

48. Winogene Redding, "Weaving Meeting Day in Gatlinburg," 449.

49. Winogene Redding, "Report of the Weaving Department—Arrowcraft Shop—May 1962"; and Meta Schattschneider, "Annual Report 1946–1947—Weaving Department." Pi Beta Phi Archives, Arrowmont.

50. Bernice Stevens, *Our Mountain Craftsmen*, 8.
51. Tina McMorran, "Report of Weaving Department—1949–1950," 1950. Pi Beta Phi Settlement School, Pi Beta Phi Archives, Arrowmont.
52. Bernice Stevens, "Tina McMorran: Combines Three Crafts in Wall Hangings," 38; and "Metallic Yarns," 48.
53. Bess L. Mottern, "Report of the Designer and Supervisor of Weaving—Arrowcraft Shop," 1965. Pi Beta Phi Archives, Arrowmont.
54. Nella Hill, interview by the author, tape recording, Gatlinburg, Tenn., 4 June 1991.
55. Cynthia Huff, "Arrowcraft Historic Textile Collection Cataloged," 16.
56. Mildred Odell Sale, "Make Your Own Treasured Souvenirs," 347.
57. Pi Beta Phi, "Summer Workshop of Crafts."
58. Jessie Harris and Marian Heard, "Summer Workshop of Crafts and Community Recreation on the Little Pigeon in Gatlinburg," 272.
59. Ethel Trainer, "News from Little Pigeon," 229.
60. Arrowcraft student enrollment records. Pi Beta Phi Archives, Arrowmont.
61. Mildred Odell Sale, "Make Your Own Treasured Souvenirs," 347.
62. Dorothy Coleman Thorman, "1963–1967 Settlement School—Art and Craft Center," 16.
63. Marian Heard, interview by the author, tape recording, Knoxville, Tenn., 18 June 1991.
64. Bernice Stevens, *Our Mountain Craftsmen*; and Bernice Stevens, interview by the author, tape recording, Gatlinburg, Tenn. 5 June 1991.
65. Allen Eaton, *Handicrafts of the Southern Highlands*, 237–43.
66. Allen Eaton, *Handicrafts of the Southern Highlands*, 245–47.
67. Southern Highlander, Inc., "Merchandise Purchases," 1938; and "Holders of Common Stock," 1937. A.E. Morgan Papers–TVA Project, National Archives.
68. Harriet Goodsell Rauch, ed., "News from Little Pigeon," 283.
69. Lula May Ogle, "The Pi Phis Prove Worth Copying," 257.

5. Appalachian School and Penland Weavers and Potters

1. Bonnie Willis Ford, *The Story of the Penland Weavers*; and A. Rufus Morgan, *From Cabin to Cabin*, 1.
2. Ralph Morgan, interview by the author, tape recording, Webster, N.C., 25 August 1992; and Louise Morgan, interview by the author, tape recording, Webster, N.C., 24 October 1992; and Lucy Morgan Tombstone, St. John's Episcopal Church, Nonah, Macon County, N.C.
3. Applachian Industrial School, *Appalachian Industrial School*; and Appalachian Industrial School, *The Appalachian Industrial School in The Mountains of North Carolina*.
4. Bonnie Willis Ford, *The Story of the Penland Weavers*, 9.
5. Lucy Morgan with LeGette Blythe, *Gift from the Hills*, 4–5; and Ralph Morgan, interview by the author, tape recording, Webster, N.C., 25 August 1992.
6. [Amy Burt?], *The Appalachian School*, 1925: 10.
7. [Amy Burt?], *The Appalachian School*, 1925: 3; and *The Appalachian School*, 1924: 6–7.
8. Diocese of Western North Carolina, "Annual Reports," 1921–33. The Diocese of Western North Carolina Archives.
9. Katherine Califf, interview by the author, tape recording, Penland, N.C., 15 July 1992.
10. Gladys Chisholm, photo album, 1932, Diocese of Western North Carolina Archives.
11. Lucy Morgan with LeGette Blythe, *Gift from the Hills*, 48–49.
12. [Amy Burt?], *The Appalachian School*, 1924: 13.
13. Muriel Earley Sheppard, *Cabins in the Laurel*, 228.
14. Bonnie Willis Ford, *The Story of the Penland Weavers*, 12; and Lucy Morgan with LeGette Blythe, *Gift from the Hills*, 54.

15. *The Appalachian School*, 1924: 15; and *The Appalachian School*, 1925: 13–15.
16. Lucy Morgan with LeGette Blythe, *Gift from the Hills*, 56.
17. Bonnie Willis Ford, *The Story of the Penland Weavers*, 14.
18. Lucy Morgan with LeGette Blythe, *Gift from the Hills*, 52–53, 60–61.
19. Bonnie Willis Ford, *The Story of the Penland Weavers*, 14–15; and Ralph Morgan, interview by the author, tape recording, Webster, N.C., 25 August 1992.
20. Bonnie Willis Ford, *The Story of the Penland Weavers*, 16.
21. Ralph Morgan, interview by the author, tape recording, Webster, N.C., 25 August 1992.
22. Margaret G. Weed, "Penland Is Training Intelligent Christian Citizens," 732; and A. Rufus Morgan, "Reviving the Art of the Mountains," 222.
23. Margaret G. Weed, "Penland Is Training Intelligent Christian Citizens," 733.
24. Bonnie Willis Ford, *The Story of the Penland Weavers*, 15.
25. Diocese of Western North Carolina, "Annual Reports," 1921–33. The Diocese of Western North Carolina Archives.
26. M.E. Vaughn to William J. Hutchins, 20 January 1923. Special Collections, Berea College.
27. Bonnie Willis Ford, *The Story of the Penland Weavers*, 17–19.
28. Jessie M. McKinney, interview by the author, tape recording, Penland, N.C., 17 June 1992.
29. Betty Morgan, interview by the author, tape recording, Penland, N.C., 7 June 1992; and Ralph Morgan, interview by the author, tape recording, Webster, N.C., 25 August 1992.
30. William Ford, interview by the author, tape recording, Penland, N.C., 21 July 1992.
31. Bonnie Willis Ford, *A Pageant of the Weavers*.
32. Bonnie Willis Ford, *The Story of the Penland Weavers*, 23–24.
33. "Penland Exhibit Enroute to Fair," Penland Papers, Louise Morgan Collection.
34. Ralph Morgan, interview by the author, tape recording, Webster, N.C., 25 August 1992.
35. Fannie Lou Bingham, "North Carolina Woman Has Sole State Exhibit," Penland Papers, Louise Morgan Collection.
36. Malcolm McDowell, "Woman Plans Fair Exhibit by Hill People," Penland Papers, Louise Morgan Collection.
37. Bonnie Willis Ford, *The Story of the Penland Weavers*, 25–26.
38. Lucy Morgan to Haywood Parker, 18 January 1934. The Diocese of Western Carolina Archives.
39. William Ford, interview by the author, tape recording, Penland, N.C., 21 July 1992.
40. Bonnie Willis Ford, "Learning From a Great Teacher," 22–23.
41. Lucy Morgan with LeGette Blythe, *Gift from the Hills*, 97.
42. Bonnie Willis Ford, *The Story of the Penland Weavers*, 18.
43. Marjorie B. Ames, ed., "Looking at the Crafts: Weaving Institute at Penland, North Carolina (Sessions August 12–16, 1930)," 34–35.
44. Lucy Morgan with LeGette Blythe, *Gift from the Hills*, 87.
45. Bonnie Willis Ford, "Learning From a Great Teacher," 23.
46. [Paul Bernat], "Looking at the Crafts," 41.
47. "Edward F. Worst Craft House, Penland, N.C.," Donation List, 24 August 1934. Jane Kessler Archives, Penland, N.C.
48. "Our Appreciation," Subscriptions List for Craft House, [1934]. Howard Ford Papers, Penland.
49. Lucy Morgan to Friends, 24 September 1935. Kathryn Conley Collection.
50. Bonnie Willis Ford, "Sixth Annual Weaving Institute at Penland," 19–22.
51. Mary V. Davis, "Tromp As Writ," 275.
52. Penland School, *Ninth Annual Weaving Institute Conducted by Edward F. Worst*, 2–6.
53. B.C. Burgess to Bishop R.E. Gribbin, 4 October 1938; B.C. Burgess to Bishop R.E. Gribbin, 16 January 1939; Lucy Morgan to Bishop R.E. Gribbin, 8 July 1935; B.C. Burgess to R.E. Gribbin, 4 October 1938; and B.C. Burgess, letter, 16 January 1939. The Diocese of Western North Carolina Archives.

54. "Last Will and Testament of Lucy Morgan," [1935]. The Diocese of Western North Carolina Archives.

55. Flossie Perisho, interviews by the author, tape recordings, Penland, N.C., 14 June 1992, 21 July 1993, 1 December 1995, and 16 August 1996; and *Mountain Milestone,* 10.

56. "Notes on the Second National Conference on Handicrafts," 1940, Penland, North Carolina; and Second National Conference on Handicrafts Invitation Flyer, 1940. Penland Papers, Archives of American Art.

57. Penland School, "Institute Roster for First Session," 1940. Penland Papers, Archives of American Art.

58. Penland School, *Twelfth Annual Session; Thirteenth Annual Session; Fifteenth Annual Session; First Winter Session;* and *1950 Sessions.*

59. Marian Heard, "A Five-Year Plan"; Marian Heard, "Report of an Exploratory Study"; and Lucy Morgan to George W. Coggin, 8 November 1944. Penland Papers, Archives of American Art.

60. Olive Dame Campbell to Lucy Morgan, 11 December 1944; and Winogene Redding to Lucy Morgan, 2 November 1945. Southern Highland Handicraft Guild Archives, Montreat College.

61. Howard Ford and Lucy Morgan, "From Penland to Independence Hall"; Steve Bland, "Independence Hall," 10–11; and Howard Ford, "Green Baize for Independence Hall from Penland Looms," 14.

62. Theresa Conley, interview by the author, tape recording, Penland, N.C., 14 July 1992.

63. Theresa Conley wrote personal comments throughout her copy of *Gift from the Hills:* 185.

64. Lucy Morgan to Miss Mihills and Mrs. Hoffman, 27 September 1945. Penland Papers, Archives of American Art.

65. Lily Mills, *Weaving Classics.*

66. Lucy Morgan with LeGette Blythe, *Gift from the Hills,* 191–201.

67. Toshie Tsumematsu, "Observation Report"; and Lucy Morgan. "European Journal," April 1949. Penland Papers, Louise Morgan Collection.

68. Susan Leveille, interview by the author, tape recording, Dillsboro, N.C., 24 August 1992.

69. Lucy Morgan to Jane and Bill Brown, 26 January 1962. Penland Papers, Archives of American Art.

70. Naoma Powell, "Ballad of Lucy M.," [1962]. Author's collection.

71. Frank H. Watson to Junius Adams Jr., 6 December 1965. The Diocese of Western North Carolina Archives.

72. Susan Leveille, interview by the author, tape recording, Dillsboro, N.C., 24 August 1992; and "Mountain Ministry."

6. The Weavers of Rabun

1. "Judge Crovatt Passes to Rest This Morning," newspaper unknown, Brunswick. Georgia. Hambidge Papers, Archives of American Art.

2. "Princess Bonnie Superbly Rendered at the Grand Last Night," "Brunswick Talent, Splendid Presentation of Opera 'Princess Bonnie' Last Night," and "Princess Bonnie, Delightful Entertainment by Brunswick Talent at The Lyceum Last Night." newspapers, Brunswick, Georgia. Hambidge Papers, Atlanta History Center.

3. American Museum of Natural History. Donation of Mockingbird (Jimmy), 9 July 1926. Hambidge Papers, Archives of American Art.

4. "To Discuss Art Drama Movement," *Passaic Daily Herald.* n.d. Hambidge Papers, Atlanta History Center.

5. Jay Hambidge, *The Elements of Dynamic Symmetry;* and Jay Hambidge, *Practical Applications of Dynamic Symmetry.*

6. Mary Hambidge, *Apprentice In Creation,* 325.

7. "New Theory of Art"; *The Random House College Dictionary,* revised edition, New York: Random House, Inc., 1975: second definition under symmetry; and "Greatest Art Discovery in Centuries Made by a Former Kansas City Man."

8. Lucy Woodhall Nicholson, "Crafts, World Balance Go Hand in Hand, Says Visitor," 2; and Eliot Wigginton, *Mary Hambidge*.

9. Jay Hambidge to Mary Crovatt, 25 May 1914, 3 August 1916, and 25 July 1916. Hambidge Papers, Archives of American Art.

10. Mary Hambidge, "Dynamic Symmetry Basis of Rabun Gap Famous Jay Hambidge Art Foundation," 20–1 and 49.

11. Muriel Noel to Mary Hambidge, 25 May 1921; and "Eva Palmer Sikelianos and the Delphic Festivals: A Commemorative Exhibition," January 16–February 3, 1967. Hambidge Papers, Archives of American Art.

12. Muriel Noel to Mary Hambidge, 28 March 1921. Hambidge Papers, Archives of American Art.

13. "Jay Hambidge Dies of Sudden Stroke"; "The United States of America Certificate of Naturalization," New York, 1912; and "Final Divorce Decree," Circuit Court, Fourteenth Judicial Circuit, Duval County, Florida, 1922. Hambidge Papers, Archives of American Art.

14. Jay Hambidge, "Last Will and Testament," New York, 1920. Hambidge Papers, Archives of American Art.

15. Mary Hambidge to Miss Hamblem, 21 September 1928, and other letters from this period. Hambidge Papers, Archives of American Art.

16. Mary Hambidge, "Dynamic Symmetry Basis of Rabun Gap Famous Jay Hambidge Art Foundation," 20.

17. "Steele-Clovis." Hambidge Papers, Atlanta History Center.

18. Mary Hambidge, *Costumes for Opera Phoebus and Pan*.

19. Karin Schaller, "Notes on Clothing by Mary Crovatt Hambidge."

20. Eleanor Steele-Reese to Mary Hambidge, 8 July 1936. Hambidge Collection, Atlanta History Center.

21. Willie Ramey, interview by the author, tape recording, Clayton, Ga., 18 May 1995, 24 September 1996, and 26 September 1996.

22. Andrew J. Ritchie, "The Weavers of Rabun," 3.

23. Eleanor Steele-Reese to Mary Hambidge, 21 November 1938. Hambidge Papers, Atlanta History Center.

24. "Mrs. Jay Hambidge Guest of Hobby Group."

25. Eliot Wigginton, *Mary Hambidge*, 18.

26. Josephine Kirpal, letters to Mary Hambidge, 1945–1957; and Eleanor Steele to Josephine Kirpal, 15 November 1950. Atlanta History Center. "On and Off the Avenue," *The New Yorker*, 17 September 1949: 82–88; and 26 November 1949: 92–96.

27. Faye Thompson, interview by the author, Hayes, N.C., 1989, and the Hambidge Center, Ga., 1990.

28. Willie Mae Ramey, interview by the author, tape recording, Clayton, Ga., 18 May 1995, 24 September 1996, and 26 September 1996.

29. Dean Beasley, interview by the author, Betty's Creek, Dillard, Ga., 1989.

30. Mary Crovatt Hambidge, *Rabun Studios*, 3.

31. *Weavers of Rabun Sample Books*, Rabun Gap, Ga.: Rabun Studios, [1938]. Hambidge Collection, Atlanta History Center.

32. "Yardage Records," 1937–1957; and "Yardage Records," [Betty's Creek] 1950–1970. Hambidge Collection, Atlanta History Center. Rabun, *Craft Shop Opening*, 1 June 1948.

33. Mary Hambidge, interview by Eliot Wigginton, tape recording, 21 July 1969. Hambidge Papers, Atlanta History Center.

34. "Rich Colors, Firm Textures."

35. "Yardage Records," 1937–1957. Hambidge Collection, Atlanta History Center.

36. "Special Materials," 1947. Hambidge Collection, Atlanta History Center.

37. "Order for U.S. Navy," 1945. Hambidge Collection, Atlanta History Center. "National Affairs: Presidential Yacht."

38. Helen Justice, interview by the author, tape recording, Rabun Gap, Ga., 21 May 1995.
39. "Wages Record," 1947. Hambidge Collection, Atlanta History Center.
40. Greta Daniel, *Textiles USA*; and "Weavers of Rabun Exhibit," press release, by the Smithsonian Institution, 4 November 1958.
41. Andrew Sparks, "Greek Culture Comes to a Mountain Pasture"; Frances Forbes Ison, "The Weavers of Rabun"; Mary Hambidge, "Dynamic Symmetry Basis of Rabun Gap Famous Jay Hambidge Art Foundation"; and "The Weavers of Rabun."
42. Ruth Kedzie Wood, "Jugtown, where they make Jugs"; and Laurence Holden, interview by the author, Hambidge Center, Ga., 1996.
43. Josephine Kirpal to Mary Hambidge, 19 October 1945; and Josephine Kirpal to Mary Hambidge, 4 November 1952. Hambidge Collection, Atlanta History Center.
44. Josephine Kirpal to Mary Hambidge, 27 September 1956; and Josephine Kirpal to Eleanor Reese, 8 November 1958. Hambidge Collection, Atlanta History Center.
45. Raymonde Alexander, "Georgia Mountains Inspire Creations by Top Designer," 21.
46. Daisy Justice, interview by the author, tape recording, Rabun Gap, Ga., 11 May 1995, 21 May 1995, 26 September 1996, and 8 October 1997.
47. Mary Hambidge, *The Jay Hambidge Art Foundation*; and Charles Ogburn, "Memorandum on Hambidge statement to IRS lawyers," 25 September 1942. Hambidge Papers, Archives of American Art.
48. Wylly Folk St. John, "Weavers of Rabun"; and "Report of Betty's Creek Community Craft School, Summer Session 1951," 1951. Hambidge Collection, Archives of American Art.
49. Andrew Sparks, "Greek Culture Comes to a Mountain Pasture," 38–39.
50. Andrew Sparks, "Greek Culture Comes to a Mountain Pasture," 39.
51. Helen Justice, interview by the author, tape recording, Rabun Gap, Ga., 21 May 1995.
52. Robert Marshall Shepherd to Philis Alvic, 25 November 1993. Author's collection. Robert Marshall Shepherd to Mary Hambidge, 15 May 1948. Hambidge Collection, Archives of American Art.
53. Eliot Wigginton, *Mary Hambidge*, 8.
54. Eleanor Steele Reese, letters to Mary Hambidge, 1935–1973. Hambidge Collection, Atlanta History Center.
55. Azoria Kanellos to Hal McWhinne, n.d. Shared by Harold McWhinne.
56. Mary Hambidge, *Apprentice In Creation*.
57. Mary Hambidge to Emily Hamblen, 20 September 1929. Hambidge Papers, Archives of American Art.
58. Mary Hambidge, interview by Eliot Wigginton, tape recording, 21 July 1969. The Hambidge Center.

7. Other Mountain Weaving Centers

1. John C. Campbell, *Southern Highland Schools Maintained by Denominational or Private Agencies*.
2. Southern Industrial Educational Association, *Quarterly Magazine of the Southern Industrial Education Association*.
3. Southern Highland Handicraft Guild, *A Catalogue of Mountain Handicrafts*.
4. Ida M. Tarbell, "Novelist Picks Nation's Fifty Foremost Women."
5. Joyce Blackburn, *Martha Berry*; and Harnett T. Kane Henry with Inez Henry. *Miracle in the Mountains*.
6. The Berry Schools, *The Southern Highlander*.
7. Harnett T. Kane with Inez Henry, *Miracle in the Mountains*, 167–81.
8. Joyce Blackburn, *Martha Berry*, 103.
9. Carol Stevens Hancock, *The Light in the Mountains*.
10. "Tallulah Falls Industrial School Annual Reports," Georgia Federation of Women's Clubs.
11. Carol Stevens Hancock, *The Light in the Mountains*.

12. Vera Connelly, "Light in the Mountains."
13. Allen Eaton, *Handicrafts of the Southern Highlands*, 76.
14. Jacqueline Burgin Painter, *The Season of Dorland-Bell*, 200–04.
15. Katherine Pettit, "The Daily Record of the Social Settlement at Sassafras, Kentucky," entry for September 23, 1901; and Jess Stoddart, *The Quare Women's Journals*.
16. Lucy Furman, "The Work of Fotched-On Women," Magazine Section, 1.
17. Wilma P. Elkins, *Winnie the Weaver*.
18. Pine Mountain, "Notes from the Pine Mountain Settlement School," 1:8, February 1923: 2; and Pine Mountain Settlement School. "Fireside Industries," progress reports, 1921–1936. Pine Mountain Papers Special Collections, Berea College.
19. Robert Boyce, interview by the author, tape recording, Art Department, Berea College, 17 May 1993.
20. Mary Sloop with LeGette Blythe, *Miracle in the Hills*.
21. Mildred Harrington, "The Magician's Trunk."
22. Nell Johnson Buchanan, "The Art of Handweaving"; and Candace Wheeler, *Home Industries and Domestic Weavings*.
23. Mary Sloop, "Weaving at Crossnore," 7.
24. "List of Teachers," 1921; and "Final Report of Vocational Classes," 1922. North Carolina Department of Vocational Education, North Carolina State Archives.
25. "Weaving Building At Crossnore Burns With Heavy Loss," 1; and Mary Sloop with LeGette Blythe, *Miracle in the Hills*.
26. Ossie Phillips, interview by the author, tape recording, Crossnore, N.C., 13 June 1995.
27. Ossie Phillips, interview by the author, tape recording, Crossnore, N.C., 13 June 1995, 15 June 1995, 12 August 1996, 24 March 1998, and 4 August 1998.
28. Sarah Corbin Robert, "Financing Our Endorsed Schools," 81–85.
29. George W. Coggin, "Trade Extension Textile Classes in North Carolina."
30. Virginia Hartley, interview by the author, tape recording, Crossnore, N.C., 20 June 1995 and 19 August 1998.
31. Pat McNelley, *The First 40 Years*; Ruth Dame Coolidge, "Vibrations From A Danish Bell"; Olive Dame Campbell, "John C. Campbell Folk School"; and Olive Dame Campbell, "Progress of the Folk School Movement," 18.
32. Bill Briggs, *The Brasstown Carvers*; and Murrial Martin, interview by the author, tape recording, Brasstown, N.C., 19 May 1995, 1 July 1995, 17 January 1997, and 17 January 1998.
33. Fred Eastman, "An Artist in Religion."
34. [Frances Goodrich], *Allanstand Cottage Industries*, 3.
35. C. Remington, "Swapping Coverlets for Shingles"; and Kathleen Curtis Wilson, *American Homespun for the President's House*.
36. Frances Goodrich, *Mountain Homespun*.
37. May L. Keller, "A Trip of Investigation to Gatlinburg," 182–83.
38. Milton Meltzer, *Violins and Shovels*.
39. Allen Eaton, *Handicrafts of the Southern Highlands*, 76–77.
40. Robert R. Madden and T. Russell Jones, *Mountain Home*.
41. Frances Harper, "A Penelope of the Carolina Mountains," 385.
42. I. Harding Hughes Jr., *Valle Crucis*, 136–39.
43. Bertha M. Nienburg, Louise R. Foeste, Rebecca G. Smaltz, and Carrie W. Graves, "The Potential Earning Power of Southern Mountaineers—Survey Forms," 1934–35. C.W. Graves, "Independent Worker–Handicraft Producers." and Women's Bureau, Department of Labor, National Archives.
44. Carrie C. Callaway, "Mountain Women Advertise Park in Big Cities of America with their Looms and Spinning Wheels."

45. "Looking Back to a Pioneer."
46. Allen Eaton, *Handicrafts of the Southern Highlands*, 250.
47. Harriet Goodsell Rauch, ed., "News from Little Pigeon," 284.
48. Allen Eaton, *Handicrafts of the Southern Highlands*, 79; and Mary Helms, interview by the author, tape recording, Russellville, Tenn., 1991.
49. Edward Dupuy with text by Emma Weaver, *Artisans of the Appalachians*, 108–9; Allen Eaton, *Handicrafts of the Southern Highlands*, 84; and Wilmer Stone Viner and H. E. S. Viner, *The Katherine Pettit Book of Vegetable Dyes*.
50. Bernice Stevens, *A Weavin' Woman*, 34.
51. Nella Hill, interview by the author, tape recording, Gatlinburg, Tenn., 4 June 1991.
52. Olive Dame Campbell to William J. Hutchins, 23 February 1926. Special Collections, Berea College.
53. William J. Hutchins to President and Mrs. Frost, 27 June 1920; and William Goodell Frost to William J. Hutchins, 3 July 1920. Special Collections, Berea College.
54. [Edith Matheny], "Development of Matheny Weaving Business in Berea," [1924?]. Special Collections, Berea College, 1.
55. [Frances E. Matheny], "A Half Solved Problem," [1920?]. 1. Special Collections, Berea College.
56. [Frances E. Matheny], "A Half Solved Problem." [1920?]; and Frances E. Matheny to William J. Hutchins, 21 October 1921. 3. Special Collections, Berea College.
57. Frances E. Matheny to William J. Hutchins, Saturday Morning [1920]. Special Collections, Berea College, 5.
58. [Edith Matheny], "Development of Matheny Weaving Business in Berea," [1924?]. "The Hand Loom Industry of Berea," Special Collections, Berea College.
59. Richard Guy, "Wooster Educator Spent Life Teaching Weaving Techniques."
60. Allen Eaton, *Handicrafts of the Southern Highlands*, 79; and Edward F. Worst, *How to Weave Linens*, 146–55.
61. Edith Matheny, *Hand Loom Weaving in the Home*, 3.
62. [Edith Matheny], "Development of Matheny Weaving Business in Berea," [1924?]. Special Collections, Berea College.
63. William J. Hutchins to Frances E. Matheny, 21 December 1923 and 27 January 1924; and Frances E. Matheny to William G. Frost, 10 October 1924. Special Collections, Berea College.
64. "College Buys Matheny Plant." [Berea Citizen], Special Collections, Berea College.
65. Richard Guy, "Wooster Educator Spent Life Teaching Weaving Techniques"; and "A Mother's Day Celebration." [Berea Citizen], Special Collections, Berea College.
66. Ernest Barrett Chamberlain, *The Churchills of Oberlin*.
67. James Watt Raine, *Have They Found Aladdin's Lamp*.
68. Churchill Weavers, "Churchill Weavers Founders."
69. Alfred H. Sinks, "Wizard of the Hand Loom."
70. David Carroll Churchill, "Final Report of Physics and Auto Mechanics," 3.
71. William J. Hutchins, "Report of Trustees' Committee on Weaving," [1922]. Special Collections, Berea College, 1.
72. Churchill Weavers, *The Churchill Loom House*.
73. Lila Bellando, interview by the author, tape recording, Berea, Ky., 17 May 1993 and 15 June 1993.
74. Alfred H. Sinks, "Wizard of the Hand Loom," 122.
75. Churchill Weavers, *Trade Price List*; and Churchill Weavers, *Churchill Hand-Woven Covers*, 11.
76. Churchill Weavers, "Catalog Price List—Retail."
77. Lila Bellando, interview by the author, tape recording, Berea, Ky., 17 May 1993 and 15 June 1993.
78. Anna Ernberg, "Report of the Fireside Industries," 1926. 4. Special Collections, Berea College.
79. E.F. Churchill, "Why Buy Handweaving?"; and Churchill Weavers, *The Churchill Loom House*.

80. Garry Barker, *The Handcraft Revival in Southern Appalachia, 1930–1990*, 23.
81. Alfred H. Sinks, "Wizard of the Hand Loom," 123.

8. Weavers and Managers

1. Winogene Redding, "Record Book, 1936–1949."
2. Sutton Christian, "Long History of Mountain Weaving Represented at Craftsman's Fair,"33.
3. Bertha M. Nienburg, Louise R. Foeste, Rebecca G. Smaltz, and Carrie W. Graves, "The Potential Earning Power of Southern Mountaineers—Survey Forms," 1934–35. Women's Bureau, Department of Labor, National Archives.
4. George W. Oakes, "Morgan's Ideas Already in Use in Settlement."
5. Bonnie Willis Ford, "Accounts Journal," 1931–39. Penland Papers, Jane Kessler Archives.
6. Winogene Redding, "Record Book, 1936–1949."
7. Ona Buchanan, interview by the author, tape recording, Newland, N.C., 6 August 1998; and Iris Brant, interview by the author, tape recording, Crossnore, N.C., 4 August 1999.
8. Jim Welsh, interview by the author, August 1998.
9. Allen Eaton to Gustav Peck, U.S. Department of Labor, 16 July 1941; and George R. Bent to Winogene Redding, 22 June 1943. Southern Highland Handicraft Guild Archives, Montreat College.
10. Meta Schattschneider, "Wage-Hour Studies," 1947. Pi Beta Phi Archives, Arrowmont School. Winogene Redding, "Record Book, 1936–1949." "Time Sheet—April 1941," 75. Pi Beta Phi Archives, Arrowmont School.
11. Winogene Redding, "Weaving Report—June 1936 to June 1, 1937," 1937. Pi Beta Phi Archives, Arrowmont School.
12. Winogene Redding, "Something About Our Weavers (draft)"; and Winogene Redding, "Record Book, 1936–1949." Pi Beta Phi Papers, Arrowmont.
13. Winogene Redding, "Record Book, 1936–1949," 37; and Winogene Redding, "Something About Our Weavers (draft)." Pi Beta Phi Papers, Arrowmont.
14. Winogene Redding, "Article Draft." *The Arrow,* [1938], 4.
15. Bonnie Willis Ford, "Accounts Journal," 1931–39. Penland Papers, Jane Kesslar Archives.
16. Gertrude Saylor, interview by the author, tape recording, Bakersville, N.C., 23 July 1993.
17. Bertha M. Nienburg, "Potential Earning Power of Southern Mountaineer Handicraft."
18. "The Hand Loom Industry of Berea," Special Collections, Berea College.
19. Bertha M. Nienburg, Louise R. Foeste, Rebecca G. Smaltz, and Carrie W. Graves, "The Potential Earning Power of Southern Mountaineers—Survey Forms," 1934–35. Women's Bureau, Department of Labor, 530, National Archives.
20. Sue Ogle, interview by the author, tape recording, Pigeon Forge, Tenn., 7 June 1991; and Doris Phillips, interview by the author, tape recording, Pigeon Forge, Tenn., 7 June 1991.
21. [Amy Burt?], *The Appalachian School,* 1925, 7.
22. Cora Morton, interview by the author, tape recording, Gatlinburg, Tenn., 12 June 1991.
23. Anna Ernberg, "Ruskin's Ideal for Humble Homes," 23; Winogene Redding, "Weaving at Gatlinburg," 869; and Bernice Stevens, interview by the author, tape recording, Gatlinburg, Tenn., 5 June 1991.
24. Bonnie Willis Ford, *Penland Weavers and Potters,* 1–2.
25. Gertrude Saylor, interview by the author, tape recording, Bakersville, N.C., 23 July 1993; and [Edith Matheny], " Development of Matheny Weaving Business in Berea," [1924]. Special Collections, Berea College.
26. Lois Whitfield, interview by the author, tape recording, Cornelia, Georgia, 23 May 1995.
27. William Morris, "The Art of the People," 182; and Pi Beta Phi, *The Pi Beta Phi Settlement School,* 11.
28. Anna Ernberg, "Ruskin's Ideal for Humble Homes," 23; [Amy Burt?], *The Appalachian School,* 6; and "Society Woman Urges Loom in Every Home." 1936. Hambidge Papers, Atlanta History Center.

29. James Watt Raine, *The Land of Saddle-Bags*, 15.
30. Max West, "The Revival of Handicrafts in America," 1580.
31. Lucy Furman, *The Glass Window*, 172.
32. Alice Green, interview by the author, tape recording, Bakersville, N.C., 1991.
33. Ossie Phillips, interview by the author, tape recording, Crossnore, N.C., 13 June 1995, 15 June 1995, and 12 August 1996, and Banner Elk, N.C., 24 March 1998, and 4 August 1998.
34. "Southern Highlands Issue"; and Evelyn Bishop, "Aunt Lizzie Reagan," 458–60.
35. Anna Ernberg to William Wade, 22 February 1911. Special Collections, Berea College.
36. Edward Dupuy with text by Emma Weaver, *Artisans of the Appalachians*, 118.
37. Frances Goodrich, *Mountain Homespun*.
38. Katherine Pettit, "Pettit Diary," 7; and Katherine Pettit, "The Daily Record of the Social Settlement," 137, 147.
39. Bernice Stevens, *A Weavin' Woman*, 17.
40. Edward Dupuy with text by Emma Weaver, *Artisans of the Appalachians*, 120.
41. Allen Eaton, *Handicrafts of the Southern Highlands*, 79, 80, 105.
42. Lily Mills, *Weaving Classics*.
43. Lucy Morgan to Edward Worst, 7 April 1944. Penland Papers, Archives of American Art.
44. Philis Alvic, "Katherine Pettit and Her Coverlet Collection"; and Philis Alvic, *The Weaving Room of Crossnore School, Inc.*
45. Allen Eaton, *Handicrafts of the Southern Highlands*, 103.
46. Allen Eaton, *Handicrafts of the Southern Highlands*, 103.
47. Eliot Wigginton, interview by the author, Clayton, Ga., June 1989.
48. Bernice Stevens, *Our Mountain Craftsmen*; and Susan Leveille, interview by the author, tape recording, Dillsboro, N.C., 24 August 1992.
49. Bess L. Mottern, "Report of the Designer and Supervisor of Weaving—Arrowcraft Shop," 1965: 4. Pi Beta Phi Archives, Arrowmont School.

9. Production

1. Fawn Valentine, *West Virginia Quilts and Quiltmakers*, 4.
2. George E. Linton, *Applied Textiles*, 3.
3. Mary Meigs Atwater, *The Shuttle-Craft Book of American Handweaving*, 21; and Mary Jo Reiter and Veronica Patterson, *Weaving A Life*, 157.
4. Michael Ann Williams, *Homeplace*, 67.
5. La Delle Allen, "Hand Loom and Fly Shuttle Weaving," 476.
6. Philis Alvic, "Summary of Weavers of Rabun Yardage: 1938–1951"; Nella Hill, interview by the author, tape recording, Gatlinburg, Tenn., 4 June 1991. and Eleanor Hjemmet, interview by the author, tape recording, Crossnore, N.C., 26 August 1998.
7. Emma Bell Miles, *The Spirit of the Mountains*, 55.
8. Meta Schattschneider, "Wage-Hour Studies," 1947. Pi Beta Phi Archives, Arrowmont School.
9. Lucy Morgan with LeGette Blythe, *Gift from the Hills*, 51–53.
10. Alice K. Waagen, "30 Years Ago in Handweaving," 18, 20.
11. Bertha M. Nienburg, Louise R. Foeste, Rebecca G. Smaltz, and Carrie W. Graves, "The Potential Earning Power of Southern Mountaineers—Survey Forms," 1934–35. Women's Bureau, Department of Labor, National Archives.
12. Berea College, "The Age of Homespun," 26–27.
13. Eliza Calvert Hall, *A Book of Hand-Woven Coverlets*, 146–7.
14. "Lee's Surrender." Crossnore School, Inc. Archives.
15. Edward F. Worst, *How to Weave Linens*, 146–55.

16. Mary Meigs Atwater, *The Shuttle-Craft Book of American Handweaving*, 240.

17. [Frances Goodrich], *Allanstand Cottage Industries*, 1909; and Jennie Lester Hill, *Fireside Industries*.

18. Edward F. Worst, *Foot-Powered Loom Weaving*; Mary Jo Reiter and Veronica Patterson, *Weaving A Life*; Mary Meigs Atwater, 141; and *The Shuttle-Craft Book of American Handweaving*.

19. Marjorie B. Ames, "Looking at the Crafts: A Group of Swedish and Norwegian Books on Weaving," 34; "Home Industries in Sweden: Arts and Crafts of the Peasant Folk"; Hannah N. Benson, "Handmade Textiles and the Stockholm Exhibition"; and Elmer Wallace Hickman, "Scandivanian Art Weaving."

20. Carol Stevens Hancock, *The Light in the Mountains*.

21. Carol Jo Evans and Helen Brown, eds., *Then and Now*.

22. Mary Hambidge to Miss Hamblem, 21 September 1928. Hambidge Papers, Archives of American Art.

23. Martha S. Gielow, *Old Andy, the Moonshiner*, 13–14.

24. Rita J. Adrosko, *Natural Dyes and Home Dyeing*; Wilmer Stone Viner and H. E. S. Viner, *The Katherine Pettit Book of Vegetable Dyes*; and Emma Conley, *Vegetable Dyeing*.

25. Lucy Morgan, *The Blue Pot*; and Allen Eaton, *Handicrafts of the Southern Highlands*, 137.

26. Berea College, *Berea Fair for Fireside Industries*.

27. Elizabeth Chesley Baity, *Man Is a Weaver*, 290–91.

28. Mary Frances Davidson, *The Dye-Pot*, 5; and Bernice Stevens, *Our Mountain Craftsmen*, 8.

29. Philis Alvic, *Mary Hambidge*, 7.

30. Toni Ford, "Perpetuating Priscilla's Craft"; and Ashton Chapman, "Dyeing Makes Life Worth Living For Penland School Instruction."

31. Winogene Redding, "Record Book, 1936–1949."

32. Jennie Lester Hill, *Fireside Industries at Berea College*, 12.

33. Elizabeth Allen Clarke Helmick, "News From Little Pigeon," March 1916: 440; and Anna Ernberg, *Fireside Industries at Berea College*, 5.

34. Bonnie Willis Ford, "The Living Tradition," 13.

35. Bernice Stevens, interview by the author, tape recording, Gatlinburg, Tenn., 5 June 1991; and Winogene Redding, "Weaving Meeting Day in Gatlinburg."

36. Philis Alvic, *The Weaving Room of Crossnore School, Inc.*, 1998.

37. Kathleen Waters Sander, *The Business of Charity*.

38. Lori D. Ginzberg, *Women and the Work of Benevolence*; and Kathleen D. McCarthy, *Women's Culture*.

39. Cora Morton, interview by the author, tape recording, Gatlinburg, Tenn., 12 June 1991.

40. Southern Highland Handicraft Guild, *A Catalogue of Mountain Handicrafts*.

41. Southern Highlanders, *The Southern Highlanders Incorporated*.

42. Janet Meany and Paula Pfaff, *Rag Rug Handbook*, 81–101.

43. William J. Hutchins to Anna Ernberg, 4 April 1928. Special Collections, Berea College.

44. Winogene Redding, "Record Book, 1936–1949," Pi Beta Phi Archives, Arrowmont; and "Production Report, August 1935 through March 1936," 1935–36. Special Collections, Berea College.

10. Financing and Fulfilling a Mission

1. Kathleen Waters Sander, *The Business of Charity*.

2. [Frances Goodrich], *Allanstand Cottage Industries*; Jennie Lester Hill, *Fireside Industries at Berea College*, 1908; and Anna Ernberg, *Fireside Industries at Berea College*, [1920?].

3. [Mary Sloop], *Weaving Department*. and [Amy Burt?], *The Appalachian School*, 1925; and Pi Beta Phi, *Arrow Craft Shop: Handicrafts*.

4. Southern Highland Handicraft Guild, *A Catalogue of Mountain Handicrafts*.

5. Churchill Weavers, *Trade Price List*. Anna Ernberg, "Report of the Fireside Industries," 1926: 5. Special Collections, Berea College. Churchill Weavers, *Churchill Hand-Woven Covers*, 12–14.

6. Pi Beta Phi, *Arrow Craft Shop*, 1941; and Winogene Redding, "Record Book, 1936–1949."

7. Anna Ernberg, *Fireside Industries at Berea College*, 5.

8. Pi Beta Phi, *The Pi Beta Phi Settlement School*, 13.

9. Winogene Redding to Olive Dame Campbell and Louise Pitman, 28 May 1946. Southern Highland Handicraft Guild Archives, Montreat College.

10. Meta Schattschneider, "Wage-Hour Studies," 1947. Arrowcraft, Pi Beta Phi Archives, Arrowmont School.

11. Louise Pitman to Dr. Arthur E. Morgan, 10 September 1941. A.E. Morgan Papers–TVA Project, National Archives.

12. [Amy Burt?], *The Appalachian School*, 1925: 11.

13. Josephine A. Robinson, "Mountain Homespun," 8.

14. Berea College, *For Berea The Beloved*, 5.

15. La Delle Allen, "Mollie Moore," 317.

16. Frances Goodrich, *Mountain Homespun*, 21; and Marguerite Butler, "A Dream Come True," 2.

17. Mary Hambidge, The Jay Hambidge Art Foundation, 2.

18. Frances Moore, "Aunt Sabrina King," 460.

19. Lucy Morgan, *The Apalachian School Department*, 3.

20. Berea College, *For Berea The Beloved*, 2.

21. Berea College, "Clover Bottom Cabin"; and Berea College, "Memorandum on Domestic Manufacture and the Stapp House," [1900?]. Berea College Special Collections.

22. Frances Goodrich, *Mountain Homespun*, 25, 28, 29.

23. Pi Beta Phi, "Settlement School Reports"; and Pi Beta Phi, "Report of Director of Settlement School."

24. Lillie Johnson, *Homespun House*.

25. Churchill Weavers, *A Tour and Background of Churchill Weavers*, 2; and Lila Bellando, interview by the author, tape recording, Berea, Ky., 17 May 1993 and 15 June 1993.

26. Robert Marshall Shepherd to Philis Alvic, 25 November 1993. Author's collection.

27. Allen Eaton, *Handicrafts of the Southern Highlands*, 90.

28. "Secretary's Report," *Southern Industrial Education Quarterly*, March and June 1919: 7–9.

29. "Allanstand Sales Records," 1931–1939. Southern Highland Handicraft Guild Archives, Monreat College.

30. Winogene Redding, "Talk on Crafts Development"; and Winogene Redding to Jean W. Schenck, Lily Mills Company, 11 September 1944. Southern Highland Hanicraft Guild Archives, Monreat College.

31. Garry Barker, *The Handcraft Revival in Southern Appalachia, 1930–1990*, 24–25.

32. Esther Bloxton to George Bent, 1 April 1942; and George Bent to Esther Bloxton, 4 April 1942. Southern Highland Handicraft Guild Archives, Montreat College.

33. Marian Heard, "A Five-Year Plan," 4.

34. Garry Barker, interview by the author, 3 April 2001.

35. "Holders of Common Stock," 31 December 1937. Norris, Tenn.: Southern Highlanders, Inc., and A.E. Morgan Papers–TVA Project, National Archives.

36. Paul B. Johnson to John E. Barr, 12 January 1939. A.E. Morgan Papers–TVA Project, National Archives.

37. "Southern Highlanders, Inc., Profit and Loss Statement," 31 December 1945: 2. Norris, Tenn.: A.E. Morgan Papers–TVA Project, National Archives.

38. "Merchandise Purchases," 1938. A.E. Morgan Papers–TVA Project, National Archives.

39. Robert G. Hart, "From The Great Smokies to Rockefeller Center."

40. Frances Goodrich, "Shuttles and Drafts."

41. "Treasurer's Reports of Student Labor Industries," 1911–1950; and "Profit and Loss Itemized State-

ments" for Fireside Industries, Men's Weaving, Cottage Weavers, and Weaving Instruction, 1907–1947. Special Collections, Berea College.

42. Pi Beta Phi, "Pi Beta Phi Settlement School Treasurer's Report."

43. Tallulah Falls Industrial School, "Final Reports," 1924–1946. Tallulah Falls, Ga.: Georgia Federation of Women's Clubs, Tallulah Falls Industrial School Archives.

44. Josephine Kirpal, "Financial Statements for Rabun Studios," 1938–1958. Hambidge Papers, Atlanta History Center.

45. Berea College, "Profit and Loss Itemized Statements" for Fireside Industries, Men's Weaving, Cottage Weavers, and Weaving Instruction, 1907–1947. Special Collections, Berea College.

46. William J. Hutchins to Member of the Prudential Committee [notes], 15 February 1932. Special Collections, Berea College.

47. McKinsey, Wellington and Company, "Berea College Survey of Woodwork-Furniture and Fireside Industries."

48. Garry Barker, interview with author, tape recording, Berea, Ky., 14 May 1991 and 20 May 1993.

49. Elizabeth Allen Clarke Helmick, "News From Little Pigeon," March 1916.

50. Pi Beta Phi, "Pi Beta Phi Settlement School Treasurer's Report."

51. Tallulah Falls Industrial School, "Final Reports," 1924–1946. Georgia Federation of Women's Clubs, Tallulah Falls Industrial School Archives.

52. Lucy Morgan to Haywood Parker, 18 January 1934. Diocese of Western Carolina Archives.

53. Bonnie Willis Ford, "Accounts Journal," 1931–39. Penland Archives, Penland School. Paul Willis, "Audit Penland Weavers and Potters," 1933. and Paul Willis, "Audit Penland Weavers and Potters," 1934. North Carolina State Archives, Raleigh; Paul Willis, "Audit The Edward F. Worst Craft House, Weaving Institute Funds, The Health House Fund," 1938. Penland Weavers and Potters, Diocese of Western North Carolina Archives, and Lucy Morgan with LeGette Blythe, *Gift from the Hills,* 99.

54. Eleanor Steele Reese to Mary Hambidge, 1935–1973. Hambidge Papers, Atlanta History Center.

55. Josephine Kirpal, "Financial Statements for Rabun Studios," 1938–1958. Hambidge Papers, Atlanta History Center.

56. Richard Guy, "Wooster Educator Spent Life Teaching Weaving Techniques"; and Alfred H. Sinks, "Wizard of the Hand Loom."

57. Max West, "The Revival of Handicrafts in America," 1622.

58. Wayne C. Nason, "Rural Industries in Knott County, Kentucky."

59. Bertha M. Nienburg, "Potential Earning Power of Southern Mountaineer Handicraft."; and Philis Alvic, "Potential Earning Power of Southern Mountaineer Handicraft."

60. Allen Eaton and Lucinda Crile, *Rural Handicrafts in the United States.*

61. Bonnie Willis Ford, "The Living Tradition," 13.

62. Winogene Redding, "Miss Redding, Director of Weaving, writes on 'Weaving in Wartime,'" 371.

63. Meta Schattschneider, "Handweaving A Way of Life," 4.

64. Sam Stahl, "Berea College."

65. Katherine Louise Smith, "A Mountain Fireside Industry," 409.

66. Mabel Tuke Priestman, "Coverlet Weaving in the South," 26.

67. Mabel Potter Daggett, "Turning Grandma's Quilts into Money."

68. Tina McMorran, "Arrowcraft Report, [1951?] " Phi Beta Phi School Archives, Arrowmont, 3.

bibliography

Manuscripts

Appalachian School Papers. The Diocese of Western North Carolina Archives. Black Mountain, North Carolina.
Brown, William. Papers. Penland School Papers. Archives of American Art, Washington, D.C.
Campbell, Olive Dame and John C Campbell Papers. Southern Historical Collection. Wilson Library. University of North Carolina–Chapel Hill. Chapel Hill, North Carolina.
Churchill Weavers Papers. Churchill Weavers Archives. Berea, Kentucky.
Coggin, George W. Papers. Divison of Trades and Industry, North Carolina Department of Education Papers. North Carolina State Archives. Raleigh, North Carolina.
Ford, Howard. Papers. Penland, N.C.
Hambidge, Mary Crovatt. Papers and Textiles. Atlanta History Center. Atlanta, Georgia.
Hambidge Papers. Archives of American Art, Washington, D.C.
North Carolina Newspaper Archives. North Carolina Collection Reading Room. Wilson Library. University of North Carolina–Chapel Hill. Chapel Hill, North Carolina.
Penland Papers. Louise Morgan Collection, Privately Held.
Penland School Papers. Archives of American Art, Washington, D.C.
Penland School Papers. Kathryn Conley Collection. Penland, North Carolina.
Penland School Papers. Jane Kessler Archives. Penland School. Penland, North Carolina.
Pettit, Katherine. Papers. Special Collections. King Library, University of Kentucky. Lexington, Kentucky.
Pi Beta Phi Historical Papers. Pi Beta Phi Archives. Arrowmont School. Gatlinburg, Tennessee.
Southern Highlands Handicraft Guild Archives. Montreat College. Montreat, North Carolina.
Southern Highlander Papers. Tennessee Valley Authority, A.E. Morgan Papers, Record Group 142, National Archives Southeast Region, Atlanta, Ga.
Special Collections, Hutchins Library. Berea College. Berea, Kentucky.
Tallulah Falls Industrial School Archives, Georgia Federation of Women's Clubs, Tallulah Falls, Georgia.
The Weaving Room and Crossnore School, Inc. Papers. Crossnore School, Inc. Archives. Crossnore, North Carolina.
The Weaving Room and Crossnore School, Inc. Photographs and Objects. The Avery County Historical Society and Museum.
Women's Bureau Records, Department of Labor. 530, 44:416/Box 232. National Archives at College Park.

Books, Periodicals, and Newspapers

Adrosko, Rita J. *Natural Dyes and Home Dyeing*. 1968. New York: Dover Publications, Inc., 1971.
Alexander, Raymonde. "Georgia Mountains Inspire Creations by Top Designer." *The Atlanta Constitution*, 5 July 1963: 21.

Bibliography

Allen, La Delle. "Hand Loom and Fly Shuttle Weaving." *The Arrow,* February 1932: 476.
———. "Mollie Moore." *The Arrow,* February 1933: 317.
Alvic, Donald. "Settlement Schools." Map. University of Tennessee, 2002.
Alvic, Philis. "Katherine Pettit and Her Coverlet Collection." Paper presented at the Women of Appalachia Conference, Ohio University, Zanesville, 26–28 October 2000.
———. *Mary Hambidge: Weaver of Rabun.* 1989. Murray, Ky.: privately printed with revisions, 1993.
———. "Potential Earning Power of Southern Mountaineer Handicraft: What the Numbers Mean In This 1935 Government Study." Paper presented at the Appalachian Studies Conference, Knoxville, Tenn., 25 March 2000.
———. "Summary of Weavers of Rabun Yardage: 1938–1951." 1990.
———. *Weavers of the Southern Highlands: Berea.* Privately printed, 1993.
———. *Weavers of the Southern Highlands: Penland.* Privately printed, 1992.
———. *Weavers of the Southern Highlands: The Early Years in Gatlinburg.* Privately printed, 1991.
———. *The Weaving Room of Crossnore School, Inc.* Newland, N.C.: Avery County Historical Museum, 1998.
———, ed. *Fiber Focus: Kentucky.* Lexington, Ky.: The Fiber Guild of Lexington, 2000.
Ames, Marjorie B., ed. "Looking at the Crafts: Weaving Institute at Penland, North Carolina (Sessions August 12–16, 1930)." *The Handicrafter,* July–August 1930: 34–35.
———, ed. "Looking at the Crafts: A Group of Swedish and Norwegian Books on Weaving." *The Handicrafter,* July–August 1930: 34.
Applachian Industrial School. *Appalachian Industrial School: A School for Mountain Boys and Girls.* [1914.]
———. *The Appalachian Industrial School in The Mountains of North Carolina.* [1915].
Atwater, Mary Meigs. *The Shuttle-Craft Book of American Handweaving.* 1928. New York: The Macmillan Company, 1961.
Baity, Elizabeth Chesley. *Man Is a Weaver.* New York: The Viking Press, 1942.
Barker, Garry. *The Handcraft Revival in Southern Appalachia, 1930–1990.* Knoxville, Tenn.: The University of Tennessee Press, 1991.
Becker, Jane S. *Selling Tradition: Appalachia and the Construction of an American Folk.* Chapel Hill: The University of North Carolina Press, 1998.
Belville, Catharine R. "The Commercialization of the Home Through Industrial Home Work." Washington, D.C.: Women's Bureau, Department of Labor, 1935.
Benson, Hannah N. "Handmade Textiles and the Stockholm Exhibition." *The Handicrafter,* January–Feburary 1931: 3–9.
Berea College. "The Age of Homespun." *Berea Quarterly,* November 1900: 26–27.
———. *Annual Circular: Berea College.* Berea, Ky.: Berea College, [1874].
———. *Berea College Work Study Program, Centennial Celebration.* Berea, Ky.: Berea College, 1955.
———. *Berea Fair for Fireside Industries.* Berea, Ky.: Berea College, 1903.
———. *Chimes.* Berea, Ky.: Berea College, 1937.
———. "Clover Bottom Cabin." *Berea Quarterly,* April 1904: 5–7.
———. *For Berea The Beloved.* Berea, Ky.: Berea College Student Industries, [1930?].
———. "Mountain Weaver Boys." Berea, Ky.: Berea College, [1929].
———. "Mountain Weaver Boys." Berea, Ky.: Berea College, [1943].
———. "Workers at Berea Tell About School Affairs." *Duluth Herald,* 18 August 1930.
[Bernat, Paul]. "Looking at the Crafts." *The Handicrafter,* November–December 1930: 41.
The Berry Schools. *The Southern Highlander.* Rome, Ga.: The Berry Schools, 1925.
Bingham, Fannie Lou. "North Carolina Woman Has Sole State Exhibit." *The Charlotte (N.C.) News,* 29 July [1934]: n.p.
Bishop, Evelyn. "Aunt Lizzie Reagan." *The Arrow,* May 1931: 458–60.
Blackburn, Joyce. *Martha Berry: Little Woman with a Big Dream.* Philadelphia: J.B. Lippincott Company, 1968.

Bibliography

Bland, Steve. "Independence Hall." *Philadelphia Inquirer*, 19 July 1956: 10–11.

Boris, Eileen. *Art and Labor: Ruskin, Morris, and the Craftsman Ideal in America*. Philadelphia: Temple University Press, 1986.

———. *Home to Work: Motherhood and the Politics of Industrial Homework in the United States*. Cambridge: Cambridge University Press, 1994.

Bradley, Louise. "Marguerite Porter Davison, Interview with John Davison." *Handwoven*, May/June 1990: 67–69.

Brady, Kathleen. *Ida Tarbell: Portrait of a Muckraker*. Pittsburgh: University of Pittsburgh Press, 1989.

Briggs, Bill. *The Brasstown Carvers*. Brasstown, N.C.: John C. Campbell Folk School, 1990.

"The Brooklyn Museum Exhibits Handicraft of the Southern Mountaineer." *The Bulletin of the Brooklyn Institute of Arts and Sciences*, [1933]: 138.

Buchanan, Nell Johnson. "The Art of Handweaving." Essay for oral presentation at Graduation of Crossnore High School, 6 April 1921.

Bullard, Helen. *Crafts and Craftsmen of the Tennessee Mountains*. Falls Church, Va.: Summit Press Ltd., 1976.

[Burt, Amy?]. *The Appalachian School*. Penland, N.C.: Appalachian School, 1924.

[———?]. *The Appalachian School*. Penland, N.C.: Appalachian School, 1925.

Burnham, Harold B. and Dorothy K. Burnham. *"Keep me warm one night": Early Handweaving in Eastern Canada*. Toronto: University of Toronto Press in co-operation with the Royal Ontario Museum, 1972.

Butler, Marguerite. "A Dream Come True." *Mountain Life and Work*, October 1931: 1–4.

Bythell, Duncan. *The Handloom Weavers: A Study in the English Cotton Industry During the Industrial Revolution*. Cambridge, England: Cambridge University Press, 1969.

Caldwell, Katherine. *From Mountain Hands: The Story of Allanstand Craft Shop's First 100 Years*. Asheville, N.C.: Southern Highland Handicraft Guild, [1990].

Callaway, Carrie C. "Mountain Women Advertise Park in Big Cities of America with their Looms and Spinning Wheels." *The Knoxville Sunday Journal*, 2 May 1930.

Callen, Anthea. *Women Artists of the Arts and Crafts Movement*. New York: Pantheon Books, 1979.

Campbell, John C. *Southern Highland Schools Maintained by Denominational or Private Agencies*. New York: The Russell Sage Foundation, 1920.

———. *The Southern Highlander and His Homeland*. New York: The Russell Sage Foundation, 1921.

Campbell, Olive Dame. *The Danish Folk School*. New York: The Macmillian Company, 1928.

———. "Flame of a New Future for the Highlands." *Southern Mountain Life and Work*, April 1925: 9–13.

———. "John C. Campbell Folk School." *Rural America*, November 1926: 12.

———. *The Life and Work of John Charles Campbell*, Madison, Wisc.: Lois Bacon, Estate Trustee, College Printing and Typing Company, Inc.,1968.

———. "Progress of the Folk School Movement." *Southern Mountain Life and Work*, July 1925: 17–18.

[Campbell, Olive Dame.] "Adjourned Session [Conference of Southern Mountain Workers]." *Mountain Life and Work*, July 1926, 23–24.

Carney, Mabel. *Country Life and the Country School*. Chicago: Row, Peterson and Company, 1912.

Carpenter, Jake. "Anthology of Death on Three Mile Creek." 1841–1916. Edited and copied by Josephine Senter Wolford. Crossnore, N.C.: Crossnore School, 1955.

Carson, Mina. *Settlement Folk*. Chicago: The University of Chicago Press, 1990.

Chamberlain, Ernest Barrett. *The Churchills of Oberlin*. Oberlin, Ohio: The Ohio Historical and Improvement Organization, 1965.

Chapman, Ashton. "Dyeing Makes Life Worth Living For Penland School Instruction." *The Tri-County News*, [1961?].

Christian, Sutton. "Long History of Mountain Weaving Represented at Craftsman's Fair." *The Arrow*, Spring 1962: 33–34.

Churchill Weavers. "Catalog Price List—Retail." Berea, Ky.: Churchill Weavers, [1940].

———. *Churchill Hand-Woven Covers*. Berea, Ky.: Churchill Weavers, 1930.

Bibliography

———. *The Churchill Loom House: By the Side of the Road.* Berea, Ky.: Churchill Weavers, [1935?].

———. "Churchill Weavers Founders." Berea, Ky.: Churchill Weavers, [1964].

———. *The Churchill Weavers: Trade Price List.* Berea, Ky.: Churchill Weavers, 1928.

———. *A Tour and Background of Churchill Weavers.* Berea, Ky.: Churchill Weavers, [1954?].

Churchill, David Carroll. "Final Report of Physics and Auto Mechanics." Berea, Ky.: Berea College, 1922.

Churchill, E.F. "Why Buy Handweaving?" *Daughters of the American Revolution Magazine,* April 1954: 398–99, 413.

Coggin, George W. "Trade Extension Textile Classes in North Carolina." Paper presented at a vocational education conference, [1937]. Coggin Papers. North Carolina State Archives/Department of Public Instruction—Vocational Education.

"College Buys Matheny Plant." *Berea Citizen,* 2 July 1936.

Conley, Emma. *Vegetable Dyeing.* 2d ed., edited and revised by Meta Lewis. Penland, N.C.: Penland School of Crafts, [1960?].

Connelly, Vera. "Light in the Mountains." *Good Housekeeping Magazine,* July 1934.

Coolidge, Ruth Dame. "Vibrations From A Danish Bell." *American-Scandinavian Review,* June 1945: 104–117.

Cotten, Jerry E. *Light and Air: The Photography of Bayard Wootten.* Chapel Hill: University of North Carolina Press, 1998.

Crunden, Robert M. *Ministers of Reform: The Progressives' Achievement in American Civilization, 1889–1920.* Urbana, Ill.: University of Illinois Press, 1984.

Daggett, Mabel Potter. "Turning Grandma's Quilts Into Money." *The Designer,* 199, 239–40.

Daniel, Greta. *Textiles USA.* New York: The Museum of Modern Art, 1956.

Davidson, Mary Frances. *The Dye-Pot.* Gatlinburg, Tenn.: privately printed, 1950.

Davidson, Alice S. *The Little Loomhouse.* Louisville, Ky.: The Lou Tate Foundation, Inc., 1997.

Davis, Mary V. "Tromp As Writ." *The Volta Review,* n.d.: 275.

Davis, Allen F. *Spearheads for Reform: The Social Settlements and the Progressive Movement, 1890–1914.* New Brunswick, N.J.: Rutgers University Press, 1984.

Davison, Marguerite Porter. *A Handweaver's Pattern Book.* 1963 ed. Swarthmore, Pa.: privately printed, 1944.

———. *A Handweaver's Source Book.* Swarthmore, Pa.: privately printed, 1953.

Dawley, Thomas R. Jr. "Our Southern Mountaineers." *The World's Work,* March 1910: 12704–12714.

"Death Claims Mrs. Ernberg, Famed Berean." *Lexington Leader,* 2 April 1940.

Dobson, Jerome Eric. "The Changing Control of Economic Activity in the Gatlinburg, Tennessee Area, 1930–1973." Ph.D. diss., The University of Tennessee, 1975.

Dorn, Jacob Henry. *Washington Gladden: Prophet of the Social Gospel.* Columbus, Ohio: Ohio State University Press, 1968.

Douglas, Clementine. "The Rural Arts Exhibition." *Mountain Life and Work,* January 1938: 8–10.

Dundee, F. Boone. "A Labor Field Day." *The Classmate* (Methodist newspaper), 30 August 1930: 7.

Dunn, Durwood. *Cades Cove: The Life and Death of A Southern Appalachian Community, 1818–1937.* Knoxville, Tenn.: The University of Tennessee Press, 1988.

Dupuy, Edward with text by Emma Weaver. *Artisans of the Appalachians.* Asheville, N.C.: The Miller Printing Company, 1967.

Earle, Alice Morse. *Home Life In Colonial Days.* 1993, American Classics edition. Stockbridge, Mass.: Berkshire House Publishers, 1898.

Eastman, Fred. "An Artist in Religion." *The Christian Century,* 6 August 1930: 963–964.

Eaton, Allen. *An Exhibition of the Rural Arts.* Washington, D.C.: Department of Agriculture, 1937.

———. *Handicrafts of New England.* New York: Bonanza Books, 1949.

———. *Handicrafts of the Southern Highlands.* New York: Russell Sage Foundation, 1937.

———. "The Mountain Handicrafts: Their Importance to the Country and to the People in the Mountain Homes." *Mountain Life and Work,* July 1930: 22–30.

Bibliography

[———]. *Old Crafts: New Horizons*. Film. Department of Agriculture, 1942.

[———]. *Patterns of Rural Art*. Film. Department of Agriculture, n.d.

Eaton, Allen and Lucinda Crile. *Rural Handicrafts in the United States*. Washington, D.C.: United States Department of Agriculture in cooperation with the Russell Sage Foundation, 1946.

Ela, Mary. "Made By Hand." *Mountain Life and Work*, Fall 1940: 1–9.

Elkins, Wilma P. *Winnie the Weaver, Sam's Branch, Knott County, Kentucky*. Lexington, Ky.: privately printed, 1996.

Ernberg, Anna. *An Appeal to the Women of America*. Berea, Ky.: Berea College, [1919].

———. *Fireside Industries at Berea College*. Berea, Ky.: Berea College, [1920].

[———]. "The Hand-Loom." *Berea Quarterly*, July–Oct. 1913: 8–14.

———. "History of Fireside Industries." *The Handicrafter*, 1928: 12–14.

———. "Ruskin's Ideal for Humble Homes." *Berea Quarterly*, January 1912: 14–23.

Evans, Wilson. "Increasing the Educational Value of the Berea College Work Program." Teachers College thesis, Columbia University, 1954.

Evans, Carol Jo, and Helen Brown, eds. *Then and Now: The Women of Englewood's Textile Mills*. Athens, Tenn.: Community Action Group of Englewood and Quality Printing Services, 1993.

Flynt, J. Wayne. *Dixie's Forgotten People: The South's Poor Whites*. Bloomington, Ind.: Indiana University Press, 1979.

Ford, Bonnie Willis. "Learning From a Great Teacher." *Mountain Life and Work*, October 1931: 22–23.

———. "The Living Tradition." *Mountain Life and Work*, October 1929: 13.

———. *A Pageant of the Weavers in Four Episodes, Four Prologues, and an Epilogue*. Penland, N.C.: privately printed, [1933].

———. *Penland Weavers and Potters*. Penland, N.C.: Penland Weavers and Potters, [1939].

———. "Sixth Annual Weaving Institute at Penland." *The Weaver*, [1936]: 19–22.

———. *The Story of the Penland Weavers*. Penland, N.C.: Penland School, [1934].

———. *The Story of the Penland Weavers*. Third printing. Penland, N.C.: Penland School, 1941.

Ford, Toni. "Perpetuating Priscilla's Craft." *Profitable Hobbies*, June 1949: 30–31, 64.

Ford, Howard. "Green Baize for Independence Hall from Penland Looms." *Handweaver and Craftsmen*, Spring 1956: 14.

——— and Lucy Morgan. "From Penland to Independence Hall." *The North Carolina Clubwoman*, February 1956: 1, 4–5.

Frome, Michael. *Strangers in High Places*. 1966. Knoxville, Tenn.: The University of Tennessee Press, 1980.

Frost, Eleanor. "Honor to Whom Honor Is Due." *Berea Citizen*, 25 September 1930.

Frost, William G. "Our Contemporary Ancestors in the Southern Mountains." *Harper's*, March 1899: 311–319.

———. "University Extension in the Southern Mountains." *Berea Quarterly*, May 1899: 9–16.

Furman, Lucy. *The Glass Window*. Boston: Little, Brown and Company, 1925.

———. "The Work of Fotched-On Women." *Louisville Courier-Journal*, 3 September 1936. Magazine Section, 1.

Gielow, Martha S. *Old Andy, the Moonshiner*. New York: Fleming H. Revell Company, 1909.

Ginzberg, Lori D. *Women and the Work of Benevolence: Morality, Politics, and Class in the Nineteenth-Century United States*. New Haven: Yale University Press, 1990.

Glenn, John Mark, Lilian Brandt and F. Emerson Andrews. *Russell Sage Foundation, 1907–1946*. 2 vols. New York: Russell Sage Foundation, 1947.

[Goodrich, Frances]. *Allanstand Cottage Industries*. New York City: Woman's Board of Home Missions of the Presbyterian Church in the USA, 1909.

———. *Mountain Homespun*. New Haven, Yale University Press, 1931. Reprinted with new introduction by Jan Davidson, Knoxville, Tenn.: University of Tennessee Press, 1989.

Bibliography

———. "Shuttles and Drafts." *Southern Industrial Education Association Quarterly Newsletter*. Reprinted from *Home Mission Monthly, November 1919*, March/June 1921: 14–16.

"Greatest Art Discovery in Centuries Made by a Former Kansas City Man." *Kansas City Star*, 23 December 1924.

Guy, Richard. "Wooster Educator Spent Life Teaching Weaving Techniques." *The Wooster (Ohio) Daily Record*, 31 July 1970: 14.

H.A.P. "Berea College." *Friends' Intelligencer*, 18 July 1903: 458–460.

Hall, Eliza Calvert. *A Book of Hand-Woven Coverlets*. 1912. Rutland, Vt.: Charles E. Tuttle Company, Inc., 1966.

Hambidge, Jay. *The Greek Vase*. New Haven: Yale University Press, 1920.

———. *The Elements of Dynamic Symmetry*. New York: Dover Publications, Inc., 1963. Reprinted from *The Diagonal*, Yale University Press, 1919–20.

———. *Practical Applications of Dynamic Symmetry*. Edited by Mary C. Hambidge. New Haven: Yale University Press, 1932.

Hambidge, Mary. *Apprentice In Creation*. Edited by Aspasia Voulis. Rabun Gap, Ga.: The Hambidge Center, 1975.

———. *Costumes for Opera Phoebus and Pan, Little Theater Opera Company: November 1930*. Hambidge Papers, Archives of American Art, 1930.

———. "Dynamic Symmetry Basis of Rabun Gap Famous Jay Hambidge Art Foundation." *Athene*, Winter 1951: 20–1, 49.

———. Interview by Eliot Wigginton. Tape recording, 21 July 1969. Hambidge Papers, Atlanta History Center.

———. *The Jay Hambidge Art Foundation*. Rabun Gap, Ga.: Hambidge Foundation, [1958].

———. *Rabun Studios*. New York City: Rabun Studios, [1938?].

Hancock, Carol Stevens. *The Light in the Mountains: A History of Tallulah Falls School*. Toccoa, Ga.: Commercial Printing Company, 1975.

"The Hand Loom Industry of Berea." *The Christian Science Monitor*, [1926].

Harper, Frances. "A Penelope of the Carolina Mountains." *The House Beautiful*, 1917: 385, 412.

Harrington, Mildred. "The Magician's Trunk." *American Magazine*, 1926.

Harris, Jessie, and Marian Heard. "Summer Workshop of Crafts and Community Recreation on the Little Pigeon in Gatlinburg." *The Arrow*, March 1948: 270–273.

Hart, Robert G. "From The Great Smokies to Rockefeller Center: The Southern Highland Handicraft Guild Brings Rural Crafts to City Markets." *Handweaver and Craftsman*, Summer 1951: 5–7, 57–58.

Heard, Marian. "A Five-Year Plan of Education Toward the Improvement and Extension of Handicrafts in the Southern Highlands." [1945]. Southern Highland Handicraft Guild Archives, Montreat College.

———. "Report of an Exploratory Study Looking Toward A Craft Education Project in the Southern Highlands." Southern Highland Handicraft Guild, [1947].

Heilbrun, Carolyn G. *Writing A Woman's Life*. New York: Ballatine Books, 1989.

Helmick, Elizabeth Allen Clarke. *The History of Phi Beta Phi Fraternity*: Pi Beta Phi Fraternity, 1915.

———. "News from Little Pigeon." *The Arrow of Pi Beta Phi*, December 1915.

———. "News from Little Pigeon." *The Arrow*, March 1916: 439–441.

———. "Pioneering in Gatlinburg." *The Arrow*, February 1917: 254–256.

———, Mrs. Richardson, and Abbie B. Lanfmaid. "A Brief History of the Settlement School." *The Arrow of Pi Beta Phi*, June 1920: 455–465.

Hickman, Elmer Wallace. "Scandinavian Art Weaving." *The Weaver*, January 1937: 20–24.

Hill, Jennie Lester. *Fireside Industries at Berea College*. Berea, Ky.: Berea College, 1908.

———. "Our Fireside Industries." *Berea Quarterly*, July 1910: 21–23.

Hoffschwelle, Mary S. *Rebuilding the Rural Southern Community: Reformers, Schools, and Homes in Tennessee, 1900–1930*. Knoxville, Tenn.: The University of Tennessee Press, 1998.

Bibliography

Holroyd, Ruth N. and Ulrike L. Beck. *Jacob Angstadt Designs Drawn from His Weavers Patron Book*. 2 vols. Pittsford, N.Y.: privately printed, 1976.

"Home Industries in Sweden: Arts and Crafts of the Peasant Folk." *The Mentor*, April 1929: 18–22.

Huff, Hennrietta McCutchan. "Memoirs of Settlement School." *The Arrow*, Summer 1967: 8–11.

Huff, Cynthia. "Arrowcraft Historic Textile Collection Cataloged." *The Arrow of Pi Beta Phi*, Fall 1994: 16.

Hughes, Caroline McKnight. "Our Industrial Work at the Settlement School." *The Arrow*, March 1916: 441–447.

Hughes, I. Harding Jr. *Valle Crucis: A History of an Uncommon Place*. Privately printed, 1995.

Hutchins, William J. "Introduction." *Southern Mountain Life and Work*, April 1925: 1.

Ison, Frances Forbes. "The Weavers of Rabun." *The Georgia Review*, Fall 1950: 159–62.

Jackson, Pearl Cashekk, ed. *Pi Beta Phi Settlement School, Chronological Outline for the Pi Phi Settlement School*. Gatlinburg, Tenn., [1927].

Jacobs, Philip Walker. *The Life and Photography of Doris Ulmann*. Lexington, Ky.: The University Press of Kentucky, 2001.

"Jay Hambidge Dies of Sudden Stroke." *The New York Times*, 21 January 1924.

Johnson, Geraldine Niva. *Weaving Rag Rugs: A Women's Craft in Western Maryland*. Knoxville, Tenn.: The University of Tennessee Press, 1985.

Johnson, Lillie. *Homespun House*. Crossnore, N.C.: Crossnore School, [1937].

Jones, Michael Owen. *Craftsman of the Cumberlands: Tradition and Creativity*. Lexington, Ky.: The University Press of Kentucky, 1989.

Kane, Harnett T. with Inez Henry. *Miracles in the Mountains*. Garden City, N.Y.: Doubleday and Company, Inc. 1956.

Kaplan, Wendy. *"The Art that is Life": The Arts and Crafts Movement in America, 1875–1920*. Boston: Little, Brown, and Company, A Bulfinch Press Book in conjunction with the Museum of Fine Arts, Boston, 1987.

Keith, Jeanette. *Country People in the New South: Tennessee's Upper Cumberland*. Chapel Hill: The University of North Carolina Press, 1996.

Keller, May L. "A Trip of Investigation to Gatlinburg." *The Arrow*, January 1911: 182–183.

Kennedy, Sayde Tune Wilson and Doris Finch. *Of Coverlets: the Legacies, the Weavers*. Nashville: Tunstede, 1983.

Lily Mills. *Weaving Classics: Original Lily Weaver's Work Sheets, Nos. 1–23, 1930–1950*. Shelby, N.C.: Lily Mills, [1950].

Linton, George E. *Applied Textiles: Raw Materials to Finished Fabrics*. 1948. New York: Duell, Sloan, and Pearce, 1961.

"Looking Back to a Pioneer." *House and Garden*, June 1942: 74.

Madden, Robert R., and T. Russell Jones. *Mountain Home: The Walker Family Homestead*. Washington, D.C.: National Park Service, U.S. Department of the Interior, 1977.

Mahoney, Olivia. *Edward F. Worst: Craftsman and Educator*. Chicago: Chicago Historical Society, 1985.

Matheny, Edith. *Hand Loom Weaving in the Home*. Berea: Matheny Weavers, [1925?].

Matthews, Alice. "Reading List on the Southern Mountaineers." Pi Beta Phi, [1911].

Mayo, Betty Driscoll. "Old Barn Becomes Craft Center." *Christian Science Monitor*, 3 March 1951.

McCarthy, Kathleen D. *Women's Culture: American Philanthropy and Art, 1830–1930*. Chicago: The University of Chicago Press, 1991.

McDowell, Malcolm. "Woman Plans Fair Exhibit by Hill People." *Chicago Daily News*, 8 May 1933.

McKinsey, Wellington and Company. "Berea College Survey of Woodwork-Furniture and Fireside Industries." Chicago: McKinsey, Wellington and Company, 1936.

McNelley, Pat. *The First 40 Years: John C. Campbell Folk School*. Brasstown, N.C.: John C. Campbell Folk School, 1966.

Bibliography

Meadows, Lorelei L. *Kentucky Textile Directory: Historic and Contemporary Collections.* Frankfort, Ky.: The Kentucky Historical Society, 1992.

Meany, Janet, and Paula Pfaff. *Rag Rug Handbook.* St. Paul, Minn.: Dos Tejedoras Fiber Arts Publications, 1988.

Meltzer, Milton. *Violins and Shovels: The WPA Arts Projects.* New York: Delacorte Press, 1976.

Messler, Isaac. "Our Co-Worker." *Mountain Life and Work,* April 1928: 7–9, 31.

"Metallic Yarns." *Handweaver and Craftsmen,* Spring 1956: 48–49.

Miles, Emma Bell. *The Spirit of the Mountains.* 1905. Reprinted with a foreword by David E. Whisnant, Knoxville, Tenn.: University of Tennessee Press, 1975.

Millard, Edward. *Export Marketing for a Small Handicraft Business.* 1992. Revised edition, Oxford, England: Oxfam/Intermediate Technology Publications, 1996.

Moore, Frances. "Aunt Sabrina King." *The Arrow,* May 1931: 460–61.

Moore, Louise. "'Arts and Crafts' Programs Reimbursed from Federal Funds." 1941. Coggin Papers, North Carolina State Archives.

Morgan, A. Rufus. *From Cabin to Cabin: The Life of A. Rufus Morgan.* Macon County, N.C.: privately printed, 1980.

———. "Reviving the Art of the Mountains." *The Spirit of Missions,* April 1930: 221–22.

Morgan, Lucy. *The Appalachian School Department of Fireside Industries.* Penland, N.C.: The Appalachian School, [1928].

———. *The Blue Pot.* Penland, N.C.: Appalachian School, [1925?].

Morgan, Lucy with LeGette Blythe. *Gift from the Hills.* Indianapolis: The Bobbs-Merrill Company, Inc., 1958.

Morley, Margaret W. *The Carolina Mountains.* Boston: Houghton Mifflin Company, 1913.

Morris, William. "The Art of the People." In *William Morris on Art and Design,* Edited by Christine Poulson. Sheffield, England: Sheffield Academic Press Ltd., 1879.

"A Mother's Day Celebration." *Berea Citizen,* [1936].

"Mountain Ministry: The Life and Times of A. Rufus Morgan, Priest." *The Living Church,* 9 April 1978.

"Mrs. Jay Hambidge Guest of Hobby Group." *Daily News-Graphic,* 22 October 1937.

Mueller, Marion Webb. "Settlement School Panorama—1945–1967." *The Arrow of Pi Beta Phi,* Summer 1967: 12–14.

Nason, Wayne C. "Rural Industries in Knott County, Kentucky." Washington, D.C.: United States Department of Agriculture, 1932.

"National Affairs: Presidential Yacht." *The New York Times,* July 1945.

"New Theory of Art." *The London Times,* 2 November 1919.

Nicholson, Lucy Woodhall. "Crafts, World Balance Go Hand in Hand, Says Visitor." *The Banner Herald* [1935], 2.

Nienburg, Bertha M. "Potential Earning Power of Southern Mountaineer Handicraft." Washington, D.C.: Women's Bureau, U.S. Department of Labor, 1935.

Oakes, George W. "Morgan's Ideas Already in Use in Settlement." *The Chattanooga Times,* 26 November 1933.

"On and Off the Avenue." *The New Yorker,* 17 September 1949: 82–88.

———. *The New Yorker,* 26 November 1949: 92–96.

Ogle, Lula May. "The Pi Phis Prove Worth Copying." *The Arrow,* February 1937: 257.

Painter, Jacqueline Burgin. *The Season of Dorland-Bell.* Asheville, N.C.: Biltmore Press, 1987.

Peck, Elisabeth S. *Berea's First 125 Years, 1855–1980.* Lexington, Ky.: The University Press of Kentucky, 1982.

"Penland Exhibit Enroute to Fair." *The Lexington (Kentucky) Leader,* 14 April 1933.

Penland School. *Fifteenth Annual Session: The Penland Scene.* Penland, N.C.: Penland School of Handicrafts, 1944.

Bibliography

———. *Mountain Milestone*. Penland, N.C.: Penland School, 1952.
———. *Ninth Annual Weaving Institute Conducted by Edward F. Worst*. Penland, N.C.: Penland School of Handicrafts, 1938.
———. *Penland School of Handicrafts: 1950 Sessions*. Penland, N.C.: Penland School of Handicrafts, 1950.
———. *The Penland School of Handicrafts: First Winter Session*. Penland, N.C.: Penland School of Handicrafts, 1945.
———. *Thirteenth Annual Session of the Penland School of Handicrafts*. Penland, N.C.: Penland School of Handicrafts, 1942.
———. *Twelfth Annual Session of the Penland School of Handicrafts*. Penland, N.C.: Penland School of Handicrafts, 1941.
Pettit, Anna F.T. "A Trip of Investigation." *The Arrow*, November 1910: 49–54.
Pettit, Katherine. "Pettit Diary: Cedar Grove at Hazard, Kentucky." 1899. Pettit Papers, Special Collections, King Library, University of Kentucky. Lexington, Kentucky.
———. "The Daily Record of the Social Settlement at Sassafras, Kentucky." 1901.
Pi Beta Phi. *The Arrow Craft Shop*. Gatlinburg, Tenn.: Pi Beta Phi Settlement School, 1936.
———. *Arrow Craft Shop*. Gatlinburg, Tenn.: Pi Beta Phi Settlement School, 1941.
———. *Arrow Craft Shop: Handicrafts*. Gatlinburg, Tenn.: Handicraft Department of Pi Beta Phi Settlement School, [1928?].
———. "Blanche Huff Pledged by Iowa Gamma." *The Arrow*, February 1932: 477.
———. *A Century of Friendship in Pi Beta Phi*: Pi Beta Phi, 1968.
———. "Comparative Statement of Operations—Arrowcraft Shop." *The Arrow*, September 1947: 81.
———. "Mattie Huff Pledge." *The Arrow*, February 1931: 333.
———. *The Pi Beta Phi Settlement School*. Gatlinburg, Tenn.: Pi Beta Phi Settlement School, [1923].
———. *Pi Beta Phi Settlement School in the Southern Mountains*: Pi Beta Phi, [1911].
———. "Pi Beta Phi Settlement School Treasurer's Report." Gatlinburg, Tenn.: Pi Beta Phi Settlement School, 1916–1950.
———. "Report of Director of Settlement School." *The Arrow of Pi Beta Phi*, 1929: 32–35.
———. "Report of Officers: Smith Hughes Department—Weaving." *The Arrow of Pi Beta Phi*, Fall 1925: 62–63.
———. "Report of the Pi Beta Phi Settlement School, 1912–1915." *The Arrow*, 3rd Annual Information Number, 1915: 72–74.
———. "Settlement School Reports." *The Arrow of Pi Beta Phi*, Fall 1926: 36–39.
———. "Summer Workshop of Crafts." Pi Beta Phi and the University of Tennessee, 1949.
Pine Mountain. *Notes from the Pine Mountain Settlement School*, February 1923.
Pollard, Mary O. "Good News from Little Pigeon." *The Arrow*, March 1915: 392–394.
Pomeroy, Sarah G. "The Business Side of the Convention." *The Arrow*, July 1910: 333–337.
Priestman, Mabel Tuke. "Coverlet Weaving in the South." *The House Beautiful*, January 1907: 25–26.
Pudup, Mary Beth, Dwight B. Billings, and Altina L. Waller, eds. *Appalachia in the Making: The Mountain South in the Nineteenth Century*. Chapel Hill: The University of North Carolina Press, 1995.
"Rich Colors, Firm Textures, Notable in Handmade Fabrics From Rabun Gap, Ga." *Women's Wear Daily*, July [1946?].
Raine, James Watt. *The Land of Saddle-Bags*. New York: Council of Women for Home Missions and Missionary Education Movement of the United States and Canada, 1924.
———. *Have They Found Aladdin's Lamp*. Berea, Ky.: Churchill Weavers, [1926].
Rauch, Harriet Goodsell, ed. "News from Little Pigeon, Craftsman's Fair of the Southern Highlands." *The Arrow*, March 1949: 282–285.
Rauschenbusch, Walter. *Selected Writings*. Edited by Winthrop S. Hudson. New York: Paulist Press, 1984.

Bibliography

Read, Phyllis J. and Bernard L. Witlieb. *The Book of Women's Firsts*. New York: Random House, 1992.

Redding, Winogene. "An Old Art Modernized." *The Arrow*, November 1929: 308–311.

———. "Miss Redding, Director of Weaving, writes on 'Weaving in Wartime.'" *The Arrow*, May 1944: 371–72.

———. "News from Little Pigeon." *The Arrow*, June 1926: 918–922.

———. "Something About Our Weavers (draft)." *The Arrow*, May 1944.

———. "Summary of the Weaving Department for 1944." 8 January 1945, Pi Beta Phi Archives, Arrowmont.

———. "Talk on Crafts Development." Paper presented at the Black Mountain Arts and Crafts Club, Warren Wilson College, Swannanoa, N.C., 1948.

———. "Weaving at Gatlinburg." *The Arrow*, May 1928: 869–872.

———. "Weaving Department Report, September 1925–May 1945." *The Arrow of Phi Beta Phi*, September 1945: 43–46.

———. "Weaving Meeting Day in Gatlinburg." *The Arrow*, May 1933: 448–449.

Reiter, Mary Jo, and Veronica Patterson. *Weaving A Life: The Story of Mary Megis Atwater*. Loveland, Colo.: Interweave Press, 1992.

Remington, C. "Swapping Coverlets for Shingles." *The Mentor*, June 1929: 34–35.

"Revives Colonial Industry in Mountains of Kentucky." unidentified newspaper, 24 March 1915. Special Collections, Hutchins Library, Berea College.

Ritchie, Andrew J. "The Weavers of Rabun." In *Sketches of Rabun County History*, Rabun Gap Nacoochee School, [1938?].

Robert, Sarah Corbin. "Financing Our Endorsed Schools." *Daughters of the American Revolution Magazine*, February 1929: 81–85.

Robinson, Josephine A. "Mountain Homespun." *Berea Quarterly*, February 1900: 7–9.

———. "Homespun "Bed-Kivers."" *Berea Quarterly*, Feburary 1902: 28–29.

Sale, Mildred Odell. "Make Your Own Treasured Souvenirs of the Smoky Mountains at the Pi Beta Phi Summer Workshop at Gatlinburg, Tennessee." *The Arrow*, May 1945: 347–352.

Sander, Kathleen Waters. *The Business of Charity: The Woman's Exchange Movement, 1832–1900*. Urbana and Chicago: University of Illinois Press, 1998.

Schaller, Karin. "Notes on Clothing by Mary Crovatt Hambidge." [1984?]. Accompanies clothing of Mary Hambidge housed at the Atlanta History Center, Atlanta, Ga.

Schattschneider, Meta. "Handweaving A Way of Life." *Design*, May 1946: 4–6.

Schneider, Dorothy and Carl J. Schneider. *American Women in the Progressive Era, 1900–1920*. New York: Doubleday, Anchor Books, 1990.

Selznick, Philip. *TVA and the Grass Roots: A Study in the Sociology of Formal Organization*. New York: Harper Torchbooks, 1966.

Shapiro, Henry D. *Appalachia on Our Mind: The Southern Mountains and Moutaineers in the American Consciousness, 1870–1920*. Chapel Hill: The University of North Carolina Press, 1978.

Sharp, Cecil J. and Olive Dame Campbell. *English Folk Songs from the Southern Appalachians*. New York: Putnam/Knickerbocker Press, 1917.

Sheppard, Muriel Earley. *Cabins in the Laurel*. 1935. Reprinted with foreword by John Ehle, Chapel Hill: University of North Carolina Press, 1991.

———. "Mountain People Aided by Appalachian School." *Asheville Citizen*, 7 November 1932.

Sinks, Alfred H. "Wizard of the Hand Loom." *Saturday Evening Post*, 21 February 1948: 30–33, 122–24.

Sloop, Mary. "Weaving at Crossnore." *Southern Industrial Education Association Quarterly*, September–December 1924: 7.

[———]. *Weaving Department*. Crossnore, N.C.: Crossnore School, [1928].

Sloop, Mary with LeGette Blythe. *Miracle in the Hills*. New York: McGraw-Hill Company, Inc., 1953.

Bibliography

Smith, Katherine Louise. "A Mountain Fireside Industry." *The House Beautiful*, May 1902: 406–09.

Smith, Betty N. *Jane Hicks Gentry: A Singer Among Singers*. Lexington, Ky.: The University of Kentucky Press, 1998.

Southern Highlanders. *The Southern Highlanders Incorporated: Handmade Gifts of Unusual Beauty*. Norris, Tenn.: Southern Highlanders, Inc., [1938].

———. *Southern Highlanders*. Norris, Tenn.: Southern Highlanders, Inc., 1937.

Southern Highland Handicraft Guild. *A Catalogue of Mountain Handicrafts by the Members of the Southern Highland Handicraft Guild*. American Federation of Arts, 1933.

———. *Frances Louisa Goodrich, 1856–1944*. Privately printed. [1944].

"Southern Highlands Issue." *House and Garden*, June 1942.

Southern Industrial Educational Association. *Quarterly Magazine of the Southern Industrial Education Association*. Washington, D.C.: Southern Industrial Educational Association, 1915–1925.

Sparks, Andrew. "Greek Culture Comes to a Mountain Pasture." *The Atlanta Journal and Constitution*, 10 November 1957: 14–15, 38–39.

St. John, Wylly Folk. "Weavers of Rabun . . . They Make Beauty with their Hands." *The Atlanta Journal*, 10 October 1948: 19–21.

Stahl, Sam. "Berea College: Fireside Industries Now Employ 60 Weavers." *Handweaver and Craftsman*, Spring 1968: 5–7, 33.

Stark, Nita Hill. "Report of the Chairman of Settlement School Committee." *The Arrow of Pi Beta Phi*, Fall 1924: 36–43.

"Steele-Clovis." Publicity Flyer. New York: Richard Copley Management, 1936.

Stevens, Bernice. *A Weavin' Woman*. Gatlinburg, Tenn.: Buckhorn Press, 1971.

———. *Our Mountain Craftsmen*. Gatlinburg, Tenn.: Buckhorn Press, 1969.

———. "Tina McMorran: Combines Three Crafts in Wall Hangings." *Handweaver and Craftsman*, Summer 1964: 14–15, 38.

Stoddart, Jess. *The Quare Women's Journals: May Stone and Katherine Pettit's Summers in the Kentucky Mountains and the Founding of the Hindman Settlement School*. Ashland, Ky.: The Jesse Stuart Foundation, 1997.

Stone, Edna L. "The Pi Beta Phi Settlement School." *The Arrow*, April 1912: 288–292.

Tarbell, Ida M. "Berea Woman Called One of 50 Outstanding Women." *Lexington Leader*, 12 September 1930.

———. "Novelist Picks Nation's Fifty Foremost Women." *Cleveland Plain Dealer*, 1930.

Tate, Lou. *Kentucky Coverlets*. Louisville, Ky.: privately printed, 1938.

Taylor, William S. "Recommendations—The Arrowcraft Program." *The Arrow*, December 1941: 164.

Thomas, Samuel W., ed. *Dawn Comes to the Mountains*. Louisville, Ky.: The George Rogers Clark Press, Inc., 1981.

Thorman, Dorothy Coleman. "1963–1967 Settlement School—Art and Craft Center." *The Arrow*, Summer 1967: 16.

Trainer, Ethel. "News from Little Pigeon." *The Arrow*, March 1951: 228–31.

Tsumematsu, Toshie. "Observation Report: Agriculture and Home Economics Extension Study Team." Kumamoto, Japan: International Cooperation Administration, 1958.

Turner, Agnes Miller, ed. "News from Little Pigeon, A Visitor's Impression." *The Arrow*, November 1926: 182–87.

Urquhart, Lewis K. "Berea's Labor Day." *Factory and Industrial Management*, July 1929: 52–55.

Valentine, Fawn. *West Virginia Quilts and Quiltmakers: Echoes from the Hills*. Athens, Ohio: Ohio University Press, 2000.

Van Dommelen, David B. "Allen Eaton: In Quest of Beauty." *American Craft*, June/July 1985: 35–39.

Bibliography

Viner, Wilmer Stone and H.E.S. Viner. *The Katherine Pettit Book of Vegetable Dyes.* Saluda, N.C.: Exelsior Press, 1946.

Waagen, Alice K. "30 Years Ago In Handweaving: Weaving as an Occupational Therapy." *Handwoven,* November–December 1984: 18, 20.

Walton, Perry. *The Story of Textiles.* New York: Tudor Publishing Co., 1925.

"The Weavers of Rabun." *Handweaver and Craftsman,* Spring 1956: 6–9.

"Weaving Building At Crossnore Burns With Heavy Loss." *The Avery (N.C.) Advocate,* 10 October 1935: 1.

Weed, Margaret G. "Penland Is Training Intelligent Christian Citizens." *The Spirit of Missions,* December 1927: 731–33.

Weimann, Jeanne Madeline. *The Fair Women.* Chicago: Academy Chicago, 1981.

Weiss, Anne. "Tales of Southern Mountain Life Are Strange As Fiction." [Boston newspaper?], 7 April 1933.

West, Max. "The Revival of Handicrafts in America." *Bulletin of the Bureau of Labor* 55 (November 1904): 1572–1622.

Wheeler, Candace. *How to Make Rugs.* New York: Doubleday, Page and Company, 1902.

———. *Home Industries and Domestic Weavings.* Privately printed, [1900?].

Whisnant, David E. *All That Is Native and Fine: The Politics of Culture in an American Region.* Chapel Hill: The University of North Carolina Press, 1983.

Wigginton, Eliot. *Mary Hambidge.* Clayton, Ga.: Rabun Printing Co., [1982?]. Reprinted from *Foxfire* 7:3, Fall 1973.

———. *Sometimes a Shining Moment: The Foxfire Experience.* Garden City, N.Y.: Doubleday/Anchor, 1986.

Williams, Michael Ann. *Homeplace: The Social Use and Meaning of the Folk Dwelling in Southwestern North Carolina.* Athens, Ga.: The University of Georgia Press, 1991.

Wilson, Sadye Tune and Doris Finch Kennedy. *Of Coverlets: the legacies, the weavers.* Nashville: Tunstede, 1983.

Wilson, Kathleen Curtis. *American Homespun for the President's House.* Washington, D.C.: Woodrow Wilson House, 1997.

———. "The Handweaving of Allie Josephine Mast, 1861–1936." In *May We All Remember Well,* Edited by Robert S. Brunk. Ashville, N.C.: Robert S. Brunk Auctions Services, Inc., 1997.

Wood, Ruth Kedzie. "Jugtown, where they make Jugs." *The Mentor,* April 1928: 32–36.

Worst, Edward F. *Foot-Powered Loom Weaving.* Milwaukee: The Bruce Publishing Company, 1918.

———. *How to Weave Linens.* Milwaukee: The Bruce Publishing Company, 1926.

index

Note: Page references for photographs are printed in italics.

Addams, Jane, 43, 58
Allanstand: articles about, 185, 188; development, 122–23; finances, 169–70, 181; marketing, 176; model for others, 10, 113, 137, 162; production, 159, 165; Southern Highland Handicraft Guild gift, 22, 73, 178–79, 189; Southern Highlanders, 23; visit to, 6, 57; weavers, 3, 86
Allen, Helen, 87
alumnae clubs of Pi Beta Phi, 61–62, 69, 74, 173, 183
American Country Life Association, 25
American Federation of Arts, 19, 25, 164
Appalachian Craft Revival. *See* Craft Revival
Appalachian Mountains: crafts development, 15, 19, 24, 30–31, 54, 73, 185; geography, 11; life descriptions, 28, 57; settlement work, 17, 35, 95, 152; weaving, 1, 49, 125, 158
Appalachian School: church support, 79, 157, 173; development, 75–76, *76*; Fireside Industries, 49–50, 80–81, 122; geography, 12, *13*, 88; leader in Craft Revival, 1; mission, 6, 9; property sale, 94; separation from Penland Weavers and Potters, 89, 184; teaching children, 8, 82, *76*, 187
Arrow, The: early weaving, 6; marketing, 61–62; Summer Craft Workshop, 70; weaving development, 2, 59, 174, 187; weavers, 8, 74. *See also* Pi Beta Phi
Arrow Craft Shop, 28, 61, 63, *176*, 183
Arrowcraft: catalogs, *181*; closing, 70; development, 60, 74; dyes, 161; finances, 67, 171, 178–79, 181; fly-shuttle opposition, 154; *House & Garden*, 28; leader, 1, 10, 113, 180; mission, 6, 73, 189; payment to weavers, 138–39, 183; pregnancy rule, 135; products, 66, 162, 164–65; production, 144–45, 156, 159, 167–68, *170*; shop, 56, 61, 176, *176*, 183; Smith-Hughes, 32, 59; Southern Highland Handicraft Guild, 23; Redding, Winogene, 60–61, 62, *65*; wage study, 65; weavers, 63–64, 135–36, *136*, 174, *175*, 187; weaving supervisors, *34*, 68–69, *68*, 71, 126, *149*, 150–51
Arrowmont School of Arts and Crafts, 33–34, 56, 70–73, 180, 189
Arts and Crafts Movement, 10, 187; American, 38, 123, 185; English, 26, 54, 143
Asheville Normal and Associated Schools, 114, 116
Atwater, Mary Megis, 129, 153, 157, 159
Avramea, Krai Elene, 44, *44*, 98

baskets, 152; Allanstand, 181; Arrowcraft, *58*, 60, 62, 136, 173; Berea, 37, 44, 167–68; demonstrating, 73; *Mountain Handicrafts*, 24–26, 114; Southern Highlanders, 24; Tallulah Falls, 115
Beard, Samuel Clemens, Jr., 28
Beasley, Dean, 103
Beaudin, Irene, 91, 148
Bebb, Hubert, 72
Beeson, M.D.R., 88
Benfield, Zada, 49, 118, *118*
Bent, George R., 51–52, 138, 178
Berea Academy, 77, 90, 118, 128
Berea College: catalog, 35; Conference of Southern Mountain Workers, 18, *20*, 127; dyes, 161; finances, 29, 48, 182–83; fly-shuttle opposition, 131, 133; geography, 11; history, 5; Homespun Fair, 37, 161, *161*; *House & Garden*, 28; instruction, 33, *41*, 49; Labor Day, 53, *53*; leader, 1, 180, 189; looms, 79, *118*, 153–54, *154*; managers, 38, *39*, 40, 43, *47*, 146; marketing, 45, 172, 173, 187; model, 10, 116,

Index

118, 128; *Mountain Handicrafts*, 25; Mountain Weaver Boys, 20, 50–53, *51*; payment to weavers, *36*, 138; pricing, 169; production, 60, 144, 149, 159, 170, *170*, *188*; Southern Highland Handicraft Guild, 22, 178; Southern Highlanders, 23, 179; student labor, 36, 44; students, 77, 117, 128, 130; weavers, 2, 7, *37*; weaving problem, 46–47

Berea Quarterly, *2*, 9, 38–40, 42, 174
Bergman, Margaret, 91
Bernat, Paul, 84, 86–87
Berry Schools, 16, 28, 47, 114, 174
Berry, Martha, 47, 114
Betty's Creek sales room, 103, *106*, 107, 177

Bidstrup, Marguerite, 22. *See also* Butler, Marguerite
Bishop, Evelyn, 60
Black Mountain College, 107
Black, Mary, 157
Blain, Sandra, 72
Bloxton, Esther, 178
Blue Ridge Industrial School, 114
Blythe, LeGette, 92
Book of Handwoven Coverlets, The, 41, 86, 122
Boyce, Sarah E., 49, 117
Bronson, 129, 159
Brown, William J., 90, *90*, 94
Burt, Amy, 12, 76, *76*, 79
Busbee, Jacque and Juliana, 106, 185
Butler, Marguerite, 78, 120, 174. *See also* Bidstrup, Marguerite

Califf, Katharine, 77
Campbell, John C., 4, 16, 17, 18, 54, 113
Campbell, Margaret, 117, 121
Campbell, Olive Dame: ballads, 19; Conference of Southern Mountain Workers, 18, *20*, 127; crafts development, *17*, *20*, 21–22, 178; Folk School, 19, 120–21, *172*; *Handicrafts of the Southern Highlands*, 27; mountain description, 11; Penland, 87, 91; Southern Highland Handicraft Guild, 33, 91; wife, 17
candlewicking, 31, 140, 153, 186
carding wool, 6, 29, 36, *37*, 125, 175
Carlson, Ester, 115, 160
Carpenter, Jake, 3
Catalogs: Arrowcraft, 62, *181*, 183; Berea, 42, 52, 175–76; Crossnore, 7; Churchill Weavers, 132; marketing, 149–50, 174–75; *Mountain Handicrafts*, 25–26, 165, 169; Southern Highlanders, *23*, 24, 165–66, 179
Century of Progress, 83, *83*, 84
chair caning, 31, 186
Cherokee, 25, 73
Chisholm, Gladys, 77
Churchill Weavers: development, 35, 54, 130, *130*, 131–32, *133*, 189; fly-shuttle, 130, 154; finances, 185; marketing, 133, 177; Penland, 87; pricing, 170, 172; production, 132, 134, *156*, *165*; Southern Highland Handicraft Guild, 134, 186; Southern Highlanders, 23, 134, 179
Churchill, David Carroll: Berea College, 46, 54, 127, 130–31; India, 130–31; Churchill Weavers, 132–34
Churchill, Eleanor, 130, *130*, 132, 134, 148, 177
Clovis, Hall, 99, *99*, 102, 107, 110, 185
Coggin, George W., 29, 30, 80, 91, 120
Colonial Coverlet Guild of America, 117
Conley, Emma: demonstrating 145, *145*; dyes, 90, 132, *160*, 161; son John, 91–92, *92*
consignment: against, 42, 171; exhibits, 52, 129; functioning, 43, 162, 180; sales, 163, 185; Southern Highland Handicraft Guild, 21
Cook, Nella. *See* Hill, Nella Cook
Cook sisters, 69, *69*, 70, 126
Copenhaver, Laura, 123
Cordell, Willie Sue, 114
cotton: clothing, 6, 28; growing, 38; mills, 57, 93, 161; yarns, 38, 93, 100, 160, 170; weaving, 40, 100, 105, 132, 134, 140, 158, 162, 166, 174
Country Life Movement, 10, 25
coverlets, 28; Allanstand, 3, 115, 122, 165, 181; Arrowcraft, 60, 66, 163; Berea, 36, 38, 40, 42, 48, 54, 163; Crossnore, 120; historic, 6, 125, 147, 148–49, 158, 160; Mast, 124; Matheny, 129; patterns, 158, *158*, *163*, 175; pricing, 169–70; production, 36, 37, 58, 132, 149, 160; weavers, 8, 67, 86
Cox, Sue Huff, 59
Craddock, C.E., 57
Craft Revival: continuing tradition, 3; leaders, 54, 82, 113, 114, 139; origins, 10, 35, 143, 174–75, 180, 186; publicity, 26, 169, 177; weaving centers, 1–2, 47, 116, 117, 144, 146, 153, 188; writing about, 1, 27, *27*, 83, 187; weaving, 159, 165
craftsmanship: quality, 54, 61, 144; standards, 21, 37, 91, 144

Index

Cranbrook Academy of Art, 94
creative outlet, 103, 143
Crossnore School, Inc.: founding, 117–18, 182; joint activities, 87; problems, 119; school class, 143; students, 118, 138; support, *15*, 16, 29–30, 119–20, 174; teachers, 49, 118; weaving, *5*, 24, 116, *118*, *119*, 177
Crossnore School's Weaving Room: catalog, 7; Daughters of the American Revolution, 119–20, 145, 149, 173–74, *173*; origin, 117–18, 169; finances, 138, 170, 182; managers, 119, 145, 147, 150; marketing, 173–74; mission, 6, 7, 9; products, *5*, 148, 149, 158, 165; production, 155, 163, 164, 181, 189; sales shop, *173*, 177; school class, 143; Smith-Hughes, 118, 119; students, 116; weavers, *118*, 139, 180
Crovatt, Mary, 96, 97, *98*, 99. *See also* Hambidge, Mary
Cumberland Mountains, 11, 38

Daggett, Mabel Potter, 187
Danforth, William H., 53
Daughters of the American Revolution: Crossnore, *15*, 118–20, 145, 163, *173*; schools, 10; weaving centers, 9, 45
Davison, Marguerite Porter, 50
Dawley, Thomas, Jr., 57
Day Law, 35
Day, Winnie Pigman, *4*, 117
de Long, Ethel, 117
Department of Agriculture: exhibition sponsor, 19, 26; Extension, 32, *32*; films, 27–28, 125; Knott County study, 185–86
Department of Labor: Fair Labor Standards Act, 32, 64–65; West study, 37, 185. *See also* Women's Bureau
Depression: conditions, 83, 153, 168, 180, 189; events, 26, 83; government agencies, 123, 186; labor, 31, 63, 85, 138, 139, 164; sales effect, 48, 49, 181, 182, 183, 184
designing for production: buyer types, 61, 66, 68; creativity, 144, 150; consumer considerations, 126, 150; inspiration, 52, 100, 121, 160; item types, 52, 69, *130*, 132, 164–66; function, 147–48; labor limitations, 48; sales ease, 48; variety, 60, 167, 168
Diagonal, The, 97
Dingman, Helen, *20*, 54

Dorland-Bell School, 114, 116
Dougherty family, 3, *124*, 125, 185
Dougherty, Leah Adams, 125
Dougherty, Sarah, 3, 125, 146–48, 150
Douglas, Clementine: development, 125–26, 146, 147, 148; leadership, 22, 87, 91; Spinning Wheel, 125–26, 185
Duffield, Georgia, 63
dyes: historic, 37, 117; process, 36, 160–61; sources, 38, 103–4, 160; dyers, 86, *104*, 121, 125, 128, *160*, 162, 166; prizes 161, *161*
Dynamic Symmetry: application, 97–98, 100, 105; expansion, 104; theory, 96–97, *97*, 102, 109

Eaton, Allen: books, 1, 27, *27*, 91, 125; development, 19; exhibition designer, 24, 25–26, *32*; facilitator, 21, 65, 81, 82; film producer, 28; researcher, 2, 3, 9, 21, 35, 38, 63, 129, 149, 161, 186; speaker, 20, *20*, 178; teaching, *34*, 71. *See also Handicrafts of the Southern Highlands*
economic development: crafts, 10, 15, 20, 30, 178, 186; motivation, 6, 9; organizations promoting, 23, *23*, 179; weaving, 53, 143; women, 1, 35, 113
Edwards, Edward B., 97
Ehle, John, 13
Episcopal Church: market, 80–81, 122, 173; schools, 75, 125; supporter, 79, 83, 84, 122
Episcopal Diocese of Western North Carolina: Appalachian School, 75, 76–77; Penland Weavers and Potters, 84, 122, 157, 173, 184
Ernberg, Anna: Berea administration, 46, 47, 128; buildings, 43, *43*, 44, *44*, 176; designing, 48; development, 41–42; Fireside model, 54, 114, 116, 143, 186; historic interest, 42; instruction, 33, *41*, 42, 49, 52, 77, 81, 127, 143, 146; loom, 45, 46, 79, 131, 153–54, *154*; marketing, 42, 45, 133, 170–71; management, 44, *47*, 48–49, 50, 162–64, 166, 168, 169, 181–83; motivation, 6, 8, 43, 54, 142; Swedish roots, 41, 149, 159
exhibitions, 19, 111; Allanstand, 57, 176; Century of Progress, 83–84, *83*; Conference of Southern Mountain Workers, 22, 24, 127; Department of Agriculture, 26–28, *32*; Homespun Fair, 37; *Mountain Handicrafts*, 24–26, 114, 121, 164–66, 169–70; museums, 106; sales events, 38, 39, 45, 52, 173; Southern Highland Handicraft

Index

Guild, 72, 73, 125; Southern Industrial Education Association, 15, 24, 178
Extension Service, 26, 32, 33, 123, 186

Fair Labor Standards Act, 32, 64–65
Federation of Women's Clubs: Georgia, 115, *163*, 176, *184*; Kentucky, 117; national organization, 9, 45
Fee, John G., 35
financial records: Arrowcraft, 59, 183; Berea, Fireside, 44, 48, 182, 183; Berea, Mountain Weaver Boys, 52; Crossnore, 120; Penland, 81, 84; Rabun Studios, 185; Tallulah Falls, 115, 183–84
financial support, 113, 162; churches, 84, 123; family help, 67, 150; independent individuals, 35, 36, 110; Pi Beta Phi, 61, 67, 74; state and federal government, 59–60, 120
Fireside Industries: Allanstand, 3, 122–23, 178; Appalachian School, development, 49, 77–78, 122; —, finances, 80–81; —, marketing, 79; —, mission, 77–78; —, production, 79–81; —, weavers, 78; Berea, brochures, 5–6, 40; —, instruction, 33, *41*, 49, 128; —, facilities, 39, 43–44; —, finances, 48, 52, 170–71. 181–82; —, Labor Day, 53, *53*; —, leader, 1, 10, 113; —, managers, 39, 44, 46, *47*, 50, 127, 146, 183; —, mission, 6; —, model, 35, 49–50, 54, 114, 117–18; —, production, 48–49, 167, 189; —, products, 48, 164, *170*; —, Southern Highland Handicraft Guild, 22; —, student labor, 44, 47, 180; —, weavers, *7*, 36, 38, 143, 187; model, 49, 60, 139, 185–86
Fishback, John, 91, 92, *92*, 148
Folk Art Center, 22
Folk Schools, 19, 20, 120, 121
Ford, Bonnie Willis: Berea attendance, 82; Penland, 7, 9, 79, 90, 84, *142*; magazine writing, 86, 87, 187; management, 89, *93*, 150; *Mountain Milestone*, 92; play, 82–83; sister, 90, *90*. See also Willis, Bonnie
Ford, Howard, 50, *51*, 82
Fowler, C.W., 81
Foxfire, 109
Frey, Berta, 71, 87
Frost, Eleanor, 38
Frost, William Goodell: Fireside support, 38, 39, 47, 53; leader, 35, 57, 153; promoting weaving,

36, 54, 145, 158; student labor, 54; weaving commission, 36–37, *36*; weaving managers, 37, 40, 41, 42, 45–46; weaving problem, 45, 127

Gatlinburg Weavers Guild, 67, 68
General Education Board, 33, 73, 91, 178
Gielow, Martha S., 15, 16, 57, 160, 177
Gift from the Hills, 92
Gilliam, David, 52
Glenn, John M., 19, 27
Goodrich, Francis: coverlets, 3, 6, 122, 148, 153, 158, 174, 187; crafts development, 122, *122*; finances, 181; marketing, 123, 153, 176; Pi Beta Phi, 57; Southern Highland Handicraft Guild, 22, 73, 123, 178; weavers, 38, 147
Graham, Hettie Wright, 39, *39*, 40, 146, 176
Graves, Caroline, 124
Great Smoky Mountains National Park: development, 2, 12, 181; impact, 63, 126, 141, 176; promotion, 124–25; Walker sister, *4*, 123–24
Greek culture: influence, 98, 100; promotion, 108, *108*, 111; understanding, 97
Green, Alice, 144
Gribbin, Bishop Robert, 88
gross sales, 31, 52, 67, 129, 181–83

Hall, Eliza Calvert, 41, 42, 86, 122, 158
Hambidge Art Foundation, 6, *14*, 108–11, 180, 189
Hambidge, Jay, 96, *97*, 98–100, *98*, 104–5, 109, 112
Hambidge, Mary: clothing, 100, *111*, 112; costumes, 100; development, 96, 147, 150; dyeing, 102, 104, *104*; Dynamic Symmetry, 96–97, 100, 102; finances, 106–7; friends, 109, 111; Georgia mountains, 14, 99, 101, 146; Greek culture promotion, 108, *108*; Greek influence, 97–98; heritage link, 6, 9; Jay Hambidge, 97–99, *98*; New York shop, 102–3, 106–7, 110; marketing, 2, 99, 101, 105–6, 174, 177, 181, 184–85; patron, 99–100, 108, 110, 177, 184–85; production, 103–5, 148, 155, 180; spinning, 103, 160; weavers, 102, *102*, *142*, 143. See also Crovatt, Mary
Handicraft Guild of the Diocese of Southwestern Virginia, 122
Handicrafter, The, 84, 85, 86, 87
Handicrafts of the Southern Highlands, 1, 19, 27, *27*, 35, 71, 91

Index

handwoven clothing, 102, *111*, 150
Hart, Robert, 180
Hayes, Susan B., 37, 38, 176
Heard, Marian, 33–34, 71–73, 91, 178
Helmick, Elizabeth Clarke, 11, 12, *12*, 57, 59
Hickman, Helen, 116
Hill, Jennie Lester, 40, *40*, 41, 42, 181
Hill, Nella Cook, 69, *69*, 70, 126
Hindman Settlement School: settlement work, 57, 94, 116–17, 189; Southern Industrial Educational Association, 16; weaving program, 4, 117, 185
homespun: Berea, 37, 68, 161; fair, 37, 161, *161*; historic reference, 1, 3, 6, 37; Mountain Weaver Boys, 51–52, 174
homework, 31
Hoppes, Doc, 84, 89
Horner, Bishop Junius, 13, 75, 77, 79, 157
House & Garden, 28
How to Weave Linens, 129, 159
Hoyle, Bascum, 79
Huff, Andy J., *56*, 58, 59, 63
Huff, Hennrietta, 58
Huff, Mattie, 59
Hughes, Carolyn McKnight, 2, 56, 58, 59
Hutchins, William J.: Churchill, 130, 131, 133; Conference of Southern Mountain Workers, 18–19, 55; Ernberg, 46–47, 49, 50, 133, 182–83; Matheny, 127–28; Southern Highland Handicraft Guild, 55; student labor, 53; weaving problem, 46, 127

indigo, 6, 37, 158, 160–61, 165
industrial arts and training: programs, 16, 29, 30, 33, 59, 75; teachers, 2, 18, 58, 59, 113, 115–16

Jay Hambidge Art Foundation. *See* Hambidge Art Foundation
John and Mary R. Markle School, 23, 114
John C. Campbell Folk School: Conference of Southern Mountain Workers, 24; craft program, 116, 121, *172*, 178; development, 120–21, 178; dyes, 161; instruction, 32–33, 34, 189; marketing, 28, 172, 179–80; Penland, 87; Southern Highlanders, 23, 179
Johnson, Lillie (Aunt Newbie), 118, 119–20, 143, 147–48, 163
Johnson, Nell, 117

Justice, Helen, 105, 109

Kanellos, Vassos, 108, *108*, 110
Kay, John, 51
Keener, Izora, *63*, *136*, 138
Keller, May Lansfield, 57
Kentucky Federation of Women's Clubs, 117
Kirpal, Josephine, 102, 106–7, 185
Knott County Department of Agriculture study, 185–86
Koch, Frederick H., 81, 87

labels, 25, 166
Labor Day, 53, *53*
LaFrance, Theresa, 91, 92, *92*
Lambert, Rev. Peter, Jr., 77
Leach, Bernard, 107
Ledford, Bess, 52
Lees McRae Institute, 16
Lily Loom House, 93, *93*
Lily Mills, 93, 148, *148*
Lincoln Institute (Shelby, Ky.), 36
Lincoln Memorial Institute, 16
linen: fabric, 105; historic, 37, 38; household textiles, 24, 115, 116, 125, 129, 144, 148, 165; *How to Weave Linens*, 129, 159; yarn, 104, 134, 144, 160, 166, 170; weaving, 40, 61, 81, 85, 117, 148, 162, 170
linsey-woolsey, 39, 159
Little Loom House, 49
Lockport Industries, 20, 81
Log House, 28, 43, *43*, *44*, 47, 176, 182
looms: abandoned, 2, 3, 4, 37, 56, 99, 175; barn, 2, *2*, 62, *62*, 125, 145, *152*, 153; counterbalance, 45, 51, 79, *154*; demonstrating, 22, 36, 63, 134; drawloom, 147, 159; Ernberg, 43, *44*, 45–46, 79, *118*, *154*; fly-shuttle, 50, 51, *51*, 54, 130, *130*, 132, 154, 166; foot-powered, 20, 51, 81, 153–54; making, 51, 77, 132, 153, 166; multi-harness, 159. *See also* warp preparation
Lowrance, Clara, 49, 118

madder, 36, 158, 160, 161
marketing: agencies, 21–22, 23, 30, 73, 123, 186; brochures, 9, 40; catalogs, 176; costs, 171–72, 182; joint promotion, 72, 73, 82, 90, 169, 179, 186; management, 48, 51, 102, 123, 125, 153,

Index

176; motivation, 6, 45, 52, 62, 169; problems, 30, 115, 129, 133, 134, 150, 166; publicity, 45, 67, 145; shops, 73, 102, 110, 177, 179, 183; strategies, 38, 177; weaving centers, 150, 162–63, 172; women's network, 164, 173, 177
Markle School of Handicrafts. *See* John and Mary Markle School
Martin, Murrial, 121
Mast family, 3, 124, 125. *See also* Mast, Josephine
Mast, Josephine, 3, 16, 124, 147
Matheny Weavers, 35, 54, 128, 129
Matheny, Edith: business, 128–29, 140, 159, 164, 187; development, 54, 127–28, 146; finances, 128–29, 185; helping others, 77; husband, 128–29; weaving problem, 127, 143; Worst, 19–20, 127, 129, 159
Matheny, Francis E., 127–29, 143
McCarter family, 59, 63, 64, 136
McCarter, Allie, 59
McMorran, Tina: designing, 69, 150; dyeing, 150, 161–62; management, 68–69, *149*, 189; studying weaving, *34*, 68, 69
Miles, Emma Bell, 2, 155
Miller, Clyde P., 88
minimum wage, 32, 64–65, 138–39
mission: Allanstand, 122; Berea, 36, 40, 42, 45, 53, 128; Crossnore, 117; Conference of Southern Mountain Workers, 18; denominational, 10, 18, 80, 122; Extension, 32; J.C. Campbell Folk School, 121; Penland, 10, 75; Pi Beta Phi, 34, 58, 62, 67, 70, 71, 73; Russell Sage, 16–17, 19; settlement movement, 4–5; shared, 5, 9, 169, 172, 174, 180, 183, 188, 189; Southern Highland Handicraft Guild, 21, 72; Southern Highlanders, 23–24; Women's Bureau, 186; writing about, 5, 9, 187
missionaries: denominational affiliation, 57, 80, 117, 122, *122*, 124; international, 54, 117, 130, 132; marketing, 45; schools, 33, 41, 124, 128; settlement workers, 39, 57
Moore, Beulah, 139
Moore, Louise, 30
Moore, Mollie, 174, *175*
Morgan, Lucy: crafts development, 78, 137, 178; development, 76–77, 146; dyes, 161; Episcopal connections, 79, 84, 157, 184; finances, 81, 88, 89, 184; historical interest, 3; instruction, *29*, 143; leader, 82, 91; learning to weave, 49–50,

77, 81, 144; management, *78*, 80, *90*, 91, 92, *93*, 140; marketing, 79, 83, *83*, 173; motivation, 77–78, 187; retirement, 85, 94–95; school, 33, 91; weaving, 78, *146*, *147*, 150
Morgan, Ralph, 82, 84, 178
Morgan, Rufus, 75
Morley, Margaret, 3
Morton, Cora, *65*, 66, 141–42, 164, *179*, *181*
Morris, William, 26, 36, 54, 143
Mottern, Bess L., 69, 150–51
Mountain Handicrafts, 25, 26, 122, 164
Mountain Life and Work, 18, 86, 87, 187
Mountain Milestone, 92
Mountain Room, 16, 24, 165
Mountain View Hotel, 59, 63, 73
Mountain Weaver Boys: development, 20, 35, 51–52, *51*; finances, 52–53, 182; management, 51–52; marketing, 52; production, 51–52, 154, 174; weavers, 51, 53, 54
mountain whites, 36, 57
Murfree, Mary. *See* Craddock, C.E.

National Youth Administration, 123
Nienburg, Bertha, 30–31, 136–37, 140, 145, 182, 186
Nikas, Mary Creety, 111
Noel, Muriel, 98
North Carolina State Fair, 79–80

Odland, Lura, 71
Ogle, Josie, 135, 162, 170
Ogle, Lula Mae, 67, 74
Old Crafts: New Horizons, 28
overshot: coverlets, 6, 50, *137*, 158, 159, *163*, 165, 170; historic, 148, 149, 159, 164, 175, 187; items, 145, 149, 167, 170; patterns, 42, 50, 120, 158, *175*; structure, 78, 155, 158

pattern draft, 40, 148, 187
Patterns of Rural Art, 28
Penland School of Crafts: classes, 88–89, 90–91, 122; development, 85, 95, 150, 180, 189; dyes, *160*; facilities, 87–88, 92–93; finances, 89, 93, 184; international visitors, 93; management, 88–89; students, 32–33, 67, 85–86, 88, 90; support, 29–30, 87, 89, 93, 143; teachers, 88, 90, *90*, 91, *92*, 148, 159, 169; Weaving Institute, *29*, 85–87, 89, *189*; workshops, 34, 88; Worst, 33, 85

Index

Penland Weavers and Potters: development, 7, 180; Episcopal affiliation, 80–81, 84, 184; evaluation, 30; finances, 81, 137, 140, 182, 184; instruction, 143; joint promotion, 143; leader, 1, 10, 15, 82, 90, 113, 181; management, 85, 140, 160; marketing, 79, 83, *83*, 175, 176; organizational activities, 72; pewter, 81–82; pottery, 81; production, 164, 167; publicity, 28, 82, 84; support, 29, 80, 143, 145; weavers, 135, 136, *137*, 140; Worst, 81

Perisho, Flossie Willis, 90, *90*

Perisho, Lester, 90

Peters, Rupert, 88, 148

Pettit, Anna, 57

Pettit, Katherine, 3, 116–17, 125, 147–48, 161

Phillips, Ossie, 120, 145, *173*

Phillips, Susan, 3

Pi Beta Phi Fraternity: communication from Arrowcraft, 6, 8, 140, 187; consumers, 9, 61, 66, *69*, 140, 173; crafts development, 113, 116, 146, *176*, 180; establishing, 57–58; founding memorial, 57, 71; investigation trip, 54, 123; management, 72, 149, 162, 171, 183; philanthropy, 9, 10, 56, 58, 67, 70–71, 74, 171, 183; settlement school pledges, 59; symbol, 61

Pi Beta Phi Settlement School: crafts education, *34*, 70; crafts development, 1, 10, 183; development, 56–58, *56*, 59–60; facilities, 34, *34*, 68, 70, 73; geography, 11, 59, 63; organizational activity, 22, 24, 28, 72, 73; support, 29, 58, 67–68, 71–72, 120, 143; students, *56*, 59, 69, 126; weaving, 2, 12, 56, 62, *62*, *135*, 136, 172

Pickett, Norman, 59

piece rate, 30, 32, 138–40, 145, 163, 183

Pigman family, 4, 117

Pigman, Una, 4, 117

Pine Mountain Settlement School: development, 117, 189; production, 165; support, 117; teachers, 120, 125, 146, 161; weavers, 157

Pitman, Louise, 121, 161, 172–73, *172*

placemats: buyers, 66, 149–50, 164; designers, 144–45, 164; marketing, 120, 133, 145, 175; production item, 66, 70, 96, 164, 165, 187, 189

Pleasant Hill Academy, 17, 49, 116–17, 121

Pollard, Mary O., 58

Potential Earning Power of Southern Mountaineer Handicrafts, 30, 64, 186

Powell, Naoma, 94

Practical Weaving Suggestions, 93, 148, *148*

pregnancy rule, 140

Presbyterian Church: education of leaders, 17, 118; exhibition space, 24; markets, 116, 123, 174; missionaries, 57, 122, *122*; sponsor of schools, 116

pricing, 67, 169, 171, 173, 188

Priestman, Mabel Tuke, 187

Progressive Movement, 5, 10, 13, 20, 27, 76

quilting, 31–32, 73, 140, 152, 186

Rabun Studios: development, 102, 107, 177; management, 107, 110, 182, 185; merchandise, 96, 103, 104; visitors, 107

rag rugs, 39, 40, 166

Ramey, Willie Mae, 102

Redding, Winogene: designing, 66, 71, 147–48; development, 12, 60–61, 146, 147, 169; leadership, 64, 68, 73, 91, 150, 178; management, 60, *60*, 64, *65*, 135, 139–40, 171, 181, 183; production, *136*, 138, 140, 163–64; teaching, 61, 63, 136, 143; writing, 6, 8, 62, 64, 67, 142, 187

Reese, Eleanor, 99, *99*, 100, 101, 102. *See also* Steele, Eleanor

retail: business, 24, 47, 126, 127, 133, 177, 178; calculating prices, 67, 171; catalogs, 133, 169; markup, 73, 170, 172; prices, 67, 133, 169, 170, 171, 172, 177; Southern Highland Handicraft Guild, 22, 24, 123, 179

rhythm in weaving, 101, 132, 156

Robinson, Josephine, 38, 174, 176

Rock House, 101, *101*, 102, *102*, 108

Rockefeller Center, *23*, 24, 28, 179, 180

Rockefeller Foundation, 33, 73, 91, 178

Roosevelt, Franklin D., 26, 63

Rosemont Industries, 123

Rural Arts Exhibition, 26, 28

Ruskin, John, 36, 42, 54

Russell Sage Foundation: crafts development, 19, 24, 25, 82; establishing, 16–17; publications, 17, 19, 27, *27*; Southern Division, 16, 17, 120

Sage, Margaret Olivia, 16

sales figures, 16, 31, 52, 69, 171

Scandinavia: design influences, 98, 115, 149, 159;

Index

folk schools, 19, 20, 120–21; models, 21, 178; weaving teachers, 41, 115, 146, 149, 159, 160

Schattschneider, Meta, 68, *68*, 138, 171, 187

Second National Conference on Handicrafts, 90

settlement house, 4, 5, 58, 68, 122.

Settlement Movement, 4, 10, 58, 146

settlement schools: Appalachian, 16, 19; movement, 4, 10; program, 33, 163, 186; teachers, 123; weaving revival, 4, 113. *See also* Pi Beta Phi, Hindman, and Pine Mountain Settlement Schools

Seven Springs Farm and Industrial School, 75

Sharp, Cecil, 19

Shawn, Ted, 98

Shepherd, Robert Marshall, 109, 177

Sheppard, Muriel Early, 12, 13, 77, 78, 91

Shirley, Eliza, 115, *115*, 116, *116*

Shuttle Crafters, 3, 125, 147, 150, 181

Sikelianos, Eva Palmer, 98

silk, 45, 100, 103, 104, 108, 166

Sloop, Eustace, 117

Sloop, Mary Martin, *5*, 14, 87, 117–19

Smith Community Life School, 126

Smith, Katherine Louise, 187

Smith-Hughes Vocation Education Bill: crafts teaching, 33, 59, 89; description, 29; evaluation, 30; state programs, 29, 80, 89; weaving support, 30, 80, 89, 118, 120, 138, 143, 162–63

Smith-Lever Act, 32

Smithsonian Institution, 106

Social Gospel Movement, 10

Southern Division of the Russell Sage Foundation, 16

Southern Highland Handicraft Guild: cooperative activities, 23, 24–25, 28, 31–32, 91, 163, 179; development, 22, 189; education, 33–34, 71, 91; exhibitions, 24–26, 114, 121, 164–66, 169; fairs, 3, 22, *22*, 73, 88, 90, 125, 145, *145*, 162, *179*; founding, 22, 55, 72–73, 82, 113; leadership, 19, 73, 90, 125; meetings, 73, 125; members, 22, 25, 28, 114, 129, 134, 154, 170, 178; merger with Southern Highlanders, 24; model, 31, 47, 186; sales, 115, 116, 170, 172–73, 178–79; shops, 22, 70, 73, 123, 178, 180; wage laws, 64–65, 138

Southern Highlander and His Homeland, The, 17

Southern Highlanders, Inc.: catalog, 23, 24, 165, 166; establishing, 23, 31, 91, 123, 179; financing, 23, 178–79; members, 28, 73, 134, 179; merger with Southern Highland Handicraft Guild, 24, 134, 180; shops, 24, 28

Southern Industrial Education Association: development, 15–16, 177–78; marketing, 16, 24, 122–23, 163; model, 57; supported activities, 16, 113, 117, 119

southern mountain workers: activities, 5, 58, 114; background, 95; crafts development, 5, 9, 42, 127, 161; organizations, 16, 18–20. *See also* Conference of Southern Mountain Workers

spinning: commercial production, 36, 51; crafts development, 1, 36, 93; demonstrating, 73, 84, 106, 114, 124–25, 145, *145*; instruction, 15, 88, 90, 98, 108; persistence, 4, 6, 99, 160, 175; production process, 36, *37*, 117, 160; supplies, 38, 39, 107, 108, 160; weaving centers, 100, 160

spinning bee, 59

Spinning Wheel, the: development, 125–26; joint promotion, 23, 28, 72, 178, 179; leadership role, 21, 72, 87; management, 126, *126*, 150, 181, 182, 185; production, 164–65

spinners: Appalachian, 3, *4*, 175; historic knowledge, 2, 3, 59, 147; production, 104, 105, 160; publicity, 84; spinning bee, 59; weaving centers, *14*, 39, 101

Stahl, Sam, 187

standards: maintaining, 91, 144, 146, 185; promoting, 37; Southern Highland Handicraft Guild, 21, 73; Southern Highlanders, 24

Steele, Eleanor, 105, 107–10, 177, 184–85. *See also* Reese, Eleanor

Stevens, Bernice, 72, 126

Stockin, Eleanor, 45

Stone, May, 116, 147

Story of Penland Weavers, The, 7, 82, 84

student labor program: Berry Schools, 114; Berea College, 33, 36, 52, 145, 166; —, finances, 44, 48, 53, 182; —, Fireside, 35, 47, 49, 167; —, Mountain Weaver Boys, 35, 51; —, problems, 46; —, management, 44, 183; Crossnore, 180

subsistence economy, 1, 5, *122*, 137

Sullivan, Mary Elizabeth Starr, 68

Summer Craft Workshop, 34, *34*, 56, 68, 70, *70*, 71–73

Swedish influence, 98, 147, 159, 160

Tabor, Grace, 41–42

Index

Tallulah Falls Industrial School: development, 115; finances, 181–82, 183–84; support, 115, *163*; students, 102, 115–16, *116*, *142*, 143; teachers, 115, 159–60; weaving program, 114–15, *115*, 176, *183*

Tarbell, Ida , 43, 46–47, 114

Tate, Lou, 49

Tennessee Valley Authority: crafts development, 23, 91, 123, 137; mission, 23–24, 79; merger with Southern Highland Handicraft Guild, 24; Southern Highlanders, *23*, 73, 134, 179; Women's Bureau study, 30, 31, 186

Thompson, Faye, 102

Travelog, 82, *82*

Tsunematsu, Toshie, 93

Turner, Emma Harper, 57

Twelve Designer Craftsmen, 72, 150

Ulmann, Doris, 25, 27, *27*, 125; photographs attributed to, *17*, *122*

University of Tennessee: crafts education, 34, *34*, 68, 70, *70*, 71; faculty, 33, 71, 91

Vaughn, Marshall, 50

Viner, Wilmer Stone, 125, 146, 161, 185

vocational education: federal programs, 29, 33, 59, 80; instruction, 29, 30, 33, 36, 128, 143, 162–63; state administration, 29, 30, 80, 143; teachers, 82, 118, 187

Voulis, Aspasia, 111

Wade, William, 42

Walker sisters, 3-4, *4*, 123–24

Walker, Anna LaGrange, 49

Walker, Elmeda, 4, 16, 122, 165

warp preparation: assistance in preparing, 78, 95; historic reference, 2; length, 103, 105, 155, 183; mistakes, 155–56; threading, 155, *156*; time involved, 32, 65, 138, 156, 162; tying on, 138, 156, 162, 183; viewing, 134; winding, 80, 93, *131*, 154–55, *155*

weave structure: Bronson, 129, 159; drafts, 155; fly-shuttle, 154; overshot, 155, 158; plain, 104; Scandinavian, 159; simple, 103, 148, 166; Summer & Winter, *146*; variety, 50, 128

Weavers of Rabun: development, 1–2, 10, 96, 150, 180; exhibitions, 106; geography, 14; management, 105; marketing, 103, 106, 110, 177, 182; production, 96, 103–4, 105, 113, 185; weavers, *102*, 105

Weaving Cabin, *79*, 80, *80*, 82, *141*

Weaving Day, 80

Weaving Institute: affiliation, 84–85; classes, 33, 85, 86, 88; facilities, *29*, 86, *86*, 87–88, 89, 176–77, *189*; Penland School, 89, 143, 180; publicity, 87; Smith-Hughes, 87; students, 85, 143, 148; transportation, 13; Worst, 19–20, 85, 147

weaving instruction: advanced skills, 69, 71, 81, 88, 116–17, *149*; apprentice model, 33, 143; content, 72, 86, 87, 89; cost, 30, 71, 80; expanding populations, 33, 85; school classes, 49, 118, 128, 162–63; weaving centers, 80, 102, 143; workshops, 33–34, 70–72, 85–87, 89, 108, 179

Weaving Room, the: development, 181, 189; geography, 177; leader, 116; management, 120, 143, 180; production, 120, 138, 139, 148, 189. *See also* Crossnore School's Weaving Room

Weaving Shed: production, 103, 104, *104*, 105; sales room, 101, 103, *106*, 177

West, Max, 37, 144, 185

Wheeler, Candace, 38, 118, 143

Whig Rose, 66, 67, 139, 144, 164

wholesale price: calculation, 67, 171; problems, 171, 172, 173, 185; sales, 73, 133, 177, 188

Wigginton, Eliot, 109

Williams, Leda, 101, *102*

Williamsburg presidential yacht, 105

Willis, Adeline, 78

Willis, Bonnie, 77, 82, 90, 187. *See also* Ford, Bonnie Willis

Willis, Flossie, 90, *90*

Willis, Laura, 108

Wilson, Ellen, 16, 24, 122, 124

Wilson, Samuel T., 57

Women's Bureau: Appalachian interviews, 64, 124, 136, 138, 141, 157; craft businesses, 31, 137; centralized work, 137, 139, 140, 163; home-work position, 30–31, 140, 141, 186; report, 30–31, 64, 139, 163; TVA study, 31, 64

Women's Clubs. *See* Federation of Women's Clubs

women's network: composition, 9, 10; consumers, 16, 79, 96, 123, 168, 177; fundraising, 24; marketing, 127, 150, 164, 172, 173; problems, 133, 134

Index

woodcarving, 26, 86, 117, 121
Woody, Cumi, 3, 85–86, 122
wool: carding, *37*, 84, 175; dyeing, 36, 103, 161, 166; fiber, 51, 52; fleece, 38, 103; historic, 6; items, 37, 38, 61, 103, 105, 110, 129, 132, 166; spinning, 4, 36, 39, 104, 105, *107*, 108, 117, 175; production, 38, 123; yarn, 99, 103, 134, 158, 160; yardage, 50, 52, 104, 155, 174
Wooten, Inez, 114
Wootten, Bayard, 13, 80, 88; photographs attributed to, *78*, *79*, *80*, *82*, *86*, *141*
Works Progress Administration, 90, 123
World's Columbian Exposition, 10
Worst Craft House, 87–88, 93, 176, 184, *189*

Worst, Edward F.: background, 20; influence, 19–20, 81; Matheny, 127–28, 159; Morgan, Lucy, 81, 83–84, 147; Mountain Weaver Boys, 50; speaker, 20, 178; Weaving Institute, *29*, 33, 85, 87–89; writing, 20, 27, 81, 129, 148, 159
Yale University Press, 97, 105
yardage: Churchill, 132; Hambidge, commissions, 105; —, exhibits, 106; —, production, 102, 103, 105, 108, 155, 166; —, sales, 96, 104–5, 182, 185; Mountain Weavers Boys, 50–52, 154; production, 40, 163, 165; Weaving Institute, 88

Zimmerman, Alice, 72

credits

Photos 1.2, 1.7, 1.8, 2.5, 2.10, 4.1–4.10, 8.1, 8.2, 8.4, 8.10, 9.10, and 10.4–10.7 courtesy of the Arrowmont School of Arts and Crafts.

Photos 1.10, and 6.1–6.10 courtesy of the Atlanta History Center.

Photos 1.1, 1.3, 1.5, 3.1–3.10, 7.6, 7.7, 9.1–9.3, 9.5, 9.7, 10.1, and 10.9 courtesy of the Berea College Archives.

Photos 7.8–7.10, 9.4, and 9.9 courtesy of the Churchill Weavers.

Photo 5.9 courtesy of Theresa Conley.

Photos 1.4, 2.1, 7.4, and 10.3 courtesy of the Crossnore School, Inc.

Photos 1.6, 1.9, and 5.1 courtesy of the Episcopal Diocese of Western North Carolina Archives.

Photo 7.3 courtesy of Dr. Emma Fink.

Photos 2.2, 7.5, and 10.2 courtesy of the John C. Campbell Folk School, Brasstown, North Carolina.

Photos 2.8, 5.3, 5.5, 5.7, 5.8, 5.10, 8.3, 8.7–8.9, 9.6, and 10.10 courtesy of the Penland School of Arts and Crafts; 5.2, 5.4, and 8.5 courtesy of the Penland School of Arts and Crafts and Bayard Wootten.

Photos 7.1, 7.2, 8.6, 9.8, and 10.8 courtesy of the Tallulah Falls School.

Photos 2.3 and 2.4 courtesy of the University of North Carolina-Chapel Hill.

Photo 5.6 from the collection of Louise Morgan.

www.ingramcontent.com/pod-product-compliance
Lightning Source LLC
Chambersburg PA
CBHW081208170426
43198CB00018B/2885